MG MIDGET
Gold Portfolio
1961~1979

Compiled by
R.M. Clarke

ISBN 1 85520 228X

Brooklands Books Ltd.
PO Box 146, Cobham, KT11 1LG
Surrey, England

Printed in Hong Kong

BROOKLANDS BOOKS

BROOKLANDS ROAD TEST SERIES

Abarth Gold Portfolio 1950-1971
AC Ace & Aceca 1953-1983
Alfa Romeo Giulietta Gold Portfolio 1954-1965
Alfa Romeo Giulia Berlinas 1962-1976
Alfa Romeo Giulia Coupés 1963-1976
Alfa Romeo Giulia Coupés Gold P. 1963-1976
Alfa Romeo Spider 1966-1990
Alfa Romeo Spider Gold Portfolio 1966-1991
Alfa Romeo Alfasud 1972-1984
Alfa Romeo Alfetta Gold Portfolio 1972-1987
Alfa Romeo Alfetta GTV6 1980-1987
Allard Gold Portfolio 1937-1959
Alvis Gold Portfolio 1919-1967
American Motors Muscle Cars 1966-1970
Armstrong Siddeley Gold Portfolio 1945-1960
Aston Martin Gold Portfolio 1972-1985
Austin Seven 1922-1982
Austin A30 & A35 1951-1962
Austin Healey 100 & 100/6 Gold P. 1952-1959
Austin Healey 3000 Gold Portfolio 1959-1967
Austin Healey Sprite 1958-1971
BMW Six Cyl. Coupés 1969-1975
BMW 1600 Collection No.1 1966-1981
BMW 2002 Gold Portfolio 1968-1976
BMW 316, 318, 320 (4 cyl.) Gold P. 1975-1990
BMW 320, 323, 325 (6 cyl.) Gold P. 1977-1990
BMW 5 Series Gold Portfolio 1981-1987
BMW M Series Performance Portfolio 1976-1993
Bristol Cars Gold Portfolio 1946-1992
Buick Automobiles 1947-1960
Buick Muscle Cars 1965-1970
Cadillac Automobiles 1949-1959
Cadillac Automobiles 1960-1969
Chevrolet 1955-1957
Chevrolet Impala & SS 1958-1971
Chevrolet Corvair 1959-1969
Chevy El Camino & SS 1959-1987
Chevy II Nova & SS 1962-1973
Chevelle & SS Muscle Portfolio 1964-1972
Chevrolet Muscle Cars 1966-1971
Chevy Blazer 1969-1981
Chevrolet Corvette Gold Portfolio 1953-1962
Chevrolet Corvette Sting Ray Gold P. 1963-1967
Chevrolet Corvette Gold Portfolio 1968-1977
High Performance Corvettes 1983-1989
Camaro Muscle Portfolio 1967-1973
Chevrolet Camaro Z28 & SS 1966-1973
Chevrolet Camaro & Z28 1973-1981
High Performance Camaros 1982-1988
Chrysler 300 Gold Portfolio 1955-1970
Chrysler Valiant 1960-1962
Citroen Traction Avant Gold Portfolio 1934-1957
Citroen 2CV Gold Portfolio 1948-1989
Citroen DS & ID Gold Portfolio 1955-1975
Citroen SM 1970-1975
Cobras & Replicas 1962-1983
Shelby Cobra Gold Portfolio 1962-1969
Cobras & Cobra Replicas Gold P. 1962-1989
Cunningham Automobiles 1951-1955
Daimler SP250 Sports & V-8 250 Saloon Gold Portfolio 1959-1969
Datsun Roadsters 1962-1971
Datsun 240Z 1970-1973
Datsun 280Z & ZX 1975-1983
De Tomaso Collection No. 1 1962-1981
Dodge Charger 1966-1974
Dodge Muscle Cars 1967-1970
Dodge Viper on the Road
The De Lorean 1977-1993
Excalibur Collection No. 1 1952-1981
Facel Vega 1954-1964
Ferrari Cars 1946-1956
Ferrari Collection No. 1 1960-1970
Ferrari Dino 1965-1974
Ferrari Dino 308 1974-1979
Ferrari 308 & Mondial 1980-1984
Motor & T&CC Ferrari 1966-1976
Motor & T&CC Ferrari 1976-1984
Fiat Pininfarina 124 & 2000 Spider 1968-1985
Fiat-Bertone X1/9 1973-1988
Ford Consul, Zephyr, Zodiac Mk.I & II 1950-1962
Ford Zephyr, Zodiac, Executive, Mk.III & Mk.IV 1962-1971
Ford Cortina 1600E & GT 1967-1970
High Performance Capris Gold P. 1969-1987
Capri Muscle Portfolio 1974-1987
High Performance Fiestas 1979-1991
High Performance Escorts Mk.I 1968-1974
High Performance Escorts Mk.II 1975-1980
High Performance Escorts 1980-1985
High Performance Escorts 1985-1990
High Performance Sierras & Merkurs Gold Portfolio 1983-1990
Ford Automobiles 1949-1959
Ford Fairlane 1955-1970
Ford Ranchero 1957-1959
Thunderbird 1955-1957
Thunderbird 1958-1963
Thunderbird 1964-1976
Ford Falcon 1960-1970
Ford GT40 Gold Portfolio 1964-1987
Ford Bronco 1966-1977
Ford Bronco 1978-1988
Holden 1948-1962
Honda CRX 1983-1987

Hudson & Railton 1936-1940
Isetta 1953-1964
Jaguar and SS Gold Portfolio 1931-1951
Jaguar XK120, 140, 150 Gold P. 1948-1960
Jaguar Mk.VII, VIII, IX, X, 420 Gold P.1950-1970
Jaguar 1957-1961
Jaguar Mk.2 1959-1969
Jaguar Cars 1961-1964
Jaguar E-Type Gold Portfolio 1961-1971
Jaguar E-Type 1966-1971
Jaguar E-Type V-12 1971-1975
Jaguar XJ12, XJ5.3, V12 Gold P. 1972-1990
Jaguar XJ6 Series II 1973-1979
Jaguar XJ6 Series III 1979-1986
Jaguar XJS Gold Portfolio 1975-1990
Jeep CJ5 & CJ6 1960-1976
Jeep CJ5 & CJ7 1976-1986
Jensen Cars 1946-1967
Jensen Cars 1967-1979
Jensen Interceptor Gold Portfolio 1966-1986
Jensen Healey 1972-1976
Lagonda Gold Portfolio 1919-1964
Lamborghini Cars 1964-1970
Lamborghini Countach & Urraco 1974-1980
Lamborghini Countach & Jalpa 1980-1985
Lancia Beta Gold Portfolio 1972-1984
Lancia Fulvia Gold Portfolio 1963-1976
Lancia Stratos 1972-1985
Land Rover Series I 1948-1958
Land Rover Series II & IIa 1958-1971
Land Rover Series III 1971-1985
Land Rover 90 & 110 1983-1989
Lincoln Gold Portfolio 1949-1960
Lincoln Continental 1961-1969
Lincoln Continental 1969-1976
Lotus & Caterham Seven Gold P. 1957-1993
Lotus Sports Racers Gold Portfolio 1953-1965
Lotus Elite 1957-1964
Lotus Elite & Eclat 1974-1982
Lotus Elan Gold Portfolio 1962-1974
Lotus Elan Collection No. 2 1963-1972
Lotus Cortina Gold Portfolio 1963-1970
Lotus Europa Gold Portfolio 1966-1975
Lotus Turbo Esprit 1980-1986
Motor & T&CC on Lotus 1979-1983
Marcos Cars 1960-1988
Maserati 1965-1970
Maserati 1970-1975
Mazda RX-7 Collection No. 1 1978-1981
Mercedes Benz Cars 1949-1954
Mercedes Benz Competition Cars 1950-1957
Mercedes Benz Cars 1954-1957
Mercedes Benz Cars 1957-1961
Mercedes 190 & 300 SL 1954-1963
Mercedes 230/250/280SL 1963-1971
Mercedes Benz SLs & SLCs Gold P. 1971-1989
Mercedes S & 600 1965-1972
Mercedes S Class 1972-1979
Mercury Muscle Cars 1966-1971
Metropolitan 1954-1962
MG Gold Portfolio 1929-1939
MG TC 1945-1949
MG TD 1949-1953
MG TF 1953-1955
MGA & Twin Cam Gold Portfolio 1955-1962
MG Midget Gold Portfolio 1961-1979
MGB Roadsters 1962-1980
MGB MGC & V8 Gold Portfolio 1962-1980
MGB GT 1965-1980
Mini Cooper Gold Portfolio 1961-1971
Mini Muscle Cars 1961-1979
Mini Moke Gold Portfolio 1964-1994
Mopar Muscle Cars 1964-1967
Morgan Three-Wheeler Gold Portfolio 1910-1952
Morgan Plus 4 & Four 4 Gold P. 1936-1967
Morgan Cars 1960-1970
Morgan Cars Gold Portfolio 1968-1989
Morris Minor Collection No. 1 1948-1980
Shelby Mustang Muscle Portfolio 1965-1970
Mustang Muscle Cars 1967-1971
High Performance Mustang IIs 1974-1978
High Performance Mustangs 1982-1988
Oldsmobile Automobiles 1955-1963
Oldsmobile Cutlass & 4-4-2 1964-1972
Oldsmobile Muscle Cars 1964-1971
Oldsmobile Toronado 1966-1978
Opel GT 1968-1973
Packard Gold Portfolio 1946-1958
Pantera Gold Portfolio 1970-1989
Panther Gold Portfolio 1972-1990
Plymouth Barracuda 1964-1974
Plymouth Muscle Cars 1966-1971
Pontiac Tempest & GTO 1961-1965
Pontiac Muscle Cars 1966-1972
Pontiac Firebird & Trans-Am 1973-1981
High Performance Firebirds 1982-1988
Pontiac Fiero 1984-1988
Porsche 356 1952-1965
Porsche 911 1965-1969
Porsche 911 1970-1972
Porsche 911 1973-1977
Porsche 911 Carrera 1973-1977
Porsche 911 Turbo 1975-1984
Porsche 911 SC 1978-1983
Porsche 914 Collection No. 1 1969-1983
Porsche 914 Gold Portfolio 1969-1976
Porsche 924 Gold Portfolio 1975-1988
Porsche 928 1977-1989
Porsche 944 1981-1985

Range Rover Gold Portfolio 1970-1992
Reliant Scimitar 1964-1986
Riley Gold Portfolio 1924-1939
Riley 1.5 & 2.5 Litre Gold Portfolio 1945-1955
Rolls Royce Silver Cloud & Bentley 'S' Series Gold Portfolio 1955-1965
Rolls Royce Silver Shadow Gold P. 1965-1980
Rover P4 1949-1959
Rover P4 1955-1964
Rover 3 & 3.5 Litre Gold Portfolio 1958-1973
Rover 2000 & 2200 1963-1977
Rover 3500 1968-1977
Rover 3500 & Vitesse 1976-1986
Saab Sonett Collection No.1 1966-1974
Saab Turbo 1976-1983
Studebaker Gold Portfolio 1947-1966
Studebaker Hawks & Larks 1956-1963
Avanti 1962-1990
Sunbeam Tiger & Alpine Gold P. 1959-1967
Toyota MR2 1984-1988
Toyota Land Cruiser 1956-1984
Triumph TR2 & TR3 1952-1960
Triumph TR4, TR5, TR250 1961-1968
Triumph TR6 Gold Portfolio 1969-1976
Triumph TR7 & TR8 Gold Portfolio 1975-1982
Triumph Herald 1959-1971
Triumph Vitesse 1962-1971
Triumph Spitfire Gold Portfolio 1962-1980
Triumph 2000, 2.5, 2500 1963-1977
Triumph GT6 1966-1974
Triumph Stag 1970-1980
TVR Gold Portfolio 1959-1990
VW Beetle Gold Portfolio 1935-1967
VW Beetle Gold Portfolio 1968-1991
VW Beetle Collection No.1 1970-1982
VW Karmann Ghia 1955-1982
VW Bus, Camper, Van 1954-1967
VW Bus, Camper, Van 1968-1979
VW Bus, Camper, Van 1979-1989
VW Scirocco 1974-1981
VW Golf GTI 1976-1986
Volvo PV444 & PV544 1945-1965
Volvo Amazon-120 Gold Portfolio 1956-1970
Volvo 1800 Gold Portfolio 1960-1973

BROOKLANDS ROAD & TRACK SERIES

Road & Track on Alfa Romeo 1949-1963
Road & Track on Alfa Romeo 1964-1970
Road & Track on Alfa Romeo 1971-1976
Road & Track on Alfa Romeo 1977-1989
Road & Track on Aston Martin 1962-1990
R & T on Auburn Cord and Duesenburg 1952-84
Road & Track on Audi & Auto Union 1952-1980
Road & Track on Audi & Auto Union 1980-1986
Road & Track on Austin Healey 1953-1970
Road & Track on BMW Cars 1966-1974
Road & Track on BMW Cars 1975-1978
Road & Track on BMW Cars 1979-1983
R & T on Cobra, Shelby & Ford GT40 1962-1992
Road & Track on Corvette 1953-1967
Road & Track on Corvette 1968-1982
Road & Track on Corvette 1982-1986
Road & Track on Corvette 1986-1990
Road & Track on Datsun Z 1970-1983
Road & Track on Ferrari 1975-1981
Road & Track on Ferrari 1981-1984
Road & Track on Ferrari 1984-1988
Road & Track on Fiat Sports Cars 1968-1987
Road & Track on Jaguar 1950-1960
Road & Track on Jaguar 1961-1968
Road & Track on Jaguar 1968-1974
Road & Track on Jaguar 1974-1982
Road & Track on Jaguar 1983-1989
Road & Track on Lamborghini 1964-1985
Road & Track on Lotus 1972-1981
Road & Track on Maserati 1952-1974
Road & Track on Maserati 1975-1983
R & T on Mazda RX7 & MX5 Miata 1986-1991
Road & Track on Mercedes 1952-1962
Road & Track on Mercedes 1963-1970
Road & Track on Mercedes 1971-1979
Road & Track on Mercedes 1980-1987
Road & Track on MG Sports Cars 1949-1961
Road & Track on MG Sports Cars 1962-1980
Road & Track on Mustang 1964-1977
R & T on Nissan 300-ZX & Turbo 1984-1989
Road & Track on Peugeot 1955-1986
Road & Track on Pontiac 1960-1983
Road & Track on Porsche 1951-1967
Road & Track on Porsche 1968-1971
Road & Track on Porsche 1972-1975
Road & Track on Porsche 1975-1978
Road & Track on Porsche 1979-1982
Road & Track on Porsche 1982-1985
Road & Track on Porsche 1985-1988
R & T on Rolls Royce & Bentley 1950-1965
R & T on Rolls Royce & Bentley 1966-1984
Road & Track on Saab 1972-1992
R & T on Toyota Sports & GT Cars 1966-1984
R & T on Triumph Sports Cars 1953-1967
R & T on Triumph Sports Cars 1967-1974
R & T on Triumph Sports Cars 1974-1982
Road & Track on Volkswagen 1951-1968
Road & Track on Volkswagen 1968-1978
Road & Track on Volkswagen 1978-1985

Road & Track on Volvo 1957-1974
Road & Track on Volvo 1975-1985
R&T - Henry Manney at Large & Abroad

BROOKLANDS CAR AND DRIVER SERIES

Car and Driver on BMW 1955-1977
Car and Driver on BMW 1977-1985
C and D on Cobra, Shelby & Ford GT40 1963-84
Car and Driver on Corvette 1956-1967
Car and Driver on Corvette 1968-1977
Car and Driver on Corvette 1978-1982
Car and Driver on Corvette 1983-1988
C and D on Datsun Z 1600 & 2000 1966-1984
Car and Driver on Ferrari 1955-1962
Car and Driver on Ferrari 1963-1975
Car and Driver on Ferrari 1976-1983
Car and Driver on Mopar 1956-1967
Car and Driver on Mopar 1968-1975
Car and Driver on Mustang 1964-1972
Car and Driver on Pontiac 1961-1975
Car and Driver on Porsche 1955-1962
Car and Driver on Porsche 1963-1970
Car and Driver on Porsche 1970-1976
Car and Driver on Porsche 1977-1981
Car and Driver on Porsche 1982-1986
Car and Driver on Saab 1956-1985
Car and Driver on Volvo 1955-1986

BROOKLANDS PRACTICAL CLASSICS SERIES

PC on Austin A40 Restoration
PC on Land Rover Restoration
PC on Metalworking in Restoration
PC on Midget/Sprite Restoration
PC on Mini Cooper Restoration
PC on MGB Restoration
PC on Morris Minor Restoration
PC on Sunbeam Rapier Restoration
PC on Triumph Herald/Vitesse
PC on Spitfire Restoration
PC on Beetle Restoration
PC on 1930s Car Restoration

BROOKLANDS HOT ROD 'MUSCLECAR & HI-PO ENGINES' SERIES

Chevy 265 & 283
Chevy 302 & 327
Chevy 348 & 409
Chevy 350 & 400
Chevy 396 & 427
Chevy 454 thru 512
Chrysler Hemi
Chrysler 273, 318, 340 & 360
Chrysler 361, 383, 400, 413, 426, 440
Ford 289, 302, Boss 302 & 351W
Ford 351C & Boss 351
Ford Big Block

BROOKLANDS RESTORATION SERIES

Auto Restoration Tips & Techniques
Basic Bodywork Tips & Techniques
Basic Painting Tips & Techniques
Camaro Restoration Tips & Techniques
Chevrolet High Performance Tips & Techniques
Chevy Engine Swapping Tips & Techniques
Chevy-GMC Pickup Repair
Chrysler Engine Swapping Tips & Techniques
Custom Painting Tips & Techniques
Engine Swapping Tips & Techniques
Ford Pickup Repair
How to Build a Street Rod
Land Rover Restoration Tips & Techniques
MG 'T' Series Restoration Guide
Mustang Restoration Tips & Techniques
Performance Tuning - Chevrolets of the '60's
Performance Tuning - Pontiacs of the '60's

BROOKLANDS MILITARY VEHICLES SERIES

Allied Military Vehicles No.1 1942-1945
Allied Military Vehicles No.2 1941-1946
Complete WW2 Military Jeep Manual
Dodge Military Vehicles No.1 1940-1945
Hail To The Jeep
Land Rovers in Military Service
Off Road Jeeps: Civ. & Mil. 1944-1971
US Military Vehicles 1941-1945
US Army Military Vehicles WW2-TM9-2800
VW Kubelwagen Military Portfolio1940-1990
WW2 Jeep Military Portfolio 1941-1945
1693

CONTENTS

BROOKLANDS BOOKS

ACKNOWLEDGEMENTS

The MG Midget of the 1960s and '70s has long been a favourite as an affordable sports car, and we published our first book of road tests about it several years ago. When the time came for a reprint, we decided to make use of the wealth of additional material which had accumulated in our archives in the meantime, and to enlarge the book into a Gold Portfolio.

We are always pleased to acknowledge the help we receive in putting our books together, and on this occasion our thanks go to Graham Paddy and Pete Taylor of Moss Europe Ltd, who kindly provided the cover photographs. Once again, motoring writer James Taylor has prepared a few words of introduction, and we have been fortunate to enjoy the co-operation and support of those who hold the copyright to the material reproduced here. We are sure that Midget enthusiasts will endorse our thanks to the managements of *Autocar, Autosport, Car and Driver, Car South Africa, Cars and Car Conversions, Cars Illustrated, Modern Motor, Motor, Motor Sport, Motor Trend, Popular Classics, Popular Imported Cars, Road & Track, Road Test, Safety Fast, Small Car, Sports and GT Cars, Sports Car Graphic, Sport Car Road Tests, Sports Car World, Thoroughbred and Classic Cars, Wheels* and the *World Car Catalogue.*

R M Clarke

The MG Midget is such a well-accepted classic sports car today that it seems hard to remember that its origins lay in the badge engineering perpetrated by the British Motor Corporation in the 1950's. In fact, BMC's Len Lord approached Donald Healey and asked him to design a cheap small sports car around Austin A35 mechanical components, and the result was badged as an Austin-Healey Sprite when it was announced in 1958.

However, MG also needed a new small sports car, and so the original "Frogeye" Sprite was restyled, using cues from the forthcoming MGB, and from 1961 was made available as the MG Midget. The Sprite continued alongside the Midget until the end of 1971 - hence the nickname "Spridget" for these cars - it was always the same car except for its badging.

In its 20 years of production, the Midget underwent hundreds of changes, and was produced in five distinct Marks, Mark Is had 948cc engines until 1962, and more powerful 1098cc types (complemented by disc front brakes) thereafter. Rear suspension changes and a power increase created the Mk.II models in 1964, and the Mk.III arrived in 1966 with a larger 1275cc engine. Rostyle wheels distinguished 1969 Mk.IV's, and the chrome grille gave way to a black one while occupants benefited from reclining seats. After January 1972, Mk.IVs had round rear wheel arches, but these did not last and the squared-off arches came back in 1974 on the Mk.V Midget. Much to the disgust of traditionalists, this had black plastic bumpers to meet US regulations, a raised ride height, and a new 1493cc engine borrowed from the Midget's long-time rival - the Triumph Spitfire.

The last Midget was built in November 1979, by which time there was no doubt that the car was outdated. It was still fun though, and that element of fun has never diminished. It is what has made the Midget such a popular classic car today - popular enough for British Motor Heritage to see commercial advantage in producing complete new Midget bodyshells from the original tooling so that enthusiasts can rebuild worn-out cars to as-new condition.

James Taylor

THE M.G. MIDGET RETURNS—and here comes one of the first off the production line.

IN introducing the 948 c.c. M.G. Midget, Abingdon returns to the type of machine which made the octagon world-famous. True, it is in most respects identical to the Austin-Healey Sprite Mk. II, but frontal treatment and a body-strip give it a somewhat different look.

With the cessation of the TD and TF models, the term "Midget" disappeared from the M.G. catalogues. It was felt that a 1½-litre car was just too big for this nomenclature, and could not justify a description which so aptly described the earlier "M", "J" and "P" series, all of which were under 1,000 c.c.

Actually the acceleration of the new Midget is better than that of the 1,250 c.c. TF, by about one second from 0-60 m.p.h. As a matter of interest, the

THE M.G. MIDGET RETURNS
948 c.c. Two-Seater Revives Famous Series—Mk. II "1600" Also Introduced

standard "P" o.h.c., 950 c.c. engine of the mid-1930s developed about 27 b.h.p., and the 1961 push-rod 948 c.c. unit develops 47 b.h.p. Maximum speed of the "P" was about 72 m.p.h., whilst the new edition can attain 85 m.p.h.

Modern independent front suspension has improved road-holding to a marked degree, and safety has been vastly increased by the use of hydraulically operated brakes. Rack-and-pinion steering is employed.

A body-cum-chassis construction is employed, reinforced by box-section body sills and a robust facia-panel structure attached to box-section members which locate engine and gearbox mounting points, together with the steering assembly units. These, in turn, are attached to a third cross-member in

SIMILAR in most respects to the new Austin-Healey Sprite, the familiar octagon is found on the radiator.

front, and just behind the rear seats a stiffening panel reinforces the wheel arches.

The rear suspension is by 15-leaves, quarter-elliptic springs to which are attached parallel radius arms to absorb braking and engine torque. Front suspension has a pressed steel lower wishbone in conjunction with a single forged steel arm at the top; rather similar to the system used on several B.M.C. cars.

Optional extras include hard-top, Smith's heater and ventilation equipment, radio and cigar lighter. Bolt-on disc wheels are standard, with 5.20 x 13

tyres. The spare wheel is located in the spacious boot.

The Mark II Series "A" M.G. has no major modifications to body or chassis, other than a revised final axle ratio. Main changes are in the o.h.v. engine, which is now of 1,622 c.c. (76.2 x 88.9 mm.), as compared to 1,588 c.c. in 1960 and develops 90 b.h.p. at 5,800 r.p.m. Compression ratio has been raised from 8.3 to 1 to 8.9 to 1. Larger valves and carburetters are employed. As a result, maximum speed is now well in excess of 100 m.p.h., with much higher cruising speeds than were possible with the 1960 type. The new axle ratio is 4 to 1.

Naturally, as regards competition work, the car now falls out of the 1,600 c.c. International class, and will have to run with 2-litre machines.

1961 CARS

MIDGET
returns to
M.G. range

The First Under-1,000 c.c. M.G. Since 1936

M.G. enthusiasts the world over will welcome the news that, for the first time since mid-1936—when the PB-type Midget went out of production—an under-1,000 c.c. model once again figures in the M.G. range.

The rationalization policy of the British Motor Corporation has been applied to its production and the new Midget is, in fact, one of a pair of basically similar models, the other being the recently introduced Mark II version of the Austin-Healey Sprite. In all their essentials the two cars are identical, but the Midget has a distinctive front, different trim and various de luxe items of finish and equipment not supplied on the standard version of the Mk. II Sprite.

Naturally it costs a little more, the basic price being £472 which, with British purchase tax of £197 15s. 10d., gives a home market total of £669 15s. 10d. This compares with the basic price of £445 (£631 10s. 10d. complete) asked for the Austin-Healey Sprite.

* * *

Power is supplied by a modified 2-carburetter version of the B.M.C. A-type engine, which has now been pro-

duced to the tune of some 1,500,000 units. With a 9/1 compression ratio, it needs 100 octane fuel. The close-ratio four-speed synchromesh gearbox has a central remote-control lever.

Although a conventional rigid axle casing is used, the rear suspension is unusual in employing quarter-elliptic springs in conjunction with parallel, super-imposed radius arms—a system which has the advantages of low unsprung weight and of concentrating the main suspension loading on the centre portion of the unitary-construction shell, the tail playing no part in supporting the weight of the car. The sole functions of the latter are to carry the six-gallon rear tank and provide a useful luggage boot in which the spare wheel is housed horizontally on the floor.

At the front, conventional independent coil-and-wishbone suspension is used, embodying pressed-steel lower wishbones and single forged upper links that also

serve as the arms of the lever-type Armstrong hydraulic dampers. The steering gear is of the rack-and-pinion type.

The Midget has Lockheed hydraulic drum brakes with two leading shoes at the front; the handbrake is on the passenger's side of the propeller-shaft tunnel and has a normal (not "fly-off") ratchet button.

The new Midget is, of course, intended primarily as a two-seater, but there is a considerable space behind the two bucket seats; if required, a cushion can be supplied as an extra to enable this space to be used for carrying a youngster. Otherwise, it can be used for stowing coats, shopping and so on, and it will, in fact, take a good-sized suitcase.

The boot has a lockable lid and straps are provided on the bulkhead to secure the detachable hood material in an envelope clear of the floor. The separate hood sticks (which are of the two-piece type with a joint in the centre for easy stowage)

The h
up, bu
on the
which

The spare wheel is stowed on the boot floor, but there is quite a fair amount of luggage space by sports-car standards.

Both bucket seats have sliding adjustment and the carpeted well behind them can take extra luggage. Flecked rubber matting covers the front floor. A large rev counter is standard; clutch and brake pedals are of pendant type, the throttle has an organ pedal.

TA/TB/TC 1936-49 TD 1950-53 TF 1953-55

also have their own envelope and fit round the spare wheel, still leaving a fair amount of room for luggage. With the additional space behind the seats in the passenger compartment, the Midget is very well provided with baggage space by sports car standards.

Unlike so many completely detachable hoods of the past, the new Midget design is neither difficult to erect nor deficient in vision—the latter thanks to a large rear window and sensibly-sized quarter lights, all in transparent plastic of the type which does not suffer from careless stowage. In addition, rigid-framed, sliding-panel side-screens can be fitted to the doors by quick-acting screws which can be operated with a coin. Both the forward and rear Perspex panels are arranged to slide.

The facia board is leathercloth covered, with a padded roll for the scuttle; a revolution counter is standard and both this and the speedometer (with total and trip mileage recorders) have a detailed scale. Other instruments comprise a fuel gauge, a water thermometer and an oil-pressure gauge. Toggle switches are used for the wipers and sealed-beam lights. Other accessories included as standard are a windscreen washer, anchorage points for safety belts and flasher-type direction indicators.

Among a long list of optional extras available from the factory are a radio set, a tonneau cover which can be arranged to cover the entire cockpit, to protect all but the driver's seat, or to cover the interior luggage space only, a heater and demister, and whitewall or heavy duty tyres; dealer-fitted accessories include a locking petrol cap, a cigar lighter, wing mirrors, twin horns, Ace Mercury wheel discs and a luggage carrier.

Externally, the new model is undeniably a good looker. Points special to the Midget include a very attractive front grille with vertical slats and the traditional M.G. trade mark incorporated in the central vertical bar, and embellishments in the form of a bright metal beading down the centre of the rear-hinged bonnet-top and a full-length flash on the body side; extending from the headlamps to the rear-light clusters, these flashes emphasize the low build. A total of five exterior colours, three types of interior trim and three hood colours are available in combinations which give a total of seven variants.

ides quite good headroom, and is easy to put - naturally looks at its sleekest when open, as 'he picture below shows the special wheel trims bought as an extra and, carrying the M.G. , give the car a real *de luxe* appearance.

M.G. MIDGET SPECIFICATION

ENGINE	
Cylinders ...	4 in line with 3-bearing crankshaft.
Bore and stroke	62.9 mm.×76.2 mm. (2.478 in.×3.0 in.).
Cubic capacity ...	948 c.c. (57.87 cu. in.).
Piston area ...	19.29 sq. in.
Compression ratio	9/1.
Valvegear ...	In line o.h.v. operated by push rods and rockers.
Carburation ...	Two semi-downdraught S.U. type HS2 carburetters, fed by AC mechanical pump, from 6-gallon tank.
Ignition	12-volt coil, centrifugal and vacuum timing control, 14 mm. Champion N5 sparking plugs.
Lubrication ...	Tecalemit or Purolator external full-flow filter. Oil capacity 7 pints (incl. filter).
Cooling	Water cooling with pump, fan and thermostat; 10-pint water capacity (plus ½ pint for heater if fitted).
Electrical system	12-volt, 43 amp. hr. battery charged by 19-amp. generator.
Maximum power	46.5 b.h.p. net (50 b.h.p. gross) at 5,500 r.p.m., equivalent to 2,750 ft./min. piston speed and 2.4 b.h.p. per sq. in. of piston area.
Maximum torque	52.5 lb. ft. at 2,750 r.p.m., equivalent to 138 lb./sq. in. b.m.e.p. at 1,375 ft./min. piston speed.
TRANSMISSION	
Clutch	Borg and Beck 6¼-in. single dry plate.
Gearbox ...	Four speeds with direct drive in top; synchromesh on three upper ratios.
Overall ratios ...	4.22, 5.726, 8.975 and 13.504; rev. 17.361.
Propeller shaft ...	Hardy Spicer, open.
Final drive ...	Hypoid bevel, three-quarter floating axle.
CHASSIS	
Brakes	Lockheed hydraulic, drum type all round.
Brake dimensions	Front and rear drums 7 in. dia.×1¼ in. wide.
Brake areas ...	67.5 sq. in. of lining (33.75 sq. in. front and rear) working on 110 sq. in. rubbed area of drums.
Front suspension	Independent by coil springs and wishbones with Armstrong lever-arm dampers.
Rear suspension...	Quarter-elliptic leaf springs with parallel radius arms and Armstrong lever-type dampers.
Wheels and tyres	Ventilated disc wheels with 4-stud fixing and 5.20-13 tubeless tyres.
Steering	Rack and pinion.
DIMENSIONS	
Length	Overall 11 ft. 5⅝ in.; wheelbase 6 ft. 8 in.
Width	Overall 4 ft. 5 in.; track 3 ft. 9¾ in. at front and 3 ft. 8¾ in. at rear.
Height	4 ft. 1¾ in.; ground clearance 5 in.
Turning circle ...	32 ft.
Kerb weight ...	14 cwt. (without fuel but with oil, water, tools, spare wheel, etc.).
EFFECTIVE GEARING	
Top gear ratio ...	15.4 m.p.h. at 1,000 r.p.m. and 30.6 m.p.h. at 1,000 ft./min. piston speed.
Maximum torque	2,750 r.p.m. corresponds to approx. 42.2 m.p.h. in top gear.
Maximum power	5,500 r.p.m. corresponds to approx. 84.0 m.p.h. in top gear.
Probable top gear pulling power...	190 lb./ton approx. (computed by *The Motor* from manufacturers' figures for torque, gear ratio and kerb weight, with allowances for 3½ cwt. load, 10% losses and 60 lb./ton drag).

M.G. MIDGET
Revived

The new M.G. Midget is reintroduced with a modern full width body which gives exceptional elbow room and a drag factor giving more than 85 m.p.h. from under 50 b.h.p.

IT has been proved many times that the production of wholly specialized cars is unprofitable and, except in special circumstances, such designs have had but a brief life. But in April, 1929 a new sports car, based upon an established tradition, was placed upon the British market. The make "M.G."; the type "M", the capacity 847 c.c.; the price R350; (The equivalent to-day of R1,050 basic; or say R1,490 in the U.K.) the established tradition; the production of a useable, roadworthy car of superior performance in its class by the adaptation of components in relatively large scale production for normal touring cars.

This "M" Type Midget used an overhead camshaft power unit and three speed gearbox which were in quantity production for the Morris 8, and this basic scheme (but with a four speed gearbox)

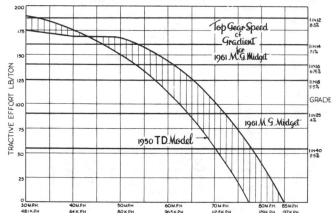

was followed in the "J" type which was in production from September, 1932 up to March, 1934 and in the "P" type which ran from February, 1934 up to May, 1936.

During this period racing versions, which resembled closely the basic design, pioneered high pressure supercharging with 28 lbs. boost giving 155 b.h.p/litre, and all independent suspension was also applied. Apart from being the first 750 c.c. car to see 100 m.p.h., and the first to cover 100 miles in one hour, the racing models of the car broke a vast number of records (some of which still stand to-day) and they were commonly first in their class in sprints, hill climbs, and long distance races.

In April, 1936, however, the overhead camshaft engine, which with three bearings and 939 c.c. had replaced the original two bearings and 847 c.c., was itself replaced by a somewhat simplified chassis with a 1,292 c.c. pushrod engine. This marked the beginning of the "T" series and in April, 1939 the "T.B." was introduced with a 1¼-litre power unit.

This was continued with slight changes as the "TC" six months from VE Day, and by the "TD" in 1950.

By 1954, 25 years after the introduction of the original "M" type, Midget engine power had nearly trebled (from 20 b.h.p to 55 b.h.p.) and road speed had risen from little over 60 m.p.h. to little short of 80 m.p.h., that is to say by some 25 per cent. It was therefore not illogical that when this model was in turn replaced by one having a more powerful 1·5 litre engine, and capable of a road speed approaching 100 m.p.h., the use of the word "Midget" seemed no longer appropriate, and, after so long and honourable history, it was put into suspense.

Now in 1961 there is a new M.G. Midget, which fits into the frame indicated by this name. Like the "P" series of 1934/36 it has an engine of 950 c.c. but despite the use of pushrod valve gear in place of an overhead camshaft it now develops 47 b.h.p. in place of 27 b.h.p. and despite a body design which has enlarged elbow room for the passengers from 34·0 ins. to 52·0 ins. the road speed has risen from little over 70 m.p.h. to 85 m.p.h.

A quarter elliptic spring with 15 leaves, each 1¾ in. wide, has the bottom and master leaf attached to a bracket below the axle tube and to contain brake and driving torque, there is a parallel radius arm mounted on the same bracket but above the axle. The two elements act therefore as two trailing arms to locate the axle end wise, and to restrain it from rotating, and the spring, with its mate, locates the whole assembly against side forces.

This arrangement has three advantages:
Reducing unsprung weight, which is particularly important in a car such as this which has a low sprung mass; the torsional forces tending to rack the structure when one wheel only passes over a bump are fed into the hull at a point where there is a massive transverse stiffening member and as the springs are relieved of driving torque wheel hop, and accompanying wheel spin, are reduced to a minimum when the car takes off from rest, or should it be traversing rough roads.

The front suspension is also slightly unconventional although of a type used on a large number of B.M.C. production cars. A normal pressed steel lower wishbone is used in conjunction with a single arm of forged steel at the top, the design being simplified further by using the damper body as the housing for the inboard upper bearing.

Rack and pinion steering

The rack and pinion steering gear gives positive control, and will run for exceptionally long periods without developing objectionable lost motion, and takes the wheels from lock to lock with 2⅓ turns of the steering wheel. With this design the inner pivot points of the short track rod may be considered part of the steering box, and as they are enclosed in flexible bellows they need no regular greasing. There are therefore only the two outer pivot bearings that need lubrication in the steering assembly and only eight other points requiring regular maintenance in the entire vehicle.

All the mechanical elements are attached to a combined body cum-chassis, which is reinforced by box section body sills and a fully enclosed central propeller shaft tunnel in the fore and aft plane, and, transversely, by a massive dash board structure integrated with the box section members which run forward to locate the engine and gearbox mounting points and the steering suspension elements. These are directly attached to a third cross member at the nose of the car, and behind the rear seats the wheel arches are tied together by yet another stiffening panel.

(Mechanical specifications follow those of the Austin-Healey Sprite II as reported in CAR, July, 1961).

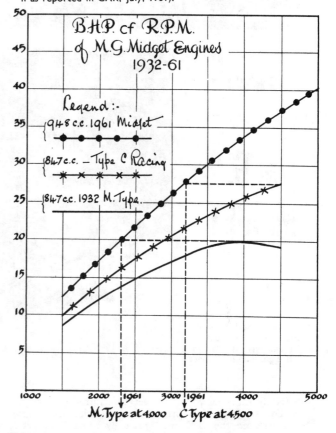

B.H.P. of R.P.M. of M.G. Midget Engines 1932-61

Legend:—
948 c.c. 1961 Midget
847 c.c. — Type C Racing
847 c.c. 1932 M. Type

M.Type at 4000   C Type at 4500

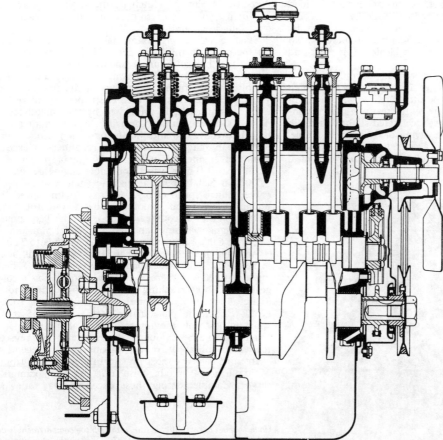

The new M.G. Midget engine gives 47 b.h.p. from 948 c.c. and provides performance whether measured in acceleration or maximum speed superior to any previous Midget Model.

1833

M.G. MIDGET

An M.G. badge is incorporated in the radiator grille, and there is a central chromed flash on the bonnet

SINCE the new M.G. Midget was introduced at the end of June, the Chancellor's tax adjustments have increased the U.K. total price by some £20; yet it remains within the £700 bracket. At this price it is still good value as a thoroughly well-planned and soundly constructed little car, and promises to regain the popularity won by its pre-war predecessors. It is no secret that the car is in effect a luxury version of the Austin-Healey Sprite II, and is thus £30 dearer with tax.

Mechanical dissimilarities are few, and the differences in performance between the Midget and the Sprite II (which we tested on 2 June) must be attributed to variations of tune, and mileage run since new by the test cars. Throughout the speed range, the Midget accelerated slightly faster in any given gear, and showed a saving of 3sec, for example, from 60 to 80 m.p.h. in top. In acceleration from rest, some of this advantage was lost by a clutch which was not ideal

for rapid take-offs. It took up the drive rather abruptly over a small part of the long and largely ineffective pedal travel, pulling engine revs below the point of maximum torque. Attempts to slip the clutch during rapid getaways resulted in clutch spin, which also prevented the car from restarting on a 1-in-3 test gradient.

Starting was always immediate, and there was no need for the choke in mild weather. After the car has stood for more than half-an-hour or so, the engine is often a little reluctant to pull straight away; this hesitance disappears rapidly as the engine warms up in the first few hundred yards, and acceleration is then crisp and responsive.

One is immediately impressed by the smoothness of the Midget's power unit. Normally the rev counter needle is held between 2,000 and 4,000 r.p.m. on the open road, but 5,000 r.p.m. may be used without roughness or excess noise from the engine. A noticeable surge of power is felt at 2,500 r.p.m. There was a noticeable engine period between 5,000 and 5,500 r.p.m., it became smooth again up to the valve bounce speed of 6,500 r.p.m. At this speed the unit remained sweet and smooth, so that a watchful eye had to be kept on the rev counter, which is standard equipment. On this an orange warning band starts at 5,500 r.p.m. and changes to red at 6,000 r.p.m.; the calibration extends to 7,000 r.p.m.

An intelligent choice of gear ratios enables full advantage to be taken of the wide span of engine power. When making a fast getaway there is a logical progression through the gears, and after reaching peak revs in bottom and second a useful range of acceleration remains in the subsequent gear. Second is particularly useful up to 45 m.p.h. for spurting past slow-moving traffic, and allows up to 50 m.p.h. Yet the docile behaviour of the engine at low revs enables the car to pull away from a walking pace in second gear.

In third gear the most practical range extends from about 25 m.p.h. to 60 m.p.h., with a 70 m.p.h. maximum in reserve. Complementing these excellent gear ratios are the

Under-bonnet accessibility is fair, although the compartment is unusually crowded on the Midget. The dipstick is below the sparking plug leads

Large amber winking indicators blend neatly with the stop and tail lamps. The rear side-screen panel is slipped forward to give access to the interior as there are no outside handles

ease and speed with which changes can be made, for the lever can be snatched from one position to the next almost as quickly as the hand can move. For fast upward changes the synchromesh cannot always quite cope, especially if the lever is pulled smartly from bottom to second. Distinctive but unobtrusive gear whine is audible in all the indirects. The gear lever is placed conveniently only a few inches from the driver's left hand on the steering wheel, and its knob is of hard plastic, insulated with rubber.

Bearing in mind the engine's willingness to rev, top gear gives just the right combination of liveliness with high-speed cruising, the road speed being just over 60 m.p.h. at 4,000 r.p.m. The fastest speed reached with the Midget was 86 m.p.h. at 5,600 r.p.m., when the engine is nowhere near the point of "running out of revs." The theoretical maximum, based on the engine's safe rev limit, would be just short of 100 m.p.h.

Factors tending to dissuade one from taking full advantage of the car's abilities were a marked increase in noise above 70 m.p.h., accompanied on this example by vibration, apparently from the transmission. The most comfortable and restful cruising rate is around 60 m.p.h., and the fuel consumption figures at constant speeds show that 60 m.p.h. is relatively economical, for at a steady 70 m.p.h. 10 miles fewer are averaged per gallon. If faster speeds are sustained, as when the car was held at 80 m.p.h. and above for long periods on M1, the oil pressure drops rapidly from its normal 60 p.s.i. maximum to nearer 40 p.s.i. Three pints of oil were consumed in 1,037 test miles, equivalent to nearly 3,000 m.p.g. At the higher speeds also, slight final drive whine was heard.

As for fuel consumption, the best figure obtained was 48·5 m.p.g. on a main road run with restrained use of the performance, but this figure dropped to 34·1 m.p.g. when the same 20-mile stretch of road was covered as fast as the car would go. In city traffic and at sustained high speeds consumption naturally increases, giving the overall figure of 33·4 m.p.g. for the entire test, but any owner in search of economy will have no difficulty in exceeding 40 m.p.g. with the Midget.

The 948 c.c. engine has a compression ratio of 9-to-1, and needs to be run on super premium grades of fuel. The lower compression ratio of 8·3-to-1 is optional to suit normal premium grades of petrol, and any increase in consumption resulting from this would probably be recovered in reduced petrol costs; performance, naturally, would be a little lower. The fuel tank holds only six gallons, so that frequent re-fuelling is necessary when the car is driven hard.

Directional stability of the Midget at speed is much affected by cross winds, and frequent correction is necessary to maintain a straight course. This characteristic is made less troublesome than it would be otherwise by the excellent precision of the rack-and-pinion steering. The control is completely free from lost movement, and with 2¼ turns of the wheel between the extremes of acceptably wide steering locks, it requires only small or even imperceptible move-

A padded roll runs along the top of the facia. Roomy pockets for maps and oddments are fitted to the inside of both doors. Right: Both seats tilt forward to give access to the rear compartment in which a seat cushion is an optional extra. An ashtray is also available at 7s 9d extra

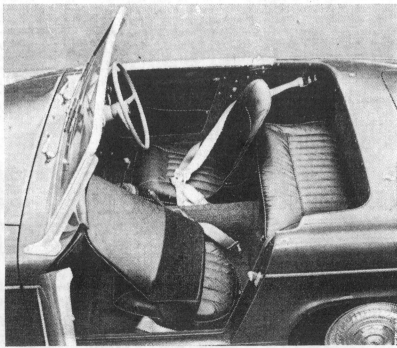

M.G. Midget . . .

With the hood in place instead of the hardtop the Midget uses the same sidescreens as are fitted to the Austin-Healey Sprite, but the car is still identifiable in this view by the full-length rubbing strip and "MG Midget" motifs on the luggage locker lid

ments of the wheel to control the car on a straight road.

When cornering the basic characteristic of the car is to oversteer, as a result of the rear wheel steering effect of the back axle, which is suspended on quarter-elliptic leaf springs. A newcomer to the car may find at first that the Midget corners unexpectedly sharply, but the handling is never vicious, and in a short time he is able to throw the Midget round corners taking full advantage of the responsive steering to correct any tendency for the tail of the car to move outwards. On winding country lanes and cross-country routes this little M.G. is really at home.

During the test some increase in travel of the brake pedal was noticed, and there was always a rather dead feel to the brakes. However, they do have a good reserve of stopping power, and fade does not occur in normal use. Pedal pressures required are fairly high, but although there is room for improvement in this respect, the driver is soon reassured that if he presses hard on the pedal the car will stop rapidly. The handbrake is controlled by a chromed pull-up lever to the left of the transmission tunnel and held the car without difficulty on the 1-in-3 test hill. The pedals are well-placed and allow easy simultaneous use of the brake and throttle.

Acceptably Soft Suspension

Extremely good bump absorption is provided by the suspension, which is softer than its layout would suggest. On secondary or badly surfaced city roads the car sits down well and does not jolt its occupants. On rough *pavé* the limited vertical wheel travel begins to tell, and the rear suspension bottoms violently on bump stops which seem to be too small.

Severe humps in the road naturally result in some firm upward movement, and when tall drivers were at the wheel they found their heads were near enough to the hardtop for them to hit it as the car bounced.

The stylish and well-made, glass-fibre hardtop with plastic interior linings may be fitted or removed single-handed in a matter of minutes. However, with the hardtop, sidescreens different from those supplied with the standard hood are necessary. As the total cost of the hardtop and sidescreens is some £73, including purchase tax, when they are ordered with the new car, most owners will probably be content with the basic p.v.c. hood as all-the-year-round weather protection. Purchase tax on the hardtop kit is not payable if it is ordered after delivery of the car, and the price is then £50.

The draught-sealing with the hood in place is about as satisfactory as one may ever hope for in a car with detachable sidescreens, and a particularly good seal is made by the rubber surrounds. The sidescreens have light alloy frames with double sliding Perspex windows allowing opening for ventilation at both front and rear. The hood fit is also good, and a metal bar sewn into the leading edge ensures a perfect overlap joint at the top of the windscreen, while the strut springs can be locked, and then released

The toolkit comprises a side-lifting jack, a wheelbrace, and a socket spanner for the sparking plugs. Storage bags are provided for the hood

when the hood is in position. When not in use the struts separate like tent poles at the centre and fold away into a bag for stowage in the luggage locker. At above 70 m.p.h. wind pressure causes the leading edge of the sidescreens to bow out.

A generously large luggage locker is provided with an exterior lockable handle—an important point since the car doors do not lock. Although the spare wheel lies flat in the centre of the boot floor there is ample room around it for carefully packed luggage. At the forward end of the compartment some space is lost when the folded hood is stowed in the bag provided. The boot is held open by a swivelling prop which proved annoyingly clumsy.

Visibility is particularly good, and the driver sits high enough to see over the steering wheel and scuttle without difficulty, and with both front wings and the bonnet in sight. The windscreen pillars are slender and offer little or no obstruction to visibility even when the car is closed. To the rear of the windscreens with the hood in place, vision is better than when the hardtop is fitted, as rear quarter windows are incorporated in the hood.

Self-parking wipers have blades as long as allowed by the depth of the windscreen, but a large portion is left unswept at both ends. The interior mirror is mounted too low and vibrates; for safety's sake we added a suction-fitting interior mirror to the screen of the test car.

Well-upholstered seats are adjustable fore-and-aft, and covered in black p.v.c. with a red-painted car. The cushion is comfortable and the backrest provides good lateral support, but it is too firm at the top, and tends to make the occupants slump forward; more support is needed in the small of the back. The occasional rear seat fitted to the test car costs £4 5s, and is adequate for two children if the adults have their seats well forward to provide rear legroom. The floor and gearbox housing are covered with dark moulded rubber flecked with red. Carpet is used behind the seats and, for protection, on the lower portions of the folding seat backrests. Both front floor mats are readily removable.

A plain but functional instrument layout is provided, with the main rev counter and speedometer on either side of the steering column. A fuel gauge is on the right, and a combined oil pressure gauge and coolant thermometer is fitted on the left, where it is partly masked by the driver's left hand on the steering wheel. Provision of a trip mileometer in the speedometer is particularly welcome. The steering wheel and column surround adjoining the facia are of yellowy

plastic material somewhat out of keeping with the character of the rest of the car.

Tumbler switches are used for the wipers and for the lamps, which are the latest sealed-reflector and filament pattern. They give ample main beam illumination for the speed potential of the Midget, and have a generously long reach on dipped beam without dazzling oncoming drivers. A switch similar to that for the lamps is mounted centrally on the facia to control the winking indicators. They are not self-cancelling, but a bright warning lamp is fitted above the steering wheel boss.

Twin windtone horns fitted to the test car are a specially desirable extra, priced at £1 12s 1d including tax. A fresh-air heater is another practically essential optional fitting, and costs £17 10s with tax. This was also among the £116 worth of accessories on the Midget tested, and gave a good flow of air through inlets with cut-off flaps to either side of the engine bulkhead. An overriding air control is fitted on the facia, and a tap on the engine allows the hot water supply to be turned off for the summer. There is no provision for a reversing lamp to be fitted. Twelve grease points require attention every 1,000 miles.

This new M.G. is an endearing little car with a remarkable capacity for nipping about among heavy traffic. It is easy and safe to drive, and certainly is approaching the ideal for the market which it is intended to serve.

M.G. MIDGET

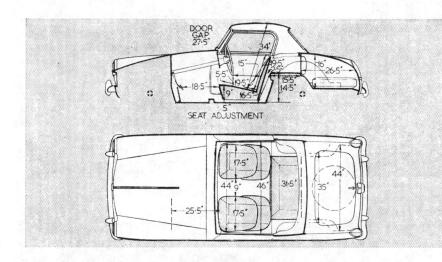

Scale ¼in. to 1ft. Driving seat in central position. Cushions uncompressed.

DATA

PRICE (basic), with open two-seater body, £472.
British purchase tax, £217 11s 5d.
Total (in Great Britain), £689 11s 5d.
Extras, incl. p.t.:
Hardtop and sidescreens, £70 16s 8d; Tonneau cover, £6 11s 3d; Heater, £17 10s 0d; Fresh air unit, £5 16s 8d; Twin horns, £1 12s 1d; Cigarette lighter, £1 12s 1d; Whitewall tyres, £7 9s 6d; Heavy duty tyres, £6 11s 3d; Radio, £30 5s 2d; Laminated windscreen, £4 0s 2d; Ace Mercury wheel discs, £16 8s 1d; Luggage carrier and wing mirror, £12 15s 2d; Rear compartment cushion, £4 7s 6d.

ENGINE: Capacity, 948 c.c. (57·9 cu. in.).
Number of cylinders, 4.
Bore and stroke, 62·9 × 76·2 mm (2.48 × 3·0 in.).
Valve gear, o.h.v., pushrods and rockers.
Compression ratio, 9·0 to 1 (8·3 to 1 optional).
B.h.p. 41.6 (net) at 5,500 r.p.m. (b.h.p. per ton laden 49·3).
Torque, 53lb. ft. at 3,000 r.p.m.
M.p.h. per 1,000 r.p.m. in top gear, 15·4.
WEIGHT: (With 5 gal fuel), 13·9 cwt (1,554lb).
Weight distribution (per cent); F, 52·7; R, 47·3.
Laden as tested, 16·9 cwt. (1,890 lb).
Lb per c.c. (laden), 2.
BRAKES: Type, Lockheed hydraulic.
Drum dimensions: F and R, 7in. dia.; 1·75in. wide.
Total swept area: 110 sq. in. (131 sq. in. per ton laden).
TYRES: 5·20—13in. Dunlop Gold Seal Nylon tubeless.
Pressures (p.s.i.); F, 18; R, 20 (normal). F, 24; R, 26 (fast driving).
TANK CAPACITY: 6 Imperial gallons.
Oil sump, 6·5 pints.
Cooling system, 10 pints (including heater).
DIMENSIONS: Wheelbase, 6ft 8in.
Track: F, 3ft 8·75in.; R, 3ft 9·75in.
Length (overall), 11ft 4·25in.
Width, 4ft 5in. Height, 4ft 1·75in.
Ground clearance, 5in.
Frontal area, 12·4 sq. ft. (approx.).
Capacity of luggage space, 11·5 sq. ft. (approx.).
ELECTRICAL SYSTEM: 12-volt; 43 ampère-hour battery.
Headlamps, 60-45 watt filaments.
SUSPENSION: Front, coil springs and wishbones, lever-type dampers. Rear, live axle, trailing quarter-elliptic leaf springs, radius arms, lever-type dampers.

PERFORMANCE

ACCELERATION TIMES (mean):
Speed range, Gear Ratios and Time in Sec.

m.p.h.	4·22 to 1	5·73 to 1	8·09 to 1	13·5 to 1
10—30	—	10·1	6·3	—
20—40	13·3	8·6	6·2	—
30—50	14·1	9·5	7·1	—
40—60	15·7	11·2	—	—
50—70	17·9	16·5	—	—
60—80	28·6	—	—	—

From rest through gears to:

30 m.p.h.	..	6·3 sec.
40 ,,	..	9·4 ,,
50 ,,	..	14·4 ,,
60 ,,	..	20·2 ,,
70 ,,	..	32·8 ,,
80 ,,	..	56·8 ,,

Standing quarter mile 21·9 sec.

MAXIMUM SPEEDS ON GEARS:

Gear			m.p.h.	k.p.h.
Top		(mean)	84·7	136
		(best)	86	138·4
3rd	..	..	70	112
2nd	..	..	50	81
1st	..	..	30	48

TRACTIVE EFFORT (by Tapley meter):

		Pull (lb per ton)	Equivalent gradient
Top	..	180	1 in 12·4
Third	..	240	1 in 10·8
Second	..	350	1 in 15·8

BRAKES (at 30 m.p.h. in neutral):

Pedal load in lb	Retardation	Equiv. stopping distance in ft
25	0·16g	187
50	0·39g	77
75	0·92g	32·8

FUEL CONSUMPTION (at steady speeds in top gear):

30 m.p.h.	51·6 m.p.g.
40 ,,	54·8 ,,
50 ,,	47·2 ,,
60 ,,	43·0 ,,
70 ,,	33·8 ,,

Overall fuel consumption for 1,037 miles, 33·4 m.p.g. (8·4 litres per 100 km.).
Approximate normal range 32-34 m.p.g. (8·8-5·9 litres per 100 km.).
Fuel: Super Premium.

TEST CONDITIONS: Weather: dry; sunny intervals, 10 m.p.h. wind gusting to 25 m.p.h.
Air temperature, 68 deg. F.

STEERING: Turning circle:
Between kerbs, L, 30ft 0in. R, 30ft 3in.
Between walls, L, 31ft 5in. R, 31ft 8in.
Turns of steering wheel from lock to lock, 2.25.

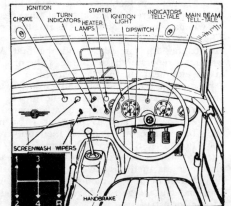

SPEEDOMETER CORRECTION: m.p.h.

Car speedometer	..	..	..	..	10	20	30	40	50	60	70	80
True speed	..	..	..	..	10	19	29	40	50	60	70	80

A Spritely Midget

The first under-one-litre MG since 1936 is undoubtedly the fastest unblown production Midget yet—and one of the simplest. With its basically BMC A-Series engine it provides nearly 50 b.h.p. per litre, and a top speed of more than 85 m.p.h.

WHEN the British Motor Corporation introduced the Mark 2 version of the Austin-Healey Sprite last summer they quickly followed it with a new MG model based on the same engine, chassis and running gear. This followed the Corporation's policy of "doubling-up" on body pressings and power-units to produce more than one *marque* from volume production components. The new MG Midget is in fact, a de luxe variant of the Austin-Healey Sprite, and there is no doubt that this likeable little sports car will gain as many adherents as its illustrious predecessors. The current Midget is the first MG to carry the world-famous tag for ten years, and the first MG to be built without a separate chassis frame. The original MG Midget (a development of the three-speed o.h.c. Morris Minor, a product of the same Nuffield Group) was introduced in 1929 and was capable of about 60 m.p.h. on its 20 b.h.p. Its cubic capacity was 847 c.c. compared to the current Midget's 948 cc, and its price at £175 makes the latest car's basic price of £472 look incredibly reasonable. The 1962 Pound Sterling is worth at most only a quarter of the 1929 Pound, so there is little doubt that modern production and business methods have given us a better product for the equivalent of less money. The modern-day Purchase Tax and Surcharge can hardly be blamed on the British Motor Industry!

The 1962 MG Midget is smart and fast, of simple easy-to-maintain design with a top speed of more than 85 m.p.h. in absolutely standard trim. So much is known about the BMC A-Series engine by the live British "speed conversion" industry that it is easy to modify the power-unit to provide a maximum speed of more than 100 m.p.h.—a performance, which for a mass-produced 948 c.c. pushrod o.h.v.—engined car would have seemed unbelievable only a few years ago.

Like its close relative the Austin-Healey Sprite Mark 2 the new MG Midget has the "one-piece" body/chassis

QUICK CHECK						
Maximum: 10 for each category						
PERFORMANCE ...	...	...	...	...	...	10
ROADHOLDING	...	...	...	...	...	8
GEARBOX	...	...	...	...	...	7
COMFORT...	...	...	...	...	...	8
FINISH ...	...	...	...	...	...	8
BRAKES ...	...	...	...	...	...	10
VISIBILITY ...	...	...	...	...	...	9
ECONOMY	...	...	...	...	...	10
STARTING...	...	...	...	...	...	10
All assessments commensurate with type of car and price tag.						

(ABOVE) *MG's have always been notable for good looks and the latest Midget maintains the breed's reputation. The available hardtop fits in very well with the general lines of the model*

(RIGHT) *The steel bonnet has a strut which is difficult to unclip from the scuttle end. When in position, the aperture is large enough to provide good accessibility. The "cast-iron" engine provides nearly 50 b.h.p. per litre. The MG grille is attractive—but not to clean!*

structure with front wings, headlamps, grille etc., all forming the front part of the structure and contributing to the rigidity. The Mark I Sprite "lift-up" bonnet incorporating headlamp nacelles, wings, and grille (with "toad-like" grin) was prone to shimmy, and there is no doubt that this new structure is a great improvement both from the appearance viewpoint, and on the score of rigidity. Perhaps a little accessibility has been lost around the front suspension and steering, but the alligator bonnet is large (and heavy!) and all engine and ancilliaries are reasonably placed for servicing.

Compared to the Mk I Sprite the new Sprite and MG Midget have larger carburetters, "hotter" camshafts, larger valves, and a compression ratio raised to 9 : 1, although the "old" ratio of 8.3 : 1 is still available for countries where fuel quality is low. Spacing of the gear ratios has been changed from the Mk I specification, and the current spacing greatly improves the performance and the fun of driving, although the synchromesh mechanism is still weak when changing down from top gear to third, and from third to second. Low gear is not equipped with synchromesh, and is harsh to engage, even at rest.

The pressed steel hull is still basically as Mk I Sprite, but the adoption of a modified rear section with wheel arches and side panels transversely tied by an eight-inch-wide fixed deck which blends into the uprights, has made it possible to ultilise 12-in. aperture behind the two bucket seats for extra luggage, or for the accommodation of children. On the test Midget a rear cushion (to match the upholstery and trim) was fitted in the rear space, but this was found to be ornamental rather than practical. There is no doubt however that for the transport of children and extra luggage the aperture provides above-average space for a sports car of less than one-litre. In addition, the stiffening of the rear body structure has made it possible to incorporate an opening lid to the sizeable rear boot, which also contains the spare wheel, hood, and tools.

The test Midget was fitted with the optional and very smart hardtop. This was secured by a simple four-point fixing, and was remarkably easy to fit. Like most hardtops however it was full of clicks and creaks when the car was on the move. The large rear window gave good visibility, and the excellent light-alloy-framed sidescreens (with sliding windows) also contributed to an above-average road view for this type of car. It is a pity that the side windows and hardtop weren't better designed to mate with each other as there were appreciable gaps where the wind-screen frame met the side windows, and more gaps where the top/rear section of the doors met the hardtop. Draughts were plentiful but the Smiths heater/demister was extremely powerful, and the car was, generally speaking, warm and snug—even when heating the interior without recourse to the booster motor. The heater takes in fresh air through a vent and trunk mounted behind the grille on the offside of the car, and is most efficient. Demisting of the windscreen in the recent cold conditions was reasonable, but rear window misting was a problem, although it was comparatively easy to reach out and wipe the area with a cloth.

Driving position was fair with bucket seats that would have gained by the adoption of thicker "thigh" padding. The seat adjustment only just provided enough legroom for a six-footer, and there is no doubt that an "undished" steering wheel (and shortened scuttle section) would contribute to a more natural driving position. The steering wheel itself was badly finished in an incongruous bronze

The interior is well trimmed. Floor mats are of a flecked plastic material, and the seats have a neat piped finish. The traditional short MG gear lever is well placed, and there are large doorpockets (not visible in photograph). One of the transverse crossmembers, incorporated in the floor structure can be seen just ahead of the driver's seat. The test car was equipped with three-point safety-belts, fitted to the standard BMC brackets

SPECIFICATION

PERFORMANCE

Through the gears:

0—30 ... ... 5.5 sec.	0—60 ... ... 19 sec.	
0—40 ... ... 9 sec.	0—70 ... ... 29 sec.	
0—50 ... ... 13 sec.		

Car mileage at completion of test: 6,350
Maximum speeds: Top, 86 m.p.h.; third, 73 m.p.h.; second, 55 m.p.h.

ENGINE

B.M.C. A-series four cylinder in-line, water-cooled. Pushrod overhead valves. Bore: 62.9 mm. Stroke: 76.2 mm. Cubic capacity: 948 c.c. Compression ratio: 9 : 1. Power-output: 46 b.h.p. (nett) at 5,500 r.p.m. (49.8 gross). Twin S.U. HS2 carburetters. Lucas coil and distributor (12-volt) ignition. A.C. mechanical fuel pump.

TRANSMISSION

B.M.C. four-speed gearbox in unit with engine. Floor control by short lever. Synchromesh mechanism on three upper ratios. Overall ratios: 1st, 13.504; 2nd, 8.085; 3rd, 5.726; 4.22:1. Reverse: 17.361. Borg and Beck single dry-plate clutch. Final drive by three-quarter floating live axle with hypoid gears. Ratio 4.22 : 1.

SUSPENSION

Independent front by unequal length wishbones, coil springs and lever-type dampers. Rear suspension by quarter-elliptic leaf springs, live axle, and lever-type dampers. Steering by rack and pinion gear.

BRAKES

Lockheed hydraulic all round with 7 in. by 1¼ in. drums. Two-leading shoes at front. Central handbrake operating on rear brakes. Pressed steel bolt-on wheels.

DIMENSIONS

Wheelbase: 6 ft. 8 in. Track: front, 3 ft. 9¾ in., rear, 3 ft. 8¾ in. Length: 11 ft. 5⅝ in. Width: 4 ft. 5⅛ in. Turning circle: 32 ft. 2 in. Kerb weight: 13 cwt. Ground clearance: 5 in. Fuel capacity: 6 gallons (Imp.). Average fuel consumption: 34 m.p.g. (100 octane). Tyres: Dunlop 5.20 by 13 tubeless.

BRAKING FIGURES

Using Bowmonk Dynometer. From 30 m.p.h. 95 per cent=31.8 ft.

PRICE

£689 11s. 5d. including Purchase Tax. Basic price £472. (Hardtop, radio heater extra).

shade. The instrument panel was well laid out with large diameter speedometer (with trip odometer as well as season) and rev.-counter, fuel contents gauge, and combined water temperature and oil pressure gauge. The facia was covered with anti-reflective black leathercloth with a padded roll across the top. There was an electric "cigar lighter", and a first-class fully-transistorised Radiomobile built-in to the left of the facia panel. Reception from this instrument was exceptional, and the instant performance from the transistorised receiver (no "warming-up" period is required) was most convenient. In spite of the radio performance however it was really only useable when the MG was travelling comparatively slowly, or when at rest as the rather high noise level of the car, particularly with hardtop fitted, made listening an ear-straining affair.

Minor controls consisted of neat tumbler switches, and push-pull cables. It was strange to note that a pull starter control is still used in addition to a key ignition switch when the majority of current cars fit the highly convenient combined key-operated ignition/starter switch. The choke control for the twin 1¼-in. S.U. carburetters had an excellent "twist-and-lock" action which made warming-up a simple affair. The winking traffic indicator control was mounted in the centre of the facia, and was a two-way tumbler switch which had to be searched for in daylight, and being set in amongst other minor controls, was almost impossible to easily locate after dark. An illuminated switch, or a steering column stalk (or even a steering wheel boss switch) would have been preferable, and a great deal safer and more efficient.

Performance of the car was exhilarating, 60 m.p.h. being obtainable through the gears in 19 seconds, with a third gear maximum of 73 m.p.h. Seventy m.p.h. was available in 29 seconds, and for give-and-take averages on crowded roads the MG Midget was a very sound bet. Handling was good, the high-geared steering (2 1/3 turns from lock to lock) contributing greatly to ease of control and enjoyment of driving. The rack and pinion mechanism was a delight to handle and in spite of the high ratio was light at all speeds—an object lesson to manufacturers of many other small cars with far lower-geared steering. There were no flat spots and the engine was most responsive at all speeds, but the spacing of the accelerator and brake pedals could be modified to advantage. Any driver with largish feet found his "throttle foot" apt to become trapped behind the brake pedal when the throttle was pressed fairly well down. The clutch was sweet throughout the test and was well up to racing-type take-offs and gear-changes.

No anti-roll bars are fitted to the MG Midget and there was appreciable roll even from low speeds, when corners and bends were negotiated. The live rear axle is mounted on quarter-elliptic springs and located by trailing links. Body roll of the Midget promotes rear wheel steering, and the car was prone to roll-oversteer from quite low speeds, but fast cornering was easy enough.

The engine was incredibly willing, and if full use was made of the gearbox, the car could be made to cover the ground in surprising fashion. The engine sounded busy at most speeds, and there was a great deal of fan noise when revs. were high. There was very little power at low revs. but the MG would trickle along without snatch in top gear providing the throttle opening was kept constant. Strong acceleration however demanded a "change-down", as befits a sports car. With its sporty camshaft the A-Series BMC engine as fitted to the Midget goes in three "stages". It starts to "go" at 1,500 r.p.m., then takes another bite at 3,500, and finally really comes to life at 5,000. The

Rear window of the hardtop is of ample dimensions, and the general finish of the car is good. unlike the Sprite, the Midget has a chromium waist strip on the body sides

rev.-counter has a technicolour section from 5—7,000 r.p.m., the final scarlet strip ending at 7,000, and the engine was very willing to enter the red in the indirects. Interior noise was understandably high (particularly with the hardtop) when the revs. were used freely, and there was a surprising amount of structure vibration, especially on the over-run. No pinking or running-on was apparent during the test runs but 100 octane fuel was very desirable with the 9 : 1 compression ratio. Warming up was rather a slow process, and during recent icy spells the car required about three miles of gentle driving before the water temperature gauge needle would show any signs of movement. The car was also prone to carburetter icing during warming-up periods.

Springing was firm but the ride improved as speed increased. In spite of the none-too-generous headroom with the hardtop fitted. the suspension was good enough to keep the driver's head from hitting the ceiling, even on bumpy roads.

The drum brakes were well up to the car's performance, and no fading could be detected at fast road speeds. Pedal pressures were light, and the action was progressive (2LS front, and leading/trailing rear). The handbrake was centrally mounted but was not equipped with the traditional MG "fly-off" action, more's the pity. Sited on the left-hand side of the propeller-shaft tunnel it was also capable of crushing the passenger's fingers if they were anywhere in the vicinity when the brake was applied—and with the low seats this was easily possible.

Taken all-round we found the new MG Midget to be a fast, non-tricky sports car that could be used for all types of motoring from fast touring to shopping. For a relatively modest outlay the Midget owner can become a competition motorist, and the various degrees of tune that can be applied to the car makes it a very worthwhile proposition. Easy to drive and easy on the eye it is the fastest MG Midget yet, and it must be the easiest to service. ★

For a small sports car the boot is a good size, and as seen here contains the folding hood and frame, tool kit, and spare wheel. For maximum carrying capacity it would be permissible to jettison all but the tool kit. There is also appreciable luggage space behind the seats within the car

The MG Midget has a deep cushion fitted behind the driver and passenger seats. With hood or hardtop in position the headroom is so restricted that it can only be regarded as a "child seat". It would seem more realistic to use the space for luggage or occasional passengers—without the cushion

MG MIDGET

No matter how you look at it, the new Midget's a real fun car.

● "It's as if the TD were reincarnated!" This was the reaction of one "classic" Midget fan to B.M.C.'s new MG Midget. A stablemate of the Austin-Healey Sprite II, it's identical to the Sprite in mechanical specifications, general body configuration and performance. While the July, 1961 C/D test of the Sprite II (and the April, 1961 Road Research Report on the earlier Sprite) is basically valid for the MG Midget, testing it has given us an opportunity to get a closer look at these inexpensive and justifiably popular sports cars.

There are some differences between the cars, just as there are differences between a Ford and Mercury, for example. And the reason why both the Sprite and Midget are sold here in the same showrooms is easily explained. In Europe, Africa or any other place, B.M.C. has Austin dealers and Nuffield dealers, but the American market is the only one where they are combined, selling both lines of cars.

The list price for the Midget is $1,939, including a tachometer and windshield washers. People who are diffident can spend $1,868 for a similarly-equipped Sprite. The difference is that the MG features better quality exterior trim, and more of it, has more luxurious seats and higher-grade floor mats.

The statement that the Midget is like a reincarnated TD or TF is valid up to a point. The car has the same handy feel of the last of the T's, but has more functional features, a slightly less powerful engine which nevertheless gives better performance and a unitized body that's solid and rattle-free. The cockpit of the new car has greater legroom and feels less restrictive, even with the top up. The seats are much more comfortable and a third person can be accommodated in the area behind the seats. A seat cushion is available for the space for $35. Visibility is better, and rather than feeling as if you are sitting on the car, driver and passenger feel as if they are in it. The trunk is a useful feature. Its shape and size are more practical than that of even the larger MGA.

Cruising speeds as high as 65 mph are taken in stride, although with the top up engine noise becomes noticeable when the revs get over the 4,000 mark at 60. The top speed we reached was an indicated 80 on level ground at 5,000 rpm. Our straightaway was not long enough to crank out the last 500 rpm to the redline

A four-wheel drift through a sweeping left-hander shows the Midget at its performance best. Stiff suspension cuts roll.

with the top down, but the Midget should equal the 84 mph top speed we attained with the Sprite.

Acceleration is businesslike, the engine winding freely to the 5,500 rpm redline or above on occasion and the exhaust pipe issuing a peppy rap. Second gear is marvelously flexible for punching through holes in traffic up to highway speeds and third gear has a similarly extended range, giving the car a good, unbreakable feel.

The steering is naturally light, perhaps a little fast at first for many people, but once you realize you only have to "think" the car around corners, its characteristics are such that you might never be happy in any other kind of car. The ride is definitely firm, leaving no doubt that you're driving a sports car. The springs are tight and the shocks quite stiff. Bumps are absorbed as much by the seat of your pants as any other suspension component.

The top and side curtains sealed well from both water and wind leaks but gave rise to several rattles, squeaks and groans. Like most owners, you'd probably find you had the top stored most of the time anyway. By the time you read this a hardtop is slated to be offered for Midgets. Its price will be slightly more than the $179 Sprite lid, but trim and shape will be different.

The handling of the car cannot be faulted. The combination of quick steering, powerful brakes and a roadworthy chassis add up to pure fun on virtually any road. So if you haven't been happy with a sports car since your TD died and you can't bring yourself to buy a 3,000, try the Midget—it's even less expensive than the TD's were. It has all the qualities a sports car should possess and, with the optional performance equipment available for it, should make a good showing on the circuit. It has all the traits experienced drivers crave yet its price and deportment should appeal to first-time sports-car buyers.

The center of attention is the shoulder-harness mount. The rear area is carpeted and a jump seat is an optional feature.

ROAD TEST: MG MIDGET

Price as tested: $2069 POE New York
Importer:
Hambro Automotive Corporation
27 West 57th Street
New York 19, New York

ENGINE:

Displacement.....................57.9 cu in, 948 cc
Dimensions......4 cyl, 2.48-in bore, 3.00-in stroke
Valve gear: Pushrod-operated in-line overhead valves.
Compression ratio...................9.1 to one
Power (SAE).............49½ bhp @ 5500 rpm
Torque...............52½ lb-ft @ 4000 rpm
Usable range of engine speeds.......900-6000 rpm
Corrected piston speed @ 5500 rpm......2490 fpm
Fuel recommended...................Premium
Mileage.........................30-33 mpg
Range on 7.2-gallon tank............215-235 miles

CHASSIS:

Wheelbase.........................80 in
Tread..............F 44¾ in, R 45¾ in
Length.........................136¼ in
Ground clearance....................5 in
Suspension: F, ind., wishbones and coil springs; R Live axle with trailing quarter-elliptic leaf springs and radius arms
Turns, lock to lock...................2⅓
Turning circle diameter between curbs....30½ ft
Tire and rim size.......5.20 x 13, 13 x 3.5D
Pressures recommended....Normal, F 18, R 20 psi
                        High speed, F 24, R 26 psi
Brakes; type, swept area: 7-inch drums, 110 sq in
Curb weight (full tank)...............1572 lbs
Percentage on the driving wheels............47.5

DRIVE TRAIN:

Gear	Synchro?	Ratio	Step	Overall	Mph per 1000 rpm
Rev	No	4.12	—	17.40	3.7
1st	No	3.20	—	13.51	4.8
2nd	Yes	1.92	68%	8.08	8.1
3rd	Yes	1.38	39%	5.80	11.2
4th	Yes	1.00	38%	4.22	15.4

Final drive ratios: 4.22 to one standard, 3.73; 4.55 and 5.38 to one optional.

ACCELERATION:

Zero to	Seconds
30 mph	6.3
40 mph	9.8
50 mph	15.2
60 mph	21.6
70 mph	33.5
Standing ¼-mile	22.8

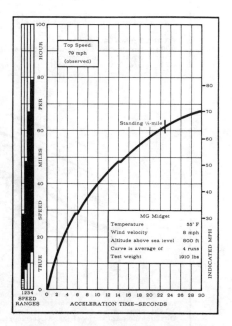

Top Speed: 79 mph (observed)

Standing ¼-mile

MG Midget
Temperature   55° F
Wind velocity   8 mph
Altitude above sea level   800 ft
Curve is average of   4 runs
Test weight   1910 lbs

Make: M.G. Type: Midget
Makers: M.G. Car Co., Ltd., Abingdon-on-Thames, Berkshire

Test Data

CONDITIONS: Weather: Windy with gusts of up to 20 m.p.h. (Temperature 32°-39°F., Barometer 29.85 in. Hg.) Surface: Dry. Fuel: Super Premium grade pump petrol (101 Octane Rating by Research Method).

INSTRUMENTS
Speedometer at 30 m.p.h.	2% fast
Speedometer at 60 m.p.h.	5% fast
Speedometer at 80 m.p.h.	5% fast
Distance recorder	accurate

WEIGHT
Kerb weight (unladen, but with oil, coolant and fuel for approx. 50 miles) .. 13¼ cwt.
Front/rear distribution of kerb weight 53/47
Weight laden as tested .. .. .. 17 cwt.

MAXIMUM SPEEDS
Mean lap speed around banked circuit 87.9 m.p.h.
Best one-way ¼-mile time equals .. 90.0 m.p.h.

"Maximile" Speed. (Timed quarter mile after one mile accelerating from rest.)
Mean of four opposite runs .. .. 81.8 m.p.h.
Best one-way time equals .. .. 83.3 m.p.h.

Speed in gears (at 6,000 r.p.m.)
Max. speed in 3rd gear .. .. .. 68 m.p.h.
Max. speed in 2nd gear .. .. .. 48 m.p.h.
Max. speed in 1st gear .. .. .. 29 m.p.h.

FUEL CONSUMPTION
54 m.p.g. at constant 30 m.p.h. on level.
53 m.p.g. at constant 40 m.p.h. on level.
46½ m.p.g. at constant 50 m.p.h. on level.
42 m.p.g. at constant 60 m.p.h. on level.
36 m.p.g. at constant 70 m.p.h. on level.
31 m.p.g. at constant 80 m.p.h. on level.

Overall Fuel Consumption for 1,172 miles, 36.5 gallons, equals 32.1 m.p.g. (8.8 litres/100 km.)

Touring Fuel Consumption (m.p.g. at steady speed midway between 30 m.p.h. and maximum, less 5% allowance for acceleration). 40.2 m.p.g.
Fuel tank capacity (makers' figure) 6 gallons.

STEERING
Turning circle between kerbs:
Left .. .. 29¼ feet
Right .. .. 29¼ feet
Turns of steering wheel from lock to lock, 2⅓

BRAKES from 30 m.p.h.
0.20 g retardation (equivalent to 150 ft. stopping distance) with 25 lb. pedal pressure.
0.51 g retardation (equivalent to 59 ft. stopping distance) with 50 lb. pedal pressure.
0.70 g retardation (equivalent to 43 ft. stopping distance) with 75 lb. pedal pressure.
0.99 g retardation (equivalent to 30½ ft. stopping distance) with 100 lb. pedal pressure.

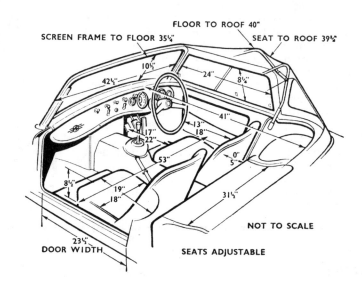

OVERALL WIDTH 4'-6"
TRACK:- FRONT 3'-9¼" REAR 3'-8¼"
4'-0¼" UNLADEN
17¼" 9¼" 19¼" 11¼"
SCALE 1:50
GROUND CLEARANCE 5"
6'-8" M.G. MIDGET
11'-5⅓"

FLOOR TO ROOF 40"
SCREEN FRAME TO FLOOR 35¼"
SEAT TO ROOF 39½"
10½" 42½" 24" 8¼"
17" 13" 41"
22" 18"
53" 0" 5"
8½" 19" 31½"
18"
23½"
DOOR WIDTH
NOT TO SCALE
SEATS ADJUSTABLE

ACCELERATION TIMES from standstill
0-30 m.p.h.	5.3 sec.
0-40 m.p.h.	8.3 sec.
0-50 m.p.h.	12.5 sec.
0-60 m.p.h.	18.3 sec.
0-70 m.p.h.	29.1 sec.
0-80 m.p.h.	59.2 sec.
Standing quarter mile	21.6 sec.

ACCELERATION TIMES on Upper Ratios
	Top gear	3rd gear
10-30 m.p.h.	12.1 sec.	8.5 sec.
20-40 m.p.h.	11.3 sec.	7.8 sec.
30-50 m.p.h.	12.5 sec.	8.4 sec.
40-60 m.p.h.	15.5 sec.	10.0 sec.
50-70 m.p.h.	20.3 sec.	—
60-80 m.p.h.	31.2 sec.	—

HILL CLIMBING at sustained steady speeds
Max. gradient on top gear .. .. 1 in 13.5 (Tapley 165 lb./ton)
Max. gradient on 3rd gear .. .. 1 in 8.2 (Tapley 270 lb./ton)
Max. gradient on 2nd gear .. .. 1 in 5.4 (Tapley 410 lb./ton)

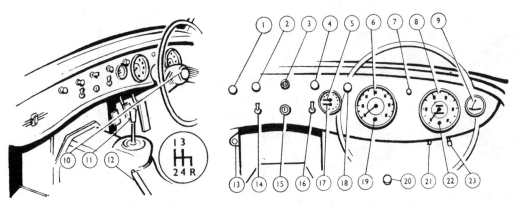

1, Choke. 2, Screen washer push. 3, Direction indicator switch. 4, Heater temperature control. 5, Oil pressure gauge. 6, Rev. counter. 7, Direction indicator warning light. 8, Speedometer. 9, Fuel gauge. 10, Horn button. 11, Gear lever. 12, Handbrake. 13, Bonnet release. 14, Screen wipers switch. 15, Ignition key. 16, Lights Switch. 17, Water temperature gauge. 18, Starter pull. 19, Dynamo charge warning light. 20, Dip switch. 21, Instrument light switch. 22, High beam warning light. 23, Trip reset.

The M.G. Midget

A Responsive Sports Car from B.M.C.

WHEN many family saloons will exceed 90 m.p.h. quite easily and not a few can exceed three figures, a sports car which will only record a mean maximum speed of 87.9 m.p.h. may seem a little tame. However, if there was ever proof of the saying that "it's not what a car does, it's the way it does it" the M.G. Midget surely provides this. Although offering weather protection and general comfort in keeping with modern standards it remains undisputably a sports car, fun to drive, and responsive to good driving.

Conventional

THE mechanical basis of the car is a platform chassis in which a mildly tuned B.M.C. Series "A" engine of 948 c.c. is coupled to its usual 4-speed gearbox, fitted in this instance with close-ratio gears. Suspension is by double wish-bones at the front and the rigid rear axle is suspended by a less common quarter elliptic leaf spring arrangement of low unsprung weight. It is not a particularly unusual specification that gives the Midget its charm, but rather the fact that conventional components have been chosen and assembled in such a way as to make up a well balanced whole.

Being small and light. (13¼ cwt. kerb weight) means that the car is at its best in accelerating from rest or low speeds. From rest to 50 m.p.h. occupies 12.5 sec. and 70 can be reached in a further 16.6

sec. Beyond this speed, which is just possible in 3rd gear, acceleration becomes less brisk and dependent on gradient and wind, borne out by the 6 m.p.h. difference between the maximile and maximum speeds. It should not be concluded from the above that the driver must work particularly hard to get performance. At lower speeds top gear gives remarkably good acceleration, 10-30, 20-40 and 30-50 m.p.h. all occupying 12.5 sec. or under. Furthermore there are no flat spots on full throttle and the car pulls away from under 10 m.p.h. more smoothly than many bread-and-butter saloons.

However, with a gearchange as light and pleasant to use as that fitted to the Midget and an engine which will rev very freely, gear changing is a pleasure rather than a chore. Some drivers

expressed a desire for more synchromesh but when really familiar with the car it is possible to make very fast changes without producing any noise. The clutch is very smooth in use but surprisingly it slipped during full throttle gear changes. This would not worry any but the hardest of drivers or those motoring competitively.

The engine fitted to our car had a 9/1 compression ratio (there is an 8.3/1 option) which demanded 100 octane petrol, but was without temperament when fed on this diet. Starting was easy under all conditions but warming up even on mild mornings was a fairly lengthy business and, until complete, response to the accelerator pedal was fluffy. This is in our experience a feature of the "A" Series engine generally, particularly those with twin carburetters. The test car showed slightly worse fuel consumption at steady speeds than previous similar models that have come our way; it was also the first one in which we recorded 90 m.p.h. but, even so, would better 50 m.p.g. at 30 m.p.h. and 30 m.p.g. at 80 m.p.h. Very hard driving (the car appropriately found its way into the hands of the younger members of our staff more than did previous examples) produced an overall consumption that could be bettered very considerably by an owner who is prepared to make a small sacrifice in performance.

(Continued overleaf)

Somewhat slab-sided in appearance, the M.G. Midget is not over-burdened with chrome. The small black spot below the door pillar is a jacking point.

In Brief

Price £472, plus purchase tax £217 11s. 5d., equals £689 11s. 5d.		
Capacity		948 c.c.
Unladen kerb weight ...		13¼ cwt.
Acceleration :		
20-40 m.p.h. in top gear ...		11.3 sec.
0-50 m.p.h. through gears		12.5 sec.
Maximum top gear gradient		1 in 13.5
Maximum speed ...		87.9 m.p.h.
"Maximile" speed ...		81.8 m.p.h.
Touring fuel consumption ...		40.2 m.p.g.
Gearing: 15.3 m.p.h. in top gear at 1,000 r.p.m.		

The M.G. Midget

Carpet covers the space behind the bucket seats and the floor and transmission tunnel are clad with flecked rubber. There are pendant clutch and brake pedals; an organ-type accelerator. Seat belts, an optional extra, were fitted to the test car and do not clutter up the interior as much as they seem to in some saloons.

Boot space is generous for so small a sports car, and at least one quite substantial hard suitcase can be accommodated as well as sundry soft or smaller items.

Good Handling

MOST pleasing of all the Midget's features is undoubtedly its handling. Starting off in it, drivers new to the car are inclined to emulate a person driving a Kart for the first time, weaving from side to side and cornering rather untidily. Soon, however, they realize that it is the other cars that they have been driving that do not steer correctly. The rack and pinion gives exceptionally light and sensitive control that reduces driver effort to a minimum and allows the car to be placed far more accurately than everyday machines. A good power to weight ratio means that when cornering the accelerator pedal can be used to control the car, which can thus be made to over- or understeer slightly to choice. Nylon corded tyres are fitted and there is little or no protest from them when cornering fast. Adhesion is very good indeed and it is possible to corner the Midget consistently fast without fatigue, making for high average speeds. On slow corners and bumpy surfaces axle tramp is notably absent.

The quality of the ride is a mixture. Firm damping allows the car to ride wave formations almost unnoticeably, but certain types of potholes can produce quite a jolt and small road unevennesses are felt. Slight scuttle shake is also noticed, more by the passenger than the driver. Naturally there is very little roll and the car is also free from pitching tendencies.

Brakes and Seats

THE brakes work well enough in ordinary motoring and pedal pressures are normal for stops from 30 m.p.h. Consistent heavy braking from high speeds does, however, show up a tendency to fade and this results in pulling to one side. The lever handbrake, placed on the passenger's side of the high transmission tunnel, is very effective and has a

pleasant action, but it can be awkward to operate when a passenger is being carried.

Although a certain amount of agility is necessary when getting in and out of this M.G., once inside there is sufficient room even for drivers over 6 ft. tall. The bucket seats are mounted so that the occupants sit very little higher than the floor with their feet almost straight out in front of them. The driver's seat only is adjustable fore and aft. A rather large steering wheel dominates the driver's side of the car and in front of him is a full range of instruments on what many find a rather Spartan facia. Passengers felt that the speedometer could have exchanged places with the rev. counter beneficially so that speed could be read by both occupants.

Like the curate's egg, accessibility of the various under-bonnet items is "good in parts". Large air cleaners are fitted to the S.U. carburetters.

The layout of the minor controls is simple and therefore good. The driver tends to rest his forearm on the gearlever when cruising and then lights, wiper, screenwash, heater and the non-cancelling flashing indicator control are all within easy reach. The heater control takes the form of a push and turn switch which determines whether air from the heater can enter the car or not and whether the booster fan is on or off. Air outlet doors by the driver's and passenger's legs can be used to direct air downwards or on to the screen. To obtain cold air it is necessary to raise the bonnet and turn off the water valve. The heater performance is good but the low mounting of the air intake makes it apt to bring

fumes into the car when travelling in heavy traffic.

Vision from an open car is naturally very good but even when the hood is up this little car has a light and airy interior and there are no blind rear quarters, a useful safety feature when pulling out of side turnings. The rear-view mirror however is not ideally placed. It obscures the nearside wing from the driver and vibrates at speed. This coupled with the inevitable movement of the plastic rear window means that it is difficult to see following cars clearly. At night the lights are very penetrating being well up to the performance of the car. The lack of any interior light other than for the instruments can however be a nuisance.

Business and Pleasure

TODAY'S cars are used more and more for business journeys and this even applies to sports cars. Therefore weather protection has to be of a very high order when the hood is in use. The one on the Midget proved almost completely weatherproof, only letting in traces of snow, renowned for its penetrating qualities. A few draughts were noticeable but could be reduced by turning on the heater which tended to pressurize the interior. The noise level with the hood up was also reasonably low for a sports car although when down, engine noise was naturally reduced considerably. In open form, but using the sidescreens, wind buffeting was not sufficient to be unpleasant and could be reduced by slightly opening the rear half of the sliding screens. Provision is made for stowing the hood, its irons and side screens neatly in the boot.

The boot itself offers a surprisingly large volume of lockable space for so small a car despite the fact that it carries the spare wheel. A simple stay is provided so that the lid can be propped open, a similar system being used for the bonnet. There is further useful luggage space inside the car behind the seats and two pockets in the doors will take small items as well as giving extra elbow room by virtue of the fact that the part of the door above the pocket is a single thickness since it does not have to accommodate a winding window. There is no cubby-hole and no ash tray is fitted.

A one-piece alligator bonnet top panel lifts up to reveal the engine. The most frequently needed item, the dipstick, is singularly inaccessible and tricky to replace, a torch being essential at night, and the distributor is even more difficult to reach. In contrast the screenwash

bottle, sparking plugs and hydraulic fluid reservoirs are near to hand.

To sum up the M.G. Midget has its faults like any other car but for those whose taste lies in small sports cars and whose circumstances allow them to own one this car can provide transport that is such fun that there would still be pleasure in driving it after tens of thousands of miles. At £689 11s. 5d. tax paid it offers an out of the run alternative to the higher priced 1-litre saloons offered by B.M.C. and, for that matter, other manufacturers.

The hood is very easily erected or taken down although it takes a little longer to stow completely. Both panels of the removable sidescreens slide so that the window can be opened at the front or rear.

Specification

Engine

Cylinders	4
Bore	62.94 mm.
Stroke	76.2 mm.
Cubic capacity	948 c.c.
Piston area	19.29 sq. in.
Valves	Overhead
Compression ratio	9.0/1 (optional 8.3/1)
Fuel pump	AC Delco mechanical
Ignition timing control	Centrifugal and vacuum
Oil filter	Tecalemit or Purolator full flow
Maximum power (net)	46.4 b.h.p. at 5,500 r.p.m.
Piston speed at maximum b.h.p.	2,750 ft./min.
Carburetters	Twin S.U. HS.2

Transmission

Clutch	Borg and Beck, 6¼ in. dia., s.d.p.
Top gear (s/m)	4.22
3rd gear (s/m)	5.726
2nd gear (s/m)	8.085
1st gear	13.504
Reverse	17.361
Propeller shaft	Hardy Spicer reverse spline
Final drive	Hypoid bevel
Top gear m.p.h. at 1,000 r.p.m.	15.3
Top gear m.p.h. at 1,000 ft./min. piston speed	30.6

Chassis

Brakes	Lockheed hydraulic, drum type, 2 l.s. at front
Brake dimensions	7 in. × 1¼ in. front and rear
Friction areas	67.50 sq. in. of lining area working on 110 sq. in. of rubbed area
Suspension:	
Front	Independent by coil springs and wishbones
Rear	Quarter elliptic leaf springs, upper radius rods and rigid axle
Shock absorbers:	
Front	Armstrong hydraulic lever arm type
Rear	Armstrong hydraulic, lever arm type
Steering gear	Rack and pinion
Tyres	Dunlop 5.20—13 tubeless

Coachwork and Equipment

Starting handle	No
Battery mounting	Engine compartment, on bulkhead
Jack	Bipod screw type with ratchet
Jacking points	On either side of body, amidships
Standard tool kit	Hub cover lever, jack and ratchet spanner, wheel nut spanner plug spanner, tommy bar.
Exterior lights	2 headlamps, 2 sidelamps/ flashers, 2 stop/tail/flasher lamps, rear number plate lamp.
Number of electrical fuses	Two
Direction indicators	Flashers, non-self cancelling
Windscreen wipers	2-blade electrical, self-parking
Windscreen washers	Hand pump
Sun visors	None
Instruments	Speedometer with decimal trip and total mileage recorder, fuel gauge, combined oil pressure and water temperature gauge, rev counter.

Warning lights	Main beam, direction indicators, ignition
Locks:	
With ignition key	Ignition switch and boot lid
Glove lockers	None
Map pockets	Two, in door panels
Parcel shelves	None
Ashtrays	None
Cigar lighters	Optional extra
Interior lights	Instrument lighting only
Interior heater	Fresh air (optional extra)
Car radio	Optional extra
Extras available	Locking petrol cap, laminated windscreen, radio, cigar lighter, wing mirror, luggage carrier, tonneau cover, hard top, heater, fresh air unit, wheel discs, white wall tyres, twin horns, rear compartment cushions.
Upholstery material	Leathercloth
Floor covering	Rubber
Exterior colours standardized	Seven
Alternative body styles	None, but hardtop available and a separate cheaper model, the Austin-Healey Sprite, uses identical basic components.

Maintenance

Sump	6½ pints, S.A.E. 30 (32° F.) 20 (32–10° F.)
Gearbox	2¼ pints, S.A.E. 30
Rear axle	1¾ pints, S.A.E. 90 Hypoid (10° F.) 80 Hypoid (below 10° F.)
Steering gear lubricant	Hypoid 90
Cooling system capacity	10 pints (2 drain taps)
Chassis lubrication	by grease gun every 1,000 miles to 11 points
Ignition timing	4° before t.d.c. (H.C.), 1° before t.d.c. (L.C.)
Contact breaker gap	0.014–0.016 in.
Sparking plug type	Champion N5
Sparking plug gap	0.024–0.026 in.

Valve timing	Inlet opens 5° before t.d.c. and closes 45° a.b.d.c. Exhaust opens 51° before b.d.c. and closes 21° a.t.d.c.
Tappet clearances (cold):	
	Inlet 0.012 in.
	Exhaust 0.012 in.
Front wheel toe-in	0–⅛ in.
Camber angle	1°
Castor angle	3°
Steering swivel pin inclination	6½°
Tyre pressures:	Front 18 lb.; rear 20 lb.
Brake fluid	Lockheed S.A.E. 70 R3
Battery type and capacity	12v. 43 amp. hr.

JOHN BOLSTER

tests

The MG MIDGET

THE M.G. Midget is a more luxurious version of the Austin-Healey Sprite or, if you prefer it, the Sprite is a simplified Midget. Both cars are identical mechanically, and they have recently been endowed with the latest long-stroke 1,098 c.c. variation of the B.M.C. A-series engine. This unit has more "punch" than its 948 c.c. predecessor, producing its maximum torque at 2,500 r.p.m. 60 b.h.p. (s.a.e.) is developed at 5,750 r.p.m., as compared with the 47.5 b.h.p. of the earlier models.

The well-known power unit has push-rod-operated valves in a cast-iron head. Twin SU carburetters are fitted and the compression ratio is 8.9 to 1. The single dry plate clutch, four-speed gearbox, and open propeller shaft are entirely conventional. A punt-type welded steel structure forms the chassis and is the basis of the body. Helical springs constitute the suspension medium in front, and at the rear a pair of quarter-elliptic springs are attached beneath the axle with radius arms above. Disc brakes are employed in front with drums behind, and the steering is by rack and pinion.

A pleasing shape has been chosen for the body, combining Italian angularity with some traditional curves. One must admit that the result is attractive, and there is plenty of room for two large people. By retaining detachable side-screens, it has been possible to hollow out the doors, to the great advantage of the driver and passenger who gain useful elbow room in consequence. The boot is largely occupied by the spare wheel but there is some useful luggage space behind the seats. This is covered by a cushion, presumably for the carriage of a baby or a dog.

The hood is very neat indeed, being easy to erect and remaining in place at maximum speed, though it does flap a little. The sidescreens have sliding panels which do not tend to creep. A useful array of proper round instruments includes a rev. counter.

Although the seats are quite comfortable, one could do with even better lateral location and a bit more support for the thighs. A pleasant driving position, giving a good all-round view, includes well-placed pedals and a central gear lever that can be reached without stretching. Pleasantly smooth except for one slight period, the engine is flexible,

and although the exhaust has a healthy note it is by no means noisy.

Over average road surfaces, the little machine gives a comfortable ride and does not tend to pitch. There is some roll, and a tendency to oversteer is noticeable. During normal driving, the steering feels light and precise. On a racing circuit, the car at first feels rather "soft" but with practice quite fast cornering may be enjoyed. Harder damper settings and an anti-roll bar would be advisable for competition work, but the standard settings are a good compromise for fairly fast touring.

The maximum speed is just under 90 m.p.h. and the engine seems content to cruise at almost any figure within its range. It revs freely, and so although the gear ratios are not particularly close, a useful 70 m.p.h. may be exceeded on third speed and 50 m.p.h. comes up on second. To cover the standing quarter-mile in less than 20 seconds must be regarded as satisfactory for a vehicle of this size and price.

Even when driven hard, the Midget returns a praiseworthy 35 m.p.g. Though the hood gives good protection, the best way to enjoy this car is to get out into the country with the top down. The very efficient heater still keeps the feet warm, and the little machine runs with great ease at quite high cruising speeds.

The easy gear change encourages one to use third speed a good deal, though the flexibility on top is perfectly normal by four-cylinder standards.

The brakes are very good indeed, taking no objection to continuous hard use. The song of the exhaust is always present, reaching quite an inspiring note at full speed, but it does not crackle or boom on the overrun, nor does it seem to attract unwelcome attention.

The appearance of the Midget, on the other hand, certainly draws some admiring glances. Although the general impression is of a sporting nature, the comfort and refinement of the interior are not inferior to normal saloon standards. The whole purpose of the car is to provide reliable everyday transportation while giving the driver the pleasure of handling a lively, responsive machine. Obviously, a sporting two-seater of this type can easily be developed much further if extreme performance is the aim, but we are dealing at present with the production Midget in standard tune.

The small M.G. is a sports car of conservative design. Yet, it has been evolved to a point where it does its job very well and goes on doing it. Of pleasant appearance and with many practical features, it represents good value for money and offers low running costs.

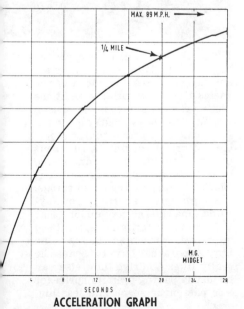

ACCELERATION GRAPH

MAX. 89 M.P.H. →

1/4 MILE

M.G. MIDGET

SECONDS

SPECIFICATION AND PERFORMANCE DATA

Car Tested: M.G. Midget sports two-seater, price £598 13s. 9d., extra: Heater £14 10s., including P.T.

Engine: Four cylinders, 64.58 mm. x 83.72 mm. (1,098 c.c.). Pushrod operated overhead valves. 8.9 to 1 compression ratio. 60 b.h.p. at 5,750 r.p.m. Twin SU carburetters. Lucas coil and distributor.

Transmission: Single dry plate clutch, four-speed gearbox with synchromesh on upper three gears and short central lever, ratios 4.22, 5.73, 8.09, and 13.50 to 1. Open propeller shaft. Hypoid rear axle.

Chassis: Punt-type chassis in unit with steel body. Independent front suspension by wishbones and helical springs. Rack and pinion steering. Rigid rear axle on quarter-elliptic springs with radius arms. Lever-type dampers all round. Lockheed hydraulic brakes with front discs and rear drums. Bolt-on disc wheels fitted 5.20-13 ins. tyres.

Equipment: 12 volt lighting and starting. Speedometer. Revolution counter. Oil pressure, water temperature and fuel gauges. Windscreen wipers and washers. Flashing direction indicators. Heater (extra).

Dimensions: Wheelbase 6 ft. 8 ins. Track (front) 3 ft. 9¼ ins. (rear) 3 ft. 8¾ ins. Overall length 11 ft. 5¼ ins. Width 4 ft. 5 ins. Turning circle 32 ft. Weight 13 cwt.

Performance: Maximum speed 89 m.p.h. Speeds in gears: 3rd, 72 m.p.h.; 2nd, 51 m.p.h.; 1st, 32.5 m.p.h. Standing quarter-mile 19.8 secs. Acceleration: 0-30 m.p.h., 4.4 secs.; 0-50 m.p.h. 9.5 secs.; 0-60 m.p.h., 16.4 secs.

Fuel Consumption: 35 m.p.g.

SAFETY '63

SO many irate owners wrote in last time we tested a car from this family (actually it had Austin Healey on the front) and complained of victimisation that we feel bound to delve just a little way into the mystic machinations of whatever sanctum it is that produces SMALL CAR's policy—and explain. You'll have noticed by now that our road tests vary in treatment as well as in length and presentation. We try to work the changes logically.

If the car we're testing is new and little-known we like to give you a fairly detailed rundown on its design and the layout of its controls as well as on the way it behaves.

If it's old and well-known we try to save your time and ours by assuming you have some idea of the basics already. Similarly we fit the test to the car's purpose; a station wagon gets heavy loads and rough farm tracks, a grand tourer a portion of grand touring, a runabout plenty of running about and so on. It doesn't always work out but that's the way we try to do things.

Accordingly a sports car or anything masquerading under that title comes in for fairly specialised appraisal. We reckon the man who buys a sports car buys it because he really likes to drive (how else can he justify paying premium price for less passenger space and less lug-

gage room?). Ergo we spend most of the test space on what we hope is constructive criticism of such vital driving factors as seating, control layout, engine and gearbox performance, roadholding and braking. And when we talk about these things in such a specialised application we apply the very highest standards, naturally.

What niggled the Sprite owners who wrote to us was that we could rave over the handling of, say, a Morris 1100 and then talk about their baby's tail-happiness when obviously we knew as well as they that the Sprite would be the better car to be in in almost any real driving emergency. Our correspond-

ents failed to appreciate that we were speaking relatively.

But to proceed to the Midget. Since we've already dealt with the Sprite in such exhaustive detail (it was the *March* issue, that man at the back) let's stick to the points which differentiate the test car (a) from its kissing-cousin and (b) from earlier models in the same common series. The car we had last time was a sort of interim model: it had the current Mark II body shape but most of the Mark I mechanicals.

Mechanical differences start with the engine, which swells to 1098 cc thanks to the same boring and stroking BMC applied to all the other cars in its non-transverse

A-series line. At 64.6 by 83.7 mm the revised engine is further than ever from being square in the modern manner but BMC seems to make up for that by building in the usual breath reserve along with a stronger crankshaft: you still don't hear of A-engines wearing out, and tuners say they have no more trouble than usual persuading the latest version to spin to a cool 8000 rpm on occasion without harm (we're still talking about fore and aft applications only, by the way).

The next change is in the gearbox, which gets the same excellent Porsche baulk-ring synchromesh setup that transformed the Mini saloons. The box also gets a rubber

coating intended to cut down whine

Modification three affects the anchor department. Lockheed 8-in discs replace the same supplier's 7-in drum brakes on the front wheels, though the drum ditto on the back remain unaltered.

What difference does all this make? Frankly, from our point of view it very nearly transforms the car. Never have we known so few changes to make such an improvement in a model's appeal.

Oddly enough the difference in performance is the one you notice least. The new engine gives nearly 10 bhp more than the old one at identical revs—55 instead of 46 bhp at 5500 rpm. Acceleration through the gears takes rather less to 40 mph and less again to 60: enough to make a difference to your point-to-point average even though the Spridget is still anything but a winner away from the lights. The precisely calibrated dashboard rev counter (still the only practical reason we can see for buying a Midget and not a Sprite, which has dreadful instruments) has an orange sector from 5500 to 6000 rpm and a red one from there on; in practice we found little point in using the orange band at all except for performance testing and in dealing with the odd cheeky Mini operator, but we fancy the car would have no objection to an occasional excursion into the beyond if you felt you must.

Of far more practical day-to-day use than the extra mechanical urge is the revised gearbox, which above all accounts for the fact that the Spridget is suddenly driveable. It has the same higher and closer ratios that distinguished 948-cc Mark IIs from their pop-eyed and rather depressing ancestors, but without the maddening clunks and graunches that greeted every

attempt at even a semi-smart shift, Instead of a misery it has become a pleasure to change gear really quickly in the latest car. Our only real regret is that first, pleasantly high and eminently usable as it is, should have remained unsynchronised and therefore out of reach to all but the bravest and most skilled. Oh, and it would be nice not to have to put up with all the unaccountable whining and grumbling that still gets past the casing.

The new brakes are an equally welcome improvement from a real driver's point of view. Thrashing older Sprites and Midgets through the lanes you often got the feeling there may be nothing there next time you stepped on the pedal, and occasionally after a really earnest mile or two there wasn't. This time we tried equally hard to make the brakes disappear. We failed.

We didn't think much of the new cockpit arrangements. The so-called crash padding strikes us (ha-ha) as an elaborate practical joke, since it seems to be fastened on *below* the bottom of the dash with skinny little metal brackets that wouldn't stop a stone. The new seats we found better than the old in that they did at least offer some thigh support, but they are still far too upright and far too skimpy. They introduce a new nuisance in the shape of over-flexibility. Standing outside the car we found we could distort the backrests up to six inches with quite mild one-handed pressure, which might give you some idea of the way they writhe.

How does the latest Midget shape up as a sports car, not just in contrast to older models but generally? We found it lively if not paralysingly fast, manageable if not breathtakingly agile, livable if not comfortable, practical if not

perfect. At £599, an acceptable score at least.

We think its styling is dreary to say the least, and we certainly don't think (see pictures) it belongs in what a 100 per cent enthusiast means by the MG genealogy. We disapprove emphatically of a seat position which makes it impossible to use the accepted sports car driving stance—right back with arms straight out and legs almost at full stretch—and which alone is responsible for the spread of that dangerous, rapacious and unfortunately quite incurable automotive disease Spridget Elbow. We laugh at BMC's provision of an optional back seat but sympathise with the reasoning behind its introduction (to keep the insurance companies quiet about third-passenger liability, otherwise a big worry).

On the other hand we approve of the way the car responds to its revised controls—steering always excellent, brakes and gearchange now in line—and we realise that its performance is enough at least to excuse the name sports car if not to justify it. We approve most definitely of the designer's compromise between ride comfort and controllability (in that respect the Midget is almost ideal). We appreciate that the car is safe and reliable even if its handling isn't of the very best (a well-driven Mini will still leave it in the twisty stretches) and we sympathise with the manufacturer in that he has obviously tried hard to provide a satisfactory standard of comfort and convenience in what is after all a grossly unsympathetic configuration.

In all, if social considerations or That Ole Fangio Feeling dictate that you must own a small, cheap sports car then we see no reason why this one shouldn't keep you quiet for a bit. ●

FACTS MG MIDGET

How much?	£599 tax paid
How fast?	92 mph
	Acceleration: 0–30 4.4 sec, 0–40 7.4 sec, 0–50 10.5 sec, 0–60 15.5 sec, 0–70 23.0 sec
How thirsty?	34 mpg
How big?	11 ft 6 in long, 4 ft 6 in wide, 4 ft high
How heavy?	1566 lb
How Hairy?	Four-cylinder water-cooled pushrod in-line engine at front driving rear wheels; 1098 cc developing 55 bhp on 8.9 to 1 compression; 8¼-in disc brakes front, 7-in drums rear; suspension by coils and double wishbones (front) and rigid axle with trailing quarter-elliptic leaf springs and links
How often?	Greasing at 12 points every 3000 miles, oil change ditto
How roomy?	Two seat two-door steel roadster, rear boot; glass-fibre hardtop available

M.G. Midget 1,098 c.c.

YOUNG blood, provided it flows red, has always craved for excitement, and the dream of cutting a dash in a fast, sleek sports car is healthy and virile. Few are fortunate enough to realize their youthful ambition to the full, but the possession of an M.G. Midget is more than a compromise. Far from a thoroughbred by birth, the current Midget still displays the traditional M.G. concept of a sports car, and loses nothing from the doubtfulness of its lineage. It is an exhilarating and predictable car to drive, with a performance that invites one to drive it hard—and to go on driving it.

For over a year now the Midget has been produced with the 1,098 c.c. power unit that was standardized by B.M.C. at last year's Motor Show, and with its two S.U. carburettors and sporting camshaft the peak power developed is 56 b.h.p. net at 5,750 r.p.m. The torque curve has a very flat shape with good bottom-end values and a peak of 62 lb. ft. quite high in the rev. range at 3,250 r.p.m. The only other difference from the car we tested in August 1961 is the adoption of 8·25in. dia. disc brakes for the front wheels and baulk-ring synchromesh in the gearbox.

On the road the extra power can be felt at once (the smaller-engined car developed only 42 b.h.p. net) and the stopwatch showed very worthwhile gains in acceleration. From rest to 80 m.p.h. took 36·9sec, almost 20sec less than before, and the mean maximum speed on a still day was 5 m.p.h. better at 89·5.

There has been no change to the gear ratios, and the indirects feel high but well spaced. First has a maximum

of 30 m.p.h., making it a useful traffic ratio, second takes the speed on to 50 m.p.h. and third 70. These speeds are the ultimates corresponding to 6,200 r.p.m. and normally one changes up at around 5,000. The electronic rev counter has an amber warning sector from 5,500 to 6,000, and a red danger zone from 6,000 to 7,000 although valve bounce limited engine speed to a safe 6,300 r.p.m.

Top gear is well matched to the power curve of the engine and the drag of the body (with its extra hardtop), for we were able to go just over peak revs in both directions on the flat. At these speeds engine noise is completely drowned by wind roar and conversation is virtually impossible.

Unusual for a test car, this Midget had covered about 16,000 miles and was over 12 months old. It had obviously

PRICES	£	s	d
Open two-seater	495	0	0
Purchase tax	103	13	9
Total (in G.B.)	598	13	9
Extras (including P.T.)			
Hardtop with special sidescreens	48	6	8
Heater	14	10	0
Tonneau cover	5	8	9
Rear seat cushion	4	5	0

Make · M.G.   Type · Midget (1,098 c.c.)
(Front engine, rear-wheel drive)

Manufacturers : M.G. Car Company Ltd., Abingdon-on-Thames, Berkshire

Test Conditions
Weather .... Dry, but dank with no wind
Temperature .... 11·0 deg. C (52 deg. F.)
Barometer .... 30·01in. Hg.
Dry concrete and tarmac surfaces.

Weight
Kerb weight (with oil, water and half-full fuel tank)
14·25 cwt (1,596lb-724kg)
Front-rear distribution, per cent F, 51; R, 49
Laden as tested .... 17·25cwt (1,932lb-876kg)

Turning Circles
Between kerbs ....L, 32ft 1in.; R, 31ft 10in.
Between walls .... L, 33ft 5in.; R, 33ft. 2in.
Turns of steering wheel lock to lock .... 2·25

Performance Data
Top gear m.p.h. per 1,000 r.p.m. .... 15·37
Mean piston speed at max. power ... 3,160ft/min
Engine revs. at mean max. speed ...... 5,820 r.p.m.
B.h.p. per ton laden .... 65·0

FUEL AND OIL CONSUMPTION

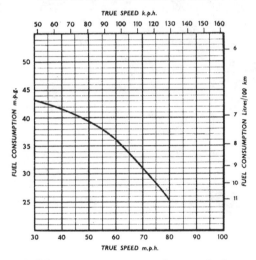

FUEL .... Super Premium Grade
(100–102 octane RM)

Test Distance .... 1,063 miles

Overall Consumption .... 29·1 m.p.g.
(9·8 litres/100 km.)

Normal Range .... 28-35 m.p.g.
(10·1-8·1 litres/100 km.)

OIL: S.A.E.30 ....Consumption 8,000 m.p.g.

HILL CLIMBING AT STEADY SPEEDS

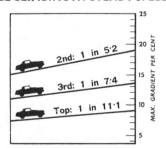

GEAR PULL	Top	3rd	2nd
(lb per ton)	41·5	300	200
Speed Range (m.p.h.)	25-38	32-47	42-56

MAXIMUM SPEEDS AND ACCELERATION TIMES

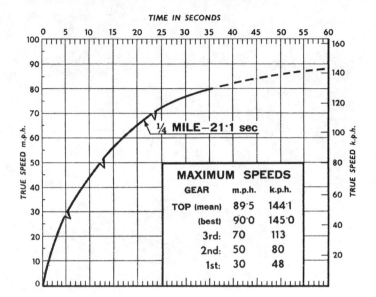

MAXIMUM SPEEDS		
GEAR	m.p.h.	k.p.h.
TOP (mean)	89·5	144·1
(best)	90·0	145·0
3rd:	70	113
2nd:	50	80
1st:	30	48

¼ MILE—21·1 sec

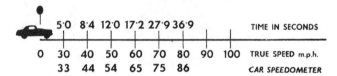

Speed range, gear ratios and time in seconds

m.p.h.	Top (4·22)	3rd (5·73)	2nd (8·05)	1st (13·50)
10—30	—	8·1	5·7	4·0
20—40	12·1	8·1	5·5	—
30—50	12·7	8·2	6·5	—
40—60	12·2	9·6	—	—
50—70	15·4	12·7	—	—
60—80	23·2	—	—	—

BRAKES	Pedal load	Retardation	Equiv. distance
(from 30 m.p.h. in neutral)	25lb	0·20g	150ft
	50lb	0·46g	65ft
	75lb	0·85g	35ft
	80lb	1·00g	30·1ft
Handbrake		0·41g	74ft

CLUTCH   Pedal load and travel—50lb and 4in.

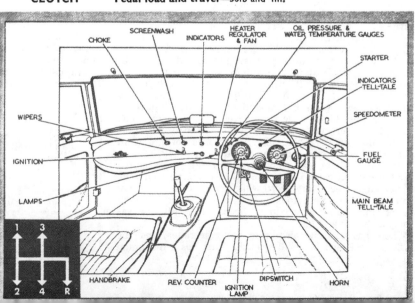

been hard used, but meticulously maintained, and this combination probably put it in nearly the same condition as an average privately owned example. Those sceptics who think that small sports cars are caned to death in a short period would soon be silenced on inspecting this one. The bodywork and interior trim were just as smart as when the car was new, and it was only in a few mechanical details that age was beginning to show.

During the test the starter had to be replaced when it played up and refused to engage its pinion in the flywheel. We missed the starting handle, for which there is no provision, but the Midget required very little impetus to fire when push-started. We also had a little trouble which was probably due to one or other of the carburettor pistons sticking, the symptoms being a sudden loss of power on two cylinders with just as sudden recovery. The exhaust manifold joint, where it meets the down-pipe, tended to leak —a fault common to many other small B.M.C. models.

The car gave indications that it was very nearly due for decarbonizing, for although there was no pinking on premium grade fuel it tended to run on unless we used super. In all other respects, apart from a perceptible whine in the gearbox on the overrun, the Midget was in a very healthy state and obviously good for very many more thousands of miles.

Pulling Power

Comparatively speaking, take-offs from rest felt a little slow and it was not until about 3,000 r.p.m. that the engine really took hold and pulled lustily. By opening the throttle delicately we were able to record some good bottom-end acceleration figures, but it usually pays to hang on to the lower gears and to change down early. The engine had no serious vibration periods, and it seemed to be a much smoother and quieter unit than the older A-series, although it made no secret that it was working hard when called upon to do so.

At the same time as they introduced the larger engine, B.M.C. installed baulk-ring synchromesh on all the A-series gearboxes, and this latest unit is by far the best they have produced. Although first has no synchromesh, a little skill at double-declutching soon makes this a practical ratio for selection on the move, and it always went in first try from rest. Movements of the remote control lever are short and very positive, with a crisp feel that encourages one to make full use of the box.

The disc front brakes were not only more sensitive than the drums they replaced, but proved far more fade resistant from speed. On one or two occasions when braking was deliberately left late from speeds in the upper eighties, the stopping power still turned out to be greater than was required by an appreciable safety margin. Combined with the high-hysteresis Dunlop C41 tyres, the brakes were easily

Carburettor adjustments call for removal of the air cleaners, and the battery is difficult to see into. For the heater fan to blow cold air, the tap on the cylinder head must be turned off by hand

capable of recording 1·0g stops from 30 m.p.h. at only 80lb pedal load, without the benefit of servo assistance.

Nestling alongside the passenger's seat cushion, the handbrake is a little awkward to reach and takes a fair amount of muscle to produce an efficient emergency stop, but it had ample purchase to hold the car fully laden on a 1-in-3 hill. Restarts were not quite possible because of the high first gear, but we did get away without any trouble on 1-in-4.

Much has been written in the past on the handling of the Midget and Sprite with their quick steering, short wheelbase and rear-wheel steering effect, but everyone who drove this car commented on how much safer it felt and how it seemed less prone to dart about at speed. One of the knacks one learns after only a few miles is to relax one's grip on the wheel and let the car find its own path, which it does very accurately. Another factor we found that transformed the handling was to increase the tyre pressure differential from the recommended 2 p.s.i. to 6 p.s.i. between front and rear. This give the car a decided understeer tendency, although some of us still preferred it as it was, when corners could be taken just as fast by a quick

With the passenger's seat right forward there is leg room for one child in the back, but this space is really meant for extra luggage. The cushion is an extra

The soft top is quick and simple to erect, once all the bits have been unpacked; it leaves fewer blind spots than the hardtop

M.G. Midget . . .

tweak on the wheel followed immediately by slight opposite lock correction.

It was more in the straight-line stability that we liked it better without the oversteer. With standard pressures it tended to weave at the slightest provocation when cruising fast, and especially when braking. Our experience with other Midgets has shown that they are also very sensitive to the type of tyres.

Even for acute corners the steering wheel seldom needs more than a wrist movement, and manoeuvres like overtaking hardly require a visible motion of the steering wheel at all; one almost seems to will the car to change course. This high-geared steering meant that when the car was deliberately made to lose adhesion in a corner on a closed test track, corrections could be made speedily and without effort.

On smooth roads the ride comfort is quite acceptable, but rough going really shows up the limitations. Suspension movements are very small, especially at the back, and with two up it is easy to bottom on the bump stops. Tackling the *pavé* was a major feat for the poor little car, which thumped and hopped its way along even at 10 m.p.h. Despite the ordeal, the body felt rigid and solid and nothing rattled except a grease cap from a front hub that came adrift inside the nave plate.

We went through a shallow water trough to test the brakes for wetting, and although they were affected, one application restored them to full efficiency. After a second run the engine cut out due to water short-circuiting the high-tension lead from the unshielded coil.

The road test car came complete with the optional hardtop that costs £48 6s 8d including special side-screens, and we therefore had the choice of three trims. Most of the time the car was run with the glass-fibre roof bolted in place, but during one fine weekend we took it off and tried the plastic-covered canvas hood. Erection is quick, even single-handed, once all the frame tubes and the hood have been unpacked from their various stowage bags, and when it is up and tensioned it makes the car almost as snug inside as does the hardtop.

We encountered heavy rain only with the hardtop on, and this was leak free on the move but tended to let water seep through the side-screen joints when left parked.

Another worthwhile extra we had was the tonneau cover

Left: Door pockets are as big as the doors themselves and make up for the lack of a glove locker. Padded coaming and pile carpets make the inside look quite plush. Right: Hood and frame tools all pack into rattle-free bags, but the spare wheel takes up most of the boot space

that adds another £5 8s 9d. This includes a rail which fits in the hood frame sockets so that the rear compartment can be closed in, and the rest of the cover then clips neatly down behind the seats.

The driver sits with his legs well offset to the right, and even with the seat right back an arms-stretch position is not possible. However, this does not in any way reduce control of the car, and all switches are easy to reach. There is no headlamp flasher; the three-position main lighting switch is close to one's left hand, where it can be used for signalling. The indicator switch is not self-cancelling but there is a bright repeater lamp (that dims when the side-lamps are lit to reduce dazzle) right under the driver's nose. while some disliked this arrangement, others soon became accustomed to it and prefered its positive action.

Although we had the extra cushion for the rear compartment, there is no leg room at all, and this makes it strictly for small children or extra luggage. Getting in and out with the roof on called for some agility, and all too often one catches some clothing on the locating dowel for the door. The doors do not lock, and stealing the car or its contents would be no problem even for the amateur.

The Perspex side-screens have metal frames with rubber sealing strips and panes sliding fore and aft. These must be opened before one can reach in and open the doors, and frost in the runners could be a problem after a night standing out in the depths of winter.

Both bonnet and boot lids have struts that have to be unclipped and fitted into clumsy slots. While that for the engine is not so important, the luggage compartment is opened much more often, usually with one's hands full, and its lid was a continual nuisance. Provided it is of the squashable variety enough luggage for two can be insinuated into the boot, but it must all come out if there should be a puncture.

Over our entire test the fuel consumption averaged 29·1 m.p.g., but this included all the performance measurements and a flat-out trip up M.1. During 500 miles of normal use the overall figure improved to 32·2 m.p.g., but even so the tiny 6-gallon tank meant refuelling stops every 175 miles or so.

The heater, which is yet another extra at £14 10s, impressed us with its high capacity to disgorge streams of really hot air around the foot wells almost as soon as the engine had started from cold. Individual trap doors can be shut for maximum demisting, and the booster fan is not unduly noisy.

Two things about the Midget stand out from our renewed acquaintance with it in its improved form. First, it is a remarkably tough and well-built little car that always feels solid and robust. Second, it is a brisk and nippy machine that has a good margin of safety in all that it does. It has many of the intangible qualities that make a sports car what it is, not the least of which is a natural charm that continually increases one's affection for it. It is the sort of car that is easy to drive well and to have fun with.

Specification : M.G. Midget

ENGINE
Cylinders ...	4-in-line, water cooled
Bore ...	64·58mm (2·54in.)
Stroke ...	83·72mm (3·30in.)
Displacement ...	1,098 c.c. (67 cu. in.)
Valve gear ...	Overhead, pushrods and rockers
Compression ratio	8·9-to-1
Carburettor ...	Two S.U. H.S.2
Fuel pump ...	AC mechanical
Oil filter ...	External, full-flow, renewable element
Max. power ...	56 b.h.p. (net) at 5,750 r.p.m.
Max. torque ...	62 lb. ft. at 3,250 r.p.m.

TRANSMISSION
Clutch ...	6·25in. dia. Borg and Beck s.d.p.
Gearbox ...	Four-speed, synchromesh on 2nd, 3rd and top, central remote control change
Overall ratios ...	Top 4·22, 3rd 5·73, 2nd 8·05, 1st 13·50, Reverse 17·36
Final drive ...	Hypoid bevel, 4·22 to 1

CHASSIS
Construction ...	Integral with steel body

SUSPENSION
Front ...	Independent, coil springs and wishbones, Armstrong lever-arm dampers
Rear ...	Live axle, quarter-elliptic leaf springs, radius arms, Armstrong lever-arm dampers
Steering ...	Rack and pinion, wheel dia., 16in.

BRAKES
Type ...	Lockheed hydraulic, disc front, drum rear
Dimensions ...	F, 8·25in. dia.; R, 7in. dia.; 1·25in. wide shoes
Swept area ...	F, 135 sq. in.; R, 55 sq. in. Total: 190 sq. in. (220 sq. in per ton laden)

WHEELS
Type ...	Pressed steel disc, 4 studs 3·5in. wide rin
Tyres ...	Dunlop C41, tubeless 5·20—13in.

EQUIPMENT
Battery ...	12-volt 43-amp. hr.
Headlamps ...	Sealed beam 40/45-watt
Reversing lamp ...	None
Electric fuses ...	2
Screen wipers ...	Two blade, single speed, self-parking
Screen washer ...	Extra
Interior heater ...	Extra
Safety belts ...	Extra, anchorages provided
Interior trim ...	Leathercloth
Floor covering ...	Carpet
Starting handle ...	No provision
Jack ...	Ratchet pillar
Jacking points ...	One each side in centre of body
Other bodies ...	None

MAINTENANCE
Fuel tank ...	6 Imp. gallons (no reserve)
Cooling system ...	10 pints (plus 1 pint for heater)
Engine sump ...	6·5 pint. Change oil every 6,000 miles; change filter element every 6,000 miles
Gearbox and over-drive ...	2.5 pints SAE 30, no change necessary after first 500 miles
Final drive ...	1·5 pints SAE 90, no change necessary after first 500 miles
Grease ...	12 points every 3,000 miles
Tyre pressures ...	F, 18; R, 20 p.s.i. (normal driving) F, 24; R, 26; p.s.i. (fast driving) F, 18; R, 24 p.s.i. (full load)

Scale: 0·3in. to 1ft.

Cushions uncompressed.

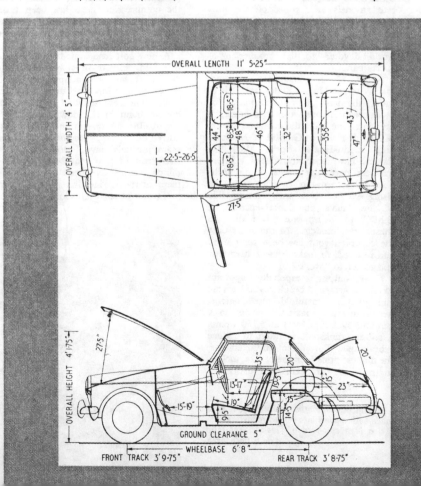

The M.G. Midget II in standard form and the Austin Healey Sprite III, with optional wire wheels

Austin Healey Sprite Mk. III and

MORE POWER, WIND-UP WINDOWS AND NEW REAR SUSPENSION

LATEST figures released by the British Motor Corporation for Austin-Healey Sprite and M.G. Midget production well exemplify the popularity of British small sports cars. Since 1958, 110,000 of these closely related models have rolled off the production line at Abingdon-on-Thames, helping to make this traditional home of M.G. cars the largest factory in the world devoted to the production of sports cars.

About 85 per cent are exported, mainly to the United States, and it is to satisfy the demand from this market for more creature comforts and to bring the cars into line with the character of the MGB, that the M.G. Midget Mark II and Austin-Healey Sprite Mark III models have been introduced. There has been particular resistance to detachable sidescreens in America, and the rising sales of rivals with wind-up side windows have no doubt encouraged B.M.C. to incorporate this feature in these latest models. At the same time the cockpit layout has been rearranged and restyled, to make it more luxurious and easier to "work" in.

Power output is especially important to enthusiasts, and besides cylinder head and exhaust manifold modifications, which increase maximum power to a genuine 59 b.h.p. (net) at 5,750 r.p.m., a stiffer crankshaft is fitted to reduce vibrations. For these improvements, the modest price increase of £24, including purchase tax, seems well justified.

Modifications to the cockpit layout have made both models into refined roadsters with a high standard of finish. Seat trim style is unchanged

Extra power from the engine has been obtained by increasing the size of the inlet valves by 0·06in. and by modifying and reshaping the siamesed inlet tracts to reduce the "uvula" which separates the ports. At the same time, the compression ratio has been raised to 9 to 1, although an 8·3 to 1 compression ratio engine is available for countries with low octane petrol.

A new cast-iron, four-branch exhaust manifold, similar in shape to that of the MGB, has been adopted to replace the older type inherited from the Austin A.35. The new manifold eliminates the double bend in the down pipe and is responsible for one of the extra horsepower of the latest engine. Crankshaft main journals have been increased in size from 1·87in. to 2·0in., while a minor change has been the abandonment of the engine driven petrol pump in favour of an S.U. electric unit.

Rear suspension has been completely revised by the adoption of half-elliptic leaf springs. It has always been a problem to make quarter-elliptic springs of the old design with a combination of low rate and sufficient lateral rigidity to locate the back axle accurately. Moreover, the whole weight of the rear of the car was carried on an anchorage point only 4in. long, requiring long, heavy channel section stiffeners to spread the loads through to the structure. The result was always a compromise resulting in a hard ride and undue roll stiffness at the rear, with a consequent tendency for the car to be very sensitive on steering.

The new springs give a better ride, and the old tendency for the car to "dart" has been eliminated without any loss of steering accuracy. The four-blade, half-elliptic springs are anchored at the forward ends in brackets, and

Neat and practical, the new instrument panel has the two main dials angled inwards slightly

Extras (including P.T.)	
Tonneau cover and rail	£5 8 9
Hardtop	£48 6 8
Fresh-air heater	£14 10 0
Wire wheels	£30 4 2

M.G. Midget Mk. II

at the rear are shackled to a plate bolted to the floor by way of the box section members which reinforce the boot floor.

With this half-elliptic rear springing the unsprung weight of two heavy axle brackets needed for the former quarter-elliptic parallelogram layout is eliminated, plus half the weight of the radius arms and approximately one third of the weight of the thick, wide, quarter-elliptic spring. It has been possible also to eliminate much of the body stiffening required by the old layout.

Thus the total weight saving all but makes up for the extra weight of the door glasses and window lifts, and the all-up weight of the latest cars is only 6lb more than that of their predecessors.

More prospective owners will welcome the change to wind-up windows, which in no way detract from the sporty appearance of the cars and yet add greatly to their general convenience. To fit wind-up glasses into the relatively thin doors of the Sprite and Midget without a major body redesign has called for curved side glasses. The gain is all on the side of the owner, for whom adequate elbow room is retained without any increase in external body width.

Small swivelling quarter vents with non-locking catches are standard equipment and a new, more rigid windscreen frame with full height cast aluminium pillars is fitted to provide a firm sealing abutment for the doors. A thin tie rod between the top and bottom rails of the screen frame prevents it "opening up" when the hood is tensioned and also provides a mounting for the driving mirror which was previously located on the scuttle, where it created a blind spot.

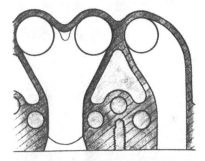
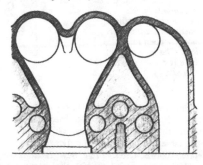

Section of the cylinder head through the ports. Above is the previous pattern, and below is the new head with better breathing capacity

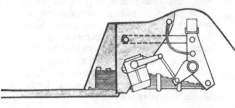
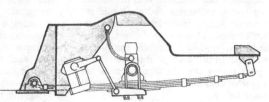

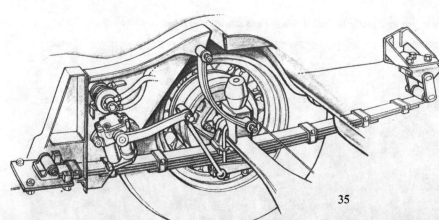

The previous type of rear suspension with quarter elliptic leaf springs and radius arms is shown in the upper left diagram. Better axle location, reduced unsprung weight and improved handling result from the new layout

ENGINE

No. of cylinders ... 4 in-line
Bore ... ... 64·6mm (2·54in.)
Stroke ... ... 83·7mm (3·30in.)
Displacement ... 1,098 c.c. (67 cu. in.)
Valve operation Overhead, pushrods
Compression
ratio ... ... 9·0 to 1 (Optional 8·3 to 1)
Max. b.h.p. (net) 59 at 5,750 r.p.m.
Max. b.m.e.p.
(net) ... ... 140 p.s.i. at 3,250 r.p.m.
Max. torque (net) 62 lb. ft. at 3,250 r.p.m.
Carburettor ... Twin S.U. HS2
Fuel pump ... S.U. Electric
Tank capacity ... 6 Imp. gallons (27 litres)
Sump capacity ... 6·5 pints (3·7 litres)
Oil filter ... Full-flow with renewable element
Cooling system Pressurized system centrifugal
pump, fan and thermostat
Battery ... ... 12 volt, 43 amp. hr.

TRANSMISSION

Clutch ... ... Borg and Beck hydraulically
operated, single dry plate, 7·25in.
dia.

Gearbox ... Four-speed, synchromesh on 2nd,
3rd and top. Central floor change
Overall ratios ... Top 4·22; third 5·73; second
8·09; first 13·51; reverse 17·32
Final drive ... Hypoid bevel, ratio 4·22 to 1

CHASSIS

Brakes ... ... Lockheed hydraulic. Front discs,
8·25in. dia.; rear drums, 7in. dia.;
1·25in. wide shoes.
Suspension:front Independent, coil springs and
wishbones, Armstrong telescopic
dampers
rear Half-elliptic leaf springs, lever arm
dampers
Wheels ... ... Steel disc, 4 studs, 3·5in rim.
Tyre size ... 5·20—13 Dunlop tubeless Gold
Seal Nylon C.41
Steering... ... Rack and pinion
Steering wheel... Three-spoke, 17in. diameter

No. of turns,
(lock to lock)... 2·25

DIMENSIONS

Wheelbase ... 6ft. 8in. (203 cm)
Track: front ... 3ft. 9·75in. (116 cm)
rear ... 3ft. 8·75in. (114 cm)
Overall length ... 11ft. 4·25in. (345 cm)
Overall width ... 4ft. 5in. (135 cm)
Overall height
(unladen) ... 4ft. 1·75in. (126 cm)
Ground clearance
(laden) ... 5in. (13 cm)
Turning circle ... 31ft. 2·5in. (9·5 cm)
Kerb weight ... 14cwt (1,566lb—714kg)

PERFORMANCE DATA

Top gear m.p.h. per 1,000 r.p.m. .... 15·37
Torque lb. ft. per cu. in. engine capacity........ 0·92
Brake surface swept by linings .... 190 sq. in.
Weight distri-
bution ... F. 52·4 per cent; R. 47·6 per cent

SPRITE and MIDGET . . .

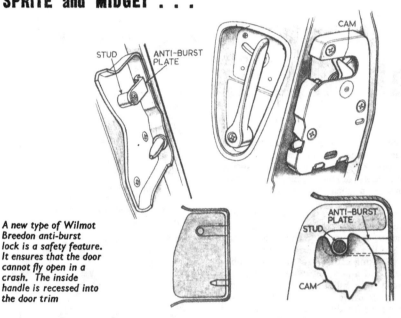

A new type of Wilmot Breedon anti-burst lock is a safety feature. It ensures that the door cannot fly open in a crash. The inside handle is recessed into the door trim

The main effect of the latest cockpit layout is to give it a designed look, rather than the appearance of having been assembled from a number of unrelated components. The new facia is handsome and practical, with the matching trip speedometer and electronic rev counter angled inwards to fall on the arc of focus of the driver's eyes. Both are clearly visible through the unobstructed upper half of the new three-spoke spring steering wheel, which has a cowled column incorporating the trafficator switch.

The instrument panel is a steel pressing taking up two-thirds of the width of the facia, and on the left-hand section (right hand for left-hand-drive cars) the fuel gauge and a combined oil pressure gauge and coolant thermometer are mounted. This section of the panel also provides a mounting for the electrical switches, choke and heater controls and screenwasher plunger. The whole of the panel and facia is finished in black crackle enamel, surmounted by a padded leathercloth roll which is extended along the tops of the doors.

On the passenger side a crushable, fibreboard parcels shelf with a padded edge provides stowage for maps and small oddments, and would collapse safely in the event of accident. The floor and transmission tunnel are covered in good quality pile carpet, and this has bound edges and rubber heel mats for both occupants.

Road Impressions

A short run in an M.G. Midget verified that the ride has been very much improved, and has a great deal in common with that of the larger MGB. The wider location base for the rear springs has allowed the manufacturers to put more rubber into the shackles. This makes for a quieter running as well as a better ride. Final drive vibration which was felt in older models is noticeably absent. Handling is particularly pleasant, light and predictable, and the necessity on certain surfaces to drive with the fingertips has gone. Particularly noteworthy is that there is ample elbowroom with two large people on board.

The Austin-Healey Sprite and the M.G. Midget were introduced as cheap, small sports cars suitable for young people to cut their motoring teeth on with safety and economy. In their latest guise they have in no sense drifted away from this precept, but rather have widened their scope, because of the comfort and convenience offered by improved suspension and weather protection, so that they now appeal to older enthusiasts looking for a small, lively car for everyday use.

Visibility is not impaired with the hood up and there is good wind protection with it removed and side windows raised

THE details of the M.G. Midget, and its companion Austin-Healey Sprite model, are well known. This is an entirely conventional small sports car, with a front engine and rear drive.

The latest Midget has a long-stroke engine of 1,098 c.c. The subject of the current test is a 1961 Midget, which originally had a 950 c.c. unit. This has been bored out to 1,080 c.c. by Speedwell but retains the less exaggerated stroke dimension of the earlier engine. In consequence, it is more suitable for sustained operation at high revolutions, the stroke being 76.2 mm. against 83.7 mm.

This particular machine is tuned almost up to Formula Junior standards, but retains an acceptable degree of flexi-

the car as well as reducing drag. The tail section of the current Midget is not well streamlined and even better results can be obtained with an early Sprite shell.

The performance of this little car on the road is very fine indeed. Although the engine is quite flexible, it is not at its best below 4,000 r.p.m., at which speed one is really in business. The power is well maintained up to 7,500 r.p.m. and so the effective band is a wide one. I was given permission to touch 8,000 r.p.m. but I obtained the best acceleration by changing up at 7,500 r.p.m., so this figure has been used in quoting the maxima in the gears. At the timed maximum speed of 105.8

an insurance policy. I covered many miles at a genuine 100 m.p.h. and the engine remained smooth and kept perfectly cool. An electric fan was fitted ahead of the radiator.

I was surprised to find that I averaged 26 m.p.g. during the flat-out performance testing. One could certainly rely on 30 m.p.g. at normal road speeds. The oil consumption was moderate and did not rise excessively at sustained high speeds.

I came to the conclusion that Speedwell have all the answers where the small B.M.C. engine is concerned. They can supply speed equipment for quite moderate tuning operations, but for the man who really wants to motor the "Clubman 85" job is the answer. You certainly can't break it, because I've tried! For further particulars, contact Speedwell Centre, Cornwall Avenue, London, N.3.

JOHN BOLSTER tests
A SPEEDWELL MIDGET

bility. It has been modified to "Clubman 85" specification, which costs £250 when the customer's existing unit is used as a basis. A special steel crankshaft is dynamically balanced, together with the light flywheel, connecting rods, and flat-top solid-skirt pistons. A new camshaft is employed with special rockers, giving extra leverage and a higher valve lift. The Speedwell light-alloy cylinder head contains large inlet valves and gives a compression ratio of 11 to 1. The manifolds are special and the carburetter is a twin-choke Weber 45 DCOE.

The exhaust system is very carefully tuned for length, and the result of all this is 89 b.h.p. at 7,000 r.p.m. with a maximum torque of 78 lb.-ft. at 5,500 r.p.m. Obviously the potentialities of such a power unit are very great.

A standard chassis is used, but great trouble has been taken to put it together about right. Commercial tolerances in assembly often cause standard Midgets and Sprites to steer badly because the designed suspension geometry is not reproduced. A Speedwell anti-roll bar is fitted in front.

Bodywork modifications include the fitting of a Speedwell "Monza" bonnet. This has central ducting to feed the water radiator, carburetter, and fresh-air intake, while the side ducts look after twin oil radiators. The cost of the "Monza" bonnet is £49 10s. A Speedwell "Clubman" hard top is also fitted, costing £37 10s. These components transform the aerodynamic stability of

m.p.h., the engine was turning at an indicated 7,300 r.p.m.

The fierce acceleration is emphasized by the standing quarter-mile time of 16.7 seconds, during which a speed of 80 m.p.h. was exceeded. Perhaps even more impressive, for so small a car, is the 0-100 m.p.h. time of 40.5 secs. The time taken to reach 80 m.p.h. from a standstill is identical to the 0-60 m.p.h. figure of a standard M.G.

Quite one of the best features of the car is the quiet exhaust system, which allows full acceleration to be used in towns. I did oil up one sparking plug in London but the car is without vice on the open road. Bucket seats, with adjustable back angles, are fitted. However, the adjusting wheel is strategically placed to catch my left funny bone during energetic manoeuvres, so I cannot praise this accessory.

Very remarkable is the stability at the maximum speed. Cars as small as this sometimes need holding at three-figure velocities but with this M.G. a couple of fingers on the wheel suffice. The over-steering tendency of the standard model has gone, the stability in side winds also being greatly improved.

To tune an engine while using the standard bottom end is either to accept rigid limitations or to risk a major blow-up. If you start off with a special crankshaft and a balancing job, you are half-way towards safe revolutions. A light flywheel is easy on the crank and, of course, the oil radiators are as good as

SPECIFICATION AND PERFORMANCE DATA

Car Tested: Speedwell M.G. Midget. Price of special engine modifications £250. Bonnet £49 10s. Hard top £37 10s.

Engine: Four-cylinders 67 mm. x 76.2 mm. (1,080 c.c.). Pushrod operated overhead valves in special light alloy head. Compression ratio 11 to 1. 89 b.h.p. at 7,000 r.p.m. Weber twin-choke carburetter. Lucas coil and distributor.

Transmission: Single dry plate clutch, four-speed gearbox with synchromesh on upper three gears and short central lever, ratios 4.22, 5.73, 8.09 and 13.50 to 1. Open propeller shaft. Hypoid rear axle.

Chassis: Standard M.G. chassis with independent front suspension by wishbones and rear axle on quarter-elliptic springs. Disc front brakes and drum rear. Extra: Speedwell anti-roll bar and wire wheels.

Equipment: Standard equipment plus oil temperature gauge and electric radiator fan with thermostatic switch.

Dimensions: Wheelbase 6 ft. 8 ins. Track (front) 3ft. 9¼ ins. (rear) 3 ft. 8¼ ins. Weight 12 cwt. (approx.).

Performance: Maximum speed 105.8 m.p.h. Speeds in gears, 3rd, 81 m.p.h.; 2nd, 55.5 m.p.h.; 1st 33 m.p.h. Standing quarter-mile 16.7 secs. Acceleration: 0-30 m.p.h. 3.2 secs.; 0-50 m.p.h. 7.3 secs.; 0-60 m.p.h. 9.1 secs.; 0-80 m.p.h. 16.4 secs.; 0-100 m.p.h. 40.5 secs.

Fuel Consumption: 26-30 m.p.g.

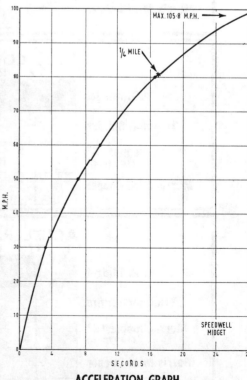

ACCELERATION GRAPH

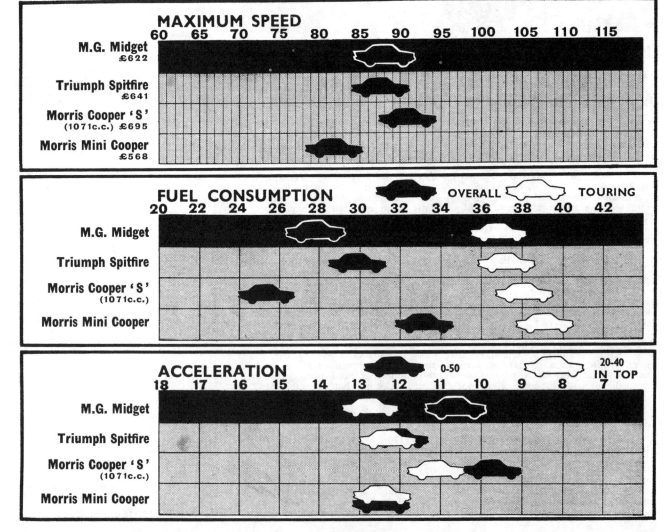

MAXIMUM SPEED

	60	65	70	75	80	85	90	95	100	105	110	115

M.G. Midget £622
Triumph Spitfire £641
Morris Cooper 'S' (1071c.c.) £695
Morris Mini Cooper £568

FUEL CONSUMPTION — OVERALL — TOURING

	20	22	24	26	28	30	32	34	36	38	40	42

M.G. Midget
Triumph Spitfire
Morris Cooper 'S' (1071c.c.)
Morris Mini Cooper

ACCELERATION — 0-50 — 20-40 IN TOP

	18	17	16	15	14	13	12	11	10	9	8	7

M.G. Midget
Triumph Spitfire
Morris Cooper 'S' (1071c.c.)
Morris Mini Cooper

O NE attraction of a small sports car like the Midget is its easy adaptability to the weather. Performance and handling are big considerations, and when the same car can offer all, so much the better. The Midget, and the Sprite before it, have always been praised for their handling, particularly for the accuracy and sensitive feel in the steering. Criticism often aimed at the Mk. I Sprite (effectively the Mark 0 Midget) was that its performance did not match its looks.

The Mark I Midget changed a lot of that, especially when the 1,098 c.c. engine came along; and now the Mark II car has found a little more power still at slightly higher revs; enough to improve the 0–60 m.p.h. time from 16·6 to 14·9 sec. (compared with the 1100 Sprite we tested). In top gear the 20–40 time is slightly worse, the 30–50 about the same while 40–60 times and beyond are distinctly better, emphasizing the raised power curve due to larger inlet valves and revised cylinder head. Although the performance figures deny it, this car does not feel any less tractable and it is quite content to potter gently.

These, however, are not the biggest changes. Wind-up windows, lockable doors and a heater are held by the early Sprite generation to detract from the original fresh air sports character. Such objection to progress is quite unfounded; the changes widen the potential market of the Midget to include many differing ages and mentalities, and either sex. The original enthusiast, probably single (there is room for little more than a portable cot behind the seats), will like the improvement in cornering stability given by semi-elliptic instead of quarter leaf springs at the rear.

Splendid controllability, good performance and nice lines make the Midget fun, and it has room for a reasonable amount of luggage behind the seats and in the boot. Big people will

Even with the hood down, wind-up windows and a big screen give plenty of protection from cold winds. The front grille distinguishes the Midget from its Austin-Healey Sprite twin.

find it a difficult fit, and knees splayed round the steering wheel will foul the window winder; the space now occupied by the window mechanism has removed the door pocket space (which previously provided extra elbow room) to cramp the tall man still further.

If you still buy a sports car primarily for sport the Midget has plenty of virtues to counteract these shortcomings.

Performance

SPORTS cars are not really meant to be driven very gently in top, but there are times when there is nothing pleasanter than pottering along, hood down, with little noise; in such moods the Midget, at around 20 m.p.h., is quite happy and can still accelerate without changing down. In top gear, 20–30 in 6·7 sec. is 0·3 sec. longer than the 50–60 time and the fastest 20 m.p.h. gap is from 30–50 m.p.h. (about 2,000–3,000 r.p.m.) emphasizing that maximum torque (at 3,250 r.p.m.) appears considerably higher in the speed range than for a family saloon.

Acceleration through the gears is good, with 0–50 m.p.h. taking only 9·9 sec., sufficient to beat most family saloons of twice the M.G.'s capacity. Trying too hard in the wet on take-off, it is very easy to get wheelspin with the lightly laden live axle.

M.G. MIDGET Mk II

Civilized cockpit: well upholstered seats, carpeted floor, and crackle finished facia. Window winding mechanism occupies the former door pockets leaving facia shelf for oddments.

Top speed is now 91·8 m.p.h. which coincides exactly with the beginning of the red sector on the rev counter at 6,000 r.p.m. Taking advantage of down grades puts the revs straight into the orange sector (at 5,500 r.p.m.); a 25-mile spell at around 5,500 r.p.m. on M1 dropped the oil pressure from its customary 55 lb./sq. in. to 40 lb./sq. in.; this was restored to normal after a short distance on ordinary roads but continuous cruising near the maximum speed is probably not advisable and certainly not effortless.

The test car was prone to running on with Premium petrol, so 100 octane grades were used for most of the time. Fuel consumptions have changed a little with the new engine, being at the most 4 m.p.g. worse than the Mk. I Midget. The overall figure of 29·2 m.p.g. represents many miles of sports motoring, but less enthusiastic driving will return figures nearer to our touring fuel consumption of 38·2 m.p.g.

Early morning starts are immediate on full choke, and less than a mile is needed on half choke before the engine is warm enough to pull evenly, although it takes considerably longer for the normal running temperature to come up.

Hill starting is all right up to 1 in 4, but on the 1 in 3 the car staggered to the top on the initial deliberate clutch slip; a long hill, as steep as this, would be too much.

Transmission

WHEN the 948 c.c. engine of the Mk. I was increased to 1,098 c.c. baulk ring synchromesh replaced the earlier not very powerful type, to make it quite unbeatable even during performance testing. The close ratios, unchanged from the previous model, are one of the best sets in production; 6,500 r.p.m. in the gears (halfway up the red sector) gives maxima of 31, 52 and 73·5 m.p.h. with rev drops on the upward changes of 2,600, 1,900 and 1,700 r.p.m. almost the progressive racing ideal.

In the lower ratios there was a certain amount of gear whine, but this seemed more the sound of well-meshed gears with no play. The excellent gearbox is supported by a not particularly light clutch, which always takes up the drive smoothly however quickly the left foot works.

To engage bottom gear smoothly every time at rest, you have first to get almost into second. Partly responsible for this, and wholly responsible for stalling under braking to a standstill, was a dragging clutch, which drops the tickover revs by 200 r.p.m.—enough to stall it with a conventional idling setting.

Handling and Brakes

DESPITE a turning circle of 30 ft. and only 2¼ turns from lock to lock, the Midget steering is unusually light, but there is plenty of feel, noticeable particularly in the wet, as the

The mirror adjusts for height. Larger dials are angled neatly upwards.

Performance

Conditions: Weather: Slight drizzle, misting rain, wind 5–15 m.p.h. (Temperature 39°F, Barometer 29·45 in. Hg.). Surface: Damp tarmacadam. Fuel: 100 octane.

ACCELERATION TIMES

0-30 m.p.h.	..	..	..	4·2 sec.
0-40	..	..	..	6·8
0-50	..	..	..	9·9
0-60	..	..	..	14·9
0-70	..	..	..	21·2
0-80	..	..	..	36·4
Standing quarter mile		..	..	20·1

On upper ratios m.p.h.	Top sec.	3rd sec.
10-30	15·4	8·6
20-40	12·0	6·6
30-50	10·6	6·5
40-60	11·7	8·2
50-70	13·5	10·3
60-80	18·4	—

The engine is reasonably accessible under the rear-hinged bonnet 1. clutch and brake reservoirs (beneath heater hose) 2. coil 3. starter solenoid 4. distributor 5. dip stick 6. oil filler cap 7. water filler cap 8. windscreen washer bottle.

The boot is large for a small sports car: total volume of cases is 3.1 cu. ft. There is more space behind the bucket seats.

front end begins to slide if too much lock is put on suddenly. As soon as one becomes accustomed to it, this gives high geared positive control of the best vintage kind, responsive in the extreme but entirely devoid of twitch. The change in rear suspension from quarter to semi-elliptic springs, giving better lateral location of the rear axle, has eliminated the lurch with which previous models were inclined to enter a corner and the consequent feeling of over-sensitivity. Handling is neutral with an easily controllable final breakaway at the back.

The Midget is particularly swervable; some of this responsiveness is due to fairly stiff springing, which can be felt uncomfortably on very bad roads as the car leaps around, but on ordinary roads the latest model is rather less harsh than its predecessor and there is never any feeling of having to hang on to the wheel; one just grips it delicately between the fingers and wills the car round corners; there is little roll,

continued on next page

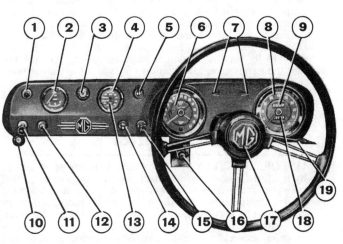

1. windscreen washer 2. petrol gauge 3. ignition starter switch 4. oil pressure gauge 5. lights switch 6. rev counter 7. direction indicator warning lights 8. speedometer 9. trip recorder 10. bonnet release 11. choke 12. wiper switch 13. water temperature gauge 14. panel light switch 15. heater control 16. dip switch (on floor) 17. horn 18. total mileage recorder 19. direction indicators.

MAXIMUM SPEEDS

Mean lap speed banked circuit ..	91·8 m.p.h.
Best one way ¼-mile	..	94·7
3rd gear at 6,000 r.p.m.	..	68·0
2nd gear at 6,000 r.p.m.	..	48·0
1st gear at 6,000 r.p.m.	..	29·0

"Maximile" Speed: (Timed quarter mile after 1 mile accelerating from rest)

Mean	..	..	..	88·0
Best	..	..	..	90·4

BRAKES

Pedal pressure, deceleration and equivalent stopping distance from 30 m.p.h.

lb.	g	ft.
25	·25	120
50	·50	60
75	·76	39½
100	·95	31½
115	·98	30½
Handbrake	·45	66½

HILL CLIMBING

At steady speed			lb./ton	
Top	..	..	1 in 10·1 ..	Tapley 220
3rd	..	..	1 in 6·4 ..	345
2nd	..	..	1 in 4·5 ..	490

FUEL CONSUMPTION

Touring (m.p.g. at steady speed midway between 30 m.p.h. and maximum, less 5% allowance for acceleration) .. .. 38·2
Overall .. .. 29·2
(=10·3 litres/100 km.)
Tank capacity (maker's figure) 6 gallons

M.P.G.
Touring = 38·2
Overall = 29·2

M.P.G. vs M.P.H. graph (y-axis M.P.G. 20 to 55; x-axis M.P.H. 30 to 90)

STEERING

Turning circle between kerbs:				ft.
Left	..	..	..	30½
Right	..	..	..	29¾
Turns of steering wheel from lock to lock	..	..	..	2¼

SPEEDOMETER

30 m.p.h.	..	..	..	11½% fast
60	..	..	..	6¾% fast
90	..	..	..	6% fast
Distance recorder	..	..	½% slow

WEIGHT

			cwt.
Kerb weight (unladen with fuel for approximately 50 miles)	..	..	13¾
Front/rear distribution	..	53/47
Weight laden as tested	..	..	17½

Test Data: World copyright reserved: no unauthorized reproduction in whole or in part.

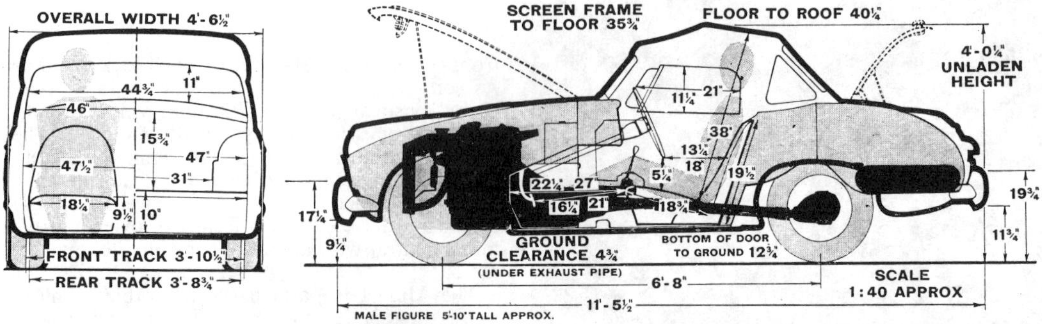
OVERALL WIDTH 4'-6½"
44¾"
11"
46"
15¾"
47"
47½"
31"
18½"
9½"
10"
FRONT TRACK 3'-10½"
REAR TRACK 3'-8¾"
SCREEN FRAME TO FLOOR 35¾"
FLOOR TO ROOF 40¼"
4'-0¼" UNLADEN HEIGHT
11½"
21"
38"
13¼"
18"
5¼"
19½"
22¼"
27"
16½"
21"
18¾"
17¼"
9¼"
19¾"
11¾"
GROUND CLEARANCE 4¾"
(UNDER EXHAUST PIPE)
BOTTOM OF DOOR TO GROUND 12¾"
6'-8"
SCALE 1:40 APPROX
11'-5½"
MALE FIGURE 5'-10" TALL APPROX.

M.G. MIDGET Mk II

and no tyre squeal to remind passers-by how fast you are going. On very bumpy corners, however, it becomes obvious that the conventional rear axle gives an indifferent sprung/unsprung weight ratio and far more wheel hop than a good independent rear suspension.

Disc brakes, now standard on the front, are effective and fade free, requiring normal pressures (50 lb. for 0·5g. stop) and 115 lb. for the maximum recorded, 0·98g. On the test hill, the handbrake, mounted on the left of the transmission tunnel (and without the traditional M.G. flyoff release) had no trouble with the 1 in 3, and proved very useful as an emergency brake with locked rear wheels recording 0·45g.

Comfort and Control

UNFORTUNATELY, rearward seat adjustment is limited by the front face of the platform over the back axle, so that even the enterprising tall owner will be unable to get himself really comfortable without major body modification or changing the seat profile. For the average man, however, the seats are very comfortable and strike an excellent compromise between a wrap-around side supporting shape and easy access.

The driving position is good for a 5 ft. 10 in. driver, with the wheel far enough away for any necessary arm twirling, although not for a completely straight arm position. A short stubby gear lever, with stiff precise movement, lies just where it is wanted, within a handspan from the wheel rim in top gear. Brake and accelerator pedals are too closely spaced and it is all too easy for a large foot to hit both, although this is ideal for heel and toe use.

However tight you have a fabric hood, it is still inclined to vibrate; the Midget's starts to do so at about 60 m.p.h. but gets little worse at higher speeds so that conversation is always possible despite any increase in carburetter noise.

The vintage days of a little bit of glass let into a fabric hood for rearward visibility have now disappeared, and current foldable transparent plastic ensures very good vision all round, with no blind spots. At night, headlights on full beam are adequate for the car's performance.

The heating system is very simple—one knob and two flaps. Pull the knob out and the heat is turned off; push in for more air and a final twist (only possible with the knob full in) turns the heater fan on. Flaps on each side of the gearbox tunnel let air onto the legs, or divert it all on to the screen when they are closed. The temperature can be varied only by allowing less hot air in or by turning off the water cock for the summer; but in winter the heater is more than adequate.

Fittings and Furniture

A NEAT crackle black facia has the two main instruments (rev counter and speedometer) canted in towards the driver, and easily visible through the three-spoke wheel. The other two are on the flat part with a combined oil pressure/water temperature and fuel gauges.

Mounted on a vertical rod, the rear view mirror can be adjusted to any position between top and bottom of the screen. Carpets now cover all metal surfaces except the doors, and rubber mats provide extra protection from sharp heels.

A small parcel shelf is situated under the facia (passenger side) and prone to damp, but most luggage will find its way to the rear compartment which will take a quite large suitcase or several small ones; the boot has plenty of room, too, despite the spare wheel.

Lockable doors were supposed to constitute a safety feature, but with the door handle at the rear, it is too easy to undo two hood fasteners and open it. The other disadvantage of this position is that it requires a universally jointed elbow to let yourself out; the passenger's interior lock was particularly stiff. Safety belt anchorages are provided, and the test car had comfortable lap strap and diagonal belts.

MAKE M.G. • MODEL Midget Mk. II • MAKERS M.G. Car Co. Ltd. Abingdon-on-Thames, Berks.

ENGINE

Cylinders	4
Bore and stroke	64·58 mm. × 83·72 mm.
Cubic capacity	1,098 c.c.
Valves	O.h.v. (pushrod)
Compression ratio	9·0 : 1
Carburetter(s)	Twin HS2 S.U.
Fuel pump	S.U. electric
Oil filter	Purolator full flow
Max. power (net)	59 b.h.p. at 5,750 r.p.m.
Max. torque (net)	62 lb. ft. at 3,250 r.p.m.

TRANSMISSION

Clutch	7¼ in. Borg & Beck
Top gear (s/m)	Direct
3rd gear (s/m)	1·36
2nd gear (s/m)	1·91
1st gear	3·20
Reverse	4·11
Final drive	Hypoid bevel 4·22 : 1
M.p.h. at 1,000 r.p.m. in:—	
Top gear	15·3
3rd gear	11·3
2nd gear	8·0
1st gear	4·8

CHASSIS

Construction	Unitary

BRAKES

Type	Lockheed hydraulic
Dimensions	Front 8¼ in. disc; Rear 7 in. drum
Swept friction area	135·28 sq. in.

SUSPENSION AND STEERING

Front	Coil spring with lower wishbone
Rear	Semi-elliptic leaf springs
Shock absorbers:	
Front	Armstrong lever arm as upper suspension link
Rear	Armstrong lever arm
Steering gear	Rack and pinion
Tyres	5·20—13

COACHWORK AND EQUIPMENT

Starting handle	No
Jack	Side lift
Jacking points	Door sill panel
Battery	Lucas 43 amp.-hr. at 20 hr. rate
No. of electrical fuses	Two (and two spares)
Indicators	Flashers
Screen wipers	Lucas single speed
Screen washers	Tudor manual
Sun visors	None
Locks:	
With ignition key	Doors and boot
With other keys	None
Interior heater	Smiths fresh air—optional
Extras	Heater, hard top, luggage carrier, twin horns, heavy duty tyres, wheel discs, Radiomobile radio
Upholstery	Leathercloth
Floor covering	Pile carpet
Alternative body types	None

MAINTENANCE

Sump	6½ pints S.A.E. 30
Gearbox	2¼ pints S.A.E. 30
Rear axle	1½ pints S.A.E. 90
Steering gear	S.A.E. 90
Cooling system	10 pints (2 drain taps)
Chassis lubrication	Every 3,000 miles to 12 points
Ignition timing	5° b.t.d.c.
Contact breaker gap	·014/·016 in.
Sparking plug type	Champion N5
Sparking plug gap	·024/·026
Tappet clearances (cold)	Inlet ·012 in., Exhaust ·012 in.
Front wheel toe-in	⅛ in.
Castor angle	3°
Tyre pressures:	
Front	18 lb. sq. in.—22 lb. } High speed
Rear	20 lb. sq. in.—24 lb. } High speed

M.G. MIDGET

MARK TWO

THE small sports car has grown up, and has done so quite suddenly in the past couple of years or so. Those who remember the early cars which bore the name "Midget"—and even those who remember the less distant past when B.M.C.'s first contribution to the small sports car field, the Austin-Healey Sprite, first appeared on the market, would find little except dimensions as points of similarity between those and the current M.G. Midget—the "Mark 2" in the line, which is, of course, similar in all respects to the current Mark 3 Sprite.

The first of the small B.M.C. sports cars, the Sprite, was an admirable machine. Small, economical and lively, with high standards of road-holding, it retained such "traditional" sports car features as detachable side-screens, limited and rather awkwardly-placed luggage accommodation, and was possessed of a performance which, although adequate, nevertheless represented only a relatively slight improvement on its less sporting companions in the one-litre category.

With the introduction of the Mark 2 Midget (and the Mark 3 Sprite) the small sports car embarked on a new era, however. The car is nowadays even more a scaled-down version of its lustier stablemates, and it combines such creature comforts as wind-up windows and much-improved interior trim with a performance of which many so-called sports cars of much greater engine capacity might well be envious.

The current model has a maximum speed comfortably in excess of 90 m.p.h., and will reach 60 m.p.h. from a standing start in around 13 seconds: a cruising speed in excess of 80 m.p.h. can be enjoyed without stress, while its fuel consumption remains extremely moderate.

The power unit is still basically the B.M.C. "A" series engine, now of 1,098 c.c. The unit has pushrod-operated overhead valves, a three-bearing crankshaft and a cast-iron cylinder head. With a nine to one compression ratio, 59 b.h.p. is developed at 5,750 r.p.m. It is a rather rough engine, but one which has plenty of "punch", and whether hot or cold it is an easy starter. Surprisingly, it is also remarkably flexible, and the top-gear performance is good: maximum torque (62 lb./ft.) is produced at 3,250 r.p.m. No snatch or unpleasantness is experienced at speeds below 20 m.p.h. in top gear, and the car will accelerate steadily from this speed to its maximum without the need for a gearchange. When cold it pulls well, although it takes several miles to reach its normal running temperature. It is extremely free-revving, and will pull maximum revs. in top gear: during our performance testing, the needle of the tachometer entered the "amber" sector of the dial when our best one-way maximum speed was recorded. The engine of the test car showed a strong tendency to "pink" when pulling hard: a change to 100-octane fuel gave no apparent improvement, and the ignition timing was

Under all conditions the car is fully-controllable, and is predictable in its handling qualities. Initial understeer promotes considerable tyre squeal: as the limit of adhesion is reached the rear end breaks away but remains easily under the driver's control. Bumps and other road surface irregularities will cause the back of the car to be thrown off-line with some violence, but the quick, positive steering enables adequate correction to be made.

Disc brakes are fitted to the front wheels, combined with drums at the rear. The brake pedal is light to use and the braking capabilities of the system give plenty of confidence. At no time during the test was any fade or uneven pulling experienced, and firm, all-square stopping power could be employed with confidence on wet and dry roads. Occasionally the front discs produced some squeal when applied firmly.

The test car had covered rather more than 6,000 miles when it came into our hands for test. There were no rattles, and the doors shut well: a further improvement on this model over the earlier car is that the doors now have outside handles, and

Right: Wind-up windows, lockable doors and swivelling quarter-lights are now featured on the Midget, together with revised instrumentation. Below right: Principal engine components and accessories are easily accessible.

suspected, although the engine did not run particularly "hot".

The gearbox is a four-speed and reverse unit, with central floor-mounted gear lever and synchromesh on the upper three ratios only. The ratios are well-spaced, and represent a noticeable improvement on earlier models, while the transmission train is quiet in operation. Only the unsynchronised first gear is rather noisy, especially on the over-run. The clutch is light to operate and in general grips well: ultra-fast gear-changes allow a slight amount of initial slip to be detected as the drive is taken up. The gear lever is precise in operation and has a short movement, although its action, on the test car, was a trifle stiff: in addition the lever possessed an annoying rattle, especially when the engine was pulling hard at high r.p.m.

Front suspension is independent, with wishbones and coil-springs. At the rear, the quarter-elliptic longitudinal leaf springs of earlier models have been replaced by springs of semi-elliptic pattern. The suspension gives a level, firm ride, and while bumps can be felt inside the car, wheel movement is well-controlled and there is a pleasing absence of axle-tramp and, on dry roads, wheel-spin is not easily induced.

can be locked. In addition, wind-up windows, their glasses having a pronounced curvature in the interests of maximum body width, and small, opening quarter-lights are now fitted. The hood is draught-free and is now secured by quick-release clips at the top of the windscreen frame: these work well and are easily and speedily manipulated when the hood is raised or lowered. In its lowered position, the hood is completely detached, and stows, with the hood-sticks, in the boot. When erect, it is fully water-proof and provides a snug interior, while the canvas retains its shape and does not flap, even at the car's maximum speed.

With the hood erect, the Midget is not the easiest car in the world to enter or leave, but once one is aboard there is a generous amount of room. The interior of the car has been given something of a face-lift, and comfortable seats, well-shaped and providing adequate support for driver and passenger, combine with a fully-carpeted and well-laid-out cockpit to provide a comfortable long-distance touring car. Front seat adjustment is limited, however, and tall drivers are less well provided for. As it is, even drivers of average height and build find the steering wheel rather too close to the chest, and additional rearward adjustment of the seat is precluded by the luggage space behind, which supplements the outside boot.

The steering itself is light and direct, with a pleasant precision which gives a good feel of the road through the front wheels and which adds to the enormous fun which driving this lively little car can provide. The wheel has three wire spokes, all of which are fitted in the lower half of the wheel so that, with the front wheels in the "straight ahead" position, the driver has an uninterrupted view of the instruments. The speedometer and rev.-counter, both of which have steady needles, are mounted at an angle so that each faces inwards for maximum visibility. The other instruments—fuel contents, oil pressure

and water temperature gauges—are mounted in the centre of the facia, together with the conveniently-placed, but unlabelled, hand controls for lights, screen-wipers, etc. The pedals are well-placed for heel and toe operation, and the gearlever is placed so as to fall conveniently to hand. Visibility all-round is good, and there is an effective heating and de-misting system. The screen-wipers clear a sufficient area of the windscreen in wet weather, but under some conditions two-speed operation would considerably assist their effectiveness: at high speed the blades tended to lift clear of the screen, with obvious deterioration in visibility.

The principal criterion for a sports car is, of course, its performance. In this direction the Midget by no means disappoints the driver. Its maximum speed, comfortably in excess of 90 m.p.h., puts it among the faster cars in the 1,100 c.c. bracket, and endows the car with a comfortable cruising speed of over 80 m.p.h., at which velocity one has the feeling that the engine is running well within its capabilities. Bearing in mind the extent to which the car is equipped, with carpets, wind-up windows and so on, its acceleration is extremely lively. From a standstill, as we have said, 60 m.p.h. can be reached in thirteen seconds. The engine develops its optimum performance in the middle range, so that only a very slight advantage is obtained by holding an intermediate ratio up to the maximum safe crankshaft speed. The gear ratios are well-spaced for a sporting vehicle, and apart from the stiffness of movement mentioned earlier—possibly a point peculiar to the individual model—the gearbox is very pleasant to use. The roadholding reaches a sufficiently high standard to permit very high average speeds to be maintained from point to point: the car's behaviour is at all times predictable and controllable, aided by the high-geared, pleasant steering, and slides can be deliberately induced and easily controlled.

Economical running has always been a feature of the small B.M.C. sports cars, and the latest Midget is no exception. Its fuel consumption must be regarded as extremely moderate in terms of the performance available, and our overall figure for the test mileage, of little short of 1,000 miles, was exactly 32 m.p.g. Very hard driving, including the taking of performance figures, reduced this figure to 30 m.p.g., and there is no doubt that many owners would improve on both these figures by a considerable margin.

 Cars on Test

M.G. MIDGET Mark 2

Engine: Four-cylinder, 64·57 mm. × 83·72 mm. (1,098 c.c.); compression ratio 8·9 : 1; pushrod-operated overhead valves; twin S.U. carburetters; 59 b.h.p. at 5,750 r.p.m.

Transmission: Single dry-plate clutch; four-speed and reverse gearbox with synchromesh on upper three forward ratios and central, floor-mounted gear-lever.

Suspension: Front, independent with coil springs, wishbones and lever-type dampers; rear, rigid axle with semi-elliptic leaf springs and lever-type dampers. Tyres: 5·20 × 13.

Brakes: Front, 8¼ in. disc brakes; rear, 7 in. drums.

Dimensions: Overall length, 11 ft. 4 ins.; overall width, 4 ft. 5 ins.; overall height, 4 ft. 2 ins.; turning circle, 32 ft. 2 ins.; dry weight, 14 cwt.

PERFORMANCE

	m.p.h.			secs.
MAXIMUM SPEED	— 97·2	ACCELERATION	0–30 —	4·0
(Mean of 2 ways)	— 95·9		0–40 —	6·6
			0–50 —	8·8
			0–60 —	13·0
SPEEDS IN GEARS First	— 30·0		0–70 —	16·5
Second	— 54·0		0–80 —	27·0
Third	— 74·0		0–90 —	35·9
		Standing quarter-mile	—	19·0

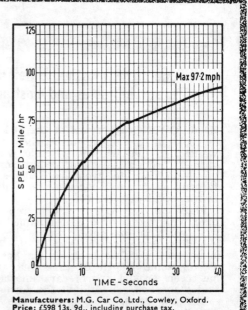

Manufacturers: M.G. Car Co. Ltd., Cowley, Oxford.
Price: £598 13s. 9d., including purchase tax.

MG MIDGET-
Traditionally Yours

One of the most mild, well-mannered of spor ts cars in its range, the Midget is one to suit all tastes and most pockets. There are few come so equipped at the price.

FOLLOWING a preview of the MG Midget, we took our time about putting the car to test. We wanted to live with it a while without being rushed through testing procedures owing to the queue of frustrated would-be Fangios who eagerly grab every new sports car as if it were their own speciality.

And, happily, we are able to report that our time with the revised and renamed Sprite was well worth the patience.

Adding flower to the test of the MG Midget is unnecessary. The basic design has been with us for some length of time and anyone who has been around sports cars knows the value that was always built into the former Sprite.

The big news, though, is in the mechanical departments. BMC, already updating the MGB and preparing to launch the MGC, wasn't ready to let the MG Midget fend for itself just on a change of name — no matter what kind of magic the name MG might conjure in the heart of the purist. So they took the best of everything and built a new car inside the current shell.

For power, engineers plucked out the proven Mini Cooper S unit of 1275 cc. They detuned it with smaller valves and a milder camshaft than used in the Coopers and held the power at 65 bhp at 6000 rpm, giving 72 lb/ft of torque at 3000 rpm. Compression ratio was kept almost the same.

The new engine really turned the little Midget on. Not that it was any slagbox before. With the former 1100 cc motor, the car was still light enough to be able to hold its own with any medium-sized sedan in traffic light derbies, yet it would be completely content to idle along at

very slow speeds without kick-back or fuss.

Not that the 1275 cc version is much different. Helped by a relatively low final drive gear ratio, the Midget is one of the most flexible sports cars around. Geared to run 15.5 mph per 1000 rpm, the 4.22 rear end brings the tachometer red line to 6300 — although the engine is just as happy to spin closer to seven grand — and a top speed of over 100 mph. The Midget would easily pull a higher rear end if you wanted some spirited cruising in the country, but as a dual-purpose sports car the ratio choice currently used is excellent for every need.

Small shortcomings do remain in the Midget design. There is a slightly cramped feeling in the driver's seat — owing to the steering wheel coming back to the driver too far. Actually, this could be turned around to read that the seat doesn't adjust back far enough to allow even a semi-straight armed driving position — and a tallish driver could well find himself experiencing slight pangs of arm fatigue on long journeys.

Whatever the driving position may be to the tall enthusiast, the car is nevertheless comfortable. Passengers have oodles of room for feet and elbows and excellent vision from a normal sitting position. With the side windows wound up and the hood down, there is hardly any wind-blown discomfort, rather a touch of fresh air wafting over the top of the windscreen lightly to fleck the occupants. For a full blast of air and a carefree feeling, simply wind the lot down and hold on to your hat.

The cockpit is fully carpeted, and this extends back to the parcel shelf behind the seats — even when the hood is folded. While overnight bags can be carried on this shelf, any other holiday luggage or parcels will fit easily into the surprisingly-large boot.

Our first impressions of the Midget gave full details of the hood and its new design, so there's

Same styling, different name. Car is very popular and MG insignia should push it to greater heights. Laminated windscreen and headlamp flasher are among optional extras. They should be standard.

Heart of the Midget Mk II is the race-proven four cylinder BMC A-series engine. Of 1275 cc, with pushrod operated ohv, twin SU down-draught carburettors and counter-balanced crank, it develops 65 bhp — reliably, if somewhat noisily.

SPECIFICATIONS

Make	MG Midget (1275)
Price	$2480
Road test mileage	348 miles

PERFORMANCE:

Top speed (fastest run)	94 mph
Speedometer indication	103 mph
Top speed (average)	93.7 mph
Rpm at max speed	6300 rpm

Speeds in gears — Equivalent rpm

First	30 mph	(6300 rpm)
Second	52 mph	(6300 rpm)
Third	70 mph	(6300 rpm)
Fourth	94 mph	(6300 rpm)

Acceleration through the gears:

0-30 mph	4.0 sec	0-60 mph	13.2 sec
0-40 mph	6.3 sec	0-70 mph	19.3 sec
0-50 mph	9.5 sec	0-80 mph	25.7 sec

Acceleration in gears:

	third	fourth
30-50 mph	5.1 sec	7.6 sec
40-60 mph	5.5 sec	7.4 sec
50-70 mph	6.2 sec	8.3 sec
60-80 mph		10.6 sec
70-90 mph		12.4 sec

Standing quarter mile:

Fastest run	18.9 sec
Average of all runs	19.1 sec

Fuel consumption:

Overall for test	28 mpg
Normal cruising	28-32 mpg
Hardie Ferodo test circuit ($1\frac{1}{8}$ mile) —	
Fastest lap	56.5 sec
Average of all laps	57.0 sec

Speedometer error:

Indicated mph:	30	40	50	60	70	80
Actual mph:	27.7	36.7	46.0	54.5	64.2	72.5

CALCULATED DATA:

Mph per 1000 rpm in top gear	14.9 mph
Piston speed at max bhp	3200 ft/min
Power to weight ratio	96 bhp/ton

ENGINE:

Cylinders	four in line
Bore and stroke	70.63 mm by 81.33 mm
Cubic capacity	1275 cc
Compression ratio	8.8 to 1
Valves	pushrod overhead
Carburettors	twin SU HS2
Power	65 bhp at 6000 rpm
Torque	72 lb/ft at 3000 rpm

TRANSMISSION:

Type	four speed, syncro 2, 3, 4
Clutch	$6\frac{1}{2}$ in. dia sdp hydraulic
Gear lever location	central floor
Overall ratios: 1st	13.5
2nd	8.4
3rd	5.7
4th	4.2
Final drive	4.22 to 1

CHASSIS AND RUNNING GEAR:

Construction	unitary
Suspension front	wishbones, coils, anti-roll bar
Suspension rear	leaf springs
Shock absorbers	telescopic hydraulic
Steering type	rack and pinion
Turns lock to lock	2 1/3
Turning circle	32 ft

BRAKES:

Type	disc front, drum rear
Dimensions	$8\frac{1}{4}$ in. dia disc, 7 in. dia drum

DIMENSIONS:

Wheelbase	6 ft 8 in.
Track front	3 ft $10\frac{1}{2}$ in.
Track rear	3 ft $8\frac{3}{4}$ in.
Fuel tank capacity	6 gals
Tyres; size	5.20-13
Ground clearance	5 in.
Length	11 ft 5in.
Width	4 ft $6\frac{1}{2}$ in.
Height	4 ft 1 in.

There's ample room on the shelf for soft baggage as well as the neat-fitting, folded hood. Seat belts anchor to rear side panels of shelf. Note full carpeting over tunnel and rear compartment.

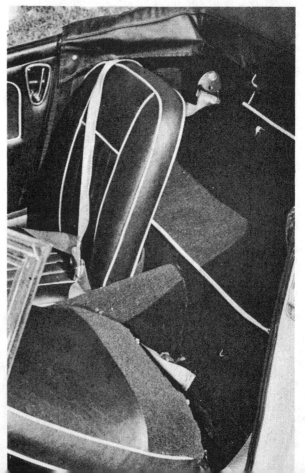

Seats are comfortable but driver's seat won't go back far enough for the tall. Steering wheel is stronger than Sprite model. Safety features are recessed interior door handles, anti-burst locks and roll bar in facia. Note handbrake location.

There are no carpets here, but the large boot is welcome. Spare wheel takes up sizeable portion of available space, but there's still room for plenty of luggage, the softer kind.

little need to go into that again. But we will applaud the company's foresight in supplying a small tonneau cover which clips over and around the folded hood, returning the car to a clean and uncluttered sight.

Handling, apart from the available extra torque, is not seriously changed. The car continues to understeer with regular tyre pressures — which probably keeps the boy-wonders out of potential trouble — but anyone with a bit of thought and driving nous can soon work out a good balance of tyre pressures to bring the car back to some semblance of neutral handling. In fact, it's damned hard to get the car to break the tail loose unless you time your actions and reactions to the split second, on the right corner with the right type of slippery road. Other than going through all of this hard work (you want to try it some-

time) you're probably as safe in the MG Midget as in any other car on the road in its class. On dirt or in the wet, the car is a ball in semi-experienced hands. Almost like a toy. It can literally be chucked around to adopt impossible angles; then brought back into line without turning a hair. A lot of the excellent handling and traction qualities found in the MG Midget can be attributed to the fact that BMC fit radial tyres as standard — a most welcome move.

So, before jumping into the big 'uns and dreaming you're a boy hero right from the start, take a trip in the Midget. It'll give you all the experience you'll want from a sports car, boasts all the features of its big brother and is one hell of a lot of fun to boot.

But at $2480, where have the cheaper sports cars gone? #

Midget is well-balanced from the rear. Locking petrol cap is optional extra. Owners can also specify a luggage carrier, full tonneau cover and anti-roll bar—at extra cost on an already expensive car.

M.G. M-Type (1929-32)　　　　　　　　　M.G. J2 (1932-34)

A Comparative Analysis of Midgets 1929 to 1965

MIDGETS have been continuously since the introduction of the M-Type in 1929, with the exception of the war years and the later '50s. All these Midgets have been astonishingly good value for money achieved as the result of the ingenuity of building a small sports car from slightly modified production saloon parts. Value, however, in the eyes of some ceased with the TF, in the eyes of others with the TC, and in the eyes of a few with the disappearance of the overhead cam, when the PB was discontinued in 1936. The proof of the pudding, however, has been in the eating. It is interesting to note that, with the exception of the P-types, sales figures from one series to another have always increased. There will, it seems, always be a generation hungry for a sports version of Morris's bread-and-butter line.

Here an attempt is made to present a comparative analysis of performance and quality in terms of value, of all Midgets, with the exception of series C, D, Q and R. Taking a pound (£1) in 1932 to be worth 20 shillings, the Westminster Bank Ltd. have kindly supplied the devaluation figures between then and now, the final figure rating the pound to be now worth 5s 3d. Using this as a financial basis, and keeping an eye on the fluctuations of purchase tax, a reasonable assessment is possible. The devaluation figures based on a pound in 1932 are these:

1932	£1	1958	6s 6d
1935	19s 2d	1960	6s 4d
1938	18s 5d	1961	6s 2d
1942	11s 0d	1962	5s 11d
1946	10s 9d	1963	5s 9d
1949	9s 1d	1964	5s 7d
1952	7s 8d	1965	5s 4d
1955	7s 3d	1966	5s 3d

Calculations are made as follows:

Comparative present day value =

$$\frac{\text{original cost} \times \text{the devaluation figure for the year}}{5/3 \ (63 \text{ pence}) \text{ being the present day value of the } 1932 \ £1.}$$

While the M-Type Midget, with its little 847 c.c. motor and all of its 20 b.h.p., has nothing in common with the current Mk. II other than its badge and the two webbing straps that retain the folded hood, no one will deny that for 1929, and for the gay young men for whom it was built, it was superb.

Having a top speed of 62 m.p.h. and a 0-60 time of 45 sec it would today be rated as expensive because at £185 then, it cost the equivalent of £705 now. But this car was a pioneer; this was the first time a small car with an interesting performance was available at anywhere near this price, and it appealed to a com-

M.G. TA (1936-39)　　　　　　　　　M.G. TC (1946-49)

Swept wing M.G. J2 (1932-34)

M.G. PB (1935-36)

pletely new section of our community.

Initially the M-Type appeared with a fabric-covered wooden body, but later with a more conventional metal one. The single overhead cam, 4-cylinder motor, even with its 2-bearing crank, was docile enough all through the rev. range, but nevertheless was noticeably happier towards the top end. Brakes have improved to such an extent since the M-Type was produced that an accurate assessment is difficult. However, fair comment can be made that in today's traffic an M-Type with the original cable brakes is somewhat of a liability unless considerable clearance is allowed at the higher speeds.

The M-Type was only the start, and after three years came the J-Type. Available at first with the cycle-type wings, and later in a swept-wing version, this model appealed as being a little more stylish. The engine was almost identical with the M's but the compression ratio had been raised from 5·4 to 6·2. The fuel tank was strapped on behind, giving what became a traditional profile, and the "noddy" appearance of the M-Type had disappeared. The J2 was 21 per cent quicker than the M. It had a top speed of 75 m.p.h., and could achieve a standing quarter-mile in 29·3 seconds. The sales were 2,300 in excess of the M,

and it was with the popular J2 that the enthusiast realized that he could push a Midget quite a long way past the makers' recommendations and get away with it—hence the J2 earned the reputation of having a rubber crankshaft.

It was indeed amazing what J2 cranks withstood, and while they did break from time to time, the problem could not be considered serious until most of the cranks in service had done considerable mileage with journals reground to well below the specifications. This was a credit to the original design, but if progress was to be maintained then something had to be done.

In 1934 the P-Type Midget appeared with a 3-bearing crank, other specifications being the same as the J2. Although top speed differed little from the J2, six seconds had been cut from the standing quarter, representing an improvement of 27·5 per cent in acceleration. The P-Type's 0-60 time of 23 sec was a 95 per cent improvement over the M of only two years earlier. The question of brakes had not been overlooked and the area was increased by fitting 12in. drums as standard, previously available only as an extra.

Road tests of the time report very favourably on the P-Type's improved suspension and roadholding, which for

pre-war standards was extremely good. The phase of P-Type production was concluded by the introduction of the PB with an extra 92 c.c., which gave an increase of 7 to 8 b.h.p. over the PA.

✱ In 1949 there was another change and the TD came out in almost complete sympathy with the Wolseley 4/44. The engine was the same XPAG unit as was fitted to the Wolseley and the TC, still developing 54·4 b.h.p. at 5,200 r.p.m. The main difference was that independent front suspension was fitted to the TD. The hard ride of 20 years' standing had disappeared. The front suspension assembly was very similar to that fitted to the Wolseley. The wheel size was reduced from 19in. to 15in., but the long, square radiator survived the onslaught of progress, and the TD made a very great impression on the market both at home and abroad. The former, however, must have been jeopardized by the crippling purchase tax. Indeed, both the TC and the TD were pioneers of sports car exports from this country to America and their contribution to British prestige cannot be over-rated.

While there was a very considerable improvement in road-holding and suspension, the TD was quite a bit heavier than the TC, yet with the same engine this resulted in very little difference in ▶

✱Continued on page 53

M.G. TD (1950-53)

M.G. TF (1954-55)

M.G. Midget Mk I (1961-1963)   M.G. Midget Mk II (1964 onwards)

M.G. Midget Analysis . . .

their comparative performances. Road tests, reports and experience do not consistently place either as being the faster—on acceleration or top speed. A slightly faster version—the TD II, developing 57 b.h.p. at 5,500 r.p.m.—was available from 1950 onwards.

During TD production between 1950 and 1953 purchase tax played havoc with value-for-money on the retail price. A TD with a basic price of £530 was loaded with £222 purchase tax. The comparative figure today for the basic price is £775, so again the manufacturers had made their contribution by changing from the TC to the TD for an increase which has a current equivalent of only £62, and was indeed worth every penny. Again this was denied to the British public who had to pay £752 for a TD which has a current equivalent of £1,095, so the value-to-cost ratio had been destroyed.

Good-looker

Worse, however, was still to come. The TF which replaced the TD in 1954 is considered by many to be the best-looking car that has ever come from Abingdon. The bonnet had been lowered, the headlamps incorporated in the wings, and the traditional flat facia panel had disappeared. Fitted with the optional wire wheels this was unquestionably a very inspiring machine. It performed on a parallel with the TD II, having the same engine and compression ratio of 8·1 to 1. This TF retailed at £780. The new styling therefore cost the public £28 over the price of the TD. The change for this price was an exceptional return for the extra money.

The Government, however, did not relent. Tax on the TF was in the region of £230 and, together with the basic price it retailed at £780 which has a current equivalent of £1,114. While the TF was a classic and quality car, and its suspension, road-holding and brakes were impeccable this was too much to pay for a Midget that was only marginally quicker than the 1939 TB.

In the following year, 1955, a new TF was available with the engine capacity increased to 1,500 c.c. developing 63 b.h.p. at 5,500 r.p.m. This gave the substantial increase in performance of about 7 per cent over the 1,250 TF and the TD II. The revised 1,500 engine, designated XPEG, was perhaps a little less robust than its predecessor, the XPAG.

Tradition Ends

The TF was the last of the traditionally styled Midgets, and there was another outcry when its production ceased. The subsequent model was the MGA, a new style incorporating the 1,500 B-series motor, and rightly it was decided that this could hardly be called a Midget. The Midget then disappeared for six years. The devaluation of the 1932 £1 during that time was 1s 1d. By an amalgamation of development costs with Austin-Healey, and a wider spread of overheads through increased production the next Midget appeared in 1961 at a very competitive price.

The 1961 Midget was a small, compact, unit-construction sports car. Its 948 c.c. motor developed just over 46 b.h.p. at 5,500 r.p.m. Its time for the standing quarter was comparable with the TC's, but its 0-60 time was almost 3 sec quicker. The basic price was £472 but purchase tax was still crippling at £217. It is interesting to compare the current equivalent of the basic price which is £554 with the corresponding figure for the M-Type, or indeed any

of the previous Midgets. This was by far the lowest price for which a Midget until then had been produced. It could offer everything except the classical configuration of its predecessors but unfortunately retailed at a comparative figure of £809. The 948 c.c. Midget was followed by an almost identical car with a 1,098 c.c. motor, and incorporating disc brakes on the front wheels. This car was 3·1 sec quicker over the standing quarter and 1·9 sec quicker on the 0-60 time.

It was now that the impediment of purchase tax was to be somewhat lightened. The 1,098 Mk. I, as it is known, cost basically £478 plus £120 purchase tax which gave a retail price of £599. This has a current equivalent of £675, and this, therefore, is the first Midget to be offered to the public for less than the M-Type of 1932. There is no need to stress the differences, or what may be termed progress. The value for money speaks for itself.

In 1964 the 1,098 Mk. II Midget came out with a curved windscreen, wind-up side window, half elliptic rear-springs and a more robust crank. This one is 2·5 sec quicker than the 1,098 Mk. I on a 0-60 time, and 0·8 seconds quicker over the standing quarter. There was a 4 per cent improvement in top speed, which according to road tests now stands at 92 m.p.h.

The Mk. II Midget is an exceptionally fine car, and at £624 is sold at the lowest comparative price at which a Midget has ever been put on the market in this country. It must represent the finest value for money that has ever come from Abingdon. Its exceptional qualities put the Mk. II in a class on its own. There are fewer than a handful of production sports cars that are anywhere near a match for a properly driven Mk. II Midget across its homeland of rural England.   **Peter Poyntz-Wright** ∎

M.G. Midget Mk. II with an Ashley fast-back hard-top

Year	Model	Basic price	Tax	Retail price	Relative value of 1932 £1	Relative value of basic	Relative value of retail	b.h.p.	Standing ¼-sec	0-60 sec
1929–32 ..	M	£185	—	£185	20s	£705	£705	20	—	45·0
1932–34 ..	J1 and J2	£200	—	£200	20s	£762	£762	36	29·3	—
1934–35 ..	P	£222	—	£222	19s 2d	£810	£810	35*	23·0	23·0
1936–39 ..	TA	£222	—	£222	18s 5d	£778	£778	50	22·8	—
1946–49 ..	TC	£412	£115	£527	10s 9d	£845	£1,079	54·4	21·8	21·1
	TC	£412	£115	£527	9s 1d	£713	£912	54·4	21·8	21·1
1950–53 ..	TD	£530	£222	£752	7s 8d	£775	£1,095	54·4†	23·2	23·6
1954 ..	TF	£550	£230	£780	7s 6d	£787	£1,114	57·3	23·0	23·3
1955 ..	TF	£645	£270	£915	7s 3d	£898	£1,264	63	—	—
1961 ..	948	£472	£217	£689	6s 2d	£554	£809	46	21·6	18·3
1962 ..	1098 I	£478	£120	£599	5s 11d	£540	£675	55	20·5	16·4
1964 ..	1098 II	£512	£111	£623	5s 7d	£546	£663	59	19·7	13·9
1966 ..	1098 II	£512	£111	£623	5s 3d	£512	£623	59	19·7	13·9

*PB 43 b.h.p. 1935–36.   †TD II 57 b.h.p.

* Continued from page 51

MIDGETS ANALYSIS

IN the article "A Comparative Analysis of Midgets—1929 to 1965," published in last week's issue of Autocar, a substantial part of Peter Poyntz-Wright's story was inadvertently omitted by the printers. We apologize to readers, who must have wondered, for example, what had happened to the famous M.G. TC, of which no mention was made other than in the captions to photographs. The "lost" galley of type follows, and should be read between the first and second paragraphs in column three of page 975, running on from ". . . an increase of 7 to 8 b.h.p. over the PA."

THE superior qualities of the P-Types, especially acceleration, were a first-class return for an increase of only 11 per cent in the retail price over the J2. Purchase tax played no part in these early years, and the P-Type price of £222, giving a current equivalent of £810, for pre-war development years, must be considered extremely reasonable.

The P-Type was the last of the overhead-cam Midgets. It *did* mark the end of an era, and there was the first of what has become a fairly regular howl of protest at any serious and progressive change made at Abingdon.

Nevertheless it was essential to keep the Midget on a parallel with standard bread and butter line. The 10 h.p. Morris-Wolseley push-rod unit was the one selected for the next Midget—the TA. A wet clutch and the innovation of synchromesh gave the sceptics ammunition, but the whole assembly performed extremely well. There was a substantial increase of 353 c.c. over the P-Types to 1,292 c.c., but it is doubtful if the increase in performance could have been achieved with a comparatively slow revving push-rod engine of this type without it.

The TA came out at the same price as the PB in 1936, retailing at £222. In terms of comparative performance it was an improvement over the P-Type. Having a 0-50 time of 15·2 sec it was 12½ per cent quicker than the PA on initial acceleration, and there was a 5 per cent improvement on top speed.

A push-rod engine in a sports car in 1936 was something of a novelty. However, it was certainly the right answer—it produced 50 b.h.p. at the comparatively low engine speed of 4,000 r.p.m., compared with the PB's 43 at a considerably higher engine speed. The extra power called for the substantial improvement in braking that was supplied by fitting hydraulically operated 9in. drums. This was the first time hydraulic brakes had been fitted as standard equipment to a Midget.

The TA was longer and lower-slung than any that had gone before, and heralded the classic lines of the post-war TC. The TA appealed to a slightly wider range of followers than the earlier designs, which were more often used for competition than fast touring.

The amazing thing is that taking comparative values the TA cost £778, which was £32 less than its immediate predecessor, the PB, and it had improved lines, power and brakes. It was only 11 per cent up on the comparative price of the M-Type of seven years earlier, over which it was 29 per cent faster on top speed.

The TA continued until May 1939, by which time some 3,000 had been built. Then followed the TB, using a slightly smaller motor of 1,250 c.c. with a dry clutch and a new gearbox that was acclaimed as being "of a new standard of mechanical perfection." The engine was a slightly faster revving unit than the TA's, and was the first with shell bearings to be fitted to a Midget. It supplied an increase in power of 4·4 b.h.p. In external appearances the TA and TB were almost identical, with a few small details that could be used for identification, but even these were inconsistent. The TB was in fact 4in. wider than the TA, but this was not immediately apparent to the observer. Unfortunately, the TB was destined for a very brief production period, and by the outbreak of war only 380 had been made.

After the war the TB was not continued, but with a few small modifications reappeared as the most famous Midget of all—the TC, a truly remarkable car that caught the imagination of thousands all over the world. It was 10 per cent quicker than the TA in achieving a 0-50 time of 13·9 sec. The springing was hard but for the first time piston-type dampers were used. The sliding trunnions in use since 1932 now gave way to shackles

At the arrival of the TC in 1945, the 1932 £1 was worth only 10s 9d, and the arch enemy of enterprise had darkened our doors—purchase tax had arrived. The manufacturers had done their share by having a prestige sports car, of exceptional performance for 1946, in series-production at a basic cost, in comparative figures, of £845. This would have been exceptional value, and the increase in price of only 9 per cent over the TA, incorporating a six-year production stoppage, is remarkable and can be attributed only to astute businessmen who were devoted enthusiasts. Unfortunately their achievement was denied to the British public who were required to pay £115 (now £234) purchase tax, which raised the comparative price to £1,079. Progress had definitely been achieved. The TC could cover a standing quarter in 21·8 sec, an increase of 34 per cent over the J2, and its 0-60 time of 21·1 is a 216 per cent improvement on the 45 sec of the M-Type.

Between 1946 and 1949 devaluation had caused a drop in value of 1s 8d in the £1 of 1932. The TC, therefore, in its later years was available at current comparative prices of down to £912, which included purchase tax. Production of the TC continued unchanged for four years. It was the last and finest of the spoked-wheel, cart-sprung Midgets, and for the more romantic enthusiast will always retain a certain magic charm, especially for those privileged in having, at sometime, owned one. ∎

MIDGET MK3 1275

IN BASIC form the MG Midget costs £736, which makes it the cheapest manufacturer's sports car on the market, bar its badge brother, the Sprite, at £724. Both are fun to drive and surprisingly civilised, though very noisy to cruise at 70 or over. With the wind-up windows and foldaway hood there's plenty of comfort even in pouring rain. The best way to enjoy a Midget is obviously with the hood down, when you can still reach 90 m.p.h. and appreciate what the pilots of those WW1 biplanes felt! The quick and accurate rack-and-pinion steering, combined with the complete dependability of the handling, make this one of the faster ways of travelling across this traffic-infested island. Acceleration isn't fantastic, with 0-60 in 12.0 secs—but combined with a wide and quite torquey power band there's very little that can actually cover ground more speedily, or more enjoyably.

Mechanically, Spridgets now have a stronger cog box and 1275 c.c. to help fend off Spitfire and S800 competition. As we all should know, this 1275 isn't such a close brother to the 'S' unit as many would wish; still, it puts out 65 horses (six more than the 1098s) and 72 lb. ft. of torque—which is 10 lb. ft. increase over the old model. Compression ratio is 8.8:1—so we used a blend of five and four star fuel on which it was quite content to trundle for just over 30 miles before demanding refreshment; we used no oil at all in over 1,000 miles.

Driving position is still of the hunched-back-and-nose-pressed-against-the-horn-boss variety, hell on earth for a six-footer. The seats offend too, being of a similar design to the MGB's and giving minimal side support—and that's something you need in a hard-driven Spridget.

Considering how little rubber it has on the road (3.5 D rims shod with C41's as standard) the car holds onto the road quite well, but in the wet controlled sliding takes over. Driving a Spridget for a short distance in rain is entertaining, but over a long distance one soon gets fed up with the poor forward vision enforced by the small screen; policemen can hide unobserved behind, too! With the soft top up the engine and rear axle noise become much more obvious, and it takes a hardy passenger to endure a constant 70 m.p.h.—especially when she can't hear her favourite song above 65!

And if you can't hear a Radiomobile, then believe us it's getting noisy in there.

The gearbox is just right, with its short lever and light, prompt action. Now that so many cars have an all-synchromesh box, we did find ourselves cursing the lack of this useful item on first though. Unlike some of our contemporaries, we found that it took some time to get first slot without some 'orrible grindings. Ratios are well spaced, returning 29, 49 and 69 m.p.h. in the first three at 6,000 r.p.m. Third is a really useful cog, taking you past main road traffic in fine style. Once on the move we usually didn't use second unless at a standstill.

We were disappointed to find that the heater is still an optional extra and that even then it doesn't provide enough warmth for winter conditions—ventilation is no problem, unless it's wet, when the interior is liable to steam up. On second thoughts that might well be a plus point with you Casanova types. . . .

Ach so, Spridgets are still good value for money and real fun to conduct. Surely BLMC could alter the seating position and bung in radials, heater and headlamp flasher at this price though?

PERFORMANCE

m.p.h.	secs.
0–30	4.0
0–40	6.1
0–50	8.4
0–60	12.2
0–70	18.1
0–80	26.8

Top speed (best) 98 m.p.h.
Top speed (mean of two ways) 96.1 m.p.h.
Price as tested £784.
Overall m.p.g. 32

Not the same as the Cooper 'S', but definitely a 1275, rocker cover an' all.

NEW SPRITE & MIDGET

M.G Midget Mark III and Austin-Healey Sprite Mark IV feature 1275-c.c. engine and sleeker, quick-fold hood

THE Mark III M.G. Midget and the Mark IV Austin-Healey Sprite are the latest versions of Abingdon's popular small sports cars and certainly the best yet! Although they look substantially the same as before, they embody two big advances—a 1275-c.c. engine based on that used in the highly successful Mini-Cooper 'S' and a true folding hood, quick to raise and lower and far better in appearance.

Power output has gone up to 65 b.h.p. at 6,000 r.p.m. (the earlier 1100-c.c. model produced 59 b.h.p. at 5,750 r.p.m.) and torque is now 72 lb. ft. at 3,000 r.p.m. (previously 65 lb. ft. at 3,500 r.p.m.). With more torque at lower revs. and more power at higher revs., the flexibility of the engine is markedly improved, as well as acceleration and maximum speed. The power unit was developed by way of a number of racing prototypes, including the class-winning Le Mans Sprites and there

The latest 1275-c.c. engine for the Midget and Sprite looks little different from its predecessor, but carries the engine number prefix 12CC. Separate brake and clutch master cylinders are visible here, and there is also a new diaphragm-spring clutch

continued overleaf

Here's the hood stowed, with its neat cover . . .

Peter Browning shows the way . . .

With the cover removed, the hood is flipped out onto the boot lid . . .

In one movement, the hood is raised and the cockpit is under cover (time so far 25 seconds from getting out of the car) . . .

Fix four poppers each side . . .

Back in the car, pull down the over-centre clips and the hood is drum-tight. Total time, just over 1½ minutes, with no practice and with a stiff brand-new hood

is plenty of scope for tuning the production version still further.

Detail mechanical improvements include the introduction of a 6½-in. diaphragm-spring clutch, which is better balanced, smoother in operation, and requires less pedal pressure; and there are now separate clutch and brake master cylinders, replacing the combined unit used previously, and meeting the latest U.S. safety regulations.

The new soft top gives the car a much more rakish line than the earlier model had, partly because the new frame has three bows instead of only two and partly because the hood line starts further rearward, giving more of a slope to the rear window. The window itself is now larger than before and rearward visibility with the hood raised is exceptionally good.

To accommodate the new top the cockpit opening has been cut back further and a new raised rim incorporated. The hood fabric is fixed at the rearward edge of the cockpit, while the frame is pivoted in mountings at either side. When folded, it sits neatly inside the edge of the cockpit and is secured with a close-fitting cover of matching hood material. To raise the hood, the cover is removed and the hood lifted up and forward in one movement, which can be done with one hand from inside the car. As the header rail is brought down and secured to the top of the windscreen with two easy over-centre clips, the fabric is automatically tensioned. All that remains is to secure the rearward sides of the hood with eight pop fasteners.

To lower and stow the hood takes a little longer, because the fabric has to be

folded neatly, but it is much quicker and simpler to stow than the old hood, and, after all, you are not usually in such a hurry to lower the hood as you are to raise it when it starts to rain!

When the hood is stowed normally it does not restrict the available space behind the seats because it folds very

In this diagram, the shaded outline shows the new hood shape, with the 'ghost' of the old hood superimposed

compactly and the cockpit has been enlarged to accommodate it. This has meant that the bulkhead between the cockpit and the luggage compartment has had to be sloped rearward, encroaching a little on the luggage space at the top, but only by a very small amount.

The hood can easily be removed altogether for racing, or to install the new hard top which will be available for this model before long.

Another interesting point is that the sleek new hood is nearly an inch lower than the old one, although the head room inside is unchanged. This is because the three-stick frame fits round the occupants' heads better. It is worth remembering, too, that the current 'MGB'-type seats which were introduced part way through the production life of the previous models are substantially lower in the car and give usefully more head room than the earlier models did. The adjustable back-rests can help in this direction, too.

A new body colour has also been added to the Sprite and Midget range. Basilica Blue is the name and it is a slinky, really deep blue, matched with black interior trim. The Riviera Blue and Primrose Yellow colours have been discontinued.

The sleeker shape of the new folding hood is well shown in this view of the M.G. Midget Mark III (type GAN4)

The U.K. prices of the new models are as follows:

Austin-Healey Sprite Mk. IV: £671 12s. 4d. (including £126 12s. 4d. Purchase Tax).

M.G. Midget Mk. III: £683 18s. 2d. (including £128 18s. 2d. Purchase Tax).

NEW CARS

'Spridgets' with bigger engines

65 b.h.p. for Austin-Healey Sprite and MG Midget

Austin-Healey Sprite Mk. IV

MG Midget Mk III

ALTHOUGH the changes made to the Austin-Healey Sprite and the MG Midget for the coming year are few in number, they are far-reaching in their effects on the character of these models and well merit the new mark numbers that have been given. The Sprite becomes the Mark IV and the Midget the Mark III. Not unexpectedly, there have been price increases. Both models go up by a total, when tax is included, of approximately £48, the new inclusive figures being £672 (basic £545) for the Sprite and £684 (basic £555) for the Midget.

Principal innovation is the fitting of a new engine—or more correctly, a new version of the basic BMC A-type unit. Larger in capacity by 16% compared with the present 1,098 c.c. unit, it gives a 10% step-up in power and an 11% improvement in torque. With virtually no change in weight, the new models should not only be much more potent but should perform with less effort.

The new engine has a bore and stroke of 70.63 mm. and 81.33 mm., giving a capacity of 1,275 c.c. These dimensions are, of course, identical to those of the well-known Mini-Cooper S, but although there is much in common with the S unit, the engine which is being used in the new Midget and Sprite has in fact, been redesigned in various respects, partly to make it more suitable for production in the very substantial numbers involved.

Both the cylinder block and the head have been redesigned for ease of casting without loss of efficiency. Because, however, the "Spridget" version is planned for a car designed to sell at a very popular price, the Nitralloy crankshaft of the Cooper engine is not used but a substantial "2-in." crank employed in its place. Valves, springs, conrods and so on are the same but a lower compression ratio of 8.8:1 is used and the output is 65 b.h.p. net at 6,000 r.p.m. compared with the 76 b.h.p. of the Cooper "S" version. For territories where high octane fuel is un-

obtainable, an 8.0:1 compression edition of the engine is available.

Also new is a diaphragm spring clutch designed to give lighter and smoother operation without loss of bite. As before, it is operated hydraulically but instead of the clutch and brake master cylinders being cast in a single unit, separate master cylinders are now employed. The reason for this is to enable a tandem braking system to be fitted readily if this should be required to comply with American or other overseas regulations.

The excellent close-ratio gearbox with unbeatable synchromesh in the three upper ratios and a very handy remote control is retained. So, too, is the remainder of the mechanical specification.

The big body change is to the hood which is now permanently attached instead of being arranged with detachable hood-irons and covering—all of which can be a nuisance to stow and a minor disaster in a sudden heavy shower. Furling the new hood is simply a matter of releasing it from the screen and unclipping four fasteners on the sides, when it can be folded down into a recess behind the seats. A neat cover can be buttoned in place to conceal it completely in settled weather. Erection is equally easy and weatherproofing is completed by raising the wind-up windows. An incidental added attraction of

the new hood is the fact that it has a more pleasing contour with a less abrupt angle at the rear.

With their added performance and improved weather protection, these new Sprites and Midgets should be more popular than ever in both home and overseas markets. Since the Mark I Sprite was introduced in May 1958, 160,000 Sprites and Midgets have been produced, of which 73½% (116,000) have been exported—mostly to the U.S. and Canada.

During this period, the type has steadily increased in both power and sophistication, although maintaining its basic objective of providing true sports-car motoring at minimum cost.

The original Mark I Sprite had a 948 c.c. engine and ¼-elliptic rear springs. In June 1961 the Mark II version with a much improved body was backed up by the first MG Midget version. Both types were given disc front brakes and 1,098 c.c. engines in October 1962. Then, in March 1964, a further increase in engine power (but not size) was made and winding windows were fitted, these constituting the Mark III Sprite and Mark II Midget which are now superseded and which have proved so popular as to call for the very high production rate (for sports cars) of 350 a week.

M

MG MIDGET/SPRITE

$2442/$2262
West Coast P.O.E.

1275 cc engine 65 BHP. New folding top. Roll up windows. Disc brakes. 30 plus MPG. Cheap to operate and fair resale value. Excellent for first-time buyer. For sake of simplicity, Sprite and Midget will be treated as one, although differing slightly in details. Manufactured by MG Car Co. Ltd., Abingdon-On-Thames, England.

Difference between Sprite and Midget is a matter of wire wheels and chrome strip. Both run on 5.20:13 Dunlop Gold Seals and have 8¼" disc brakes up front and 7" by 1¼" drums on the rear.

The engine in the Sprite Mk 1V for 1967 is the 1275 c.c. block from the Austin Cooper 'S'. It is detuned to 65 HP from the normal 75 HP, mainly for lower production costs: For example, a normal forged crankshaft is used instead of the more expensive nitrided steel crank of the 'S'. It is the latest version of the 'A' type series engine that has been proven over the years as a reliable unit. As with all British cars, the electrics are Lucas and the carburetors are S.U.

The car is quite conventional in every respect and the front suspension is basic independent with coil springs and wishbones. Rear suspension is by semi-elliptic springs. These came in on the 1964 car which helped to reduce roll oversteer inherent in the live axle on quarter-elliptic design units.

The clutch is 6½" dia. diaphragm-spring type and is hydraulically operated. The gearbox, like the MGB, has no synchro on first gear. The lever has a short throw and speed shifting is quite easy. Reverse is difficult to select and requires a sharp snap to the lever to engage. This proves to be difficult for small females on new cars. Once mastered and with the passage of time however, it does loosen up. Rear axle follows standard BMC practice and the final ratio is 4.22:1.

Although the seats are the same as those on the MGB, the Spridget is 6" narrower and has 3" less headroom.

Unquestionably the most popular cars in SCCA racing, 'Spridget' suspension is firm and predictable. This is the easiest and least expensive machine for the new racer.

Despite their rather diminutive dimensions the 'Spridgets' will accept drivers of almost any reasonable size. Instruments are complete but are a bit low for easy reading.

For a small car a surprising amount of luggage can be stowed in Midget or Sprite. Top is well made, weather-proof and still permits good visibility. Finish is good.

This makes the car too cramped for the six-foot-plus driver. He can get in with the top down but with it erected, the sideshow is something. The dash is quite spartan with the bare essentials for enthusiast driving. Tachometer and Speedometer are angled for easier scanning and are framed by the steering wheel. The water/ oil pressure gauge and fuel gauge are the only other instruments in the car and are standard Smith gauges. The switches on the dash are unmarked and reference to the handbook is required to fathom their use.

The heater is inadequate and the air circulation round the driver's feet is poor. The heater control works in reverse, when the knob is in, the heat is on. A twist to the right operates the fan. In the summer, there is a tap on the engine which, when closed, allows only 'cold' air to flow through the system.

The Midget has similar chrome trim to that of the MGB

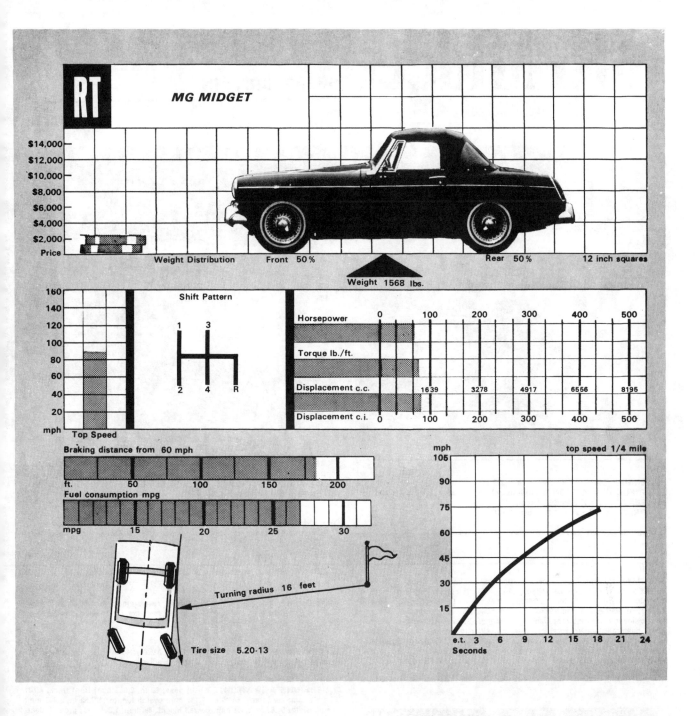

RT

MG MIDGET

Price: $14,000 / $12,000 / $10,000 / $8,000 / $6,000 / $4,000 / $2,000

Weight Distribution Front 50% Rear 50% 12 inch squares

Weight 1568 lbs.

Shift Pattern
1 3
2 4 R

Top Speed (mph): 160 / 140 / 120 / 100 / 80 / 60 / 40 / 20

	0	100	200	300	400	500
Horsepower						
Torque lb./ft.						
Displacement c.c.		1639	3278	4917	6556	8195
Displacement c.i.	0	100	200	300	400	500

Braking distance from 60 mph
ft. 50 100 150 200

Fuel consumption mpg
mpg 15 20 25 30

Turning radius 16 feet

Tire size 5.20-13

mph top speed 1/4 mile
105 / 90 / 75 / 60 / 45 / 30 / 15

e.t. 3 6 9 12 15 18 21 24
Seconds

and the 'family' relationship has been used in the advertising campaigns. The Sprite has exactly the same body shell but is completely devoid of any frills and has disc wheels.

Both cars have the new folding convertible top which is a simple thing to operate over the previous one, which was even more difficult to stow than the present one on the MGB.

Both cars are tightly built and there are few rattles in either.

The original 'bug-eyed' Sprite came along in 1958 and was pretty stark in every way. The current body style was introduced in 1961 when disc brakes were added. In 1964, roll up windows were adopted and the car began to offer more creature comforts than its predecessors.

The current machine is the latest in this line and has proven to be a popular successor. The resale value of these

cars is sound and some of the old bug-eyes are becoming almost as hard to find as TD & TC's. It is unlikely that they will ever be quite the classic models of their ancestors but a good used one will still bring well up in the three figure range. Generally, used Sprites and Midgets will sell at close to book values and this is as good an assurance that the owner can have.

The Spridget is well balanced (50/50) and can be thrown around to a great degree. There is plenty of warning as the rear end begins to slide and part of the fun in owning this car is to be able to use this technique in slaloms. The rack and pinion steering is super sensitive and new owners are easily spotted as they overcorrect on the straight roads. The low c.g. of these cars makes this one of the surest small cars on the road and its overall package from the handling aspect is a good buy for the money.

MG Midget

ENGINE CAPACITY 77.80 cu in, 1,275 cu cm
FUEL CONSUMPTION 31.4 m/imp gal, 26.1 m/US gal, 9 l × 100 km
SEATS 2 MAX SPEED 92 mph, 148 km/h
PRICE IN GB basic £ 555, total £ 684

ENGINE front, 4 stroke; cylinders: 4, vertical, in line; bore and stroke: 2.78 × 3.20 in, 70.6 × 81.3 mm; engine capacity: 77.80 cu in, 1,275 cu cm; compression ratio: 8.8; max power (DIN): 65 hp at 6,000 rpm; max torque (DIN): 65 lb ft, 9 kg m at 3,000 rpm; max engine rpm: 6,000; specific power: 51 hp/l; cylinder block: cast iron; cylinder head: cast iron; crankshaft bearings: 3; valves: 2 per cylinder, overhead, push-rods and rockers; camshafts: 1, side; lubrication: eccentric pump, full flow filter; lubricating system capacity: 7 imp pt, 8.46 US pt, 7 l; carburation: 2 SU type HS 2 semi-downdraught carburettors; fuel feed: electric pump; cooling system: water; cooling system capacity: 10.50 imp pt, 12.68 US pt, 6 l.

TRANSMISSION driving wheels: rear; clutch: single dry plate, hydraulically controlled; gearbox: mechanical; gears: 4 + reverse; synchromesh gears: II, III, IV; gearbox ratios: I 3.200, II 1.916, III 1.357, IV 1, rev 4.114; gear lever: central; final drive: hypoid bevel; axle ratio: 4.220.

CHASSIS integral; front suspension: independent, wishbones, coil springs, lever dampers as upper arms; rear suspension: rigid axle, semi-elliptic leafsprings, lever dampers.

STEERING rack-and-pinion; turns of steering wheel lock to lock: 2.30.

BRAKES front disc (diameter 8 in, 203 mm), rear drum; area rubbed by linings: front 135 sq in, 870.75 sq cm, rear 55 sq in, 354.75 sq cm, total 190 sq in, 1,225.50 sq cm.

ELECTRICAL EQUIPMENT voltage: 12 V; battery: 43 Ah; generator type: dynamo, 22 Ah; ignition distributor: Lucas; headlamps: 2.

DIMENSIONS AND WEIGHT wheel base: 80 in, 2,032 mm; front track: 46.31 in, 1,176 mm; rear track: 44.75 in, 1,137 mm; overall length: 137.62 in, 3,495 mm; overall width: 54.87 in, 1,394 mm; overall height: 49.75 in, 1,264 mm; ground clearance: 5 in, 127 mm; dry weight: 1,510 lb, 685 kg; distribution of weight: 52.4% front axle, 47.6% rear axle; turning circle (between walls): 32 ft, 9.8 m; tyres: 5.20 × 13; fuel tank capacity: 6 imp gal, 7.1 US gal, 27 l.

BODY convertible; doors: 2; seats: 2.

PERFORMANCE max speeds: 29 mph, 46.7 km/h in 1st gear; 49 mph, 78.9 km/h in 2nd gear; 69 mph, 111 km/h in 3rd gear; 92 mph, 148 km/h in 4th gear; power-weight ratio: 23.2 lb/hp, 10.5 kg/hp; carrying capacity: 353 lb, 160 kg; acceleration: standing ¼ mile 20.1 sec, 0 — 50 mph (0 — 80 km/h) 9.9 sec; speed in direct drive at 1,000 rpm: 15.5 mph, 25 km/h.

PRACTICAL INSTRUCTIONS fuel: 98 oct petrol; engine sump oil: 6.40 imp pt, 7.61 US pt, 3.6 l, SAE 20W-30 (winter) 20W-40 (summer), change every 6,000 miles, 9,700 km; gearbox oil: 2.25 imp pt, 2.75 US pt, 1.3 l, SAE 10W-30 (winter) 20W-40 (summer), change every 6,000 miles, 9,700 km; final drive oil: 1.50 imp pt, 1.69 US pt, 0.8 l, SAE 90; greasing: every 3,000 miles, 4,800 km, 10 points; tappet clearances: inlet 0.012 in, 0.30 mm, exhaust 0.012 in, 0.30 mm; normal tyre pressure: front 18 psi, 1.3 atm, rear 20 psi, 1.4 atm.

VARIATIONS AND OPTIONAL ACCESSORIES oil cooler; wire wheels and knock-on hubs; anti-roll bar on front suspension; hardtop.

M.G. Midget III 1,275 c.c.

AT A GLANCE: Latest version of popular small M.G.—Austin-Healey range. Slightly better acceleration and mid-range torque than previous model. Robust engine and transmission, with full range of B.M.C. tuning equipment available. Excellent gearchange but no synchromesh on bottom gear. M.p.g. little affected by more powerful engine. Sports car ride and handling in best M.G. traditions. Faultless brakes. New hood a great improvement, but cramped seating not changed. Inadequate heater control.

MANUFACTURER
The M.G. Car Co. Ltd., Abingdon-on-Thames, Berkshire.

PRICES

Basic	..	..	£555	0s	0d
Purchase Tax	..		£128	18s	2d
Total (in G.B.)	..		£683	18s	2d

EXTRAS (inc. P.T.)

Wire wheels (factory fitted)	..	..	£30	14s	7d
Heater	..	..	£14	15s	0d

PERFORMANCE SUMMARY

Mean maximum speed	93·5 m.p.h.
Standing start ¼-mile	19·7 sec
0-60 m.p.h.	14·6 sec
30-70 m.p.h. (through gears)	16·1 sec
Fuel consumption	30 m.p.g.
Miles per tankful	180

EIGHT-AND-A-HALF years of consistent development by the B.M.C. sports car factory at Abingdon have improved the Sprite-Midget range in nearly every respect. Few Mark I Sprite owners would argue that their version is still the best, and they would be hard put to recognize many parts of the latest car. Our test car on this occasion was the M.G. Midget Series III which, apart from the badges and some trim details, is identical with the Series IV Austin-Healey Sprite. In fact the first M.G. Midget appeared as a more luxurious version of the new Series II Sprite in June 1961, and the latest 1,275 c.c. engined car is really the fourth distinct development.

The original Midget had the 948 c.c. engine, a much simpler facia design, styling almost identical with the latest car, sliding windows and a " build-it-yourself " hood. Later this model was given the new 1,098 c.c. engine and disc brakes became standard. In March 1964 the Mk. II model appeared, fitted for the first time with wind-up windows and half-elliptic rear springs, plus revised interior trim. Finally the latest Mark III version was released just in time for the last Earls Court show. Production cars are only now appearing

on British roads, as there have been some delays in building up output and the vast majority of Midgets are destined for valuable export markets.

Though the latest car has a 1,275 c.c. engine, superficially the same as that of the famous 1275S Mini-Cooper, it has been detuned somewhat to keep down the cost. In place of the Cooper S's nitrided-steel crankshaft there is a normal forged one, and the Mark II Midget camshaft timing replaces that of the S. Compression ratio is down a little, valves and ports a little restricted, and both inlet and exhaust manifolds are the same as on previous Midgets. There has been no change to gearbox or rear axle, though a diaphragm spring clutch is now fitted. Claimed power output is 65 b.h.p. at 6,000 r.p.m. instead of the 59 b.h.p. at 5,750 r.p.m. of the previous model.

Because the new car has 6 b.h.p. more than the 1,100 c.c. which it replaces, and because there has been a negligible weight increase with no change to the gearing, we were expecting to find significant performance gains. Mysteriously, the 1,275 c.c. car was only just as lively as the 1,100 we last sampled in April 1964. This car, in its turn, was *much* livelier than a previous 1,100 test car with 3 b.h.p. less (56 b.h.p.). We can

Autocar Road Test number 2118

Make: M.G.

Type: MIDGET III 1,275 c.c.

TEST CONDITIONS
Weather: Frosty and clear. Wind 5-10 m.p.h.
Temperature: 2 deg. C. (36 deg. F.)
Barometer: 29·6 in. Hg.
Surfaces: Dry concrete and asphalt

WEIGHT
Kerb weight: 14·2cwt (1,589lb-721kg) (with oil, water and half-full fuel tank)
Distribution, per cent F, 52; R, 48.
Laden as tested: 17·9cwt (2,011lb-912kg)

Figures taken at 5,400 miles by our own staff at the Motor Industry Research Association proving ground at Nuneaton.

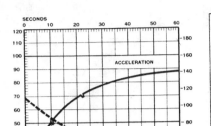

MAXIMUM SPEEDS

Gear	m.p.h.	k.p.h.	r.p.m.
Top (mean)	93·5	150	6,070
(best)	95	153	6,170
3rd	71	114	6,300
2nd	50	81	6,300
1st	30	48	6,300

Standing ¼-Mile 19·7 sec 68 m.p.h.
Standing Kilometre 37·4 sec 82 m.p.h.

FUEL CONSUMPTION

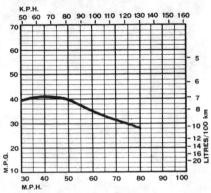

TIME IN SECONDS	4·6	7·0	9·9	14·6	20·7	33·2	
TRUE SPEED M.P.H.	30	40	50	60	70	80	90
INDICATED SPEED	31	42	52	62	72	83	93

Mileage recorder 1 per cent over-reading.

Test distance 1,179 miles.

(At constant speeds—m.p.g.)

30 m.p.h.	40·0
40	41·2
50	40·0
60	35·4
70	31·7
80	28·5

Typical m.p.g. 30 (9·4 litres/100 km)
Calculated (DIN) m.p.g. 28·8 (9·8 litres/100km)

Overall m.p.g. 28·4 (9·95 litres/100km)

Grade of fuel, Premium (96·8-98·8 RM)

OIL CONSUMPTION
Miles per pint (SAE 10W/30) 800

Speed range, gear ratios and time in seconds

m.p.h.	Top (4·22)	3rd (5·73)	2nd (8·09)	1st (13·50)
10—30	—	7·7	4·7	3·3
20—40	10·6	7·5	4·4	—
30—50	9·8	6·5	5·4	—
40—60	10·0	8·0	—	—
50—70	12·4	10·2	—	—
60—80	17·1	—	—	—

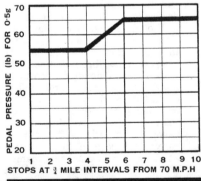

BRAKES (from 30 m.p.h. in neutral)

Load	g	Distance
25 lb	0·19	158ft
50 ,,	0·44	68 ,,
75 ,,	0·70	43 ,,
100 ,,	1·00	30·1 ,,

Handbrake 0·42 72 ,,
Max. Gradient, 1 in 3
Clutch Pedal: 35 lb and 4in.

TURNING CIRCLES
Between kerbs L, 32ft 0in.; R, 31ft 3in.
Between walls L, 33ft 3in.; R, 32ft 6in.
Steering wheel turns, lock to lock, 2·3.

HOW THE CAR COMPARES:
MAXIMUM SPEED (mean) M.P.H.

60	70	80	90	100
M.G. Midget III
B.M.C. 1275S Mini-Cooper
Fiat 850 Coupe
Sunbeam Imp Sport
Triumph Spitfire II

0-60 M.P.H. (secs)

30	20	10
M.G. Midget III
B.M.C. 1275S Mini-Cooper
Fiat 850 Coupe
Sunbeam Imp Sport
Triumph Spitfire II

STANDING START ¼ MILE (secs)

30	20	10
M.G. Midget III
B.M.C. 1275S Mini-Cooper
Fiat 850 Coupe
Sunbeam Imp Sport
Triumph Spitfire II

M.P.G. OVERALL

20	30	40
M.G. Midget III
B.M.C. 1275S Mini-Cooper
Fiat 850 Coupe
Sunbeam Imp Sport
Triumph Spitfire II

PRICES

M.G. Midget III	£684
Mini-Cooper 1275S	£849
Fiat 850 Coupé	£865
Sunbeam Imp Sport	£665
Triumph Spitfire II	£678

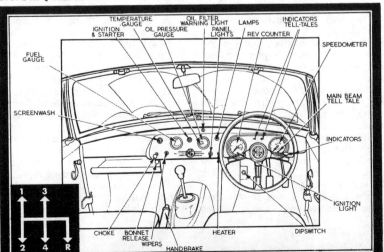

The M.G. Midget's Mk I Sprite ancestry is still evident below waist level. The chromium strip which permanently attaches the back of the hood to the body is the only outward feature identifying the Mk III from its predecessor

M.G. MIDGET III

only assume now that the 1964 test car was perhaps in better-than-average form at the time, while the subject of this test is a thoroughly representative 1,275 c.c. Midget. Comparison of its performance with other sports cars having similar power-weight ratios confirms this, and two owners of late model 1,100s reckoned that there were, indeed, substantial gains with the new car.

With its bigger, though less highly tuned engine, the new Midget is more docile than before, needing little cosseting to develop its full performance on the open road. The torque delivery is smooth throughout the range, and no Midget owner should be frightened away from town traffic jams by thoughts of temperament. In top gear the little car can be trundled along at a mere 800 r.p.m. (12 m.p.h.) and can be acceler-

ated smoothly, without snatch or hesitation from 10 m.p.h. if necessary. Acceleration figures for this range were not taken, as the practice is not likely to be used on such a sporting car.

By the time 2,000 r.p.m. is reached, everything is beginning to swing together, though most owners will be stirring the gear lever about to make sure the needle is always above 4,000 r.p.m. It is all too easy to over-rev, unless a careful watch is kept on the rev-counter, and there is little doubt that well over 6,500 r.p.m. could be seen in the indirect gears. In deference to the danger markings on the rev-counter we changed gear at 6,300 r.p.m. when conducting performance tests; the engine was then well on to the meat of the power curve at the same road speed in the next gear. The fastest standing starts were achieved by using 4,500 r.p.m. and controlled clutch slip off the line.

Full choke is needed for rapid cold-starts, though the engine warms up

quickly, and the choke knob can be pushed home after the first half mile or so. When thoroughly warm, helped by the perfectly balanced S.U. carburettors on this test car, the idling speed is a gentle 700 r.p.m.

At higher speeds, however, mechanical noise increased quite considerably. At 70 m.p.h. the engine is turning at 4,550 r.p.m. and this, together with the usual wind noise around the hood, made normal conversation difficult. Reception from the optional Radiomobile was excellent, but difficult to enjoy because of the high noise level. There appears to be no sound-deadening material between the engine bay and the cockpit. Despite the low overall gearing, and the spirited way in which we usually drove the car, its oil pressure never fluctuated; most of the time this stabilized at between 70 and 80 p.s.i. If anything, the car is a little over-cooled, for we never managed to get the water temperature above about 162 deg. F. (72 deg. C.), which is just about the thermostat-opening point.

▶

The very functional cockpit has its tachometer and speedometer angled towards the driver's line of vision. The driver can erect the hood without getting out of the car

Left: Accessibility to the oil filter, distributor and battery is not easy. The handwheel in front of the heater assembly controls the heater temperature. Right: Boot space is limited by the spare wheel and hood cover. The stay is held by the clip at the corner of the boot lid

M.G. MIDGET III

One of the delights of every Austin-Healey Sprite and M.G. Midget has been the splendid gearbox and gearchange. With the gear lever knob only inches from the steering wheel rim, it really does "fall readily to hand"; gearchange movements are short, ultra-light and just as fast as required. Though the baulk-ring synchromesh is efficient on top, 3rd and 2nd, the Midget is one of the few British cars which has an unsynchronized bottom gear. At low speeds in traffic the driver often feels the need to thrust down into bottom gear for a speedy take-off, but we found more than usually accurate double-declutching was needed to make a silent change. All the indirect gears, particularly bottom (with straight-cut teeth) are noisy, and somewhat harsh.

Perhaps, too, the ratios are a little widely spaced, yet somehow the Midget's change typifies everything that is enjoyable in sports car driving, and an owner will find himself "stirring up the cogs" just for the fun of it. The latest clutch is a diaphragm spring type. Though smaller than before, its operation was smooth, and no amount of abuse caused any judder or slipping.

No red-blooded young owner (or *Autocar* tester, for that matter) would think of driving such a lively little sports car slowly, and the overall fuel consumption must have suffered a little because of the use we gave it. During 1,200 miles of exuberant motoring we averaged 28·4 m.p.g.; this compares very well with 29·7 m.p.g. for the 1964 1,100, and 29·1 for an earlier (1963) 1,100 Sprite. Steady speed fuel consumption measurements above 50 m.p.h. were very similar to the earlier model, but at lower (traffic) speeds, the new car was much thirstier. As compression ratio is only 8·8 to 1, normal premium fuel is perfectly adequate.

As with all previous Sprites and Midgets, the 6-gallon fuel tank is really much too small. On our test car a gauge fault meant that barely 110 miles (and about 4 gallons) were completed before the unsteady needle began to indicate "Empty." A normal fuel range, without taking risks, would be 150 miles; though barely adequate by day, a long night journey might present problems when filling stations are few and far between.

Big improvements were made to the Midget's rear suspension when the Mark II was introduced in 1964; the original cantilever quarter-elliptics were replaced by conventional half-elliptic leaf springs. Since then there have been no important changes, and the Mark III Midget handles just like the previous model. Following the very best M.G. roadholding traditions, the ride is firm, perhaps even a little choppy on minor roads, while the steering is light, positive and direct. Urging the little car down simulated "rally roads" seemed to need only tiny wrist movements on the wheel, and the Midget must be one of very few cars which seems to go exactly where it is pointed. With very little understeer to make rapid direction changes untidy, the little car's handling is delicately balanced and enjoyable. When pressed really hard, the tail begins to break away apologetically; this can be curbed by the merest flick of opposite lock, almost without thinking. In fact, the Midget must be one of the safest cars on the road when in the right hands. Roll is strictly limited at all times, and damping firm.

Predictably, the little car does not enjoy being forced down rough roads, which can provoke some occasional axle tramp. The structure felt impressively rigid at all times.

Fade-free braking and a predictable pedal response is now expected from modern disc-drum systems; the Lockheed layout fitted to this Midget was no exception. In normally hard road use, there was no increase in pedal travel, and even the rigorous fade tests carried out at MIRA did not show up any limitations. The hand-brake (surprisingly not with a fly-off release) was efficient, allowing 42 per cent braking when used alone, and holding the car easily on a 1-in-3 test gradient.

The latest Midget's driving position is disappointing and somewhat cramped. Late model Mark II Midgets were given revised seats, similar to those of the MGB, which are retained on the new model. Their back rests are thicker than before, with less bucket shaping, though they hold passengers in place quite well against high cornering forces. Unfortunately the thicker back rests have restricted the small living space still more, and drivers taller than 5ft 8in. found it difficult to get comfortable. Rearward seat adjustment is limited by a structural bulkhead behind the slides, while the steering wheel and facia panel are uncompromisingly near to the driver's shoulders. The now customary straight-arm driving position is quite impossible in the Midget, and long-legged drivers found their legs wrapped unhappily around the steering column. Heel-and-toe gear changing is possible without effort, but there is no real resting place for an unoccupied clutch foot.

To be really in fashion, modern sports car must have a foldaway hood; that fitted to the new Midget is much better than the previous type and certainly the most worthwhile improvement in the new car. Two stout overcentre catches and a couple of press studs attach the hood to the screen rail. Furling the hood to its stowed position can be done in one sweep from inside the car. The press-studs near to the door hinges should be released, or the hood fabric might be torn in folding down. When erect, windproofing is excellent, and during our fortnight's test there were no water leaks. Though the new hood has a lower profile than before, there seemed to be ample headroom for tall passengers. When furled, part of the useful stowage space behind the seats is obstructed; there is a neat hood cover.

The Midget's heater is still a £15

extra though it woud be difficult to order a car for home delivery without one. Its control and adjustment is crude and unsatisfactory for many conditions. A water tap under the bonnet controls supply of warm water to the matrix, while the only air or temperature control in the car is by opening or closing flaps in the foot-wells. A switch on the facia operates the booster fan. There are no fresh air vents.

For such a small car the luggage boot seems quite large, though the floor is practically filled by the spare wheel, jack and tools, and the surfaces are unlined. The boot lid, like the bonnet, has to be propped open by a stay. On our test car the boot-lid stay was already damaging paintwork near its clip.

The small-sized popular-price sports car market is expanding all the time, and buyers continue to demand improvements in performance and specification. By regular power increases and trim changes B.M.C. have kept abreast of the trends; undoubtedly the M.G. Midget will be with us for some time yet. ∎

SPECIFICATION: M.G. MIDGET III (FRONT ENGINE, REAR-WHEEL DRIVE)

ENGINE

Cylinders	4, in line
Cooling system	Water; pump, fan and thermostat
Bore	70·6mm (2·78in.)
Stroke	81·3mm (3·2in.)
Displacement	1,275 c.c. (78 cu. in.)
Valve gear	Overhead, push rods and rockers
Compression ratio	8·8-to-1
Carburettors	2 S.U. H.S.2
Fuel pump	S.U. Electric
Oil filter	Full flow with renewable element
Max. power	65 b.h.p. (net) at 6,000 r.p.m.
Max. torque	72 lb. ft. (net) at 3,000 r.p.m.

TRANSMISSION

Clutch	Borg and Beck diaphragm spring 6·5in. dia.
Gearbox	4-speed, synchromesh on Top, 3rd and 2nd
Gear ratios	Top 1·00; Third 1·36; Second 1·92; First 3·20; Reverse 4·11
Final drive	Hypoid bevel, 4·22 to 1

CHASSIS and BODY

Construction	Integral, with steel body, fold away hood

SUSPENSION

Front	Independent, coil springs, wishbones, lever-arm dampers
Rear	Live axle, half-elliptic leaf springs, lever-arm dampers

STEERING

Type	Cam Gears, rack and pinion
Wheel dia.	15·5in.

BRAKES

Make and type	Lockheed disc front, drum rear
Servo	None
Dimensions	F, 8·25in. dia. R, 7.0in. dia. 1·25in. wide shoes
Swept area	F, 135 sq. in.; R, 55 sq. in. Total 190 sq. in. (237 sq.in.) per ton laden)

WHEELS

Type	Wire-spoked centre lock (optional extra). 3·5in. wide rim
Tyres—make	Dunlop
—type	C41 Nylon tubed cross-ply
—size	5·20—13in.

EQUIPMENT

Battery	12-volt 43-amp. hr.
Generator	22 amp. d.c.
Headlamps	Lucas sealed beam 45/40-watt
Reversing lamp	None
Electric fuses	2
Screen wipers	Single speed, self parking
Screen washer	Standard, manual plunger
Interior heater	Extra, fresh air type
Safety belts	Extra, anchorages built in
Interior trim	Leather seats, PVC hood

Floor covering	Carpet
Starting handle	No provision
Jack	Screw pillar
Jacking points	One each side, under door
Windscreen	Zone toughened
Underbody protection	Cellulose paint only
Other bodies	Hardtop

MAINTENANCE

Fuel tank	6 Imp. gallons (no reserve) (27 litres)
Cooling system	10·5 pints (including heater) (6 litres)
Engine sump	6·5 pints (3·7 litres) SAE 10W/30. Change oil and element every 6,000 miles
Gearbox	2·2 pints SAE 30. No change necessary after first 500 miles
Final drive	1·5 pints SAE 90. No change necessary after first 500 miles
Grease	10 points every 3,000 miles
Tyre pressures	F, 18; R, 20 p.s.i. (normal driving). F, 22; R, 24 p.s.i. (fast driving).

PERFORMANCE DATA

Top gear m.p.h. per 1,000 r.p.m.	15·4
Mean piston speed at max. power	3,200ft./min.
B.h.p. per ton laden	81·1

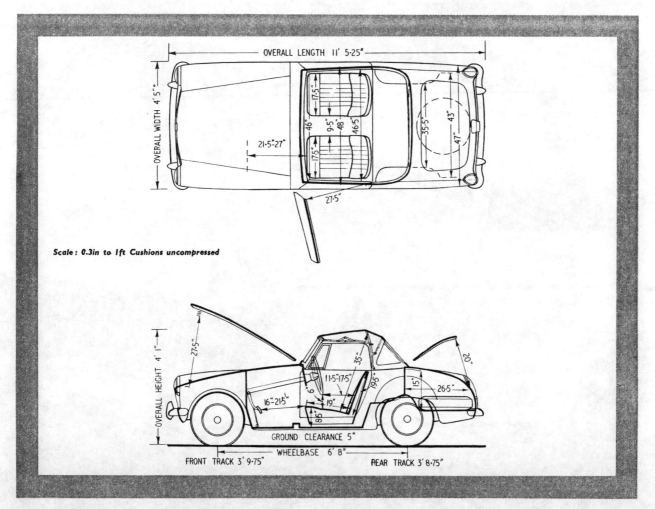

Scale: 0.3in to 1ft Cushions uncompressed

OVERALL LENGTH 11' 5·25"
OVERALL WIDTH 4' 5"
OVERALL HEIGHT 4' 1"
GROUND CLEARANCE 5"
WHEELBASE 6' 8"
FRONT TRACK 3' 9·75"   REAR TRACK 3' 8·75"

Road Test: MG Midget Mk.III
SAFETY FASTER, ALREADY

Two major changes denote the Mk. III Sprite and MG Midget: a 1275-cc engine and a fold-down top. The engine enhances the performance and the top completes the general convenience and weatherproofing that make it a more modern sports car. After that what do you say? Well, you look at the car and then the base price of $2095 for the Sprite and $2250 for the Midget (wire wheels and trim make the difference). Then you have to conclude that both are outstanding buys on the low end of the sports-car price scale.

The ride and handling remain pretty much unchanged; a bit choppy on the ride and relatively good in the corners. The power plant, developing 65 horsepower at 6000 rpm, features a nitrided crankshaft. It gets the little machine through the standing quarter-mile in 19.4 seconds and from 0-60 mph in 12.7 seconds. It may do even better with more break-in time than our test car had. Gas mileage averages about 28 miles per gallon for normal commuting and around-town running, quite a bit higher on the highway. Top speed is close to 90 mph, depending on which direction the wind is blowing.

Still unchanged, but a relatively minor annoyance is the non-synchro First in the quick-shifting four-speed gearbox. The brakes, with 8¼-inch discs front and seven-inch drums in the rear, are excellent. Body dimensions are the same; entry and exit are cramped but, once you're seated, there's ample room.

With more performance and the absence of the do-it-yourself convertible top, the car is an even more attractive buy for someone who wants a solid, fun-type tiddler that'll take them most anywhere for the lowest in both purchase *and* operating costs. We happened to have four different cars at home during the Midget's test period. Somehow, it was always the one we hopped in to go someplace. It got the job done the quickest and easiest.

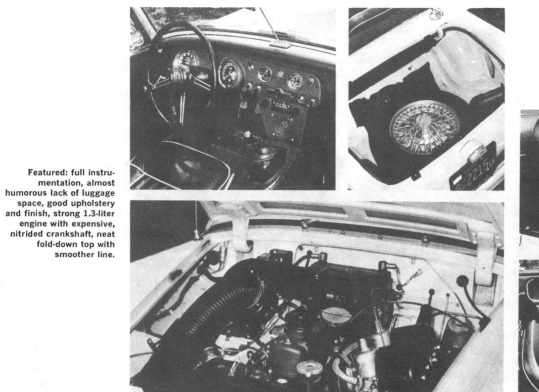

Featured: full instrumentation, almost humorous lack of luggage space, good upholstery and finish, strong 1.3-liter engine with expensive, nitrided crankshaft, neat fold-down top with smoother line.

GORDON CHITTENDEN PHOTOS

MG MIDGET III
TRIUMPH SPITFIRE Mk 3

Basic sports cars that continue a proud tradition

THE MG MIDGET and the Triumph Spitfire are basic sports cars, the type most likely to mark the driver's first ownership of the breed. As such, they meet certain classic requirements and have a set of special traits that set them apart from their more sophisticated (and expensive) brethren.

One of the more subtle requirements of a proper sports car is that it have a proud name earned in road racing competition. Most manufacturers have learned the value of building a proper reputation of this type and those that don't almost inevitably end up wondering why their products never achieve the same degree of acceptance and respect. There's no question about the pedigree of the Midget and Spitfire in this field and the driver never has to suffer that vague unease that results from not being sure whether his car is or isn't a true sports car.

They also meet the most important all-round requirement for a sports car—responsiveness. If a sports car is anything, it is responsive—with steering that is quick and accurate, clutch action that is crisp, a gearbox with positive feel, brakes that can be used hard and often. All-out brute performance is far less important than the feeling that you are in complete control and directing the machine rather than holding on and trying not to do anything foolish.

There are still more characteristics. In a basic sports car there should be an awareness of things mechanical going on under hand, foot and seat. A bit of row under the hood when the accelerator is depressed, for instance; a businesslike exhaust note; even a little gear whine isn't unacceptable. There should also be instruments. Before their first sports car, most drivers have never had the pleasure of knowing a full set of instruments at work, felt the satisfaction of just kissing the

Open seam behind Midget wheel remains from days when whole front end lifted. Functional lid now starts at grille.

Raised front bumper on Spitfire will take getting used to. Entire front end swings open for ultimate in availability.

redline with the tach needle, or the doubt and dread that come with the rise of the water temperature and the accompanying descent of the oil pressure. Warning lights, in comparison, are as sterile as a dead battery.

Perhaps not strictly necessary but nonetheless acceptable in the basic sports car are certain minimum standards of habitability. They don't have to offer armchair comfort for the occupants or boxcar volumes of luggage space. And even something out of date, like a non-synchromesh first gear, can be tolerated simply because it makes the driver a part of a great tradition. It's appalling to think there are millions of drivers who've never known the satisfaction of a perfectly executed double-clutched downshift into a non-synchro first gear.

It isn't easy to think of two cars that fulfill all the requirements for the basic sports car any better than the MG Midget and the Triumph Spitfire.

THIS ROAD TEST is of the latest version of each of these models, the Midget Mk III and the Spitfire 3. (The Roman and Arabic designations are those of the manufacturers, by the way.) The major change for both cars is that each now has a 1.3-liter engine. As you are no doubt aware, the MG Midget differs from the Austin Healey Sprite only in name and trim. The original Sprite came along in 1958, a stark 1-liter sports car with frog-eye headlights on the hood. The current body style was introduced in 1961 along with a 1098-cc engine and disc brakes at the front. The Midget nameplate

made its debut at the same time so that the second-series Sprite was the original-series Midget and the Midget has been one number behind ever since. In 1964, the Midget II adopted roll-up windows and semi-elliptic rear springs to reduce the tricky roll oversteer inherent in the live-axle-on-quarter-elliptics design.

The new Midget III's 1275-cc engine is similar to that used in the Mini Cooper S but is detuned from 75 bhp to 65 which allows lower production costs (a normal forged crankshaft can be used, for example, instead of the more expensive nitrided steel crank of the S) and yet continue the Midget's reputation for reliability and long life. There is a net increase of 6 bhp over the Mk II's 59, though, so the performance is somewhat better.

The other major change in the Midget III is the new top. This is now a proper convertible top that goes up and down easily and accurately and is a great improvement over the roadster-style build-it-yourself top.

The Triumph Spitfire has a somewhat shorter history than its opposite number from BMC. It was introduced in 1962, underwent minor revisions and a power increase (from 63 to 67 bhp) in 1964 and is now offered in $3000 fastback form as the 95-bhp, 2-liter GT6 as well as the basic roadster with the 75-bhp, 1296-cc 4-cyl engine. It is somewhat more modern than the Midget in one respect as it has independent suspension at both ends while the Midget has a live rear axle.

The 1296-cc engine of the 3 is based on the 1300 Triumph instead of the 1147-cc unit used before. This engine has in-

MG MIDGET III
ROAD TEST RESULTS

PRICE
List price................$2255
Price as Tested............2434

ENGINE & DRIVE TRAIN
Engine, no. cyl, type..inline 4, ohv
Bore x stroke, mm....70.6 x 81.3
Displacement, cc/cu in..1275/77.5
Compression ratio.........8.8:1
Bhp @ rpm...........65 @ 6000
  Equivalent mph...........90
Torque @ rpm, lb-ft...72 @ 3000
  Equivalent mph...........46
Transmission type...4-spd manual
Gear ratios, 4th (1.00).....4.22:1
  3rd (1.36)...........5.73:1
  2nd (1.92)...........8.09:1
  1st (3.20)...........13.5:1
Synchromesh...........on top 3
Final drive ratio..........4.22:1

GENERAL
Curb weight...............1560
Weight distribution (with
  driver), front/rear, %....50/50
Wheelbase, in..............80.0
Track, front/rear......46.3/44.8
Overall length............137.4
  Width.................56.5
  Height................48.6
Frontal area, sq ft.........15.3
Steering type.......rack & pinion
  Turns, lock-to-lock........2.3
Brake type, f/r........disc/drum
Swept area, sq in...........190

ACCOMMODATION
Seating capacity, persons......2
Seat width..............2 x 17.5
Head room................39.0
Seat back adjustment, degrees..0
Driver comfort rating (scale of 100):
  For driver 69 in. tall........70
  For driver 72 in. tall........60
  For driver 75 in. tall........45

PERFORMANCE
Top speed, high gear, mph.....93
Acceleration, time to distance, sec:
  0–100 ft.................4.0
  0–250 ft.................6.7
  0–500 ft................10.5
  0–750 ft................13.8
  0–1000 ft...............16.5
  0–1320 ft (¼ mi).........19.9
  Speed at end, mph........69
Time to speed, sec:
  0–30 mph.................4.3
  0–40 mph.................6.7
  0–50 mph................10.2
  0–60 mph................14.7
  0–80 mph................31.0

BRAKE TESTS
Panic stop from 80 mph:
  Deceleration rate, % g.....81%
  Control.................good
Fade test: percent of increase in
  pedal effort required to maintain
  50%-g deceleration rate in six
  stops from 60 mph.......60%
Overall brake rating........good

SPEEDOMETER ERROR
30 mph indicated.....actual 29.2
40 mph.....................38.8
60 mph.....................58.0

CALCULATED DATA
Lb/hp (test weight).........29.4
Cu ft/ton mi..............87.2
Mph/1000 rpm (high gear)...15.4
Engine revs/mi............3900
Piston travel, ft/mi........2080
Rpm @ 2500 ft/min........4690
  Equivalent mph...........71
R&T wear index............81
Brake swept area, sq in/ton...200

FUEL
Type fuel required.......premium
Fuel tank size, gal..........7.5
Normal consumption, mpg...23–25

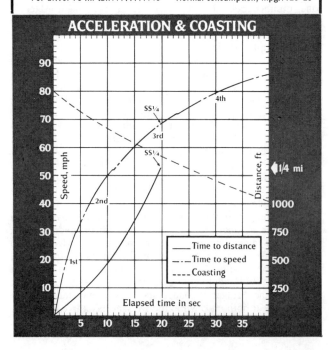

ACCELERATION & COASTING

Speed, mph / Distance, ft

SS¼   4th   3rd   SS¼   2nd   1st   ¼ mi

— Time to distance
-·- Time to speed
--- Coasting

Elapsed time in sec

Midget interior is small and snug; neat top is great improvement over earlier version; engine now has 1275 cc and 65 bhp.

dividual inlet ports instead of siamesed, the combustion chamber shape is improved and there is a cast iron manifold in place of the fabricated headers used on the Spitfire 2. Other mechanical changes include slightly larger brake calipers which should contribute to longer pad life and a new lift-over-and-clamp top that is superior to the old one in every way.

There are also changes in appearance that distinguish the 3 from earlier versions. The front bumpers have been raised to a more practical height, back-up lights are standard and the sharp-eyed will note that the exhaust pipe is slightly larger in diameter and now terminates at the right rear instead of the rear center. In the cockpit there is a smaller steering wheel, which gives the driver a bit more leg room, and there is a nice polished-wood setting for the instruments.

In size, the Spitfire is bigger than the Midget, longer in wheelbase and overall length (83.0 and 147.0 vs. 80.0 and 137.3) and heavier in curb weight (1680 vs. 1560 lb). In straight-line performance, the Spitfire is the quicker of the two, getting through the standing quarter in 19.3 to the Midget's 19.9 sec and having an edge in top speed of 100 to 93.

Both cars handle very well. The Midget is well balanced with a 50/50 weight distribution (compared to 54/46 front/rear for the Spitfire) and there is still a dependable bit of roll oversteer built into the rear suspension that makes it great fun to drive a little bit sideways. Predictably, the different rear suspension systems of the two cars makes for somewhat different handling. The overall effect is that the Spitfire rides and handles better over uneven road surfaces, as it should with independent rear suspension, has less initial oversteer with comparable steering effort but transfers to final oversteer more abruptly—again as you would expect with swing axles.

From the driver's point of view, the Midget seems to be better assembled, to have fewer rattles and to be more of a piece. The engine is smoother than the Spitfire's and the controls all seem to be happier with each other. For example, the Spitfire's throttle linkage has an "over-center" feel which requires a delicate touch to make small changes in throttle opening while the Midget's throttle action blends in unobtrusively well with the operation of the other controls. The Spitfire also has a slightly skewed shift pattern that takes

Spitfire has new wood-finished instrument panel; engine is uncommonly accessible; interior is roomier than Midget.

TRIUMPH SPITFIRE Mk 3
ROAD TEST RESULTS

PRICE
List price.................$2373
Price as tested...........$2672

ENGINE & DRIVE TRAIN
Engine, no. cyl, type..inline 4, ohv
Bore x stroke, mm.....73.7 x 76.0
Displacement, cc/cu in..1296/79.2
Compression ratio..........9.0:1
Bhp @ rpm............75 @ 6000
  Equivalent mph............101
Torque @ rpm, lb-ft...75 @ 4000
  Equivalent mph.............64
Transmission type...4-spd manual
Gear ratios, 4th (1.00)......4.11:1
  3rd (1.39)..............5.73:1
  2nd (2.16)..............8.87:1
  1st (3.75).............15.4:1
Synchromesh............on top 3
Final drive ratio..........4.11:1

GENERAL
Curb weight, lb.............1680
Weight distribution (with
  driver), front/rear, %....54/46
Wheelbase, in..............83.0
Track, front/rear.......49.0/48.0
Overall length.............147.0
  Width...................57.0
  Height..................47.5
Frontal area, sq ft..........15.1
Steering type.......rack & pinion
Turns, lock-to-lock.........3.8
Brake type, f/r........disc/drum
  Swept area, sq in.........205

ACCOMMODATION
Seating capacity, persons........2
Seat width..............2 x 19
Head room.................39.0
Seat back adjustment, degrees...0
Driver comfort rating (scale of 100):
  For driver 69 in. tall........85
  For driver 72 in. tall........75
  For driver 75 in. tall........70

PERFORMANCE
Top speed, high gear, mph....100
Acceleration, time to distance, sec:
  0–100 ft....................3.8
  0–250 ft....................6.6
  0–500 ft...................10.3
  0–750 ft...................13.4
  0–1000 ft..................16.1
  0–1320 ft (¼ mi).........19.3
  Speed at end, mph..........70
Time to speed, sec:
  0–30 mph...................4.1
  0–40 mph...................6.1
  0–50 mph...................9.3
  0–60 mph..................13.6
  0–80 mph..................28.0

BRAKE TESTS
Panic stop from 80 mph:
  Deceleration rate, % g.......74
  Control..................good
Fade test: percent of increase in
  pedal effort required to maintain
  50%-g deceleration rate in six
  stops from 60 mph.......15%
Overall brake rating.....very good

SPEEDOMETER ERROR
30 mph indicated......actual 27.3
40 mph......................37.5
60 mph......................57.5

CALCULATED DATA
Lb/hp (test weight).........27.0
Cu ft/ton mi................85.1
Mph/1000 rpm (high gear)....15.9
Engine revs/mi............3760
Piston travel, ft/mi........1880
Rpm @ 2500 ft/min........5000
  Equivalent mph.............82
R&T wear index..........70.8
Brake swept area, sq in/ton...202

FUEL
Type fuel required.......premium
Fuel tank size, gal...........9.9
Normal consumption, mpg..22–24

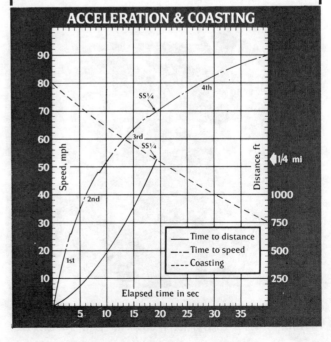

some getting used to while the Midget's shift lever is right where it should be and works just the way it should. The Midget is also quieter in everything except first gear and the engine seems willing to wing along at any reasonable speed without complaint. We did notice that after several miles of only moderately high cruising speed (70) in the Midget the oil pressure dropped from 60 to 45 psi, which suggests that the addition of an oil cooler might not be a bad idea if long periods of hard running are anticipated.

The Spitfire engine is rougher than the Midget's, noisier at low revs and with more vibration at speed. Triumph does offer overdrive on the Spitfire (which BMC does not offer on the Midget) and that would make touring more pleasant as no one really enjoys hearing a rough little 4 buzz out more than 4000 revs per mile at 70 mph.

The luggage and storage space is roughly the same for both cars. The spare tire and tools occupy a good share of the space in the trunks of both but the odd-shaped area left there and behind the seats is sufficient for even serious touring if you don't demand hard-sided luggage for your pliable belongings. Both cars are extremely agile for traffic and parking, the very tight (24-ft) turning circle of the Spitfire permitting close-quarter maneuvers almost unparalleled in modern motoring. The heater of the Midget is, frankly, abominable and there is no provision for bringing fresh air into the cockpit except through the heater, whose hot-water valve is reached only by looking under the hood. The Spitfire's heater, though also with a one-speed blower, is better and there are two underdash vents for fresh air.

There are many virtues in the Midget's small bulk—such as easy, accurate handling, confident maneuvering in tight quarters—but there are also several penalties to be paid. The driver compartment is so small as to be barely satisfactory for a 5-9 driver (see Driver Comfort Rating) and all but impossible for any driver much over 6 ft tall. The Spitfire is much more satisfactory in this respect.

It must be noted, though, that for comparably equipped cars, the Midget costs about $200 less. And for most drivers getting into their first sports car, $200 is a serious quantity of money. But whichever one the buyer chooses, he is assured of many miles of motoring pleasure in the great sports car tradition. They're good cars, both of them. You can't go wrong.

MIDGET ON THE LOCAL SCENE

BMC's 1275 cc Midget hits here in January with quick-fold hood and close ratio gearbox. The first car won't be ready till some time in December so we bring you this brief impression run per courtesy of Bill Yates, Sydney northside sports car dealer who provided an identical imported unit.

WHEN we broke the news of BMC's switch to the MG Midget as its economy sports car on the local scene we predicted a good reaction from buyers. Unfortunately production delays have meant there aren't any buyers yet, but we got that favorable reaction from everyone — would-be buyers, dealers, and enthusiasts in general.

That doesn't prove anything about MG engineering — only that the average guy is a little susceptible to status symbols and the MG name is THE status symbol when you're talking in terms of everyday average-income sports cars.

But the MG Midget comes here with some pretty important improvements. The main one is the 1275 cc engine, but in terms of comfort the new quick-folding hood is also important. Additionally there's a close ratio gearbox and 6¼ in. diaphragm clutch.

The Midget should go on sale here in January at a purchase price of some $2500 — whereas the Austin Healey Sprite sold for $2198. Absorbing a large portion of that extra $300 of your money is a new 1275 engine based on the Cooper S type mill, but detuned by use of more economical components to yield 65 bhp (the 1100 Sprite was rated for 60 bhp when it went out of production). There's also a close-ratio gearbox and this makes the most significant difference to the car's performance.

Yates had the car finely detailed when we picked it up and we went over it thoroughly before our workout. Externally it's the old familiar Sprite. The bodywork is of course the same, apart from the badge engineering changes and the detail tidy-up work that accompanies the new hood treatment. This is very well tailored, with neat chromed Dzus-fasteners and full width protective chrome moulding along the back plus a half-tonneau when the hood is slipped away. Simulating an emergency hood erection, we tried yanking it up at about 10 mph — one hand, while driving round a park. It was easy. We don't recommend it for the road though.

The interior is done out in the same black finish of the Sprite — crinkle finish dashboard, black plastic monkey grips and window winders, vinyl door trims and seats with white beading. The door-openers are located at shoulder point in a chrome recess. Needless to say, they're awkward.

The car still shows many traces of its economy heritage that aren't exactly in keeping with its new BIG price. The doors swing open on the old leather straps — no door stays — and, worst of all, the car still only has single-speed windscreen wipers. The cockpit is far too cramped, and a tall driver becomes miserable after a few miles of city driving, unless he likes a wheel in his stomach all the time.

The rest is all good. The handling is fantastic — especially with new power which opens up all sorts of new avenues in high speed cornering. We didn't get a chance at high-speed stuff, but on a twisty mountain section the car tracked like a steam train and didn't want to hang out sideways

Cockpit area is cramped for tall drivers, has similar trim to Sprite. Wood rim is not standard.

Best feature of the new car is the quick-fold hood. It can be pushed down or up one-handed.

New Midget has same body as old Sprite, but really goes with 1275 cc engine and cr gearbox.

anywhere. The steering is still delightful (even if the wheel is too close) and the gearbox is at least 100 percent better than the old one. The ratios are very well mated to the power and torque curves and you always have a suitable cog for the situation. You can pick up first with a double shuffle at 10 mph or more, with no hint of protest from the box and the notchy lever moves positively from gate to gate.

Ride depends on how fast you want to go. We tried 16 psi all round and found it very comfortable for town use while still giving incredibly good handling if you do want to squirt it. With more pressure you increase handling and detract from ride. About 28 psi would be a maximum unless you want to go racing.

The figures in the accompanying chart are from English sources who tested an identical car. They point out 100 mph is quite realistic under good conditions, which is quite a step-up from the Sprite's normal 85-90 mph performance. #

Hood stores behind seats under smooth-fitting half-tonneau, a great improvement on old system.

MG MIDGET 1275

Performance
Acceleration:

Standing quarter mile	19.1 secs
0-30 mph	4.2 secs
0-40 mph	6.4 secs
0-50 mph	9.2 secs
0-60 mph	13.0 secs
0-70 mph	19.1 secs

Maximum speed: 95 mph (see text)
Fuel consumption:
  Touring: 33 mpg; Hard Driving: 30 mpg.

meet the midget

THERE'S a good deal of commonsense behind BMC's decision to drop the Austin Healey Sprite and replace it with the almost identical MG Midget.

Despite the fact that MGs aren't the force in competition that they used to be, the name still commands a lot of respect, and consequently draws customers like flies to a honey pot.

The Austin Healey name-tag, while appreciated by the hard core sports car initiates, didn't have the same appeal to run-of-the-mill customers.

The Sprite continues in production back in the Old Dart, but you won't be able to buy one here.

MG dealers have been importing Midgets independently of BMC for some time—since the Sprite went out of production, in fact—but local manufacture will begin at BMC's Zetland establishment soon.

We recently spent a few hours behind the wheel of the Midget, and we'll shortly be getting it for a full-length road test.

The motor is the B-series donk, producing 65 bhp from 1275 cc (bore 70.61 mm, stroke 81.28 mm). Torque is a useful 72 lb. ft. at 3000 rpm. This motor, although it's been around for some years, is the best thing about the Midget.

Smooth, responsive, and economical, it is.

Transmission is a four-speed with synchro on upper three ratios only. When will BMC introduce synchro on first to all its gearboxes? It's long overdue.

The gearchange is very good. Although the car had done less than 150 miles, there was none of the stiffness or baulkiness we've come to expect from BMC boxes.

The lever moved through the gate smoothly, and was absolutely no effort to use. Gearbox ratios are well chosen.

Comfortwise, the MG isn't really very different from the superseded Sprite. The seating position is low, and although the seats are reasonably comfortable you rely more on the doors than the seats to keep you located in vigorous cornering—and they get pretty hard after making contact with the shoulders a few times.

The steering wheel is too high set by today's standards and sitting behind the wheel is a strictly vintage sensation.

Instrumentation is reasonably comprehensive—speedo, tacho, fuel, water temperature, and oil pressure.

Retail price of the Midget hasn't been fixed yet, but when the Sprite went out of production it was selling for $2207. Bet your boots the MG will cost more than that. ●

FIRST impressions CAN be misleading. Last month when we had a brief exploratory run in BMC's new baby MG — the Midget — we weren't too impressed.

We felt then that it had a vintage feel about it — almost as if it was a reincarnation of some earlier MG. The steering wheel is too big, and too close to the operator's chest, the ride is overly firm, without the suppleness we've come to expect of modern sports-cars, and the handling was, to say the least, most unsporty.

None of these things have changed. But after spending a week with ESK 290, we find them not nearly as hard to live with as we had imagined they would be.

What wasn't obvious when we first drove the car was the tremendous revvability of the motor, and the quite good performance it offered. With only a few miles up the car was of course very stiff, and completely lacking in the flexibility we found so enjoyable when we drove it later.

What's new?

Basically, the Midget is just the Austin Healey Sprite with the name changed. BMC found that the magic of the octagonal MG nameplate was attracting buyers — the MGB is the country's best-selling sports-car, despite a price tag considerably in excess of the Sprite, Honda and Spitfire.

So they did the obvious thing, phasing out the Sprite in the second half of 1967 and introducing the MG Midget in early 1968.

Most important single difference between the two cars lies in the engine compartment. The Sprite used a tuned 1098 cc. motor and it produced 59 bhp at 5750 rpm and 65 lb. ft. of torque at 3500 rpm.

The Midget uses a 1275 cc. motor — basically the Mini Cooper S unit but detuned to the extent of smaller valves and a milder camshaft — which produces 65 bhp at 6000 rpm and 72 lb. ft. of torque at 3000 rpm. Compression ratio is slightly down from 8.9 to 8.8 to 1.

The Sprite was never a difficult car to drive in traffic. It's light weight and the flexibility of the 1100 motor were sufficient to allow it to potter along with the best of the family sedans. Imagine then how much better the Midget is with considerably more torque developed at lower rpm.

It's a great potterer — at the same time having a good reserve of performance on tap, irrespective of the gear ratio used.

Speaking of gear ratios brings us to a piece of news that will definitely interest potential Midget buyers. If they haven't already done so, BMC will shortly fit synchromesh to first gear.

MG midget
what's in a name?

That will be an improvement, although we never had difficulty engaging first on the move — either by double declutching, or just gritting our teeth and crunching it in.

Part of the Midget's flexibility is no doubt due to a final drive ratio which many critics feel is too low. The Midget's tachometer is red-lined at 6300 rpm but the 4.22 final drive ratio allows the car to run to 7000 rpm in top without any trouble at all. That gives it an outright top speed of 107 mph — because it is geared to do 15.5 mph/1000 rpm.

We did the right thing though and backed-off the throttle on our top speed runs, going through the traps with the tacho on the red line. This gave us 93.7 mph in both directions.

If you chose to ignore the red line, the Midget's top speed is a fair and square 107. Incidentally, BMC say the motor is capable of standing 7000 rpm without breaking to pieces.

Appointments

Like the Sprite that's gone before, the Midget offers pretty reasonable comfort for two people.

The seats are pleasant to sit on — more so, we think, than the Sprite's — although they look the same. They don't provide that hip-hugging support essential for ultimate comfort at speed, but by wedging oneself against the door and seatback and belting up with the standard seatbelt it is possible to stay firmly located.

The cabin area is fully carpeted, and a handy shelf behind the rear seats is also nicely trimmed with carpet. A good feature of this shelf area is that it is not made completely useless when

Sprite replacement turns out a much better car than we had at first expected

MG midget

the hood is stowed. With the top down, there is still room for a considerable amount of soft luggage in addition to that area provided in the miniscule boot.

The Midget's hood is a considerable refinement over the Sprite's — not so much in the mechanics of erecting and lowering as in mode of stowage.

Once it is folded up, it can be neatly hidden under a half tonneau — and, as we've already said, it doesn't seriously interfere with stowage.

Visibility is not brilliant in any direction, but this is not unusual in sportscars. The windscreen is rather low, and the mini wipers sweep only a small area.

Handling, brakes

The Midget is a very strong understeerer, and while we appreciate that this feature makes it a safe vehicle for the young and somewhat inexperienced drivers who will buy it, it is not the least sporty.

The color action pictures of the MG show BMC rally ace Evan Green at the wheel. Despite his considerable skill and daring, he just wasn't able to induce a tail-out oversteer attitude at any stage of our photographic sessions, and he tried handbrake turns and all!

We subsequently pumped the front tyres (Dunlop SP41 radials are standard) up to 30 psi and this reduced the understeer quite a bit.

On dirt roads, of course, the tail hangs out. Acceleration on loose surfaces causes the rigid rear axle to tramp and dither, and on very rough sections the front tyres chafe on the wheel arches.

Steering is rack and pinion, and

very direct at 2.3 turns lock to lock. Sharp and sensitive on good surfaces, it produces a lot of feedback and chatter on poor roads. A touch more self-centring would help, too.

One of the Midget's most outstanding features is its superb braking ability. It is one of only two cars we've so far subjected to our crash braking test that has recorded a full 1g stop. And it did this not once but twice in succession. See our performance panel for more details.

The Dunlops SP41s, which have a legendary reputation for stickiness, are obviously contributing considerably to the Midget's braking.

Performance

We've already talked at some length about the Midget's top speed. Acceleration is most respectable. The

car ran a best S.S. ¼-mile of 18.8 sec. and averaged 18.9, and accelerated to 60 in 12.5 sec.

Mid-range acceleration is good. The car's flexibility is such that it will run along on a whiff of throttle and take off strongly when the throttle is opened.

The average owner could expect 33-34 mpg. We achieved this in our normal running around, dropped the consumption to 27 when we did our performance runs. The six-gallon fuel tank is totally inadequate.

There's nothing really new about the MG Midget except the name — it's a collection of bits with which we're all pretty familiar. However, it's a mixture that blends well, and one that is easy to like.

We like it — despite our earlier misgivings. We're sure young sports-car enthusiasts will like it, too. ●

Manufacturer: BMC (Aust.) Pty. Ltd., Zetland, Sydney.
Test car supplied by them.
Price as tested: $2480.

SPECIFICATIONS

ENGINE
Water cooled, four cylinders in line, cast iron block, three main bearings.

Bore x stroke	70.6 x 81.2 mm.
Capacity	1275 cc. (77.9 cu. in.)
Compression	8.8 to 1
Carburettor	Twin SUs
Fuel pump	Electrical
Fuel tank	6 gallons
Fuel recommended	super
Valve gear	pushrod ohv
Max. power (gross)	65 bhp at 6000 rpm
Max. torque	72 lb./ft. at 3000 rpm
Specific power output	51 bhp/litre
Electrical system	12v, 43 amp hr. battery

TRANSMISSION
Four-speed manual with synchro on upper three ratios. Single dry plate clutch.

Gear	Ratio	Mph/1000 rpm	Max. mph
1st	3.2	5.0	30 (6000)
2nd	1.916	8.3	50 (6000)
3rd	1.257	11.6	70 (6000)
4th	1.00	15.5	98 (6300)
Final drive ratio	4.22 to 1		

CHASSIS

Wheelbase	6ft. 8in.
Track front	3ft. 10¼in.
Track rear	3ft. 8¼in.
Length	11ft. 5in.
Width	4ft. 6¼in.
Height	4ft. 1in.
Clearance	5in.
Kerb weight	14 cwt. 35 lb.
Weight distribution front/rear	52.4/47.6%

SUSPENSION
Front: Independent by coils and wishbones with tubular shock absorbers.
Rear: Rigid axle with semi-elliptic leaf springs and tubular shock absorbers.
Brakes: 8¼in. disc, 7in. drum. 190 sq. in. of swept area.

Steering	Rack and pinion
Turns lock to lock	2-1/3
Turning circle	32ft.

Wheels: Knock-off wire with 5.20 by 13 tubeless radial tyres.

PERFORMANCE

Top speed	94.1 mph
Average (both ways)	93.7 mph
Standing quarter-mile	18.9 sec.

Acceleration

Zero to	seconds
30 mph	3.7
40 mph	6.0
50 mph	9.0
60 mph	12.5
70 mph	16.5
80 mph	25.1

	3rd	top
20-40 mph	5.7	—
30-50 mph	5.5	8.0
40-60 mph	6.3	7.4
50-70 mph	6.7	7.7

BRAKING: Ten crash stops from 60 mph.

Stop	percent G	pedal pressure
1	95	80 lb.
2	100	90 lb.
3	100	100 lb.
4	95	95 lb.
5	95	95 lb.
6	95	100 lb.
7	90	105 lb.
8	85	110 lb.
9	80	110 lb.
10	80	120 lb.

Comments: Rear brake lock-up on stops 4 and 5.
Consumption: 27 mpg over 112 miles, including all tests; 34.1 mpg in normal country and suburban use.

Speedo error:

Indicated mph	30	40	50	60	70	80
Actual mph	28.1	37.8	47.4	56.4	66.1	75.2

 MG MIDGET 1275
COBURN IMPROVED

SMALL sports cars are fun, of that there can be no doubt—we have tried a few lately including standard MK3 Spitfire, standard 1275 Midget and even more fun a converted 1275 Midget, this is the one we are on about now. The Midget started life as a 1098 c.c. 1965 model and thus it stayed until those friendly men at Coburn improvements stuffed a 1275 go-unit and box into it. Not content with that they then made sure that the engine was a good one by carefully balancing the moving bits and lightening the flywheel. More urge still comes from the Janspeed exhaust manifold and 1½ in. S.U. carbs. We went and got the Midget from Coburn's at Hampstead (London) one fine and clear day—perfect sports car weather in fact; while we were waiting for the car to have service completed we had a little chat to Mike—whose in charge of the workshop side—and Fred Curtiss, their financial wizard. Both of them stressed that the car wasn't meant to be really hot, just a pleasant road car. Well they were vindicated both ways, 'cos the car went well enough to justify the absence of bumpers and the rather imposing power bulge on the bonnet, and yet was as flexible as the standard Spridget in town.

Quick we said—well we think 0–78 in 16.4 secs. is good going for a Midget, specially when you consider that the little car would pull 6500 in top on any straight worth the name! We had the feeling that given time it would pull a bit more than this—but we had to stick to a six five rev limit anyway. The only thing that disturbed us was the racket from the gearbox when in 4th travelling over 70 m.p.h. In fact, our test was to be cut short by trouble with the gearbox after doing the 0–70 acceleration run—we nearly cried. However we manfully fought off the urge and called it a day after working out that the Midget would pull 100 m.p.h. at 6500 r.p.m.

It's very nice having a reasonable amount of "go" under the bonnet of most cars, and it's even nicer having some "go" in a small sports machine. After all, that is what they're built for. In practical terms this means you can nip in and out of traffic at the drop of a hat—or your great

hairy fat foot! As the Spridgets are quite small motors you'll probably find you can run the beast too.

Sometimes after our test it was discovered that Coburns had been supplied with a 948 c.c. Spridget gearbox which has the bronze bushes as opposed to the 1275s needle roller bearings—makes a big difference that!

In spite of these bothers we would like to thank Mr. Tony Wynter of Bexley, Kent, for letting us try his Midget.

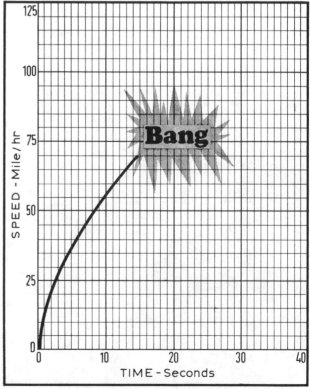

"Bang" shows what happens if you use the wrong gear box.

THE SPRIDGETS

**1969 Prices
Not Available**

1275 cc engine 65 BHP. New folding top. Roll up windows. Disc brakes. 30 plus MPG. Cheap to operate and fair resale value. Excellent for first-time buyer. For sake of simplicity, Sprite and Midget will be treated as one, although differing slightly in details. Manufactured by MG Car Co. Ltd., Abingdon-On-Thames, England.

The Sprite and the Midget are just a chrome strip and a set of wire wheels apart. Both cars are powered by a 1275 cc block from the Austin Cooper 'S'. It is the newest version of the 'At' type series engine that has always been the 'Old Faithful.' For lower production costs, the engine is detuned from 75 HP to 65 HP. Several less expensive parts are used in this detuning. A normal forged crankshaft instead of the expensive nitided steel crank, is one example of the detuning. Carburetors are S.U. and it has a Lucas electrical system.

The suspension system is the same as the previous model and proves to be more than adequate for the Spridgets. Front suspension is basic independent with coil springs and wishbones. Semi-elliptic springs provide the rear suspension.

The Spridget is well balanced (50/50), and with this factor and the good suspension system, the car can be thrown about safely. It is very responsive and gives warning before the rear end starts to slide. It makes a versatile slalom car with these handling characteristics. The rack and pinion steering is really hair trigger sharp and it takes a little practice to stop overcorrecting the car.

Although the wire wheels set the cars apart they both have 8¼" disc brakes on the front and 7 by 1¼" drums on the rear. Excellent braking power is provided for the weight of the car. 5.20 × 13 Dunlop Gold Seals are the standard tire which comes on the cars.

The clutch is 6½" diameter diaphragm-spring type and is hydraulically activated. There is still no synchro on first gear. Speed shifting is made easy because of the short throw on the shift lever. A sharp jerk is required to secure reverse gear, but this loosens up with use, time and practice. The rear axle standard ratio is 4.22:1.

Each year the Spridgets have added a few more 'pure luxury' features. A most welcome one is the easy folding top which was added last year. It is a very well made convertible top and is truly weather proof. Visibility is good when this top is up. The only problem it presents is to an over six foot driver. The tall driver finds no head room when the top is up.

The Spridget has 3" less headroom and is 6" narrower than the MG B, but it contains the same seats. So the only real loss of space is in the head room.

The steering wheel frames the tachometer and speedometer, which are nicely tilted for easy viewing. The water/oil pressure gauge and the fuel gauge are standard Smith instruments. The whole dash has a simple, uncluttered look with only the essentials there for the driver. Unmarked switches were a nuisance, but all that will be changed with the arrival of the '69s.

The heater control is confusing because it is on when the knob is in and vice versa. The fan operates with a right twist. The heating system is not adequate for real comfort, due mostly to poor circulation. For hot weather driving, there is a tap on the engine which when closed, allows only 'cold' air to flow through the system.

The Sprite and Midget have the same body shell, but the Sprite has no chrome trim and plain disc wheels.

The chrome trim on the Midget is similar to that on the MG B. This current body style was brought out in 1961 and continues to look new and clean. In 1964 the roll up windows were added to make the car more weatherproof. The windows and the new folding top have added much to the comfort and convenience of both passengers and drivers. The car is also almost rattle free due to good, tight construction.

This machine has proven to be popular and a good seller. The resale value is about the book value and a good used one will bring up in the three figure range. This car may never become a classic like the bug eyed earlier models, but will maintain a reasonable value after providing inexpensive driving pleasure.

This Spridget remains an outstanding buy for road racing, slalom driving and for pure fun for the low budget sports car buyer. ♠

Spare wheel, tools and still room for a case or two in the Spridget trunk.

The engine that has made hotted-up Spridgets quite a force in 'H' production racing . . . 1275cc and 65bhp standard.

Just like the rest of the car, the interior is neat, compact and stylish.

Nothing pretentious about the small MG or Healey. The Spridget looks just what it sets out to be — a little fun car.

Sprite Midget
Data in Brief

DIMENSIONS

Overall length (in.)	132
Height (in.)	48
Turning diameter (ft.)	16
Fuel tank capacity (gal.)	approx. 7

WEIGHT, TIRES, BRAKES

Weight (lbs.)	1568
Tires	5.20 x 13
Brakes, front	disc
Brakes, rear	drum

ENGINE

Type	4 cylinder
Displacement (c.c.)	1275
Horsepower	65

SUSPENSION

Front	independent coil springs
Rear	semi-elliptical

DESCRIPTION—MG MIDGET

It's harder than ever now to tell the Midget from the Sprite, as the chrome strip is no longer fitted down the centre of the MG bonnet. Both use a version of the BMC A-series engine with a capacity of 1,275 c.c. and developing 65 bhp net at 6,000 rpm. This is not the 1275S Mini-Cooper unit, which is more expensive and turns out 76 bhp.

The gearbox has a crash first gear and overall gearing is 15.4 mph per 1,000 rpm in top. Disc front brakes are 8.25in. dia. and there is no servo assistance. Rear drums are 7 x 1.25in.

Front suspension uses wishbones and coil springs with the arms of the dampers acting as upper wishbones. An anti-roll bar is optional; it was not fitted on the test car. At the rear half-elliptic leaf springs are used, with a live axle and lever-arm dampers. Steering is by rack and pinion.

Cross-ply Dunlop C41 tyres are the standard wear, on 3½in. rims and 13in. wheels. Optional wire wheels were fitted on the test car with the same size rims.

Performance—Midget

From rest, changing up at 6,500 rpm (of which more anon), the Midget reaches 50 mph in 9.5 sec and 60 mph in 13.8 sec. At the ¼-mile post, which is reached in 19.3 sec, the speed is exactly 70 mph. The recommended "brief" maximum engine speed is, in fact, 6,300 rpm. At these revs, the tachometer in the test car was indicating only 5,800 rpm and we therefore considered it in order to use this extra amount. The engine showed no signs of distress, but it is a sobering thought that an owner could unknowingly use 6,800 rpm!

DESCRIPTION—TRIUMPH SPITFIRE

The stylist "bone in its teeth" front bumper makes the MK 3 Spitfire, introduced in March 1967, easily distinguishable from its predecessors. Engine capacity went up from 1,147 c.c. to 1,296 c.c. at the same time. Peak power is now 75 bhp at 6,000 rpm.

Front discs are 9in. dia. and work without a servo; rear drums are 7 x 1.25in. The gearbox has standard Herald ratios and no syncromesh on bottom. Overall gearing is 15.8 mph per 1,000 rpm in direct top.

A separate chassis of basically cruciform shape is used. Front suspension is by means of double wishbones, in conjunction with coil springs, telescopic dampers and an anti-roll bar. At the rear, swing axles are used in conjunction with a transverse leaf spring. Longitudinal location is provided by a radius rod each side. Steering is by rack and pinion.

Standard tyres are 5.20-13in. Dunlop C41 cross-ply, mounted on 3.5in. pressed steel wheels. The test car was fitted with the optional 145-13in. Dunlop SP68 radial-ply tyres mounted on 4.5in. wire wheels. Amongst the other optional extras fitted were an overdrive, tonneau cover, heater, sun-vizors and auxiliary lamps.

The speedometer, on the other hand, over-reads by a modest 2.5 per cent, whilst the odometer is accurate. Maximum speed is 93 mph and the best one-way 94 mph. The latter represents 6,100 rpm—well over the 5,500 rpm (equivalent to 85 mph) recommended as the limit for continuous operation. With the hood down, the maximum speed drops to 88 mph.

It is almost impossible to resist the temptation to drive the Midget really hard. Certainly, this was its fate during the time it was in our hands. Yet, in the course of ordinary road

running, it returned as many as 34.8 mpg. Performance testing at MIRA, always a thirsty business, yielded only 26.4 mpg, but the average for the whole of the test period was a creditable 29.8 mpg. No measurable quantity of oil was used during the 800 miles we covered in the car.

Performance—Spitfire

The Spitfire's mechanical tachometer is much more accurate than the electronic type used in the Midget. At the maximum permissible engine speed of 6,500 rpm, it reads just under 6,400 rpm. Using this as the change point, 50 mph comes up from rest in 9.9 sec and 60 mph in 14.0 sec. The standing ¼-mile takes 19.4 sec, 70 mph coming up just 0.1 sec later. We used the overdrive (an optional extra) when taking these figures, engaging it at 74 mph on third gear. As the maximum speed in overdrive third is 92 mph, top gear was not required when taking the standing-start figures.

The speedometer over-reads by 5 per cent and the odometer by 2 per cent. Maximum speed, achieved in direct top, is 92 mph. The best one-way speed of 93 mph represents an engine speed of 5,900 rpm—just under the 6,000 rpm continuous-use limit. Engaging the overdrive drops the speed by only 1 mph (down to 91 mph). The best one-way figure remains at 93 mph, but the revs are down to only 4,700 rpm. Lowering the hood reduces the maximum speed to 87 mph.

Despite hard driving, the Spitfire returned an overall petrol consumption figure of 31.3 mpg. The oil consumption, however, was less satisfactory, a pint being used every 250 miles or so.

2 CAR TEST
MG Midget Mk III
Triumph Spitfire Mk 3

NOJ 47F

Performance Differences

It would be difficult to find two more evenly matched cars. Their acceleration times differ by only a few tenths of a second and there is only 1 mph between their maximum speeds. Even lowering the hood has exactly the same effect on the maximum speed of both. The Spitfire has a slightly better petrol consumption, but this is offset by its considerable thirst for oil. Both offer approximately the same accommodation and are aimed at the same market. Yet they differ enormously in character.

The Midget is at its best when being hurled along a winding country road. Its beautifully light and precise gearchange encourages the enthusiastic driver to strive to get the best out of it and its low overall gearing merely adds to its nimbleness. The Spitfire, on the other hand, is a better proposition for long journeys on fast roads. Its higher gearing is an advantage under such conditions and its appeal can be further enhanced by specifying an overdrive.

Although the gearchange is so delightful on the Midget, the transmission is not without its shortcomings. All the indirect gears whine noticeably and the lever rattles quite badly at times. It also lacks syncromesh on first gear—an omission it shares with the Spitfire. The latter's gearbox, on the other hand, is very much quieter. Neither does the lever rattle but its travel, especially across the gate, is considerably greater and the change always feels a trifle "sticky".

The Midget has better spaced ratios but is only just able to re-start on a 1 in 3 gradient. With its lower first gear, the Spitfire copes with great ease.

In heavy traffic, the Midget is the pleasanter car to handle, despite its inferior visibility. This again is partially due to its better gearchange

Ultimate handling on the same bend at the same speed. The Midget (above) understeers safely on regardless while the Spitfire (below) jacks up at the rear and oversteers with power on

and lighter clutch. A more important factor is its better throttle response and cleaner carburation. The Spitfire has a marked tendency to surge at small throttle openings, especially at low speeds.

Ride and Handling—Midget

"Safety Fast" has long been an MG slogan and the Midget is a car that is really worthy of it. Chassis design is quite conventional and there is little to explain why the handling should be so outstanding. Good weight distribution and the use of a torsionally stiff monocoque body structure probably play a large part but some of it must be the result of careful suspension "tuning".

The little car feels ideally balanced. There is enough understeer to impart stability but not enough to cause embarrassment. The steering is very light and precise. One knows exactly what is happening at the front wheels, yet there is no unpleasant "fight". Response is instantaneous, yet the car doesn't feel in the least "twitchy". There is very little body roll and one has to try really hard to produce any signs of wheel-lifting. Most impressive of all is its incredibly forgiving nature. There can be precious few cars on the market with such inherently safe handling characteristics. Its only peculiarity is a tendency to veer to the right with power on and to the left with power off, but this is not even noticed after a while.

Such good handling qualities in a conventionally designed small car often involve ride penalties and the Midget is no exception. The ride is firm—almost choppy—over poor surfaces but the excellent seats effectively insulate the occupants. No matter how rough the going, the body structure gives an impression of absolute rigidity.

Ride and Handling—Spitfire

Our test car was equipped with 4.5in. wide wire wheels, shod with 145—13in Dunlop SP68 tyres—both optional extras. Past experience suggests that these make an appreciable contribution to the car's cornering capabilities and we found that it does handle very pleasantly indeed in all normal circumstances. Pushed hard enough, however, its basic swing-axle characteristics become very evident. The outer rear wheel suddenly tucks under, causing the tail-end to break away viciously. It must be emphasised that this only happens when cornering pretty hard and that reasonably prudent driving on public roads presents no problems. Although we have no wish to malign the reputation of this very pleasant sports car, we make no apology for referring to its handling limitations. Its stablemates, the GT6 and Vitesse, now have a completely redesigned rear suspension system. What a pity that the Spitfire has not been included.

The steering is rather low-geared, a feature that is emphasised by too large a steering wheel (16in dia.). As a result, response is not very rapid for a small sports car, but the effort is low and there is just the right amount of castor action. Straight-line stability is good and there is virtually no "fight", even on rough roads.

The ride is quite good but it suffers from considerable bump-thumping on rough roads and the body creaks a great deal. There is also a trace of scuttle shake. The result is that rough roads are heard and sensed, rather than felt.

Ride and Handling Differences

Driven moderately, there is really very little to choose between the handling of the two cars. The Midget has lighter and more responsive steering but the Spitfire has a slight edge in terms of directional stability.

Pushed to the limit, however, the Midget remains completely predictable and safe, whilst the Spitfire oversteers quite viciously. Although we acknowledge that it provides an alert driver with reasonable warning of its intentions, there is always the possibility of having to take sudden evasive action. In addition, it has been designed specifically to appeal to the sporting fraternity, many of whom, quite properly, enjoy driving at a brisker pace than average. We feel that the Spitfire doesn't provide the margin of safety they have a right to expect from a car of this type.

As far as ride is concerned, the Spitfire has the advantage. This is multiplied to some extent by the Midget's superior seats with their adjustable back-rests. Other features in favour of the Midget are the lower level of bump-thumping (possibly because it was fitted with cross-ply tyres) and the rigid feel of its body structure. The majority of people, however, clearly prefer the riding properties of the Spitfire.

Noise—Midget

The Midget suffers from wind noise especially around the top of the windscreen and wind-up windows. There is also flapping of the hood fabric against the hood irons at about 40 or 50 mph before wind pressure inside billows it out taunt.

Gearbox and transmission whine are very noticeable, especially in the intermediate gears, until they become drowned in the overall engine and wind roar, which also drowns speech from the radio however loud the volume. A harsh drive-line vibration sets up at speeds above an indicated 85 mph in the Midget, which cannot be passed and only gets progressively worse with speed.

Bad surfaces do little to transmit noise through the C41 tyres and awareness of road noise generally is absent other than tyre squeal caused by exuberant cornering.

Noise—Spitfire

The Spitfire is an extremely different story with tyre thump from indifferent surfaces coming through the radial tyres in a disturbing and very noisy way.

Loose stones thrown up against the underside of the tyres sounded like lead shot peppering the metal; some form of underseal would considerably reduce this. Also, under severe left-hand cornering, as the tyres sideslipped cum juddered on the road surface, a tremendous hammering came from the region of the gear lever housing showing that the engine-gearbox unit was making body contact somewhere in the bulkhead area.

When crossing washboard-like surfaces apparent scuttle shake added to the impression that more rattle was being generated than could actually be recognised. In spite of this, however, the Spitfire was far quieter for high speed cruising especially as overdrive reduced further the already lower level of engine and mechanical noise.

A bad exhaust boom comes in around 3,000 rpm in the Spitfire, but this passes away with increase in revs. A drive line vibration comes in at 85 mph with or without overdrive engaged.

Brakes

Both cars employ the front disc, rear drum brake arrangement, with both providing adequate braking power for moderate braking effort. Neither showed any tendency to lock-up prematurely under heavy braking, no pulling or

extreme fade under repeated application could be induced, the only apparent discomfort to the systems being some smoking of the Midget discs. This is not a fair criticism however, because the safer nature of the Midget led to its being driven harder for many more laps of the test course at MIRA, due to its fun appeal.

Fittings and Furniture
Spitfire

Seat adjustment was adequate to provide an almost straight arm driving position for a just short of 6ft driver, but the bucket back could not be altered for rake. With the seat well to the rear the release catch for the hinged backrest was all but inaccessible. The bucket back provides good sideways hold when cornering, but the comfort factor of the seat was not very high with little leg support. A rest for the left foot made the task of staying firmly in the seat somewhat easier.

The non-fly-off handbrake is located for easy use on the top of the transmission tunnel and the gear lever is nice and close to the wheel rim.

Gear positions are canted over towards the right and the steering wheel column slightly left to complete the 'twisted' set up, but acclimatization comes easily. The cockpit is carpeted and a kick-panel on the inside of the door is a good feature to avoid the muddy smears usually found on the inside of sports car doors. The door opening handle is located awkwardly near the door bottom but the window winder is sensibly placed and is free from the knuckle-barking obstacles. Small parcel shelves each side have open fronts.

Instruments are clustered centrally in a glossy wood facia panel making reading impossible without removing the left hand from its ten-to-two driving position. All the push pull or turn control knobs have their functions marked on them. The heating-ventilation system is effective, the steering column mounted lamp selector stalk includes a flasher and the overdrive stalk is on the right hand beyond the direction indicator stalk.

The hood is released by two levers from the windscreen to fold readily back into the space behind the seats once the securing studs around the base are released. A cover secures and protects the hood neatly in its stowed position.

Two levers on the bonnet sides allow forward hinging of the entire front to give very good access to the mechanicals. A smallish boot accommodating the spare wheel, will take the usual limited soft bag luggage.

Fittings and Furniture
Midget

A very comfortable seat provides excellent back and leg support with rake of the seat back adjustable. Forward leg room adjustment is restricted by the rear bulkhead so that a jack-nifed, wheel-in-lap driving position is necessary for a tall person. Because of the support given by the seat however this cramped position surprisingly caused no discomfort at any time, and lateral hold is provided by the close proximity of the transmission tunnel and door. The gear lever is centrally placed on the hump of the transmission tunnel for very light fast gear changes. Foot controls include an organ throttle pedal and a dip switch cum left foot rest.

Difficult to find quickly without groping, the handbrake lever is situated on the passenger side of the transmission tunnel, and gets enveloped by a passenger. The three-spoked wheel affords a perfect view of the speedometer and rev counter which are angled towards the driver. The dashboard although old-fashioned in appearance is functionally efficient with all switches easily accessible. Heating-demisting

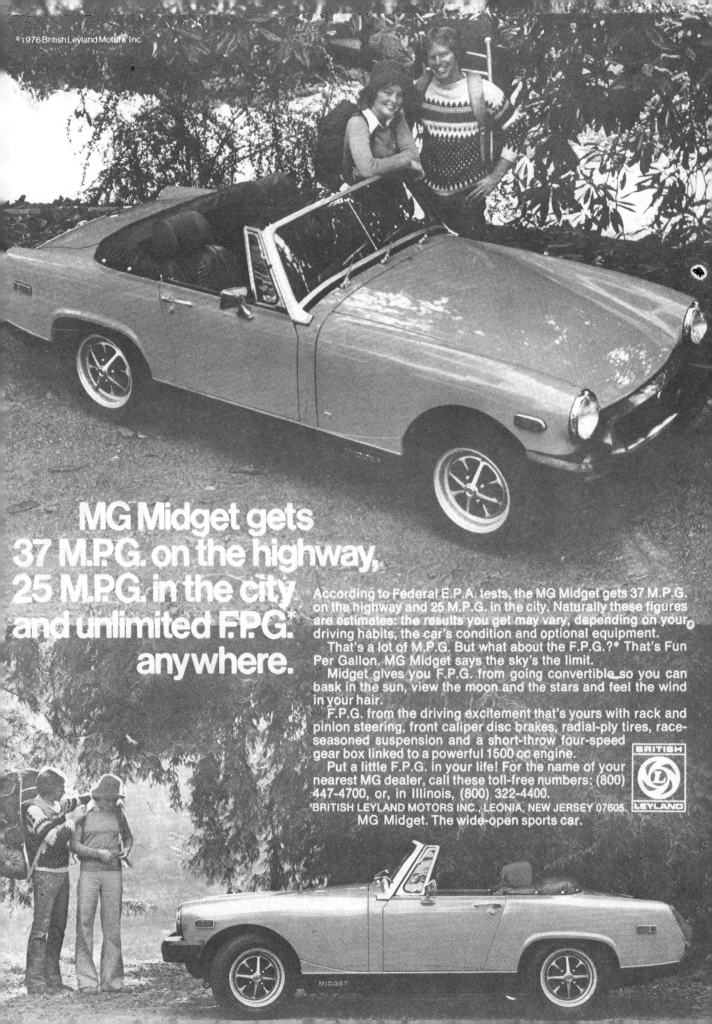

MG Midget gets 37 M.P.G. on the highway, 25 M.P.G. in the city and unlimited F.P.G.* anywhere.

According to Federal E.P.A. tests, the MG Midget gets 37 M.P.G. on the highway and 25 M.P.G. in the city. Naturally these figures are estimates: the results you get may vary, depending on your driving habits, the car's condition and optional equipment.

That's a lot of M.P.G. But what about the F.P.G.?* That's Fun Per Gallon. MG Midget says the sky's the limit.

Midget gives you F.P.G. from going convertible so you can bask in the sun, view the moon and the stars and feel the wind in your hair.

F.P.G. from the driving excitement that's yours with rack and pinion steering, front caliper disc brakes, radial-ply tires, race-seasoned suspension and a short-throw four-speed gear box linked to a powerful 1500 cc engine.

Put a little F.P.G. in your life! For the name of your nearest MG dealer, call these toll-free numbers: (800) 447-4700, or, in Illinois, (800) 322-4400.

'BRITISH LEYLAND MOTORS INC., LEONIA, NEW JERSEY 07605.

MG Midget. The wide-open sports car.

BRITISH LEYLAND

Above: With no front anti-roll bar, the Midget leans a lot in a corner, but remains stable and tidy right through. At the rear, the tyres are smoking from the sideways scrub

Right: Safety fast is the MG slogan, and speed holds no perils in the Midget. It is quick and tidy through corners always

controls are equally simple but efficient and opening quarterlights give fresh air at the expense of extra wind noise at speed. The bonnet release catch under the facia was very stiff on the test car and access to the engine compartment is reasonable.

The hood releases from the windscreen to fold back into the space behind the seats to be held in place by a neat cover. Erecting the hood needs quite some strength to clip it back into the windscreen and is a somewhat lengthy job.

Criticism must be levelled at the door opening catches, which are recessed high up near the rear edge and need considerable finger strength to operate.

Personal View

Choosing between two cars can sometimes be a difficult task. In this instance, however, there is absolutely no doubt in my mind.

The two are very similar in many ways, yet possess entirely different characters. Agility and excellent handling are the Midget's outstanding features, whilst effortless cruising, a more refined power train, rather more space and a better ride are the Spitfire's forte. There is one important point I must make clear at this stage —noise, especially wind noise, would deter one from buying a small sports car for long distance work. It would be primarily a fun machine. In this capacity I consider the Midget to be a far better proposition. Tweaking the engine—say to Cooper S standards—would make it even more fun.

It is only fair to record that my initial reactions were very different. I dislike the Midget driving position intensely and thought the power train (mainly the gearbox) lacked refinement. It still possesses these faults, of course, but I have grown to like the little car to such an extent that I am no longer aware of them. Never before have I undergone such a complete and rapid change of heart. DRT

Personal View

Choosing between the two cars in my case tends to avoid the main issue somewhat, because I find a pretty clear cut case for using

SPECIFICATION
MG MIDGET

		Maximum speeds
rpm	**mph**	
6,050	93	Top
6,500	74	3rd
6,500	52	2nd
6,500	31	1st
		Acceleration
ind. mph	**sec**	**mph**
31	4.0	0-30
41	6.4	0-40
51	9.5	0-50
62	13.8	0-60
72	19.3	0-70
82	27.8	0-80
19.3 sec	70 mph	**Standing ¼-mile**
Top (4.22)	3rd (5.73)	mph
—	8.5	10-30
10.8	6.7	20-40
10.0	6.7	30-50
10.5	7.4	40-60
12.9	9.6	50-70
18.2	—	60-80
29.8		**Overall mpg**
31		**Typical mpg**
Negligible		**Oil—**
consumption		**miles per pint**

FRONT ENGINE, REAR-WHEEL DRIVE

ENGINE
Cylinders	4, in line; 3 main bearings
Cooling system . .	Water; pump, fan and thermostat
Bore	70.6mm (2.78in.)
Stroke	81.3mm (3.20in.)
Displacement . . .	1,275c.c. (77.8cu.in.)
Valve gear	Overhead; pushrods and rockers
Compression ratio .	8.8-to-1 Min. octane rating: 99 RM
Carburettors . . .	Twin SU HS2
Max. power . . .	64bhp (net) at 5,800rpm
Max. torque . . .	72lb.ft. (net) at 3,000rpm

TRANSMISSION
Gear ratios	Top 1.0
	Third 1.36
	Second 1.92
	First 3.20
	Reverse 4.12
Final drive	Hypoid bevel, 3.90-to-1

SUSPENSION
Front	Independent, coil springs, wishbones, Armstrong lever arm dampers
Rear	Live axle, half-elliptic leaf springs, Armstrong lever arm dampers.

STEERING
Type	Rack and pinion

BRAKES
Make and type . .	Lockheed discs front, drums rear, no servo
Dimensions . . .	F. 8.25in. dia.; R. 7in. dia.; 1.25in. wide shoes

WHEELS
Type	Wire-spoked centre lock (extra). 3.50in. wide rim
Tyres—make . . .	Dunlop
—type . . .	C41 crossply tubeless
—size . . .	5.20-13in.

SPECIFICATION

TRIUMPH SPITFIRE

Maximum speeds

	mph	rpm
Top	92	5,850
3rd	74	6,500
2nd	47	6,500
1st	27	6,500

Acceleration

mph	sec	ind. mph
0-30	4.5	31
0-40	6.9	41
0-50	9.9	51
0-60	14.0	62
0-70	19.5	72
0-80	27.8	83

Standing ¼-mile	70 mph	19.4 sec
mph	3rd (5.73)	Top (4.11)
10-30	7.8	—
20-40	7.0	10.2
30-50	6.9	10.4
40-60	7.3	11.4
50-70	9.6	13.1
60-80	—	17.1

Overall mpg		31.3
Typical mpg		33
Oil—		
miles per pint		250

FRONT ENGINE, REAR-WHEEL DRIVE

ENGINE
Cylinders . . . . 4, in line; 3 main bearings
Cooling system . . Water; pump, fan and thermostat
Bore 73.7mm (2.90in.)
Stroke 76mm (2.99in.)
Displacement . . 1,296c.c. (79.2cu.in.)
Valve gear . . . . Overhead; pushrods and rockers
Compression ratio . 9.0-to-1 Min. octane rating: 99 RM
Carburettors . . . Twin SU HS2
Max. power . . . . 75bhp (net) at 6,000rpm
Max. torque . . . . 75lb.ft. (net) at 4,000rpm

TRANSMISSION
Gear ratios . . . . Top 1.0
Third 1.39
Second 2.16
First 3.75
Reverse 3.75
Final drive . . . . Hypoid bevel, 4.11-to-1

SUSPENSION
Front . . . . . Independent, coil springs, wishbones, anti-roll bar, telescopic dampers
Rear . . . . . . Independent, swing axles, transverse leaf spring, radius rods, telescopic dampers

STEERING
Type . . . . . . Rack and pinion

BRAKES
Make and type . . Girling discs front, drums rear, no servo
Dimensions . . . F. 9.0in. dia; R. 7in. dia.; 1.25in. wide shoes

WHEELS
Type . . . . . Wire spoked centre-lock (extra), 4.5in. wide rim
Tyres—make . . . Dunlop
—type . . . SP68 radial ply tubed
—size . . . 145-13in.

Above: Whoops! Under full power the Spitfire swing axles eventually take over and flick the back out at the ultimate cornering speed

Left: What happens when there is more roll than wheel travel at the rear. As the outside wheel tucks under, tail end grip reduces

either car for a specific set of circumstances. If my journey was relatively short or around town or a blast of a distinctly sporting nature, then the Midget is the easy choice. Its solid feeling, compact and freely buzzing nature together with the gearbox which is a delight to snick around, tied with the utterly predictable handling, promises something which will not catch me out at an inconvenient moment. Its limitations however concern the very squashed but not cramped sitting position as my knees actually rest up against the underside of the dashboard. However the organ throttle pedal and the very comfortable seat with plenty of back support makes a journey very bearable. My main disappointment is the high noise level which discourages use of the Midget on long motorway journeys. The ride is very firm and distinctly sporting with little noise to convey the hard work being put in by the tyres.

It should now be pretty obvious that my choice would be the Spitfire, if a lot of boring mileage had to be covered. Provided it is not driven in too sporting a fashion, it has remarkably long legs with little noise discomfort other than the harsh tyre thump present over rough surfaces. The overdrive does nothing to assist performance at all but makes life so much more pleasant. I did not find the creature comfort level to be very high due to the poor fit of the seat around my back, and the offset position of the pedals with the non-organ type throttle pedal. The instruments in the centre of the

dashboard which were completely obscured by my left hand did nothing to ease the physical discomfort caused by removing it every time a speed check became necessary.

There was nothing to choose between the brakes or the fresh air aspects of the two cars, although maybe the Spitfire hood was easier to stow and erect.

If the situation arose whereby one was to be mine, the two were side by side and I had one set of keys, the tyre dust would settle on the Spitfire as my Midget buzzed off.　　CJH

PRICES

The price of the basic Midget, inclusive of Purchase Tax, is £768 13s 1d, with the heater now standard. The equivalent Spitfire costs £796 1s 5d, the heater accounting for £14 7s 3d.

The specification of the two test cars was very similar except that the Spitfire had an overdrive, sun visors and radial-ply tyres. Excluding these three items (the first two are not available for the Midget, in any case) the prices for the cars as tested are £849 12s 7d and £886 13s 0d, the Spitfire being the more expensive by £37 0s 5d. Note that these prices include a pair of safety belts at £6 10s 0d and a Radiomobile installation at £33 0s 0d, as well as the more usual extras like wire wheels and a tonneau cover. If overdrive is counted as well, the Spitfire goes up to £943 9s 1d, £93 16s 6d more than the Midget.

BLMC Sports Cars

Exterior styling and interior trim changes only for 1970 Sprite and MGs; no changes to mechanical specification. Prices up.

THE BLMC factory at Abingdon, the biggest one in the world devoted solely to the production of sports cars, will suffer little disruption of schedules as a result of the introduction of the 1970 models of the MGB, MG Midget and Austin-Healey Sprite.

Changes in all three cars are confined to interior trim and exterior finish and fittings. Mechanically they continue entirely unchanged; basically, the cars follow the trend towards greater comfort and luxury in this type of vehicle.

Exterior alterations to both the small and medium-sized cars are very similar. All three have new matt-black grilles, twin rear bumpers with the number plate between them, and Rostyle wheels. The Sprite and Midget also have matt black lower side panels carrying the name of the car. The BLMC corporate badge makes an appearance on the front wings of each car.

Cross-ply tyres are still standard; radial-ply tyres and wire-spoke wheels are options. Auto-

matic transmission continues as an option on the MGB and MGB GT.

A new feature of all three interiors is the provision of fully-adjustable reclining seats. The dashboards have been redesigned to improve safety still further, and now incorporate rocker-type switches. The interiors of the smaller cars are now fully carpeted, and a gear-lever gaiter is fitted.

As far as prices are concerned, the Midget costs exactly the same as the Sprite for the first time in its life; previously, it has always cost slightly more. Both models are now £818. The MGB is now £1,125, and the MGB GT £1,254.

The colour range for 1970 is all-new, except for the retention of British Racing Green. There are four other colours (shared with the new Mini Clubman and 1300GT ranges); glacier white, blue royale, flame red and bronze yellow. Interiors are in black only.

The MGB roadster has changed in parallel with the GT. Note the Rostyle wheels which are now standard; wire wheels continue as an option

From the front, the latest MGB GT is recognizable by the new matt-black grille. This car is fitted with radial-ply tyres, but cross-plies are standard

Seen here at the Press introduction, the Sprite and the Midget now differ only in badges; everything else—including price—is identical. Recognition points on the 1970 cars include the matt-black windscreen surrounds and lower side panels. The grille layout is new

MIGHTY MIDGET

JUST A FEW days after last month's MOTOR SPORT pages went to Press I was pleasantly proved a liar. For in that issue I had noted that "in general, the traditional art of making two-seaters move that little bit faster has died out", following this uncertain ruling up with the declaration that a modified 1275 Sprite, or Midget, call it what you will, had never passed through my hands. British Leyland Special Tuning personnel were the people responsible for this month's about face, laying on a day of modified motoring which included four sporting two-seaters among a batch of entertaining machinery. You can read about that enthralling exercise in "Performance News", for here we want to concentrate on the outcome of that day, which for us was one hot week with one exceedingly "hot" MG Midget. After all there are not many steel-bodied, 1,300-c.c. cars which will exceed 110 m.p.h., record 0-60-m.p.h. runs in the low nine-second bracket *and* average 29.1 m.p.g. under irksome conditions.

However, the introductory words above should not be taken to mean this Special Tuning Midget is a perfect form of transport for even the most ardent enthusiasts among you, for there were snags—nearly all of which arose from the lack of preparation time, in turn prompted by our eagerness to borrow the car. Activities which can be classified as enjoyable have a tendency towards being either illegal, immoral or fattening, according to the proverb, and this Midget is nearly always in the first category when travelling at its normal pace on British roads, and possibly is slightly imbued with the second quality too as anything which gives such illicit pleasure must surely be!

Before looking at these pleasures in more detail let us first look at what Abingdon's resourceful works did to concoct such a potent little brew. The engine and ancillaries are the major story in this case because in the scramble to prepare the car chassis mods were left aside. Excepting the installation of fade-resistant, Ferodo DS11 grade, disc brake pads at the front, there are no modifications apart from power unit ones. In essence the engine is a full race example of the venerable "A" series, enlarged from 1,275 c.c. to 1,293 c.c. by means of a 20-thou. cylinder rebore (so I still have not tried a modified 1275—J. W.).

From the top BL modifications consist of a full race 11-stud cylinder head along well proven Mini-Cooper S-type lines; this head is just one stage short of the ultimate in siamese port layout at £65, whereas the big (1.406 in.) valve head is another £10. The valve train features a number of strengthened items, as well as lightened tappets, which allows the regular use of 7,500 r.p.m. for as long as the noise is appreciated, with an absolute limit recommended at 7,800 r.p.m. The standard pistons are dished, keeping the compression down below 9 to 1, but were replaced by flat-top forged pistons giving a ratio of 11.5 to 1 within those enlarged bores.

The standard connecting rods appear to be exceptionally robust items and are not changed for racing use. The crankshaft story is slightly involved because twice during the 20,000 plus Mk. 4 "Spridget" (*i.e.*, both badge derivatives) production run there had been a nitrided crankshaft installed as standard. Unfortunately this is not the case at present, so this £30 treated shaft was necessary on "our" current production example. As one would expect on a "works" sort of motor car the reciprocating parts which have to endure all those crankshaft revolutions are carefully balanced in a highly successful attempt to eliminate vibration anywhere throughout the usable power band. Among the sundry engine changes one also finds a larger capacity sump and revised pump pick-up, a modified distributor with vacuum advance disconnected, and a 16s. dynamo pulley which has a smaller diameter to stop the risk of the electrical system over-revving itself.

Deeper breathing for the unit comes from a pair of 1½-in. choke HS4 SU carburetters (standard have 1¼-in. chokes) partially masked by glass-fibre inlet trumpets, a suitably re-shaped standard inlet manifold is used together with a very effective extractor exhaust system. The latter emphasises the effect of the racing camshaft profile utilised on the test car so that at certain r.p.m. one gets a smooth power bonus. The camshaft is coded C-AEG 595 which seems an insignificant detail, but remember that the oil-pump drive was changed for the 1275-powered versions so this is the current coding for the old 648 or 649 cam: the legendary device which has featured in so many successful BLMC racing engines, and lined a few sharp boys' pockets with different manufacturer's labels attached!

The result of all this engine work is to raise maximum power from 65 production brake horsepower at 6,000 r.p.m. to a roistering 95-97 b.h.p. at 7,500 r.p.m. In other words the output is not doubled but the 13.4-cwt. car gains an extra 30 b.h.p., to sharply boost the power-to-weight ratio to the point where it is better than that boasted by a production Lotus Seven. Of course one can buy a 120-b.h.p. Holbay unit for the Seven, but that is another story.

In order to judge this Midget against some sort of known quantity we took along a Lotus Seven S4 on the collection trip to Abingdon-on-Thames. We found the Midget as we have described it, plus a pair of headlamp cowls. A seemingly pointless item for the headlamp units suffer through a scattering effect on main beam and not even supreme optimists could claim the aerodynamics were significantly improved. SOK 94H, the Midget's registration number, struck a chord in the author's mind for, just two weeks previously, he had reluctantly (it was sunny!) handed back SOK 95H, another of the current Midgets which have adjustable seat backs and mock leather-rim steering wheels as standard equipment. 95H had the latest 4.5-in. rim sports steel wheels, whereas the modified Midget's Pirelli Cinturato tyres rested on 4-in. rim width wire wheels. Latest Sprites and Midgets also suffer, in my opinion anyway, from an overdose of matt black paint, but the interior changes do improve the driving position considerably—although those over six foot are still unlikely to feel at home in the car because all seat adjustment is limited by the steel carpeted shelf behind them.

The Midget set off from Abingdon with the tonneau cover on and hood down. In the week that followed the hood lay undisturbed and only once did we have to bail out a soggy interior. There is a way of travelling from Abingdon to Henley almost entirely on country roads and this we elected to do, the two open cars being at their most enjoyable over this terrain. With a standard 3.9-to-1 final drive and a considerably extended r.p.m. range the Midget proved to be at home winding up through the gears, holding 2nd gear up to an easy 60 and 3rd up to over 80 m.p.h. Frequently the Lotus Seven pilot would look down at his gear-change in a vain attempt to find a corresponding 5th gear as the Midget accelerated away at 90, keeping up a respectable urge forward until the speedometer needle fell off the clock at 100 and the r.p.m. needle indicated 6,000 plus. A very happy cruising pace is an honest 80-85 m.p.h. with the throttle eased back. The Midget pilot had his problems though: first the tachometer was standard, reading 7,000 r.p.m., stopping abruptly at this point, and secondly the brakes and road-holding were nowhere in the same league as the super smooth and thrustful engine. To solve the first dilemma we hung on for the count of two after 7,000 r.p.m. were indicated, or simply waited for the speedometer needle to indicate two or three m.p.h. more: so far as we know the car is still giving reliable service! The second problem was a lot more fun to solve, for the Midget is one of those delightful machines that can be tossed around by even a moderate driver and still return to base unscathed. Our cornering style was to brake and change down rather earlier than one would

CONTINUED ON PAGE 97

DATA SHEET— MG MIDGET

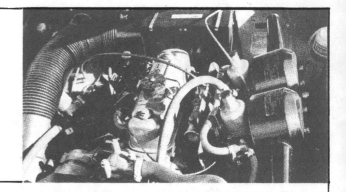

Manufacturer: BLMC (Aust.) Pty. Ltd.
Test car supplied by: BLMC, Zetland, NSW.
Price as tested: $2670

ENGINE

Water cooled, 4 cylinders in line. Cast iron block, 3 main bearings.

Bore x stroke	70.6 x 81.2mm
Capacity	1275cc
Compression	8.8 to 1
Carburettor	twin SUs
Fuel pump	electrical
Fuel tank	6 gallons
Fuel recommended	super
Valve gear	p'rod ohv
Max. power (gross)	65 bhp at 6000 rpm
Max. torque	72 lb. ft. at 3000 rpm
Specific power output	51 bhp/litre
Electrical system	12v, 43 amp hr battery, at 20-hr rate, alternator.

TRANSMISSION

Four speed manual, with synchro on upper three ratios. Single dry plate clutch.

Gear	Ratio	Mph/1000 Rpm	Max. mph	
Rev.	4.100	4.5	28	6250
1st	3.200	5.8	36	6250
2nd	1.916	9.6	60	6250
3rd	1.357	13.6	85	6250
4th	1.000	18.5	102	5500

Final drive ratio .... 3.9 to 1

CHASSIS

Wheelbase	6ft. 8in.
Track front	3ft. 10¼in.
Track rear	3ft. 8¾in.
Length	11ft. 5in.
Width	4ft. 6½in.
Height	4ft. 1in.
Clearance	5in.
Kerb weight	14 cwt. 35lbs.
Weight distribution front/rear	52/48 percent
lb/bhp	29.5

SUSPENSION

Front: Independent by wishbones, coil springs and lever-action hydraulic shock absorbers.
Rear: Rigid axle with semi-elliptic leaf springs and telescopic hydraulic shock absorbers.
Brakes: 8¼in disc, 7in. drum, 190 sq. in. of swept area.

Steering	rack and pinion
Turns lock to lock	2 1/3
Turning circled	32ft. (av.)

Wheels: Knock-off wire with 145 by 13 tubed radial tyres.

PERFORMANCE

Top speed	102 mph
Average (both ways)	102 mph

Standing quarter mile .... 18.6 sec.

Acceleration
Zero to	seconds
30 mph	4.0
40 mph	5.8
50 mph	8.8
60 mph	12.0
70 mph	16.2
80 mph	22.5

	3rd	top
20-40 mph	6.0	8.8
30-50 mph	5.6	9.3
40-60 mph	6.0	9.4
50-70 mph	7.9	10.1

BRAKING: Five crash stops from 60 mph.
Stop	percent G	pedal pressure
1	95	80
2	95	90
3	100	90
4	95	95
5	95	95

Consumption: 26 mpg over 114 miles including all tests; 32 mpg in normal country and suburban use.

Speedo error
Indicated mph	30 40 50 60 70 80
Actual mph	30 38 47 56 66 75

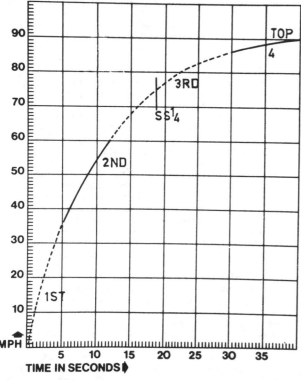

ACCELERATION CHART

TOP
4
3RD
SS¼
2ND
1ST
MPH
TIME IN SECONDS

HOW MG MIDGET COMPARES

MAXIMUM SPEED (mean) M.P.H.
70 80 90 100 110 120 130

MG Midget ($2670)
Toyota Corolla 1200 coupe ($2567)
Fiat 850S coupe ($2509)
Mazda R100 ($2835)

0-60 M.P.H. SECONDS
25 20 15 10 5

MG Midget
Toyota Corolla 1200 coupe
Fiat 850S coupe
Mazda R100

M.P.G. Overall
10 20 30 40

MG Midget
Toyota Corolla 1200 coupe
Fiat 850S coupe
Mazda R100

STANDING START ¼ MILE (secs)
20 10

MG Midget
Toyota Corolla 1200 coupe
Fiat 850S coupe
Mazda R100

MG

NSW BCL·015

MIDGET

Detail improvements and a "mod" paint job give the MG Midget a new lease of life — even if the concept is outdated

THE MG Midget makes a great road test car. You pick it up on a Friday, enjoy a sunny weekend with the fast-folding hood down, then hand it back on Monday morning.

Past that, its practical limitations will try even the tolerance of the "young-at-heart".

It is a tremendous fun car, is great to learn about real "driving" and relishes an aggressive technique.

But to own, it needs to be a fourth car for when the mood suits or a bachelor-catcher town commuter for

the career girl. Alternatively, it forms a basis of great potential for the serious club motor sport aficionado.

We handed the keys back to the British Leyland after a 300-mile test having loved every moment in the endearing little roadster, but quite happy to step out.

The latest version, the Midget Mk. Two has been updated to keep in-vogue with the "seventies swingers". New grille and rear bumperette treatment plus a black, chrome-stripped sill section re-juvenate the basic "Spridget" body introduced seven years ago, as the second series Austin-Healey Sprite.

Apart from the dress pizzazz and additional safety gear, the Mark Two Midget differs in only one mechanical specification — the rear axle ratio. But this seemingly innocuous item has transformed the small sporty. In our road-test of the first Australian Midget in Modern Motor, February 1968 we commented how the car needed a "taller" final drive. And that is what British-Leyland has given the Mark Two — uprated on numerical values from 4.222 to 3.9 to 1.

Theorists would tell you that will reduce acceleration but increase top speed. In fact, and due to the Midget's low-tune 1275 cc Morris Cooper engine, the tremendous torque keeps acceleration up and also gives higher speed in all gears.

We saw 6250 (start of the red tacho sector) in the indirect gears and 5500 rpm in top — equivalent to 101 mph, and increase of seven mph over the 4.222 to 1-geared Midget.

Improved handling

The revised gearing which gives maxima of 35, 60 and 86, has the indirect benefit of transforming the handling also. Because the car is on peak torque at higher speeds, it is easy to flick around in a most controlled way. There is still pronounced initial understeer but a strong prod of the accelerator lets the enterprising driver use power oversteer where he wants.

The direct, if stiff steering (the test car had 4000 miles up and the steering still seemed "sticky") and excellent control ergonomics — gearshift, pedal location and brakes — give a feeling of mastery and confidence. It is easy to see why the Midget wears such a high insurance loading as the less experienced driver would exploit this confidence too far.

Perhaps the only handling vice comes from the quite low ratio of track to wheelbase size and soft springing which makes the car "dive" noticeably while cornering on a trailing throttle. This roll oversteer can be used successfully to "set-up", the Midget for tight cornering, especially on banked turns where the tail will lean into the banking in an oversteer attitude without really needing opposite lock. Used this way the Midget's handling is a real delight with the car showing magic response.

Less endearing is the trait of engine torque reflex. Driving on a straight road, the Midget will alter course dramatically with throttle movement. Hard acceleration to trailing throttle swings the nose left, trailing to power-on a less dramatic pull to the right. Although the suspension is to sports cars standards, it is quite soft which allows the torque reflex such advantage.

But over dirt roads, the suspension wins and you can forget most of that

bone-jarring-sports-car-ride idea. The back axle is sufficiently well located to handle even the worst corrugations

The front — on coils and double lever action shockers — is supple enough to keep directional stability high. We can now see why John Sprinzel put up such a good show in the London-to-Sydney Marathon when all critics decried the baby, over-laden Midget as a toy. Up to Broken Hill on the third last day Sprinzel lay first private entrant outright before he broke a front stub axle. Despite its diminutive size, the body cross-members and sub-frames make the Midget a solid, rattle-free car.

Whilst the Midget could not be taken too seriously — except as extreme personalised transport for those prepared to accept its crudities — it is an uncompromising sports car.

And the 1970 definition of a sports car is a ragtop — for there are many sedans for the same money which will match the Midget in performance, braking and even handling.

New fittings

But no sedan can offer a one-handed drop top, without even climbing out. That's one of the strong features carried over from the last Midget model. The top comes down by flipping two catches, undoing some press-studs and folding the steel-framed hood back behind the seats. It is neat, simple and easy-to-use.

An anti-roll bar, multi-laced wire wheels and oil cooler are UK market, extra-cost options which come in the Australian ckd packs as standard.

These combine with the 1970 additions of vinyl-bound, alloy-spoked steering wheel, reclining seats, laminated windscreen and radial ply tyres to up-date the Midget. Twin reversing lights, a combined flasher/dip switch, indicators, horn stalk, a fresh-air heater and new thicker carpets make the Midget more livable and comfortable.

British-Leyland even says the Midget is quieter but we'd dispute that. At peak rpm in third, the mechanical wail announces the Midget's flight several miles back. There is less gearbox noise in this model but first is still

un-synchronised and screeches the familiar Morris whine under a heavy right foot.

Despite the noise, the new Midget does seem more accommodating. The test car was not fitted with a heater, only a fresh air plenum chamber with dash control for side flaps into the foot-wells. It is a lucky dip whether you get the billed-as-standard-equipment heater, as they are omitted from some ckd kits. Even with the hood down, night travel would be cosy with this addition. We found, with no heater the cockpit warmed-up from engine and transmission heat — eventually.

While the new flasher stalk is better ergonomically than the floor dipper, it is stiff and hard to use. Other switch gear also is lacking pre-thought on easy operation. The wiper and washer controls live on the far left which would be great for lhd cars but calls for hands off the wheel on rhd cars. As the dash is so close, the all important wipers and washers could be at finger-reach.

The US export car gets three-blade wipers. Why, British Leyland, do we not get them here with twin-speed motors and power washers? At $2670, crying "cost" is not justification.

For those who like the Midget but not its wind-in-the-hair there is an optional hardtop which makes the cockpit cosier but defeats much of the aim of this low-cost drop-head.

The little Midget commands considerable respect as a serious attempt to build a not-so-serious car. It is tight and safe for the clientele it will attract. But it is not very good value and with the tremendous insurance loadings it attracts there will be little change from $3000 once you've put the car on the road with all accessories, registration and insurance.

If you can put up with the crudities, looking down the barrel of diesel bus exhausts, being spattered with mud and slush on wet days and not being able to see around that Mini in front, then the Midget will soon start winning you. Certainly, outside city smog, it has to be a groovy way to get your favourite bird to the beach.

But, like we said, it was no struggle giving it back when the time came. ●

MG SERVICE TEST MIDGET

SPACE UNDER THE HOOD IS LIMITED BUT YOU CAN GET AT MOST ENGINE COMPONENTS WITHOUT SERIOUS DIFFICULTY. YOU'LL PULL PARTS TO GET AT OTHERS

It takes a bit of British-style stiff-upper-lip to be a weekend mechanic with an MG Midget. There's no job on the checklist that's absolutely impossible for a weekender, and no special tools are required, but several things will take substantially longer than one would really like to spend.

The spark plugs on the in-line four-cylinder engine are right out there in the open and should be a cinch. (They were on earlier models, but the inclusion of an anti-smog air pump has blocked off access to the No. 1 spark plug.) You can just fit a spark plug socket over the plug, but you can't fit the ratchet wrench onto it, for the air pump is in the way. Happily, pulling the air pump is not a complex job (a couple of bolts), but it does take a bit of the joie de vivre out of the work. The rating is fair and four points.

The air pump is mounted over the generator, which adds to the time to remove this unit (an anachronistic DC type). Fortunately, once the air pump is off, all the generator nuts are reasonably accessible. The nut that retains the adjusting bracket appears to be buried, but it really is no problem. A 9/16-inch wrench (box or open end) fits on rather easily. The generator removal rating is fair-to-good and six points.

The fan belt also is affected by the air pump location, and for this job I was not so forgiving. Because the air pump is an add-on, its drive belt is on the outside. To change a generator belt, therefore, you must take off the air pump belt first. The rating is fair and four points.

The distributor is on the right side and mounted somewhat low. A flexible oil line is routed over the distributor cap about two inches away, presenting a minor in-

convenience. The distributor lock (a pinch-bolt-and-nut arrangement) looks impossible to reach, but if you've developed any artistry at snaking wrenches into tight places, you'll find no real difficulty. Once you've got the wrench on (a 7/16-inch box does nicely), there's actually a fair bit of room to swing the handle. The rating is fair to good and six points.

The ignition points are accessible without removing the distributor, although you might want to move the oil line out of the way. The rating is fair to good and six points.

Battery cables are almost a pure pleasure. The ground cable is an absolute cinch. The starter cable is a two-piece design, one section from battery to starter switch, second section from starter switch to starter. Everything is moderately accessible

(Continued on page 97)

Compartment is crowded considering small 4-cylinder engine. Air pump for anti pollution equipment is up front on the left.

Air pump is relatively easy to remove. Wrench is on top bolt and the lower bolt is just about as accessible as the top one.

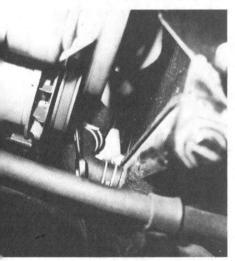

Protruding wrench holds generator adjusting bracket nut. No problem when found.

You've got to snake wrench onto pinchbolt nut that holds the MG distributor in place.

Distance from front spark plug to air pump is minimal so the pump must be removed.

Battery cables are no problem to replace. Battery itself is behind heater. Starter switch (see finger) is alongside heater.

There are five places you've got to place wrench to remove air filters but they're all wide open and the job is quite simple.

MG MIDGET

and the rating is good and seven points.

The oil filter is a remove-from-underneath proposition. It's that hoary replaceable element design that if slightly misaligned when installing results in massive oil leaks. If the Triumph Spitfire can use a spin-on cannister filter, so can the Midget. The rating for this item is poor and zero points.

The air filters (two, one for each of the one-barrel SU carburetors) are held by four bolts (plus a bracket with a nut) and replacing them may take a minute longer, but it's easy. The rating is good and eight points.

The carburetors each are held by two nuts (one on top, one on the bottom). The top nut is visible and easy. The bottom nut is invisible but just about as easy. The rating is good and seven points.

Torquing cylinder head bolts is an absolute cinch on MG engines, and the Midget is no exception. The rocker cover comes off in seconds (unlike most other cars) and the job is a 10-minute proposition. The rating is good and the full eight points.

The brake master cylinder sits alongside the clutch master cylinder the driver's side of the engine compartment. A sheet metal housing

Brake master cylinder is on driver's side next to clutch master cylinder. Cover plate has been removed which allows master cylinder to be rebuilt right on the car.

covers much of them,but it takes only the removal of a sheet metal plate to expose almost everything.

With this plate off, it's a simple matter to rebuild the master cylinder on the car.

However, replacement of the master cylinder requires prior removal of the entire housing, held by several screws, several of which are less than totally accessible. The rating is fair and four points.

The fuel pump is an SU electric, mounted at the gas tank. Although this means that the rear of the car must be jacked up and supported on safety stands for fuel pump replacement, the electric pump has its advantages (no vapor lock, for one). And once you've got the rear up, it is wide open. So the rating is fair and four points.

Midget heavy repairs are what

you'd expect in a tight little sports car. The engine has to be removed in order to replace the transmission, which makes a clutch close to a six-hour job. However, a starter takes less than 45 minutes, which is neither good nor bad. The factory time for a cylinder head gasket is about 2.6 hours, which includes cutting a valve. Mere gasket replacement can obviously be done in less than two hours, which is good.

The overall rating for heavy repairs is fair and four points. There's no reason why the engine has to come out to replace a transmission (it isn't true on other British sports car or on American cars), and the relatively low rating is based on that problem.

There isn't any way to replace the starter without getting underneath, and dashboard bulbs are not easy, so the Midget fails to win the bonus points for these items. The speedometer cable is no problem, however, and two bonus points are awarded for that.

With this issue, Service Test adds two bonus points if the upper and lower radiator hoses can be removed without unusual difficulty or getting underneath. The Midget did not pick up bonus points for this.

The point total is 70, which is somewhat low, even for a sports car. However, it is worth repeating that special tools are not needed, and in fact, everything can be done with the most basic of weekend mechanic's tools. It just takes a little longer. ●

CONTINUED FROM PAGE 91

normally, then let the engine wail away happily to push the Midget round. The back wheels can be slid out to fantastic attitudes in safety, but for public road work only the very slightest of steering corrections should ever be necessary, though one can save a little steering effort by merely applying power to turn out of a side road—leaving the rear wheels to look after the navigation.

Younger people who drive a Midget in this stage of tune will probably enjoy the same love-hate relationship with the gearbox as we did. When the non-synchromesh 1st gear goes in correctly at 25-30 m.p.h. there is immense satisfaction, but if those teeth clash, what a sadistic idiot one feels! A good blip of the throttle is an essential part of the double de-clutching routine, but even though this helps I would honestly rather have all straight-cut gear teeth and no synchronisers, or a synchromesh box to the standards offered by Ford and Fiat. Apart from this 1st gear routine, the change is excellent from the stubby lever and a competition clutch does its job superbly as one feeds in 3,000 r.p.m. plus as part of the normal getaway routine.

There is a full range of modifications to improve both handling and braking at Abingdon, but as explained we were left practically bereft in both these departments—only stopping giving us any anxious moments. The lesson is obvious, even for brisk road use the braking should be improved before the converted Sprite is used. It sounds all so obvious, but the exhilaration of new found power can lead normally safe drivers into trouble if the brakes are not up to par. This was demonstrated for me when the Midget simply could not draw back from a high-speed overtaking manoeuvre while the Lotus did, and all so easily.

The Midget was used for all our normal routine traffic work and ran steadily throughout with the water temperature needle occasionally crawling as high as the N for normal mark. Oil pressure never dropped below 40 lb. per sq. in., but was a little worrying at anything over a consistent 5,500 in 4th (90-95 m.p.h.) when it would drop back from 60 to 45lb. per sq. in.—and no less. We could detect no surge during hard cornering (nicknamed "Advanced Aerobatics" by a pilot friend who drove with us!) but were nevertheless disappointed that oil

pressure was not maintained to a more reassuring level with the sump definitely full. Flexibility for traffic work depends on the driver feather-footing until 3,000 r.p.m., the bulk of the engine's power output coming in at 4,500, which feels like 2,000 revs on a standard Sprite anyway.

Altogether a fabulous little car for blowing away the dullness of everyday life at a reasonable price. The engine modification parts cost in the region of £200, an Austin Healey Sprite is just over £800, so the final cost will be in the £1,100-1,200 bracket, depending on who does the engine assembly and how much more one wants to do in the handling department. What is far more practical and likely is that a large number of Spridget owners will fit all or some (I *would* suggest a less energetic camshaft for most uses) of the parts we have discussed and will derive even more enjoyment from these likeable open sports cars.—J. W.

PERFORMANCE

Acceleration :				
0-30 m.p.h.	3.0 sec.	0-70 m.p.h.	13.5 sec.
0-40 „	4.8 „	0-80 „	18.2 „
0-50 „	6.8 „	0-90 „	26.7 „
0-60 „	9.25 „		

Gear speeds (at 7.000 r.p.m.) :

1st	38 m.p.h.	3rd	82.5 m.p.h.
2nd	60 „		

Top speed (hood down) :

Best .. .. 114 m.p.h.   Mean.. .. 110 m.p.h.

Average : 112 m.p.h.

Speedometer : Over-reading by 1.5 m.p.h. from 60 to 90 m.p.h. indicated.

Fuel consumption : 29.1 m.p.g. overall.

Converters : British Leyland Special Tuning, Abingdon-on-Thames, Berkshire.

Chapter Twelve in the continuing story of...

THE MIGHTY SPRIDGET

Defying the principles of planned obsolescence, the 1970 Midget stands as a permanent sporting fixture in a rapidly changing automotive scene. John Crawford goes on marathon test to determine this veteran's life expectancy.

Far Left: Midget in technicolor and wide-view. New Mark Two has detail grille restyle and some other detail touch-ups, but there are more under-the-skin changes.

Above Left: Back sill panels and reversing lights are worthy dress-up and function extras to mark the new Mark Two.

THE Midget/Sprite, or as it's known in the trade the Spridget, has been around close on 12 years. The basic car hasn't changed all that much, but owners of early cars would have to drive the current BLMC offering to see how far things have progressed.

In 1958, BMC released a low priced fun car called the Sprite. It was intended to be a bit on the revolutionary side, incorporating a few new design features such as retractable headlights, but after doing its sums, the marketing team found the concept was moving quickly out of the low-priced field.

Obviously, the revolutionary bits had to be dropped.

The 1970 MG Midget isn't all that revolutionary, in fact compared with current design, it is pretty old hat. But, BLMC has been in the car business long enough to know you don't bite off the hand that feeds you. The Spridget has been, and still is, a big money earner for the Corporation and there's no sense in doing a drastic re-work and pricing yourself out of the market. The Spridget is tried and true and is still really the only reasonably priced, genuine sports/fun car available.

The Midget hasn't gone the way of its older brother, the "Boulevarde B". Certain concessions have been made in the interests of comfort and, most importantly, competition — not so much racing type competition, but market type. The Midget has been popular in Britain and Australia, but its success on the American sales graph was the clincher that led BLMC to update its baby in much the same way as European car makers have done when their cars have faced US opposition.

During its 12 years, the Spridget's major changes have been a slightly different body, disc front brakes, new motor and an improved convertible type hood. Other changes have mostly been details — important to the overall improvement, but still minor. The Spridget, the best selling sports car on the Australian market, still manages to do well overseas, despite the number of competitors in its price and specification range.

The secret of this tremendous success must lie in the fact that the Midget is a very honest motor car. It doesn't pretend to be anything more than it is. The car still has some annoying shortcomings, but, at this stage, the only thing that would improve the car further is a completely new design.

The MG Midget sells in Australia for $2643, quite a bit more than when the car was originally introduced (even allowing for cost-of-living increases). It has also progressed greatly.

THE MIGHTY SPRIDGET

The changes over the first Midget (or the fifth Sprite if you wish) are new seats (adjustable for rake), padded leather-covered steering wheel, rear bumperettes instead (of full width bumper bar), reversing lights, blacked out sill panels, new grille and the new one-hand operated hood.

The engine and transmission unit remains unchanged and, departing from the parent plant policy, BLMC in Australia offers wire wheels as standard. In Britain, Midget owners get steel disc wheels with Rostyle type wheel covers (same as Triumph 2.5 PI).

The new seats are great. The adjustment provides enough movement to suit most drivers, particularly the girls. New padding makes them pleasant to sit on, but BLMC (in line with what we think must be British car makers' general policy) still persists in putting those annoying little seat adjusters on its products. The Japanese and Continentals (even Americans) provide a prominent cranked lever with a large plastic knob on the end, and its about time British Leyland spread the change through its entire model range.

The leather-padded steering wheel is good to hold and after driving the car for a while you begin to wonder why this sort of extra wasn't added long ago. But on the Midget, this fitting does cause problems. With the plastic wheel (early cars had plastic spokes, later cars wire spokes) you could always see the instruments, but now, apart from arranging the wheel in a sympathetic position, or aiming your eyesight through the drilled holes in the spokes, it is damn near impossible to see the cluster and practically dangerous to look at if you are driving at speed. Short of re-shaping the angle of the spokes there isn't a quick, cheap way out.

BLMC has added a multi-purpose stalk (flashers, high-beam, horn, headlamp flasher) to the right hand side of the steering column and this also gets all hung up with the steering wheel. The multi-purpose stalk seems closer to the wheel than the blinker-only wand it replaces and with your hands firmly gripping the steering wheel the stalk is easy to bump and occasionally hard to use. The main problem is that the wheel itself is a larger diameter than the plastic ones it replaces. The increased diameter is probably cheaper because the same wheel is used for the Midget and MGB. The "B" requires a large steering wheel to reduce steering effort — the Midget doesn't.

However, steering through the rack and pinion is still light and positive on the Midget and with almost three turns lock to lock, only a small movement is needed to send it off on a new path.

Still on debit points, the test Midget had a badly fitted boot lid. On reflection, gappy, ill-fitting boot lids have always been a Sprite trademark. The hood fitted tightly, but after a couple of ups and downs a sudden draught developed. We tried raising and lowering the hood a couple of more times, but

Mag-alloy wheel options on this English Spridget don't make local sense because of standard wire centre-locks. British car has standard disc wheels.

couldn't solve the problem. Together with hood flap, we suffered a steady three knot gale over our legs. Then the rains came — inside the car as well as outside. BLMC assured us Midget hoods normally fit snugly and claimed this unit had seen a hard life. We still feel the hood needs improvement.

British Leyland shows a standard heater-demister on its brochures for the Midget, but this is not fitted in Australia due to a problem with the CKD packs from England. B-L Australia ordered its basic packs from Britain with the heater-demister included and, on assurance from the parent company, printed its brochures and publicity material. The CKD packs arrived on the wharves without the heater units and British Leyland put the car on the market here without them. The cars will have heaters fitted by January 1971 (compulsory, anyway, under Australian safety design rules) and there will be a slight price adjustment. If you want a heater now go see your friendly B-L dealer who can give you details of the rather finicky conversion. Alternatively, national heater firms may help out.

The little car is easy to ventilate, however, if you're travelling with the hood raised because of the underdash vent and quarter lights, plus the wind-up windows. One benefit of the new hood arrangement is that you no longer have to stow the hood in the boot. It folds up neatly around the rear of the passenger compartment and has a storage tonneau built-in. This neatly flips over the folded top and fastens to the back wall of the bathtub. The boot space saved is still obstructed by the spare wheel lying flat on the floor, but that can't be improved without major structural alterations.

With a bit of juggling, it is surprising how much you can fit into the small capacity compartment - particularly soft luggage. Spridget owners will notice one interior change — the loss of the metal surround for the gear lever. This was nearly a traditional part of the design, but it has been replaced by an attractive stitched vinyl glove. This feature may also cut down noise from the transmission.

The test car had a little backlash from the differential and the gearbox did give out a few groans, but after a week in the car it is obvious BLMC engineers have tried to quieten it. With extra soundproofing and an extra muffler, the car sounds quite subdued, but when you wind it up there is enough noise to let you know that everything is working.

Performance on the MG Midget MK, Two is unchanged from that of the previous model. It performs well and is quite reliable, but a few more horses would help. The Spridget's big feature over the years has been its chuck-about-ability. This is a point raised many times over the years in road tests of the Sprite/Midget, but one which is an endearing quality.

MG Midget 1970-71 vintage can be picked by new grille treatment, black sill panels. Australian Midgets get centre-lock wires as standard equipment — English versions get discs.

It is a real fun car, a great first car for the young driver and it has good enough road manners to forgive the uninitiated. It is no wonder that Sprite/Midget owners start modifying their cars. The Midget has such forgiving handling qualities and responds so well to extra tuning that even after the initial joy of owning and driving you can practically make a different car of it and start enjoying the car all over again.

The Sprite was always a safe understeerer. The car was easy enough to provoke into a tail-out attitude and the original suspension set-up lasted until the Mark Three. Front suspension featured coils and wishbones with quarter elliptics and live axle at the rear — lever action shockers all round. With the Mark three, came a change in the rear suspension, and semi-elliptics made the ride better at the expense of a little more understeer.

The next handling and suspension change came with the official factory fitting of a front anti-roll bar. Sprite owners had been fitting this accessory themselves for some time and they were a must on racing Sprites. BLMC included them in the specifications and price only on the first Midget.

Sprite brakes have always been adequate for the job but before WHEELS got down to recording some braking figures, the stoppers on the test car seemed a bit spongy. As the figures on the performance panel show, the brakes performed well. With 8½ in. discs on the front and 7 in. drums on the rear the car pulled up straight from a 60 mph panic stop.

Controls generally are light, the clutch gives the impression it will stand up well to fast starts and changes and the gearbox ratios seem well enough spaced for good performance (more about ratios in a moment). However the gearbox had two failings, one not previously noticed on Spridgets before. Firstly, there is still no first gear syncro, but more importantly the change from second to third was diabolical.

During our test with many different and competent drivers we continually suffered missed changes and often snicked first on the way through. The driver really has to concentrate hard for a clean change because a close gate and lack of spring protection, slides the lever into first instead of third.

According to the brochures, the gearbox is a close ratio one, but inspection reveals the ratios are in fact unchanged. There is a close ratio box for the Midget, but unfortunately it isn't available as an optional extra (only through the special tuning department at Abingdon).

The Midget Mark Two engine is unchanged and is the rugged and reliable 1275 cc S-type unit. The important features of this block over previous A-series units are: Larger main and big end bearings, increased capacity combustion chambers, bigger valves and improved cooling passages. The advertised horsepower is 65 bhp produced at 6000 rpm, but the obvious feature of the powerplant is the generous (relatively) amount of torque available. This makes the car an easy handler round town and, of course, helps the car's cruising ability and fuel consumption figures.

Although the tacho is redlined from 6400 and peak power is developed at 6000 the engine puts up a vocal complaint when pushed over 5500. It still

New interior is marked by new seats, leather-alloy wheel, and vinyl boot for the gearlever extension.

operates well in the high rev range and, despite what sounds like valves bouncing off pistons, the engine will run right up to seven grand (although it runs out of breath long before that). The oil pressure and water temperature remained constant throughout the test.

The Midget engine is still fed by 1¼ in. SUs. The car cruises well, if a little noisily, at around 75-80. The speedometer accuracy was in question all the way up the range. Over 60 mph the readings became increasingly optimistic with the meter reading 100 mph at 6000 (actual speed 95).

One other gauge which Midget owners must learn to watch is the fuel contents. WHEELS recorded an overall consumption figure on test of 30 mph but the tank holds only a miserable six gallons and the needle seems to drop very quickly. A larger tank is necessary, but here we get back to basic design problems and, short of a new rear end redesign, there is sufficient room to instal a larger fuel tank.

The Midget seems to have its section of the sports car market to itself, but the car doesn't compete with some of the sports sedans now on the market, especially those from Japan, in terms of equipment and value for money.

Its success is its sporting concept — one which enthusiasts find highly acceptable. It is a strange anomaly in the automotive world that sports cars gain wide market acceptance, with lower value-for-money standards than would be acceptable for any sedan or sporting coupe.

This situation has lasted for years and shows no sign of winding up. British Leyland certainly doesn't have an alternative for the Midget planned — so it could be with us in similar form for quite a while yet. Give it at least three years.

TECHNICAL DETAILS

MAKE: . . . . MG
BODY TYPE: . . . . Two-seater sports
OPTIONS: . . . . .radio
MILEAGE START: .5400
WEIGHT: . . . .(714 kgm) 1575 lb
MODEL: . . . . MIDGET
PRICE: $2643
COLOR: . . . . .Mustard yellow
MILEAGE FINISH: .5604

FUEL CONSUMPTION:
Overall . . . . 28 mpg
Cruising . . . . 30 mpg

TEST CONDITIONS:
Weather . . . . .dry
Surface . . . . .bitumen
Load . . . . 2 persons
Fuel . . . . super

SPEEDOMETER ERROR (mph):

Indicated	30	40	50	60	70	80	90
Actual	28	38	47	56	65	75	84

PERFORMANCE
Piston speed at max bhp . . . . .(970 m/min) 3200 ft/min
Top gear mph per 1000 rpm . . . . 16.1 mph per 1000
Engine rpm at max speed 6200
Lbs (laden)per gross bhp (power-to-weight) 26 lb per 65 bhp

MAXIMUM SPEEDS:
Fastest run . . . .(148 kph) 92 mph
Average of all runs . . . .(138 kph) 86 mph
Speedometer indication, fastest run . . . .(156 kph) 98 mph

IN GEARS:
1st . . . . (48 kph) 30 mph 5500 rpm
2nd . . . . (80 kph) 50 mph 5500 rpm
3rd . . . .(112 kph) 70 mph 5500 rpm
4th . . . .(138 kph) 86 mph 5500 rpm

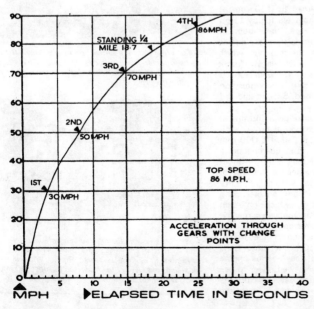

STANDING ¼ MILE 18·7
4TH 86MPH
3RD 70 MPH
2ND 50 MPH
1ST 30 MPH
TOP SPEED 86 M.P.H.
ACCELERATION THROUGH GEARS WITH CHANGE POINTS
MPH ▶ELAPSED TIME IN SECONDS

ACCELERATION (through gears):
0-30 mph . . . . 3.4 secs
0-40 mph . . . . 5.5 secs
0-50 mph . . . . 7.9 secs
0-60 mph . . . . 11.0 secs
0-70 mph . . . . 14.9 secs
0-80 mph . . . . 20.8 secs

	2nd gear	3rd gear	4th gear
20-40 mph	3.9 sec	5.9 sec	8.6 sec
30-50 mph	4.4 sec	5.5 sec	8.5 sec
40-60 mph	3.0 sec	5.8 sec	8.0 sec
50-70 mph	—	7.2 sec	8.6 sec

STANDING QUARTER MILE:
Fastest run . . . . 18.7 secs
Average all runs . . . . 18.7 secs

BRAKING:
From 30 mph to 0 . . . . .1.9 secs
From 60 mph to 0 . . . . .3.4 secs

ENGINE:
Cylinders . . . . .Four
Bore and Stroke . (70.61 mm) 2.78 in. x (81.28 mm) 3.2 in.
Cubic Capacity . . . . (1275 cc) 77.9 cu in.
Compression Ratio 8.8:1
Valves . . . . pushrod overhead
Carburettors . . . . . twin SU-type HS.2 semi-downdraught
Fuel Pump . . . . SU electric
Oil Filter .full flow
Power at rpm . . . . .65 bhp @ 6000
Torque at rpm . . . . (10.9 kg/m) 72 lb/ft @ 3000

TRANSMISSION:
Type . . . . .four speed, syncro on 2nd, 3rd, 4th
Clutch:
(16 cm) 6.5 in. diaphragm spring hydraulically operated.
Gear lever location . . . . .centre floor
Ratios:

	Overall	Direct
1st . .	12.5	3.2
2nd . .	7.5	1.9
3rd . .	5.3	1.4
4th . .	3.9	1.0
Final Drive . .	3.9 to 1	

CHASSIS AND RUNNING GEAR:
Construction . . . . .Monocoque
Suspension front . . . . . . Coils, upper and lower wishbones
Suspension rear . . . . Semi-elliptical and live rear axle
Shock absorbers . . . . Lever action
Steering type . . . . Rack and pinion
Turns l to l 2¼
Turning circle . . . . (8.4 m) 32 ft
Steering wheel diameter . . . . (39 cm) 15½ in.
Brakes type . . . . Front disc, rear drum
Dimensions . . . .(20.9 cm) 8.25 in. x (17.8 cm) 7 in.

DIMENSIONS:
Wheelbase . . . . (203 cm) 80 in.
Track front . . . . (118 cm) 46.3 in.
Track rear . . . . (116 cm) 45.3 in.
Length . . . .(350 cm) 137.4 in.
Height . . . . (124 cm) 48.6 in.
Width . . . . (140 cm) 54.9 in.
Fuel Tank Capacity . . . .(27.3 litres) 6 galls

TYRES:
Size . . . . 145 x 13
Pressures . . . . (2.65 kg/m) 30 lb/sq in. x
(1.95 kg/m) 28 lb/sq in.
Make on test car . . . . Dunlop

GROUND CLEARANCE:
Registered . . . .(12.7 cm) 5 in.

AUTOTEST

MG MIDGET MK III
(1,275 c.c.)

AT-A-GLANCE: BLMC's familiar small sports-car in latest paintwork and trim, with some detail improvements. Higher gearing increases top speed slightly but not acceleration. Excellent handling, firm ride, good value and good fun.

MANUFACTURER
British Leyland Motor Corporation Ltd., (MG Division), Abingdon-on-Thames, Berkshire.

PRICES
Basic	£692	0s	0d
Purchase Tax	£213	14s	9d
Seat belts (approx.)	£10	0s	0d
Total (in G.B.)	£915	14s	9d

EXTRAS (inc P.T.)
*Tonneau cover and rail	£11	15s	0d
*Radial ply tyres	£9	2s	9d
Wire wheels	£32	12s	9d
Oil cooler	£13	1s	1d
Anti-roll bar	£3	18s	4d
Hard top	£65	5s	7d
Headrests (pair)	£10	8s	1d

*Fitted to test car

PRICE AS TESTED £936 12s 6d

PERFORMANCE SUMMARY
Mean maximum speed	94 mph
Standing start ¼-mile	19.6 sec
0-60 mph	14.1 sec
30-70 mph through gears	15.8 sec
Typical fuel consumption	30 mpg
Miles per tankful	180

THERE are, surprisingly, still too few contenders for the role of the young man's (or young woman's) first sports-car. With still-steeper insurance one might have thought that the demand for a proper open two-seater of acceptably nippy performance, nimble handling, sports-car appointments and—by today's inflated standards—middling low price, was bigger than ever. At £906 Austin-Healey Sprite-cum-MG Midget in its latest form still remains perhaps the best car of the type available. Performance, though good, is still not as good as a number of saloon cars, but the Midget (which is the "badge" we tested) is undeniably a true sports-car.

The body shape dates back to 1961 when the highly distinctive "frog-eyed" Sprite was restyled to a more conventional—and perhaps less original—shape. Later, a more important change in one way, the unusual quarter-elliptic leaf-sprung back axle was altered to ordinary half-elliptic springing which more or less eliminated the car's marked and—once you'd got to know it—amusing tendency to slight rear-axle steer. The faithful BMC A-series engine fitted has gradually gone up in capacity and power; it stands now at 1,275 c.c. in the inexplicably mild 64 bhp at 5,800 rpm form. (Its saloon stablemate the MG1300 Mk II is allowed 5 bhp more and is at some points slightly faster). Most recent alterations are a 3.9-to-1 final drive (in place of 4.22), black paint on the sills giving the effect of particularly heavy side-flashes, the words "Midget" in heavy chrome also on the sides, nave-plateless wheels (wire-wheels remaining an option), and self-propping boot and bonnet stays (at last).

From the performance point of view, the gearing change is the most important, the overall figure going up from 15.4 to 16.5 mph per 1,000 rpm on the Michelin ZX 145 SR-13in. radial-ply tyres on the test car (cross-ply tyres are standard). (Owners with other tyres fitted there should note that in this particular size there are different rev-per-mile figures for the various makes, giving different overall gearing.) Previously the same-size Midget's top speed of 93 mph was seen after peak-power engine speed—6,000 rpm—but the higher-geared test car achieved 94 mph mean at 5,700 rpm, with a best figure on one leg of MIRA's banked circuit in good conditions of 96 (5,800 rpm). One does not notice much difference in cruising refinement subjectively, though there is obviously some improvement. Fuel consumption overall, compared with the lower-geared car which took part in the Midget-Spitfire double test (*Autocar* 10 April 1969), seems hardly affected. We averaged 29.6 mpg over 1,270 miles with best and worst consumptions of 26 and 35 mpg, depending of course on how one responded to the car's obvious willingness to work hard.

Acceleration is very slightly slower, to a degree only noticed by the ink-recording stopwatch. Showing the double-test car in brackets, from a standing start 50 mph comes up in 9.6sec (9.5), 60 in 14.1 (13.8), the ¼-mile in 19.6 (19.3), and 80 in 29.7 (28.3); the new car will however just achieve 90 mph within the length of MIRA's twin horizontal mile—in 51.3sec—which the other would not. Corresponding figures for the MG 1300 MkII are respectively 9.4sec, 14.1, 19.6, and 28.3, with 90 mph seen at 49.2sec.

Good car in traffic

Such cold comparisons are not to the Midget's advantage, and do less than justice to its likeable character. Coupled with good smooth-road handling and brakes (of which more anon), and good visibility whether or not the hood is down, the performance is more than enough to provide the keen driver with a lot of fun. Clearly what advantages the little MG has are at their best in traffic; one has more than enough go to stay master of most traffic situations. The engine is always willing, beginning to pull hard from 3,000 rpm, though not baulking if you ask it to work from speeds only a little above its tickover. Recommended brief maximum speed is 6,300 rpm on the revcounter, which under-read by 100 rpm at this speed, but the engine feels happy to go higher without signs of valve-bounce. Exhaust and mechanical noise from the engine are not obtrusive; it is the gearbox which offends most clearly here. First gear would not seem out of voice in one of the lower-priced Vintage-period popular cars. It is very noisy on most examples we have tried. Second and 3rd are only somewhat better.

Gear ratios are well-chosen, giving maximum speeds of 33, 55 and 78 mph at 6,400 rpm. Useful maxima for everyday use at 6,000 rpm are 31, 52 and 73 mph. The gearchange is extremely precise, with nothing rubbery about it, and very much in character for the type of car. The Midget shares with its main competitor the Triumph Spitfire the distinction of lacking synchromesh on 1st gear, which omission stands out more clearly as the years roll by. One learns to judge engine and road speeds correctly for double-declutching changes down, but it isn't easy here. On the other hand the renowned flexibility of the A-series engine will enable the lazy or less-skilled driver to use 2nd instead in many instances. The clutch is equally tolerant, coping adequately with the

considerable revs needed to re-start two-up on the 1-in-3 test slope.

The Midget's steering is everything a sports-car's ought to be—light, very accurate, highly responsive, highly geared and, once the rack is fully run-in, giving good feel without too much kickback. There is no slop worth mentioning, so that on first driving it, having got out of almost any other car, one tends to "over-steer". The car's obviously rigid construction shows through to the driver on a twisty road; it feels very much all one piece. Slippery roads are fun in the Midget, which is unusually well balanced. Handling characteristics are completely safe; slight initial understeer changing progressively to middling tail-breakaway when you try really hard. There is no suggestion of treachery at any stage, though such a light car obviously badly needs all-independent suspension. Ride is distinctly firm, the live-axled back end hopping outwards somewhat on bumpy bends taken quickly. As usual with an open car one is not conscious of suspension noise to any degree.

Brakes are unassisted discs front, drums

Unlike several other sports-cars, the Midget's hood does not need a lot of practice to furl properly

This view shows how comparatively little three-quarter-rear vision is lost by the large-windowed hood. Rubber-faced overriders are a sensible feature

Neat trim lines still, though you can only buy the car now with the black side-strip paint. There are no nave-plates on the wheels. Right: Wide-angle, lens-distorted view of the Midget in its most pleasant form, with hood down

rear. They work well, giving 1g stopping power on a dry track with the rear wheels just locking at a not-too-heavy 80lb pedal pressure. There is adequate fade resistance for all normal purposes, though anyone using the car at all competitively does well to fit hard pads and linings (available, like much other speed equipment at extra cost, from British Leyland Special Tuning at Abingdon). The handbrake holds the car facing up or down the 1-in-3 slope.

The driving position remains somewhat old-fashioned. Taller drivers have to sit closer to the large steering wheel than they may prefer, and have just enough legroom. The quickness of the steering means that the first objection doesn't matter too much; the second could only be improved by a major redesign of the car. Door openings are rather cramping for getting out, and the too-stiff door releases are much too far back for easy reach. There is however a pleasant feeling of snugness once you're in the very comfortable driving seat. No major control is remote from you, the gearchange falls readily to hand, and the pedals are well arranged.

Heel-and-toe changes come easily, and there is room to rest the left foot on the foot dip-switch. The horn is in the most natural place, the large padded centre of the steering wheel, and makes a surprisingly "quality" noise. Visibility is of course superb with the hood down, except perhaps through the somewhat fussy clutter of the front quarter-lights. It is better-than-average with the hood up, with no serious blind spots.

The facia is pleasingly straightforward, with no ostentatious transatlantic lips and jowls. One would however like to see some extra attention paid to more efficient design—combination of wiper and washer switch and plunger for one thing and, on each door, a more substantial-feeling but less stiff-winding window handle. When it broke away from its fixing screws we learnt that the quite generous parcel shelf on the passenger's side is made of something resembling cardboard. Uprating the crude water-valve may increase the heat output, but it does nothing towards proper control of temperature.

Hood erection and furling is easier than on most British sports-cars. The windscreen-frame clamps need a lot of effort, so does buttoning down the hood-cover press-studs. If one fitted a wireless it would, with the hood up, only be any real use at slow speeds, as wind noise becomes too loud above 60 mph. Keen enthusiasts who prefer to carry out their own servicing will find the Midget's engine accessibility pretty good. They will however need a lot more in tools than comes with the car—in the usual scruffy bag lying loose in the boots of so many British cars. Boot space is limited by the spare wheel, but careful stowage with squashy bags will get quite a lot in.

As stated at the beginning, there is not very much competition for the Midget (and the Sprite). It is a model that fills a large need, and one we would like to see developed considerably without losing its worthy character of sports-car primer for the not-so-well-off younger driver (and slightly dashing shopping car for two-car families). As it is, it remains an excellent little car which certainly achieves its primary object—that of being fun to drive. □

ACCELERATION

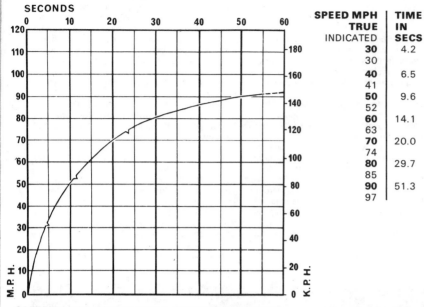

SPEED MPH TRUE INDICATED	TIME IN SECS
30	4.2
30	
40	6.5
41	
50	9.6
52	
60	14.1
63	
70	20.0
74	
80	29.7
85	
90	51.3
97	

SPEED RANGE, GEAR RATIOS AND TIME IN SECONDS

mph	Top (3.9)	3rd (5.29)	2nd (7.47)	1st (12.48)
10-30	—	8.0	5.5	4.0
20-40	10.7	7.4	5.2	—
30-50	10.4	7.2	6.3	—
40-60	10.7	8.3	—	—
50-70	12.3	10.3	—	—
60-80	16.9	—	—	—
70-90	31.8	—	—	—

Standing ¼-mile
19.6sec 69 mph
Standing kilometre
36.6sec 85mph
Test distance
1,270 miles
Mileage recorder
0.7 per cent
over-reading

PERFORMANCE
MAXIMUM SPEEDS

Gear	mph	kph	rpm
Top (mean)	94	151	5,700
(best)	96	155	5,800
3rd	78	126	6,400
2nd	55	89	6,400
1st	33	53	6,400

BRAKES

(from 70 mph in neutral)
Pedal load for 0.5g stops in lb

1	55-50		6	55-50
2	55-50		7	55-50
3	52-48		8	55-52
4	52-47		9	55-50
5	53-48		10	55-50

RESPONSE (from 30 mph in neutral)

Load	g	Distance
20lb	0.16	188ft
40lb	0.34	89ft
60lb	0.57	53ft
80lb	1.0	30.1ft
Handbrake	0.37	81ft
Max. Gradient 1 in 3		

CLUTCH
Pedal 35lb and 4.5 in.
MOTORWAY CRUISING

Indicated speed at 70mph	74mph
Engine (rpm at 70mph)	4,240rpm
(mean piston speed)	2,260ft/min.
Fuel (mpg at 70mph)	35.7
Passing (50-70mph)	10.4sec

COMPARISONS

MAXIMUM SPEED MPH

MG 1300 Mk II 2-door	(£968)	97
Ford Escort 1300GT 2-door	(£966)	95
MG Midget Mk III	**(£906)**	**94**
Triumph Spitfire 4 Mk 3	(£876)	92
Mini 1275GT	(£894)	86

0-60 MPH, SEC

Ford Escort 1300GT 2-door	12.2
Triumph Spitfire 4 Mk 3	14.0
MG Midget Mk III	**14.1**
MG 1300 Mk II 2-door	14.1
Mini 1275 GT	14.7

STANDING ¼-MILE, SEC

Triumph Spitfire 4 Mk 3	19.4
Ford Escort 1300GT 2-door	19.5
MG Midget Mk III	**19.6**
MG 1300 Mk II 2-door	19.6
Mini 1275 GT	19.8

OVERALL MPG

Triumph Spitfire 4 Mk 3	31.3
Mini 1275GT	30.2
MG Midget Mk III	**29.6**
Ford Escort 1300GT 2-door	27.5
MG 1300 Mk II 2-door	26.8

GEARING (with 145-13in. Michelin ZX tyres)

Top	16.5 mph per 1,000 rpm
3rd	12.15 mph per 1,000 rpm
2nd	8.62 mph per 1,000 rpm
1st	5.16 mph per 1,000 rpm

TEST CONDITIONS:
Weather: Fine. Wind: 5-10 mph. Temperature: 16 deg. C. (60 deg. F). Barometer: 29.7in. hg. Humidity: 40 per cent. Surfaces: Dry concrete and asphalt.

WEIGHT:
Kerb weight 13.8 cwt (1,546lb—702kg) (with oil, water and half full fuel tank). Distribution, per cent F. 52.5; R. 47.5. Laden as tested: 17.3cwt (1,934lb—878kg).

TURNING CIRCLES:
Between kerbs L. 32ft 3in.; R. 32ft 0in. Between walls L. 33ft 7in.; R. 33ft 4in., steering wheel turns, lock to lock 2¼.

Figures taken at 3,200 miles by our own staff at the Motor Industry Research Association proving ground at Nuneaton.

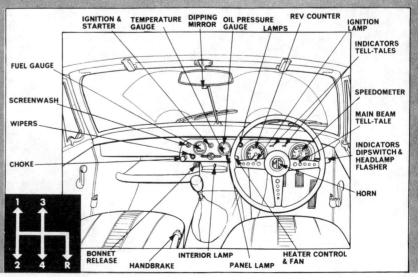

CONSUMPTION

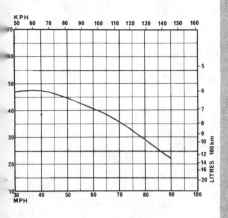

FUEL

At constant speeds—mpg)

30 mph	47.0
40 mph	47.6
50 mph	44.9
60 mph	40.4
70 mph	35.7
80 mph	28.5
90 mph	22.8

Typical mpg . . . 30 (9.4 litres/100km)
Calculated (DIN) mpg 32.5 (8.7 litres/100km)
Overall mpg . . . 29.6 (9.5 litres/100km)
Grade of fuel Premium, 4-star (min. 97 RM)

OIL

Miles per pint (SAE 10W/40) 1,200

SPECIFICATION FRONT ENGINE, REAR-WHEEL DRIVE

ENGINE
Cylinders . . . . 4, in line
Main bearings . 3
Cooling system . Water; pump, fan and thermostat
Bore . . . . . 70.6mm (2.78 in.)
Stroke . . . . 81.3mm (3.20 in.)
Displacement . 1,275 c.c. (77.8 cu.in.)
Valve gear . . . Overhead: pushrods and rockers
Compression ratio 8.8-to-1 Min. octane rating: 97 RM
Carburettors . . Twin SU HS2
Fuel pump . . . SU electric
Oil filter . . . . Full-flow, renewable element
Max. power . . 64 bhp (net) at 5,800 rpm
Max. torque . . 72 lb.ft (net) at 3,000 rpm

TRANSMISSION
Clutch . . . . Borg and Beck diaphragm spring 6.5in. dia.
Gearbox. . . . Four speed, synchromesh on 2nd, 3rd and top
Gear ratios . . . Top 1.0
Third 1.357
Second 1.916
First 3.2
Reverse 4.14
Final drive . . . Hypoid bevel 3.90-to-1

CHASSIS and BODY
Construction . . Integral, with steel body

SUSPENSION
Front . . . . . Independent, coil springs, wishbones, lever-arm dampers, optional anti-roll bar (not fitted to test car)
Rear . . . . . Live axle, half-elliptic leaf springs, lever arm dampers

STEERING
Type . . . . . Rack and pinion
Wheel dia. . . . 16in.

BRAKES
Make and type . Lockheed discs front, drums rear, no servo
Dimensions . . F 8.25in. dia
R 7in. dia 1.25in. wide shoes.
Swept area . . F 135 sq. in., R 55 sq. in.
Total 190 sq. in. (220 sq. in./ton laden)

WHEELS
Type . . . . Pressed steel perforated disc, four-stud fixing (wire wheels optional) 4.0 in. wide rim.
Tyres—make . . (cross-ply standard) Michelin on test car
—type . . ZX radial ply tubeless.
—size . . 145-13 in.

EQUIPMENT
Battery . . . . 12 Volt 43 Ah
Generator . . . Lucas C40 28 amp d.c.
Headlamps . . Sealed beam, 120/90 watt (total)
Reversing lamp . Standard
Electric fuses . . 4
Screen wipers . Single speed, self-parking
Screen washer . Standard, manual plunger
Interior heater . Standard, water-valve
Heated backlight Not applicable
Safety belts . . Extra, anchorages built in
Interior trim . . Pvc seats, pvc headlining
Floor covering . Carpet
Jack . . . . . Screw pillar
Jacking points . One each side in centre of body
Windscreen . . Toughened
Underbody
protection . . Phosphate treatment under paint

MAINTENANCE
Fuel tank . . . 6 Imp. gallons (no reserve) (27.3 litres)
Cooling system . 6 pints (including heater)
Engine sump . . 6.5 pints (3.7 litres) SAE 10W/40. Change oil every 6,000 miles. Change filter element every 6,000 miles.
Gearbox . . . . 2.5 pints SAE 10W/40. Top up every 12,000 miles.
Final drive . . . 1.5 pints SAE 90EP. Top up every 12,000 miles
Grease . . . . 7 points every 3,000 miles
Tyre pressures . F 22; R 24 psi (normal driving) F26, R 28 psi (fast driving) F 22; R 26 psi (full load)
Max. payload. . 350 lb (159 kg.)

PERFORMANCE DATA
Top gear mph per 1,000 rpm 16.5
Mean piston speed at max. power . 3,200 ft/min.
Bhp per ton laden 74

STANDARD GARAGE 16ft x 8ft 6in.

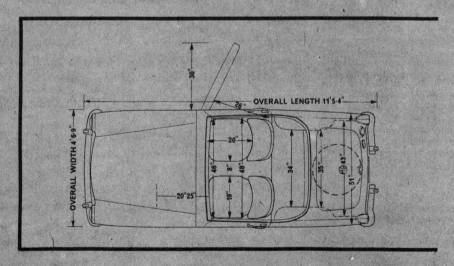

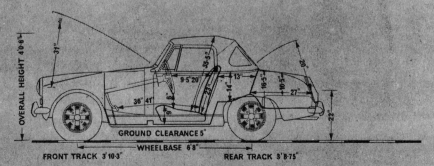

SCALE 0.3in. to 1ft
Cushions uncompressed

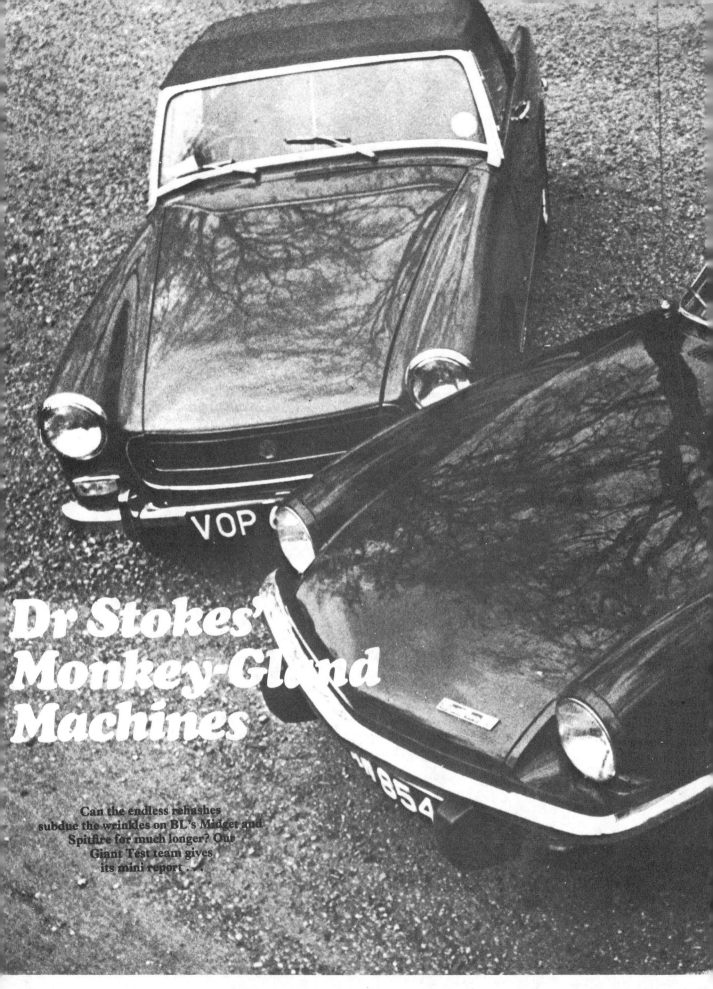

Dr Stokes' Monkey-Gland Machines

Can the endless rehashes subdue the wrinkles on BL's Midget and Spitfire for much longer? Our Giant Test team gives its mini report . . .

PERFORMANCE	
MG Midget	Triumph Spitfire
0–30 3.9	0–30 4.4 seconds
40 5.9	40 6.4
50 9.5	50 10.5
60 13.8	60 15
70 19.0	70 23.8
80 28.2	80 34.1

MAXIMUM SPEED	
96mph	91mph

FUEL CONSUMPTION	
27mpg	28mpg

FOR	
Higher performance	Reasonable performance
Lower price	Good handling
Smaller dimensions	Better roadholding
	Lower noise levels
	Roomier cockpit

AGAINST	
Cramped driving position	Poor ride
Poor ride	
Indifferent roadholding	

CAR june 1971

71

▶YOUNG ENTHUSIASTS—not to mention a few other categories of driver—have been choosing between MG Midget and Triumph Spitfire for quite a while now. Having decided to ignore small GT saloons and go the sports car route there's precious little else to consider. Kit cars are ruled out for the majority by inferior marketing, lack of service facilities and guarantees as much as anything else—a lot more people would buy Ginettas and the like if they knew more about them because they are very good. So it comes back to what the big manufacturers have to offer—and that's not much. The British-based American trio are content, as are most Continentals, to leave this specialised field to British Leyland.

Even if there were challengers they would find BL's pair pretty well entrenched. The Midget, now priced at £970, in its present basic form has been around for 10 years and its ancestry stretches back to 1958 when the Austin Healey Sprite, from which it is derived, came on the scene. The Midget is no more than a Sprite by another badge but now that the Healey name for trade use is reverting to Donald of that ilk (and will next be seen on a Jensen-built sports car) the Sprite part of the duo is due to disappear ere long.

The cousin/rival Triumph, £55 dearer, isn't that much younger. But, like the Midget, it's received enough modifications and improvements over the years to maintain much of its original appeal. On the Spitfire the latest batch of changes concerned the appearance and (belatedly) the suspension.

Let's deal with the looks first. The big change was around the tail, where the fussy, rounded rump was sliced off to be replaced by a cleaner, notched transom copied from big brother Stag. At the front the ugly raised seams along the wing tops were removed. The panel joint was moved down to the side of the wing and is now made by folding the sheet metal inwards rather than out. The top of the wing was re-finished with a razor-edge. At the same time the headlamps got painted instead of chrome bezels and the nose treatment was tidied up in detail. The overall result is a cleaner, altogether more pleasing shape that has lost all the cheapness imparted by the chrome-tipped wings of earlier models. It's a pity the budget didn't run to similar treatment for the rear wings. They still have the shiny strip but at least it's not so noticeable there.

The Midget changed rather less at its last facelift. It got some black paint along the rocker panels in a partially successful attempt to make the lines less dumpy. Some chunky-patterned steel wheels became standard, with wires an option as on the Spitfire, and the bonnet and boot were equipped with self-propping stays.

Black paint or no, the Midget is a full foot shorter than the better-proportioned Spitfire. And it looks it from most angles.

On getting in you will probably conclude that all 12 inches have been saved in the cockpit. The cramped quarters of the Midget come as an instant reminder of its aged basic design. Back then, it seems, a significant number of people thought it all right to be cramped into a sports car, arms akimbo and legs splayed. Today they don't with the result that the cockpit is best suited to midgets or sub-teenage children. Unfortunately the cockpit room has stayed unchanged over the years but the seats have become thicker and plusher. Since kids are unlikely to be driving it and midgets are in short supply (that was unintentional, I promise) the cockpit poses a problem for the rest of us. Even with the very limited seat travel used up the largish wheel is still stuck in your chest and you're sitting bow-legged at the pedals. Facia and windscreen are disconcertingly close, and so is everything else in the cockpit.

The Spitfire seems almost roomy by comparison. Six-footers can get far enough away from wheel and pedals for comfort and to drivers of all shapes and sizes the higher seating position means better visibility than in the Midget.

In both cars there's a space behind the seats that comes in handy for tucking away small objects. Or it does when the hood is erect. Furled, the soft top hogs most of this compartment.

The hoods currently in use have come a long way from those of the earliest Midgets and Spitfires. They can be folded down in proper convertible style, the frames remaining attached to the body. On the Spitfire plastic covers are used on the rails passing near the occupants' heads. In both instances raising or lowering the top is several minutes' work, best done by two people although one can cope quite well alone. As ever, the windscreen rail clamps have a tensioning function and need more muscle than many a woman can muster even in a crisis like rain.

Even the frailest woman, however, should have little trouble with the rest of the controls. The Triumph's are particularly light to use, though some might want a servo or at least more progressive action on the rather dead brake pedal, while the Midget's gearchange was stiffer than it should have been. Experience shows that these boxes improve with age...

The customary sports car instrumentation of speedo and tacho, fuel level, oil pressure and water temperature gauges occurs on the Midget. The Spitfire relies on a warning light for oil pressure. We thought the layout of the instruments, also the minor controls and switches, ill-considered —in fact, confusing—on both.

This is all the more a pity when you remember that sports machines like these are supposedly *the* cars for enthusiastic drivers. But enthusiasts, according to the gospel of British Leyland, don't mind that sort of thing. Neither, apparently, are they supposed to mind the inefficient heating and ventilation systems of this pair. The Midget has opening quarterlights, the Spitfire not, but both had gaps between hood and windscreen or window through which fresh air could enter. Neither car has proper direction-controllable fresh air outlets. And the heating controls function with all the precision and predictability of an ageing geyser.

There are other things too that you have to put up with in these 1971 sports cars. Wind roar plus mechanical noise (and the usual terrible transmission whine in the Midget) and suitably burpy exhausts combine to make a din that precludes conversation above 60mph. Even at a meagre 40 or so the Spitfire is becoming a trifle wearing and the Midget is already downright noisy.

Equally tiresome is the ride on anything but a billiards table of a surface. Bumps, especially the kind that abound on country lanes, soon have the Spitfire joggling like a massage machine. The harder sprung Midget feels the bumps even more. So do its occupants.

These high noise levels and rotten ride qualities were once supposed to be part of the fun— an inescapable part of high performance motoring. Well, Chapman proved years ago with the Lotus that suspension doesn't have to be hard to work correctly.

Saloon designers have found ways of sound damping that would apply to. the Triumph and MG. And in any case the performance is not all that high for 1971!

The days when sports cars were automatically the masters of the saloon are over. We would back a comparable GT saloon, say Ford's 1300 GT Escort or the 1275 GT Mini, to match the Spitfire and Midget lap for lap on a racing circuit. The saloons have been catching up in both handling and performance over the last few years and some of them are now level-pegging if not ahead of the alleged sports cars.

Until last autumn, in fact, we would have doubted the Spitfire's ability even to equal some of its more staid rivals when it came to cornering. Up to that date, you will recall, its Herald parentage meant that it was cursed with the same swing-axle rear end. This meant that initial understeer switched abruptly and prematurely to oversteer as the high rear roll centre jacked the back up and let the wheels droop in a classic positive-camber knock-kneed pose. The effect could be induced even earlier and for the novice even more unsettlingly by driving into a corner and then lifting off.

Eventually, rather late in the day, Triumph put a stop to this. The current Mk IV Spitfire has not the wishbone-geometry rear end of the once similarly afflicted GT6 but an ingenious modification of existing components. Only the master leaf of the transverse rear spring is clamped to the chassis. The rest of the leaves are held via a rubber pad on to a pivot so that they still support the car's weight but can also rock about their axis. Thus practically all roll stiffness has been eliminated from the rear end. At the front it has been increased by a corresponding amount with a thicker anti-roll bar. So the Spitfire rolls no more than before, which is to say very little, but with nearly all the roll loading on the outer front tyre it is now a reformed character. It still starts out with understeer but that changes to near neutral handling as the *g* force increases and only changes to oversteer at an advanced stage and then in a highly controllable fashion. So the Spitfire has gained in both handling, for it can now be thrown around with abandon *and* confidence, and roadholding, inasmuch as that sheer cornering power is now a good deal higher than before. All this still with the basic swing axle...

Such developments put it rather a long way ahead of the poor old Midget. Hampered by its leaf-sprung back axle, harder suspension settings as well as stiff damping, plus an inordinately short (6ft 8in) wheelbase the MG remains very much a leaper from crag to crag. Bumps easily unsettle a sometimes tenuous grip on the road, making it hard to tell when axle hop ends and unadulterated oversteer begins. The cramped driving position does little to encourage dashing tactics.

Like the Spitfire, the Midget has a disappointingly dead-feeling disc front/drum rear brake system.

Being based largely on bits and pieces from saloons this pair have extremely familiar engines. The A series unit in the Midget and the Spitfire's ex-Standard engine share the usual basic features: three main bearings, for instance, and pushrod valves, not to mention constricted porting and other things that impede development. Notwithstanding this, Triumph manage to get a respectable 63bhp out of the 1296cc capacity, with the knowledge that there's more to come just from changing to the long-stroke crank used in the 1500 saloon. But there could be a problem here with bearings.

Journal sizes went up less than a year ago in an attempt to increase bearing life; higher loadings from enlarged capacity could put the engineers back to square one.

The Midget's aged but still willing A series is fractionally more efficient, producing one extra bhp from 21 fewer ccs. For some reason we have yet to fathom BLMC is keeping some power up its corporate sleeve here for the similarly-engined MG 1300 gets an extra six bhp which wouldn't come amiss in the two-seater. Nor would it mean any loss in flexibility for the Midget is more than sufficiently amenable to lugging along in too high a gear if a lazy driver insists. The Spitfire is not so happy under these conditions, losing out not so much on tractability of the power unit as in the snatch that overrun all too easily builds up in the multi-jointed transmission.

Talking of transmission, though, the Spitfire does score easily in the cog-changing part of the drive line. For a start, it now actually has synchromesh on bottom gear (where *will* all this development end, one wonders) while the Midget continues to lack this feature—almost alone among 1971 cars. Just to compound the felony, first is none too easy to

engage on the move, and sometimes at rest, even with competent double-declutching. The Spitfire scores again by making overdrive available as an extra-cost option. It works on third and top and is controlled by a switch built into the gear knob. Very convenient.

The presence of overdrive does a lot for fuel consumption (in addition to enhancing general drivability) which in our hard-driving hands averaged around 28mpg, though many an owner is probably getting better than 30. Another factor here was the recent step up in axle ratio from 4.11 to 3.89 to one. The other side of this coin is of course that the higher final drive knocks something off the acceleration. In this case the Spitfire certainly felt a little less lively than earlier models and confirmed our fears by its acceleration figures.

The Midget, gaining from its much lower weight, proved quicker by a useful amount all the way up to maximum. Initial acceleration would have been even better were it not for a recent increase in the ratio of that accursed first gear. Fuel consumption at 27mpg was only slightly heavier.

Neither car stood out as a sparkling performer in ultimate terms. There are plenty of 1300s around that can match their acceleration and top speed. The difference is that these other 1300s are saloons, with four seats.

So why buy a little two-seater unless you're a masochist? Well, there's no doubt that they're fun to drive. Sitting down there with that long bonnet out front, amidst all the mechanical clamour, you feel part of the action in a way you never can in a saloon. Then there's that huge 20th century myth about sports cars that has permeated the whole Western world: they do things for a young man's style, and make implications about his virility that no small saloon can match. Which, you might sardonically point out, is why they sell so well in America where extroverts are thicker on the ground. They're an incitement to quick motoring. They make every journey feel an epic of automotive adventure.

The Midget feels outdated now though the much more modern Spitfire should be good for a few more years yet—especially with the boost of a 1500 engine. But manufacturing costs are soaring for these relatively limited output cars and are being forced up even higher as the parental saloons are discontinued as times change. ●

The engines of the Midget (top) and Spitfire are old faithfuls, the 1275cc MG unit dating back to Morris Minors of the 1950s. Strangely, in MG form it gives less power than in the Cooper S. The Spitfire unit is shared with the Herald and in updated form with the Toledo, and also dates from way back in the days when Standard made cars

The Spitfire interior (top) is more simple and functional than that of the MG, with better leg room and a more satisfactory facia. The Spitfire's hood can be unclipped and folded fairly quickly but the MG's takes longer

Atlantis Midget

Apart from the word Atlantis signwritten on the back and sides of he car, it looks exactly like an ordinary MG Midget. But the 1600 GT Ford engine makes it almost 50 per cent more powerful than the standard 1275cc Mark 4 Spridget, just enough to beat an MGB. The idea is good and the engine installation is well carried out: we feel that the Atlantis conversion would deserve great praise but for one major drawback—the test car tended to overheat in traffic jams and cook the occupants, though an electric fan would probably have cured this defect.

The Ford engine always started up very easily, the distinctive Cortina-type noises seemed pleasantly incongruous in these unaccustomed surroundings. We have always liked the Spridget for its fun value, despite the somewhat antique layout, but as David Martell of Car Preparations points out, the Spridget's performance is now equalled by many medium-sized family cars and has acquired an image of impotence as a result. With a top speed of over 105 mph and 0-60 mph time of 10.3 sec. Car Preps' Atlantis is hardly underpowered and with the optional 3.727:1 back axle ratio replacing the standard 3.9:1 unit it gains longer legs for more relaxed high speed cruising. At the same time the extra torque of the big engine makes the Atlantis even smoother and more flexible than standard.

The ordinary Midget is good for 95 mph, but the Atlantis has another 11 mph to go—as might be expected with such an engine swap the performance improvements are very noticeable to the driver right through the range. To drive a Spridget quickly it must be used to the rather meagre limit, whereas the Atlantis version can outpace most of the traffic without stretching itself. The engine in the test car was not one of the '71 series Kent motors, so a new Atlantis would be 5 or 6 per cent more powerful.

Steady driving at low speeds proved very economical—up to 50 mph it was using less petrol than the standard Midget or the MGB—but once the second choke comes into use it gets much more thirsty as the overall figure of 24.4 mpg shows. The Sprite we tested last year recorded a creditable 30.2 mpg overall. Cruising at high speeds there is very little to choose between the three cars shown in the performance tables. The MGB, of course, was able to keep its fuel consumption down to a minimum by means of the well-geared overdrive.

Car Preps fit a 12 gallon fuel tank as standard which gives the Atlantis a useful range of up to 370 miles or about 300 miles when driven hard.

At £1166 the Atlantis is £196 more than the standard Midget and £142 less than the MGB. Whether it's worth paying the extra and getting the more spacious and comfortable MGB is a matter of personal taste, but Spridget fans will be pleased to note that the Atlantis retains the essential character and behaviour that has made the standard car so popular over the years.

The gearchange is pleasing to use, though the Ford box is not quite as light and notchy as the BL unit. The gear ratios provide the following speeds in the intermediates at 6500 rpm: 31, 49, 82 mph. The 'B' is the same in first and second but 76 mph is the limit in third. At 70 mph the Atlantis is revving at a fraction under 4000 rpm and we felt that it is a pity that there is no more room in the transmission tunnel for an overdrive system: the engine could easily have coped with a higher gear for economical cruising.

There were no radius rods on the rear axle and we were surprised to find that axle tramp was by no means excessive. Radius rods are available if customers want them badly enough, but the standard transmission can take the extra power without twisting itself in a knot.

The only modification at the rear end is a

Car: MG Midget (Motor Road Test on Austin-Healey Sprite 10.10.70)
Tuner: Car Preparations Ltd, 8 Union Street, Bedford, Beds
Telephone: Bedford 56768
Conversion: Ford 1600GT engine and gearbox into MG Midget bodyshell; Panhard rod; ⅝in. front anti-roll bar; higher final drive; 12 gallon fuel tank; DS11 brake pads and servo-assistance

	Atlantis Midget 1600cc	Austin-Healey Sprite 1275cc	MGB 1798cc
Maximum speed			
Lap	106.1	95.0	105.0
Best ¼ mile	106.6	96.8	108.3
Mean Maximile	103.6	94.7	102.2
Best Maximile	104.2	96.8	105.8
Acceleration			
	sec	sec	sec
mph			
0- 30	3.7	4.0	3.6
0- 40	5.5	6.5	5.7
0- 50	7.5	9.3	7.8
0- 60	10.3	13.5	11.0
0- 70	14.3	19.1	14.9
0- 80	19.6	28.5	19.8
0- 90	27.7	45.7	27.5
0-100	38.5	—	39.2
Standing ¼ mile	17.8	19.3	18.2
Standing Km	33.0	36.2	33.6
In Top			
mph			
20- 40	8.8	9.9	9.1
30- 50	8.7	9.6	8.8
40- 60	8.9	9.8	8.6
50- 70	9.5	11.7	9.9
60- 80	10.6	16.0	11.3
70- 90	12.8	—	13.9
80-100	19.2	—	21.0
In Third			
mph			
10-30	6.2	7.1	6.6
20-40	5.7	6.8	6.1
30-50	5.6	6.8	5.9
40-60	5.6	7.4	6.1
50-70	6.3	9.4	7.2
60-80	9.4	—	8.9
Fuel consumption			
Steady mph			
30	54.0	46.9	47.4*
40	49.7	45.3	40.2
50	41.6	42.5	40.9*
60	36.2	39.6	32.9
70	32.1	34.1	33.8*
80	28.8	29.0	24.8
90	23.5	23.8	24.4*
100	18.5	—	16.6
Overall	24.4	30.2	23.7
Touring	31.4	36.3	29.2
*Overdrive			

Panhard rod. We did not have the opportunity to try a car without this device, but with it the rear end behaves very well in corners. The go-kart feel of the Midget is retained on the Atlantis, the car being as controllable as ever. Kerb weight is up by about 60 lb., but by siting the engine well back in the chassis, Car Preps have achieved a front/rear weight distribution of 50/50. Despite a ⅝ in. anti-roll bar on the front suspension there is more of a tendency for the body to roll in corners: the extra weight also manifests itself with a little more plunging of the suspension on bumps and more dive in the front suspension under heavy braking. We felt that stiffer shock absorbers might have helped to cut down transient body movements. Yet the steering remains light and responsive and we all felt that we could chuck the car into corners with complete confidence.

One particularly masochistic road tester drove 100 miles across country in the pouring rain with the hood down and David Martell's *Led Zeppelin II* tape blaring away at full volume. He claimed that the extra power made this an exhilarating experience, and confirmed that the wet weather handling

Car Preparations have made a neat job of installing the Ford 1600 GT motor in the Midget

on the 4½J Michelin ZX radials is very safe and predictable. The most satisfying way to drive the Atlantis, as with any Midget, is to set it up for a corner on mild oversteer and power it through with a touch of opposite lock. The point is that the Atlantis responds to such treatment as well as the standard car, yet has the power to make it even more enjoyable.

The brakes—which have a Lockheed servo and DS11 pads at the front—are very effective and transmit plenty of feel to the driver so that under emergency stop conditions it is easy to tell exactly when the wheels are on the point of locking up. Even with the servo the pedal needs to be pushed quite hard, but the effort required is acceptable.

Inside the cockpit everything is standard and our usual criticisms apply. The driving position, pedal layout, and gearlever position are good but the minor controls are poorly arranged. The rev counter was accurate at steady speeds but there was too much float at other times. The ride is acceptable but rather bumpy. The exhaust system on the

CONTINUED ON PAGE 118

Morris Garages

Above: Midget Mk III is distinguished by recessed flat black grille with MG medallion instead of vertical bars used on earlier versions. Dimensions and body shape remain the same but with a number of detail changes.
Left: Small size of the Midget can be gauged from the size of the driver. Wire wheels are standard but disc wheels can be ordered.
Bottom: The cockpit of the Midget, adequate in the Mk I for six-footers, has shrunk over the years due to modifications, some of which were NOT the desire of the builder. Roll-up windows cut lateral room but required dash padding and thick seats really cramp it.

Comparison

From 1923 to the present, the products that have rolled out of the doors of the old Morris Garages and later, Abingdon-on-Thames, have been alternately praised and damned, eulogized and slandered, under- and over-rated—often with good reason on either account. In all the years during which MGs have been built it is likely that 99 out of a hundred of them have been driven harder and with more enthusiasm than the builders ever thought possible. Such treatment engenders praise for the cars that can seemingly absorb the punishment and criticism because the treatment inevitably results in things falling off. But MGs have always been that way and remain so to this day.

The comments one hears about MGs in many ways recall those made by U.S. Navy people concerning British wartime ships: often uncomfortable, wet, bluff and straightforward almost to the point of crudity—but they got the job done. So it is with the MG; blunt, strong and, by today's standards of sophistication, almost crude, they accomplish their purpose (which we will explore momentarily) in a manner

both surprising and admirable. Where other, more complicated cars accommodate themselves to the road, the MG fights back gamely and tenaciously—and usually wins.

The makers of MG have always been long on heritage and while the current series of MGs have been with us in one mark or modification or another for roughly a decade, the ancestry of some of the major bits and pieces goes back a good deal further than that. The engine in the MGB, for example, is the B-Type BMC unit originally designed for the Austin A-40 while the power unit in the Midget originally saw the light of day in the Austin A-20 and the Morris Minor Mk II. To

make the point even stronger, the MGB rides on a chassis and suspension that is essentially identical to that of the MGA, first introduced to the world in the Fall of 1954, though with a slightly lower spring rate to reduce the original harshness and increase road compliance. At first glance, and even at a second, this would seem to shout *obsolescence* in words of brass. A better description would be "well proven" though that is often used as a euphemism for "obsolete." Probably "matured" describes things more accurately, simply because that is exactly what has happened to these supposedly venerable components

Morris Garages

and to the cars themselves. The first MGB engine was a direct development of the last of the MGA units which in itself was a thorough redesign of the earlier B-Type engines. Though sharing the same 3.5-inch stroke, the new engine was given a 3.2-inch bore which brought the displacement up to 1798cc (109 c.i.). Two years later another redesign gave it five main bearings instead of the classic three and brought the horsepower up to 98. In 1968 the necessity of adding an air injection pump to reduce pollution brought the power back down to 92 at 5400 in spite of what appears to be roughly a Stage II type of tune which includes a 180-degree tuned exhaust header

Above: As with the Midget, the MGB has been given detail changes throughout the decade. Among the latest are the recessed grille and placement of the Octagon on the grille instead of the front of the hood.
Left: Perhaps the biggest and most welcome change is the new top, replacing the old Erector-set that had to be disassembled and stowed in the trunk when not in use. It's stiff but far more satisfactory.
Bottom: The major change in the interior is the thick padding that replaces the earlier attractive dash to satisfy U.S. requirements. It also covers the former glove compartment.

among other things. This is the plant that powers the current MGB and MGB GT. And in spite of the fact that by today's standards this is lawn mower and garden tractor power, an MGB will do what MGs have been doing for nearly half a century when in its own sort of country, which is to suck the headlights out of more prosaic machinery including a number of our own more respectable domestic passenger cars.

The Midget, too, is the result of a number of developments though not all of them always for the best. Along about 1960, John Thornley and the men of Abingdon were given the job of updating and revising the popular "Bugeye" Sprite. As Thornley admits, they got rid of the froglike look just about the time it was catching on, an accomplishment that still infuriates Sprite enthusiasts. At the same time they decided to do a bit of what BMC (and latterly BLMC) critics called "badge engineering" and with minor trim changes and a slight rise in price, hung the MG octagon on the newly designed car and revived the old Midget name with the inevitable result that both cars became known as Spridgets, an appellation that hangs on to this day although the Sprite badge has been discontinued for several years.

These first Spridgets, like the Bugeyes before them were true roadsters with all that the word implies, including arm, shoulder and leg room along with the less desirable properties of being windy and, on rainy days, wet. They were also, thanks to the quarter elliptic rear springs inherited from the Sprite, bouncy and overly responsive. A new redesign seemed to be in order, whereupon, enter the MG Midget Mk II and the Sprite Mk III. The rear springs gave way to a parallel semi-elliptic

design similar to that of the MGB. Making the Spridget even more like the MGB, they also added roll-up windows and more thickly padded seats. The Spridget was now more comfortable, with less tendency to dart around with minor wheel twitches and was also reasonably dry in wet weather, provided you took care to roll the windows up *after* you closed the doors and not before. It also had considerably less arm and shoulder room, thanks to the thicker doors. Along with all this came an engine change with an increase in displacement to 1098cc, up from 948.

Then along came Safety and Emissions and Chief Engineer Sydney Enever gave the little machine another overhaul. The engine size went up to 1275cc, the same as that of the hottest Mini-Coopers, to offset the crippling effects of emissions tuning, including an air pump. This engine gives a rated 62 bhp at 6000 rpm but even

more important, a healthy increase in torque to 72 lbs.-ft. at a low 3000 rpm which produced enough low-end torque to make the Midget competitive with the MGB at stoplights and other low rpm activities although the advantage tends to fall off as speeds get up toward the top end. As matter of fact, we tend to doubt that peak rpm figure of 6000 since performance in terms of acceleration fell off after 5000 rpm in any gear. Another change, dictated by the safety bureaucrats rather than any rational engineering or styling reasons is the addition of even thicker seats with tall headrests, a thickly padded dash and more padding on the doors. The result is that the latest Midget is definitely on the cramped side for anyone over about five feet, nine inches and 165 lbs., where the first Sprites and Spridgets could accommodate a six footer with ease. What hap-

Morris Garages

pened was that the thick dash moved the steering wheel back, the seats won't go back as far as they used to go and the pedals are where they always were. In consequence a six-foot-plus driver can't get far enough back and the short driver is too close to the wheel when the pedals are in the right place. The person who cut his sports car teeth on TC and TD Series MGs or on a Triumph TR-2 can learn to live with it, especially now that they have made the seats so that they tilt back, but others not so trained and truly shriven in the MG cult find the situation so annoying as to make the whole car unappealing. All of which is a shame because if the car is in the kind of situation for which it was designed and driven with the realization that it is, after all, not a Formula car and doesn't handle like one but rather takes to flinging with the abandon that characterized its earlier namesakes, it can be an appealing little car indeed. All this in spite of the number of built-in aggravations, many of which were no fault of the builder's in the first place.

And then there is the MG about which one hears very little slander and that usually from those who have never been exposed to one—the MGB GT. The GT is beyond a doubt the most civilized MG ever built, including the various sedans of past years. One might suspect that it would be little more than an MGB with a roof. In one sense it is and in another it is much more. It handles very much like the roadster except that it seems a bit smoother in steer characteristics and with better balance. This last is explained when the car is weighed. Our particular example weighed 1,170 lbs. at the front and 1,190 lbs. at the rear and it would be hard indeed to find a car nearer to a 50/50 distribution than that. In a steady-state turn, as on a 200-ft. circle, it also shows significantly less understeer than the roadster with 3.5 degrees for left turns and 3.0 for right turns where the roadster shows well over 4 degrees in both directions. In terms of absolute lateral g forces it holds almost as well with .72g as compared with the .75 showed by the roadster, a small difference that could likely be explained by the differences in tires as well as the 120 lbs. more weight of the GT.

What all that does *not* tell you is how comfortable the coupe can be under almost any conditions. With the windows up it is even quiet inside and with them down, surprisingly free from wind buffeting. There is definitely some noise with the windows open, both from the road and from the exhaust, which to those in the car has a definite, strong drone—but only to those *inside* the car or close to it. This is the result of a rather clever bit of deception on the part of the folks at Abingdon. They know that the usual sports car driver in general and the MG driver in particular likes to hear a bit of a rap in the exhaust

note. They also know that such a rap is not popular with all segments of the general body politic. On the MGB and GT they have put a rather large, efficient but free-flowing muffler all the way to the rear which damps out all that pipe resonance that gives the distinctive snore to a free-flow system. But just behind the point where the secondary pipes of the header system come together they have placed a resonator that is more sounding board than anything else. Its resonance is heard as the distinctive drone associated with MGs since the Year One. It sounds nice to the occupants and to those standing nearby but it doesn't disturb the neighbors or the law. Clever. We wouldn't have noticed it at all but for the fact we dinked one on a rock and changed its state of "tune" to the point where it actually sounded like an uncorked pipe from inside the car. We searched for 10 minutes for the pulled or separated pipe before we discovered the source of the snarl. A whack with a hammer restored the tone to its former muted snore.

Now all of the foregoing is very well and good but it really doesn't give a true indication of what MGs—or any other sports cars—are all about. It is as patently unfair to "test" a sports car on a drag strip and a succession of city streets and freeways as it is to run a Cadillac limousine at a road course and winding byways and call either a definitive test. In consequence we

Top: The weight distribution of the MGB GT is almost exactly 50/50 and the handling as with all the cars tested is solid and secure without the bounce once associated with MGs in general. The GT is a cruiser. Above: The Midget engine (left) is derived from the Austin A-type block and now has 1275cc displacement with 62 hp even with the air pump. The MGB engine (right) is an expanded version of the B-type block with 1798cc, 92 bhp at 5400 rpm. Its best feature is torque with 110 lbs.-ft. at a low, low 3000 rpm which allows tremendous range since it will rev willingly beyond its normal peaking speed to 6000 and over. Bottom: The rear end treatments of all the cars has remained pretty much the same except for backup lights and Midget bumper.

Morris Garages

used the MGs to inaugurate a test loop of just on 1,000 miles that will be used whenever practicable in the future. This loop runs from Los Angeles to Reno and back. The course runs over a long stretch of freeway to the foothills of the Sierras, up through the winding, two-lane Highway 49 through the Gold Rush country, then across the mountains to Reno, back down the spine of the Sierras to the Mojave desert and thence back to Los Angeles. On this loop there are sections that duplicate conditions in every part of the country from the byways of the East through the flat straights of the Midwest to the freeways of the West. There are switchbacks, grades, undulating lanes and one legal flat-out stretch.

On this loop we rediscovered what MGs are and are not all about. What they are NOT all about (with the exception of the GT) is freeways. In an MG a freeway is one long interminable, boring drag strip without end. This part left us with the feeling that a warning buzzer should sound in an MG, especially the Midget, after one

continuous run of 50 miles on a freeway at which point you have five minutes to find an offramp and some sort of thoroughfare with turns and speed variations. If ignored—BOOM!—you're vaporized and the car goes off looking for someone more appreciative.

What MGs ARE all about are the mountains and the tighter, twistier the road and the higher the altitude to about 7,000 feet the better. From about 3,000 feet up the MG—Midget, B or GT—comes into its own and doesn't begin to suffer altitude bronchitis like ordinary cars until the 7,000 foot level is reached. There is some loss of power but very little compared to your average V8 family sedan. This is partially the characteristic of a properly tuned four-cylinder engine and partially due to the S.U. carburetors which are to a great extent self-compensating for altitude in regard to mixture control. As a result, the MG still has a power reserve to accelerate up grades and around switchbacks and lesser turns and the handling to use it. Where more prosaic machinery is huffing for breath and tip-

CONTINUED ON PAGE 118

	MGB GT	MGB	MG MIDGET
Engine	4-Cylinder, in-line OHV	4-Cylinder, in-line OHV	4-Cylinder, in-line OHV
Bore & stroke—ins.	3.15 x 3.5	3.15 x 3.5	2.8 x 3.2
Displacement—cu. in.	109 (1798cc)	109 (1798cc)	78 (1275cc)
HP @ RPM	92 @ 5400	92 @ 5400	62 @ 6000
Torque: lbs.-ft. @ RPM	110 @ 3000	110 @ 3000	72 @ 3000
Compression Ratio/Fuel	8.8:1/Premium	8.8:1/Premium	8.8:1/Premium
Carburetion	2 S.U. HS-4	2 S.U. HS-4	2 S.U. HS-2
Transmission	4-speed, all synchro	4-speed, all synchro	4-speed, synchro 2-3-4
Final Drive Ratio	3.91:1	3.91:1	3.73
Steering type	Rack and pinion	Rack and pinion	Rack and pinion
Turning Diameter (curb-to-curb-ft.)	32	32	28
Wheel Turns (lock to lock)	3.0	3.0	2.3
Tire size	155Rx14	155Rx14	145Rx13
Brakes	Disc front/drum rear	Disc front/drum rear	Disc front/drum rear
Front Suspension	Unequal length A-arms, lever shocks, sway bar	Unequal length A-arms, lever shocks, sway bar	Unequal length A-arms, lever shocks
Rear Suspension	Live axle, semi-elliptic leaf springs, lever shocks	Live axle, semi-elliptic leaf springs, lever shocks	Live axle, semi-elliptic leaf springs, lever shocks
Body/Frame Construction	Unit steel	Unit steel	Unit steel
Wheelbase—ins.	91.0	91.0	80.0
Overall length—ins.	152.5	152.5	137.4
Width—ins.	59.9	59.9	56.6
Height—ins.	49.4	49.4	48.6
Front Track—ins.	49.25	49.25	46.3
Rear Track—ins.	49.25	49.25	44.8
Curb Weight—lbs.	2,360	2,240	1,635
Fuel Capacity—gals.	12	12	8
Oil Capacity—qts.	4.8	4.8	4.0

PERFORMANCE

	MGB GT	MGB	MG MIDGET
Acceleration			
0-30 mph	4.1	4.0	4.8
0-45 mph	7.4	7.8	8.9
0-60 mph	12.8	13.1	15.2
0-75 mph	20.8	21.5	26.9
Standing Start ¼-mile			
Mph	72.7	74.0	69.5
Elapsed time	19.0	19.3	20.0
Passing speeds			
40-60 mph (3rd)	6.2	6.7	7.5
50-70 mph (3rd)	7.7	8.1	9.9
Speeds in gears*			
1st ...mph @ rpm	28.5 @ 5500	28.5 @ 5500	29.0 @ 5500
2nd ...mph @ rpm	45.0 @ 5500	45.0 @ 5500	49.5 @ 5500
3rd ...mph @ rpm	70.0 @ 5500	70.0 @ 5500	69.0 @ 5500
4th ...mph @ rpm	96.2 @ 5500	96.2 @ 5500	96.2 @ 5500
Mph per 1000 rpm (in top gear)	17.5	17.5	17.5
Stopping distances**			
From 30 mph	31 ft.	29 ft.	29 ft.
From 60 mph	133 ft.	134 ft.	134 ft.
Gas mileage range	25-28	25-28	25-30

Speedometer error

MGB GT — Car speedometer

	30	45	50	60	70	80
Electric speedometer	30	44.8	49.3	58.9	68.7	78.2

MGB — Car speedometer

	30	45	50	60	70	80
Electric speedometer	28.0	42.0	47.2	56.1	65.0	75.0

MG MIDGET — Car speedometer

	30	45	50	60	70	80
Electric speedometer	29.0	44.0	49.0	59.0	68.9	77.8

*Speeds in gears are at shift points (limited by the length of track) and do not represent maximum speeds.
**Stopping distances are averages of 6 hard stops just short of lockup.

MG MIDGET

NOW, HERE IS ONE YOU CAN DO THINGS TO IF YOU HAVE THE TIME. OUR RATING IS GOOD.

By PAUL WEISSLER

SERVICE TESTING

■ Some 13 years ago, I purchased an Austin-Healey Sprite. The price was under $1800, making it the lowest-priced sports car on the market. For that kind of money, one bought two seats and handling, not long-lasting quality. The car required a good deal of work after a while, but happily most routine service was quite easy.

British Leyland's contract with Donald Healey ran out, and the Healey marque was dropped as a result. The Sprite lives on, however, as the MG Midget, and I subjected a Midget to a PIC Service Test. There have been some changes over the years. The price tag is in excess of $2500, which probably isn't that much of an increase. The quality isn't enormously better, and the serviceability is a bit worse, primarily because of anti-air pollution hardware.

No. 1 spark plug, for example, is blocked by an air pump, which helps control exhaust emissions. The pump is held by two bolts that are reasonably accessible, so spark plug replacement gets a fair rating and 5 points.

The generator is under the air pump, and once you've got that off, the generator is a snap. The pre-smog control generator was a five-minute job to yank; the current one is perhaps a 10-minute job. The rating is fair to good and six points.

The fan belt also gets a fair to good rating and six points.

The air filters (two of them) are held by five bolts, which seems excessive. But they are all accessible so replacement gets a good rating and seven points.

The oil filter faces downward and you must get it from underneath. The car is low-slung, so you'll have to jack it up and fit a safety stand.

The filter itself is a spin-on. Someone apparently convinced the British that the bolt-held container with a replaceable element and an O-ring gasket was not a pleasure to change.

I have rated other British cars with replaceable element oil filters harshly (zero points for the filter). So although this filter points downward and requires jacking the car, I feel that the incorporation of the spin-on

Engine compartment of MG Midget holds a conventional in-line four-cylinder pushrod powerplant with dual carburetor setup.

Air pump blocks access to the No. 1 sparkplug. Fortunately, removal of the pump poses no serious problem in this case.

Air cleaners are held by five bolts but at least that's three less than on the Jaguar V-12 which we test in this issue.

Hand reaches down behind heater air duct to slip wrench on to battery cable at starter switch. Room is limited but adequate.

All head bolts can be tightened with torque wrench without special adapters. Rating is good and a full eight points here.

Two bolts hold brake master cylinder, one of them a toughie. Ratchet, extension, universal joint and socket just makes it.

(13 years late) is commendable. The oil filter rating therefore is fair and five points.

The distributor is on the right side of the engine and in the pre-smog control days was moderately accessible. The space is a bit tighter these days what with hoses, but it's still quite tolerable. The rating for the distributor lock (a pinch-clamp) is good and seven points; the rating for the ingnition points is fair and

five points.

The battery cables are surprisingly good. There is a two section cable to the starter. One section goes to the starter switch under the heater air duct, the second from the switch to the starter itself. If your hands aren't too big you can get to all connections without undue hardship. The rating is good and seven points.

The head bolts are very nice. Two bolts

SERVICE TESTING CHECKLIST	
(Max. 8 points each)	
1. Spark plugs	7. Cylinder
2. Ignition	head bolts
breaker points	8. Fuel pump
3. Distributor lockbolt	9. Battery cables
or locknut	10. Air filter
4. Generator	11. Oil filter
5. Carburetor	12. Brake master
6. Fan belt	cylinder
13. Heavy repairs	
Bonus Points	
(Max. 2 points each)	
1. Dashboard bulbs	3. Starter motor
2. Speedometer Cable	4. Radiator Hoses

hold the rocker cover and all head bolts are readily accessible with an ordinary socket. This is one thing that hasn't changed a whit from the original model. The rating is good and the full eight points.

The fuel pump is an electric unit in the rear. This requires jacking up the car to change, but I believe remotely-mounted electric fuel pumps are essentially good, and while this location doesn't match that of the Subaru (on the firewall), I give it a fair rating and five points.

The carburetors are twin sidedraft SU units, each held by a nut at the top and bottom. The bottom nut in each case is a braille item, but not particularly difficult. The rating for carburetor replacement is good and seven points.

The master cylinder is held by two nuts and bolts. The rear nut and bolt is a minimum accessible item (the only way I found was to use a socket with a U-joint on the bolt head), so the rating is fair and four points.

The Midget picks up five bonus points. The radiator hoses can be changed from the top, but it's a struggle, so this item gets just one of two possible points. Dashboard bulbs and the speedometer cable connection get the full two points each. The starter gets nothing.

The Midget gets a fair rating and four points for heavy repairs. An engine pull-and-refit is factory-rated as a five-hour job, a clutch more than six hours and a head gasket about two and a half. Parts availability has always been reasonably good but the service available in dealerships is spotty in quality.

The Midget's total of 81 points is pretty decent for a sports car. But it's still just a four-cylinder (in-line) rig and in this era of overhead-cam engines, it's a simple pushrod. Happily, it requires no special tools, so if you've got the time, you can get the job done. ●

CONTINUED FROM PAGE 111

Atlantis heats the passengers feet to an uncomfortable degree, while the tendency to engine overheating in congested traffic makes a misery out of commuting. The temperature gauge rises rapidly when the car is left ticking over and there is no way of preventing the extra heat from getting into the cockpit area and cooking the occupants' feet and legs. It looked as if the plastic fan blades had been shortened to fit into a restricted space and were thereby rendered ineffective. A thermostatically controlled electric fan in front of the radiator might have made all the difference.

Sports cars as we know them today are very old fashioned because steps have not been taken by the major manufacturers to develop up-to-date ideas on engine and transmission layouts and suspension systems. The reason is simple: big companies are reluctant to spend large sums of money on advanced sports car design so long as they fear that forthcoming international safety regulations will drive lightweight sports cars off the road. Many enthusiasts fear that true sports cars are near the end of the road anyway, but in the meantime we can still derive pleasure from driving in the country with the hood down in cars like the Atlantis. We should take advantage of the opportunity while it still exists. ■

Morris Garages

CONTINUED FROM PAGE 115

toeing around, the MG is up on the step and motoring.

The GT is, of course, at home anywhere and is handy in the hill country but the two roadsters really come into their own in that milieu, especially at night with the top down. If you've been used to riding around in cars with solid roofs, you suddenly discover there's a whole big world out there. You not only see it and hear it, you smell it, and in that sort of country, the sort of country where the MG and Midget are most at home, the air is so clean it stings your nose. And you know without looking that the farmer over *there* is growing corn and the house on the hill has a hardwood fire going on the hearth. It's an experience that is getting increasingly harder to find these days.

Perhaps we should carp about such things as archaic tops, lack of luggage space in all but the GT and all those other things that others have caviled over when concerning themselves with the various MGs. But somehow we can't. The tops on both the B and the Midget *are* somewhat inconvenient but are vastly improved over the former Erector set types that used to prevail on all British sports cars. At least they are installed and folding, even if a bit stiff. MGs have NEVER had much in the way of luggage space and there's no real reason why they should change at this late date. And as for the rest of the carping from critics both freelance and professional, the people from Abingdon have managed to make and sell more than 250,000 MGBs and at least half that many Midgets. You can find them any day on most any piece of twisting pike, happily ignoring their stiff tops and minimal luggage space and leaving the bigger "now" cars in their wake. And *that's* what MGs are all about./MT

118

MIDGET MODS

Some driving impressions of the latest MG Midget Mk. III

Generally neat and functional if not outstandingly pretty, the latest Midget's appearance is improved by the rounded rear wheel arches. Its Mk I Sprite ancestry is still evident from the curved bonnet-to-side member join line behind the front wheel arch

Some small changes made to the highly successful MG Midget last January gave us an opportunity to once again sample this old-fashioned but still very enjoyable small sports car. They also marked the final fare-well to production of the mechanically identical Austin-Healey Sprite, whose frog-eyed quarter-elliptic rear sprung ancestor began a minor success story for what has become British Leyland.

THE obvious recognition points for the car spotter are the Rostyle wheels—a big improvement on the very bogus-looking affairs previously fitted in our opinion—and the enlarged, round-eyelidded rear wheel arches, also we think much nicer than the previous flat-topped ones. Most useful of the unseen changes is the adoption of a $16\frac{1}{2}$ per cent larger capacity for the petrol tank, now a nominal 7 gallons instead of only 6. Inside the cockpit there are now improved quality carpets, softer 'safety' door pulls, a larger gearlever knob—a small but very

welcome change on any sporting car—and rocker switches instead of toggles.

It is still noticeable how much of the highly individual character of the old Mk 1 Sprite there is about even this latest Midget. Certainly the very amusing but not very high-grip tail-happiness of the original car disappeared long ago with those quarter elliptics, but the same snug 'right' feeling is still there. Particularly if you have been spoilt by the not inconsiderable number of motor cars around which go faster, you tend to get into the Midget ready to be disappointed.

And certainly its performance is not startling. There isn't any syncromesh on first gear, not on the one we drove anyway. The ride is pure sports car, and the tight little cockpit though roomy enough for even a six-footer imposes a close-to-the-wheel driving position that will take some people right back to its namesake of 40 years ago.

But—and the 'but' is a good one—there is something about the little beast. Its steering is most marvellously quick by modern standards, also completely accurate in the way that only a good rack and

AOH 619K

MIDGET MODS...

pinion set up can be. The gearchange is a delight, and one enjoys getting a proper change into first right again. Its size makes it simplicity itself to poke through gaps, remembering always that the same factor dictates more than usual care on the part of the driver for fear he may not be seen. And although the stiff springing makes it hop about somewhat on bumpy country bends, it never hops too far, and the roadholding on Michelin X's is very

good. So much so in fact that one has to restrain oneself from having a go at all sorts of other people through a series of corners, Minis included.

One joy of even the simplest sports cars is that usually (though not always) one is very comfortably placed, whether driver or passenger. The Midget is no exception, because the driver soon gets used to the old-fashioned driving position, and certainly feels one with the car. The seats hold one quite well. Heel-and-toe work with the pedals is easy, unlike the arrangement on the Midget's big brother the MGB which always to my amazement needs some work on the throttle pedal before it can be driven properly. With the hood up visibility is not bad, but as usual the car comes into its own with the hood down. Getting the top down is still not

nearly as simple as it ought to be—we wish someone at British Leyland would take a long careful look at the incredibly simple arrangement on the Alfa Romeo 1750 Spider Veloce—you can if you feel like it put that up or take it down whilst driving gently.

It is fortunate for British Leyland that no one has ever seriously attempted to challenge their position in the admittedly limited small sports-car market; both the Midget and its less successful rival from Triumph would do well with a combined re-think. That does not alter the fact that the Midget is still the right way for the young man who is keen on driving to start (assuming he can find a tolerant insurance company). The reason is that this little MG is true fun, which is what a sports car is for in any language. **Michael Scarlett**

Rocker switches and a better carpet are the principal changes visible here inside; the driving position is very snug, suiting the relatively high-geared steering. Under the bonnet there are no immediately obvious modifications; accessibility is good. The boot allows just enough room for a weekend's squashy luggage for two

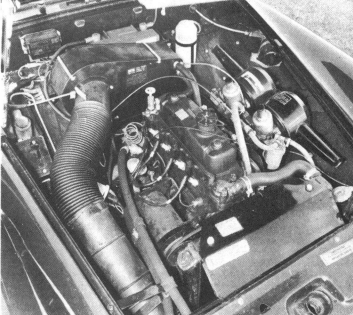

THE M.G. MIDGET Mk. III

Still a sports-car—the long-lined MG Midget in cleaned up 1,275c.c. Mk. III form

I LET A colleague collect the new Jensen-Healey sports-car and write the test report on it last month because it had to be gathered in from West Bromwich, which meant travelling there by train, and as a motoring writer I have an objection to this form of transport. But curiosity decreed that I drive the car, and having agreed to return it to its makers, how was I to get home to remote Wales? It was Ivor Greening, obliging Press Officer at British Leyland's Austin/Morris Division, who came to the rescue. I had asked if I could sample the newest MG Midget and when he promptly agreed and as promptly said it would be delivered to our offices in London, I countered by saying I would collect it from Longbridge.

So it came about that Jensen's well-known delivery driver wafted me across to the great Austin plant on the outskirts of Birmingham, a place which seems to me the true home of the enormous BL empire and where I once used to go for the release of so many then new BMC models, the revolutionary Mini included—there was even one visit, just after the war, when I went to collect a road test A40 in my own car, a 1934 Austin 7, and the chap on the gate directed me to the *museum*, believing that anyone in such an old Austin must be delivering it thereto!

Anyway, that is how I came to be driving away from Birmingham in an MG Midget III, with its safer minor controls on the facia but otherwise the same little Midget we have known for many years. Hood high to an Alvis 12/50 (really, as you would know if you saw it parked behind Tom Rolt's duck's-back at Prescott), this is a *small* sports-car, but it rides very well, remembering the ever-present problem of making a light, fast car hold the road, although I concede that somewhat stiff half-elliptic back springs make it weave a bit on rough surfaces. But it hangs on well round fast bends, helped in the case of the test car by Michelin "X" tyres, and if the 1,275-c.c. engine is rather noisy and there is some whine from the gearbox, how can you complain, for this is a no-nonsense sports-car and these intrusions merely enhance the pre-war tradition of such cars? The gear change itself is good, if you overlook a baulky first-gear, the driver's seat was unexpectedly comfortable, and as the miles went by at mostly an indicated 65-70 m.p.h., I grew to enjoy the MG more and more. The hood clips securely to the screen rail and does not drum but its poppers make it difficult to erect or stow in a hurry—you tend, therefore, to drive the Midget in open guise only if the weather is "set fair". In absolutely torrential rain of cloud-burst proportions the hood kept all the dirty weather out, which was more than could be said in the case of the more expensive Jensen-Healey, and it scarcely restricts rearward vision, as the rear-quarters have transparent panels.

I suppose many readers will think it folly to invest in such a car when you can enjoy more scientific handling from a Mini. But if you are young enough not to be encumbered with the clobber older people accumulate and seem to want to carry in their cars, if there are just two of you and you want fun, the MG Midget provides it. There is not room for much luggage in the lockable boot and the angled shelf behind the seats is for baggage, not a third human. Accept that, and the *Midget* somehow seems a more eager car to drive, to handle more tautly than a saloon and its disc front brakes made it safe to drive

quickly, nor did it seem as vulnerable in heavy traffic on account of its diminutive size as I had expected.

In sober fact this MG is flat out at a bit more than 90 m.p.h. and the 0-60 acceleration time isn't scintillating, being in the order of 14½ seconds. But that there was something essentially likeable about this unpretentious miniature two-seater, BL's toy fun-car, was emphasised by the difficulty I had in keeping the Production Manager's and my assistant's hands off it, although normally they are, respectively, Alfa Romeo 2000 GTV and Reliant Scimitar mounted . . . Certainly this friendly little MG served us well, and gave me an economical 36.7 m.p.g. of 4-star petrol in fast main-road driving. The only fly in the proverbial ointment is that it now requires as much as £1,103 to acquire one. A.R.M. says of the car:—

For some years I have turned my nose up at the MG Midget—mainly because it can boast of no technical ingenuity whatsoever, the engine is frankly outdated by a decade and the performance leaves it struggling to keep up with a number of saloons. When I have seen young men driving about in shiny new M.G. Midgets I have thought "what stick in the muds they must be". For the same money they could have built themselves something like a Ginetta G15, rear-engined, overhead camshaft, performance with economy and superb handling. So, once in a while, the choke comes away in your hand but to my mind the 1970s idea of a sports car is something in which you lie back in the cockpit, with finger tip steering, lightning brakes and some stylistic flair. Definitely not a solid old Midget which has hardly changed in ten years.

Having said all that I must say that I enjoyed driving the Midget far more than I ever expected. British Leyland have had a fair bit of experience at building the machines and they have certainly got them as right as they will ever be. For a start the car is now very much more comfortable than in the early days. However, the door catches on the inside are still extremely nasty and are ideal for breaking your finger nails on but otherwise the fixtures and fittings give no cause for complaint. I had the hood up and down a couple of times and found that on erecting the weather protection a quick application of the right foot in the appropriate place speeded up the proceedings!

The performance was very much better than I had remembered. That A series engine in 1,275 c.c. form may be old fashioned but it still does the job extremely well, if a little harshly. The gearbox proved an absolute delight to use being extremely quick apart from the lack of synchromesh on first, while the brakes stop the car well. Considering its lack of sophistication the suspension works effectively, the low centre of gravity obviously helping.

My re-acquaintance with the Midget allowed me to see this little car in a new light. I still would advise any young man who wants a small sports car and has some spirit and adventure left in him to look at the machines produced by the smaller manufacturers but there is no doubt that the Midget will provide reliable, sporty, open air motoring.—A.R.M.

MG

It's the same old friends behind the octagon, wearing some new colors and detail trim.

The British, praises be, stubbornly refuse the thought that the sports roadster is a dead issue. Giant British Leyland has many marques of sports cars available in the world, and their line up includes the sacred octagon of MG. The announcement of the new model came just in time to make our deadline, consequently we can't bring you any personal observations on the '73 MGs. However the spec sheets indicate that there is no major change in any of the three MGs. Most of the new bits are to conform with safety and emission regulations in this country. All the MGs now have reclining bucket seats and the handy inertia reel harness, and the MGB has some new creature comfort devices as well.

The MG Midget is the surviving "Spridget" today. The word Spridget was coined some years back to describe the Sprite/Midget line of BMC; the cars differed mainly in trim and in the design of the grill. Badge engineering went out the door when BMC merged into British Leyland, in fact the entire Austin Healey line, including the Sprite, was gradually phased into history. The big changes in the MG Midget occurred last year when it got fancy mag style wheels and radial ply tires as standard equipment. At the same time the dash was redone and the glove box gained a locking door. Detuning a shade to run on low lead gas has cost the Midget some in horsepower. The 77.9 cubic inch, in line four cylinder is now rated at 54.5 net HP. Just think for a minute, that the same basic engine, in the Mini Cooper, just five years ago was rated at an honest 90 horsepower. The smallest of the MGs is one of the few cars still on the market without a synchro first gear on a four speed manual transmission. The crash into first gear does give one a nostalgic feeling, but it does seem a bit archaic. A nice fitting top, roll up windows, a reasonable sized trunk, and all the expected dials and knobs make the Midget a real fun car in the 2500 dollar range.

The MGB convertible and the GT look much the same on the outside, but there have been some big changes inside. New on the exterior is the 1973 grill treatment of criss cross metal design and it is painted black. The chrome grill surround is heavier and more MGish in appearance than in recent years, and the badge is back in its proper place, cen-

The MGB gets a new grill and interior trim in its eleventh year. Fine body design is still current and the MGB is every inch a real sports car.

tered on top of the grill. Inside both of the Bs have new arm rests and a restyled steering wheel, plus a new leather covered gear shift knob. The GT has all new seat upholstery on the reclining buckets; it is a brushed nylon fabric for coolness and it is specially treated to make it flame retardant. The MGB comes in some nifty sounding colors for 1973 ... things like Black Tulip and Lime Flower describe a deep purple and a pale green. The windshield wiper arms are no longer chrome, the passing of an era for sure, but the matt black treatment eliminates distracting reflections. The roadster windshield is still overpowered by three wiper blades, needed to cover the required area of some state laws.

Under the hood the 109.8 cubic inch four cylinder engine is the same old pal. New and special valves have been fitted to handle the run-on that is often a byproduct of low octane or low lead gasoline, and the horsepower has sunk from 92 to 78.5. However usable power and torque remain much the same despite the paper ratings. The transmission is the familiar four speed, all synchro unit, and the underpinnings, with front disc brakes and radial tires, are the same as

The MG Midget is budget priced and features full instrumentation, reclining bucket seats, inertia reel safety harness and standard radial tires.

MGB
Data in Brief

...NSIONS

...ase	91 in.
...ength	153 in.
...	49.4 in.
...	59.9 in.
...front/rear	49/49.3 in.
...g type & ratio	rack & pinion
...acity	12 gal
...e capacity	3 cu ft (Rdstr)
...passenger load	2 passengers
...diameter	32 ft
...eight	2220 lbs

...NE — Standard

...	in line, 4 cylinder OHV
...ement	1798cc/109.8 cu in.
...ower	78.5 (SAE net) at 5400 rpm
...	NA

...ELINE

...ission	4 speed manual, all synchro
...xle ratio	3.91:1

...KES

...	10.75 in. disc
...	10 in. drum

...PENSION

...	independent, wishbones, coil springs, hydraulic shocks
...	live axle, semi elliptic leaf springs, hydraulic shocks

...ELS & TIRES

...., type & size	mag style, steel, 14 in.
...ype & size	155 SR×14 Radial

...Data not available
— Data not applicable

MIDGET
Data in Brief

...ENSIONS

...ase	80.0 in.
...length	137.6 in.
...	48.6 in.
...	56.6 in.
...front/rear	44.3/44.8 in.
...g type & ratio	rack & pinion
...pacity	7.25 gal
...ge capacity	NA
...passenger load	2 passenger
...g diameter	32.0 ft
...eight	1560 lbs

...NE — Standard

...	in-line, 4 cylinder OHV
...cement	1275cc/77.9 cu in.
...ower	54.5 (SAE net) at 6000 rpm
...	NA

...VELINE

...ission	4 speed manual, synchromesh on top 3
...xle ratio	4.22:1

...KES

...	8.25 in. disc
...	7.0 in. drum

...PENSION

...	independent, wish bones, coil springs, lever arm shocks
...	live axle, semi-elliptic leaf springs, lever arm shocks

...ELS & TIRES

..., type & size	mag style, steel 13 in.
...ype & size	145×13 radial

...Data not available
— Data not applicable

MGB GT fastback coupe is the only hardtop in the line. It has nice things like flow through ventilation, and a bag of interior improvements.

in former editions.

The MGB roadster is now going into its eleventh model year, and it may be getting a bit long in the tooth, as the English say. It is still impossible to put the top up or down without a struggle, but that may be part of its charm. The GT is just a few years younger than the roadster, and much the same in concept allowing for the hardtop and station wagon type rear door and deck. The prices range from 3500 to 4000 dollars, and that price range is filled with cars of all descriptions in the U.S. Still, with the precise rack and pinion steering and the willing powerplant, the MGB is a real fun car on the road, and perhaps the essence of a true sports car. The MG... are fully equipped with instruments, re... clining seats, and all that, and they now have inertia reel type safety harness a... well.

While the MGB may be a mite primi... tive compared to other sportsters in it... class, it is now, as always, a delight to drive on a demanding piece of roadway. If the B is getting a shade old fashioned the buyers don't seem to mind. MG... sales keep going up and up in this country, so the demand is still out there in America ... perhaps for any car that bears the mystical nameplate of MG.

Basil's Mighty Midget

MG MIDGET

This little tear-away was anothe[r] from Wales' workshop—British [Leyland] Special Tuning Department to you. [One] time I pompously thought my own [racing] days had come to an end when I [sold] off my battered "Frogeye" some se[asons] ago. However, a few minutes in th[is car] instantly reminded me of the uniqu[e thrill of] a baby sports car. Its ability [to dart] through traffic, blast up to a ge[nuine 100] mph down the straights and th[en swing] controllably in tail-out fashion r[ound the] turns, must make it our fun car fo[r 1971.]

Some will remember the amazing [ST] Spridget which clocked an incre[dible 117] mph down the straight at MIRA a[nd main-] tained a genuine 112 mph on a la[p, on] January 16, 1971. This time Abing[don] opted for a milder tune, stage 2 in [the] result, however, is no less impressi[ve.]

Modifications are confined to the [head] of the engine and the chief item is a [polished] and gas flowed cylinder head. This [goes] with a competition gasket and a set [of N64Y] plugs. To help its breathing, the [standard] 1⅛in. SU carburetters are replaced [by a pair] of more man-sized 1½in. ones with n[ew needles.] Exhausting is now done with a [tubular] manifold and a straight-through sile[ncer, while] the original distributor is replaced [by a] competition one. The total will ligh[ten your] pocket by approximately £140, bu[t] the results are particularly worthwh[ile.]

The standard article requires 13[.5 sec. to] reach 60 mph and manages 95.0 mph [flat out.] The ST car, however, rushes up to 6[0 mph in] a mere 10.0 sec. and lapped MI[RA at a] respectable 103.3 mph, touching 10[7 mph] on the fastest flying quarter mile. [This sug-] gests an increase in power of som[e 40 per] cent which is very healthy when you [consider] the relative simplicity of the mods.

It is at this stage that we normal[ly start] to talk about the reduction in l[ow-speed] torque and the lumpy tick-over. Bu[t in this] case the improved breathing and ret[ention of]

the standard camshaft have graced the Sprid-get with better torque throughout the range, knocking no less than 5 sec. off the 60-80 mph time in top. The tick-over, of course, remains unaffected.

You will now appreciate why the car is so enjoyable to drive, for it is utterly viceless. No climbing on the cam, no stalling at lights, just put your foot down and it goes. What about all the petrol in gulps? Well, I'm afraid it doesn't do that either. If you look at our table, you will see that the ST car is more economical throughout the range. The lower touring consumption is explained by the potentially higher cruising speed and the lower overall figure by the fact that our lead-footed testers were enjoying themselves. So it would seem that the Midget betters the standard car on every count so far. Yet surely there must be something to criticise?

Well we did have a slight moan about the suspension. The car had been lowered all round and initially we thought the handling had been improved. Pushing a bit harder, however, showed that it was hitting the outside rear bump-stop under fast cornering, causing rather sudden oversteer—very interesting. The ride, too, had suffered, for the car would bottom regularly when travelling fast over undulating country roads. It transpired that an old set of rear spring leaves had been fitted by mistake. We have

since tried the car with the correct ones and found the handling to be first-rate. Like the standard car, it understeers gently under power, but there is plenty in reserve to kick the tail out; or for those that don't pursue the joys of sideways motoring, the nose will tuck in nicely on a trailing throttle. So however you drive, it's quick, safe and very controllable. After the modification we had no complaints about the ride either, which seemed as standard, and typical of a small sports car.

The stiffer rear springs and lowering kit for the front are all normal ST parts, available from any Special Tuning or British Leyland distributor, as are all the engine parts used in the conversion.

Our final thoughts on the car were this—that in days of rising insurance, continuing indifferent weather and packed roads it is becoming increasingly difficult to justify the cost of a sports car. We thought the Sprid-get, however, could easily be woven into the lives of a great number of keen motorists, male and female either single or married. For this is a car that would genuinely double as the wife's shopping car during the week and as a potentially successful autotest machine at the weekend. If you enjoy a baby sports car with plenty of steam you'll like this one—we did.   **Gordon Bruce**

Car: MG Midget (Motor road test, October 10, 1970).
Conversion by : BL Special Tuning, Abingdon, Berks.
Tel : Abingdon 251.
Conversion : Stage II. Polished, flowed cylinder head (C-AHT 463), £65. Twin 1½in. SUs (C-AUD 224) £25.74. Installation kit for carbs (C-AJJ 4040), £14.25. Distributor (C-27H7766), £13. Set N64Y plugs (C-37H4208), £3.20. Head gasket (C-AHT 188), £1.85. Exhaust manifold (C-AHT 11), £17. Stiffer rear springs (C-AHA8272), £9.50. Lowering kit, front suspension (C-AJJ3322), £2.45. Total: £151.99.

	Full race ST Midget	ST's Milder Midget	Standard Midget
Maximum Speed mph	mph	mph	mph
Lap	112.0	102.3	95.0
Best ¼ mile	117.0	104.7	96.8
Mean maximile	107.1	100.0	94.7
Best maximile	111.1	101.1	96.8
Acceleration			
mph	sec	sec	sec
0- 30	3.5	3.3	4.0
0- 40	5.0	5.1	6.5
0- 50	7.1	7.2	9.3
0- 60	9.2	10.0	13.5
0- 70	13.1	13.8	19.1
0- 80	16.6	18.8	28.5
0- 90	22.9	27.5	45.7
0-100	33.8	—	—
Standing ¼ mile	17.2	17.4	19.3
Standing km	—	—	36.2
In top			
mph			
20- 40	—	8.9	9.9
30- 50	17.4	9.0	9.6
40- 60	11.5	8.5	9.8
50- 70	9.5	9.1	11.7
60- 80	11.7	10.9	16.0
70- 90	13.7	14.0	—

In third mph					
10-30	...	...	...	6.3	7.1
20-40	...	...	...	6.3	6.8
30-50	...	...	...	5.8	6.8
40-60	...	...	...	5.7	7.4
50-70	...	...	...	6.6	9.4
60-80	...	...	...	8.5	—
Fuel consumption					
Steady mph				mpg	mpg
30	...	...	...	54.8	46.7
40	...	...	...	50.3	45.2
50	...	...	...	44.9	42.5
60	...	...	...	38.6	39.5
70	...	...	...	35.5	34.1
80	...	...	...	30.4	29.0
90	...	...	...	26.5	23.5
Overall	...	...	...	25.8	30.2
Touring	...	...	...	34.8	36.3

New at the Show

Cars you won't have seen before

MG Midget 1500 and "soft-nose" MGBs

SOME FAIRLY significant changes to British Leyland's sports car range are announced for the opening of the Motor Show, the MG Midget being the car most affected. Most of the changes are dictated by the need to standardize the cars as closely as possible with those delivered to the American market, which remains the biggest single outlet for them; and this in turn calls for modifications to improve crashworthiness and exhaust emissions.

For the MG enthusiast, the most interesting change is the adoption of a new engine of 1,491 c.c., developed from the Triumph 1500 unit. It proved easier to make this engine meet both the American regulations – for which purpose it is quite heavily modified – and the European ECE15 emission limits. The 1500 engine is hardly any bigger than the original 1275 power unit, and the only changes needed to make it fit the Midget shell were a redesign of the exhaust manifold and new air filters.

The 1500 engine, like the one it replaces, can trace its ancestry back to a much smaller ohv power unit of 1950 vintage – in this case, the Standard 8 engine rather than that of the Morris Minor. Oddly, both ancestors were of 803 c.c. capacity. It is difficult to quantify the power increase due to the bigger engine, since British Leyland quote 65 bhp (DIN) for the 1500 as against 65 bhp (net) for the 1275. The DIN method is the tougher, so the new car has some power margin – though not much. Peak power speed is down from 6,000 to 5,500 rpm. Torque is up, naturally, from 72 lb. ft. to 76·5, still at 3,000 rpm. Gearing remains the same, with a 3·9 final drive and 145-12in. tyres, giving 16·4 mph per 1,000 rpm.

Together with the change in engine, the transmission has been altered in detail, with a new gearbox derived from the single-rail design used in the Marina 1·3; this has wider ratios than the previous Midget gearbox. The propeller shaft is a new single-piece design.

Midget is both longer and heavier with 5 mph bumpers, makes up for it with increased power of 1500 engine. Note revised rear wheel arch shape caused by structure change to carry through loads

The power and torque increase of the 1500 engine will be welcome, because the weight of the car is up by some 200lb.; this is due not to the power plant, but to the adoption of American-standard 5 mph bumpers, front and rear. These are moulded in urethane foam, over a steel armature base, and the body structure has had to be strengthened to carry through the loads; as a consequence of this, the shape of the rear wheel arch has changed. The ride height has been increased by an inch (by changing the front crossmember mounting, and re-cambering the rear springs) to meet the bumper height requirement. Overall length is increased by a fraction over 3½in., and is now 11ft 9in.

"Soft-nose" MGB is modified on same principle as Midget. Steel armature inside deformable urethane cover provides spring and strength

MGB changes

There are no power unit changes in either the standard or V8 MGBs, but like the Midget they too receive 5 mph bumpers of the same general construction. Local body shell changes provided sufficiently rigid bumper mounting points, but again the ride height has had to be changed. The 1·8-litre cars are now 1½in. higher; the V8 ride height was already an inch higher, so another half-inch was all that was required.

The collapsible steering column previously used in the V8 is now standard on all MGBs, together with twin column-mounted stalks controlling lights/direction indicators and wash/wipe, the second also operating the overdrive when it is fitted. The V8 instrument pack, with 80mm speedometer and rev counter, also becomes standard.

Like the Midget, the 1975-standard MGBs will be rather heavier, while their overall length has been increased by 5in. with the fitting of the new bumpers. Since power output stays the same, there will inevitably be some loss in performance, but the penalty will not be great. *Autocar* hopes to test both the Midget and an MGB in the near future.

TWIN TEST

SPITFIRE 1500 v MIDGET 1500

The engine and gearbox are the same, the suspensions are different yet both go round corners at much the same speed. So which of BL's two mini rag tops do you choose ?

Of all Britain's volume car producers British Leyland alone fosters the two-seater open sports car cult. Nobody else except small concerns like Jensen, Morgan and Panther really wants to know. It's all because of economics, as those ugly, energy-absorbing Federal bumpers at each end of the MG serve to underline. Were it not for the lucrative American market, British-built volume production sports cars just would not exist.

For this very same reason (economics) BL sports car development has lagged in recent years. The MGB series, Midget and Spitfire are essentially the same as they were when launched about a decade and a half ago. The only new sports car to emerge from BL's enclaves for years is the TR7. And that's to be available only as a closed car.

Paradoxically for the Midget and Spitfire, the American exhaust emission regulations have been a blessing in disguise. Both cars now sport Triumph 1500 cc twin-carburetter engines in place of different 1300 cc mills, in a bid to meet the desired low level of exhaust pollutants. The result is more (though still rather mediocre) power, better straight-line performance and, in the Spitfire's case, better fuel economy.

The two rag tops also share the same gearbox—a Marina unit wtih single-rail selector mechanism and all-synchromesh shift. Unlike the MG, the Spitfire is also offered with the useful option of an overdrive.

Which marque to choose has long been a quandary of those sports car enthusiasts whose budgets could stretch only to something bordering the price of a base-model saloon. Popularity in Britain has been split evenly between the two—or we should really say three as Sprite sales figures have been coupled with the MG's. In the States, where enthusiasts relate strongly to the MG cachet the Abingdon car has been highly popular for years, though it's not until its 115,234 overseas sales have been coupled with those of the discontinued Sprite (103,118) that the Spitfire's 171,000 figure is topped. So the pair are fairly evenly matched in terms of popularity.

Despite the engine and gearbox similarities of the two cars the obvious preferences for one marque over the next will exist (so long as Sir Don Ryder's model rationalisation scheme doesn't affect them) if only because the cars over the years have been pitched at slightly different markets.

The MG is more the old school, hard sprung, seat-of-the-pants type of driver's car while the Spitfire is overtly more sophisticated and a bit more expensive. The Triumph costs £1689 in its most basic guise compared with the MG at £1560, while if you add the extra cost of the overdrive and comfort option pack plus laminated screen, then the Spitfire's cost rises to £1875.

To find out if the Spitfire's extra £300 cost is worth it we took the cars on a twin test convoy.

PERFORMANCE

It was in October last year that BL announced the Triumph 1500 engine for the Midget and Spitfire, though the latter had been sold in the States (more successfully than ever, incidentally) with this unit for two years previously.

The engine changes endow the Spitfire with 10 extra bhp (now 71 at 5500 rpm) and a further 14 lb ft of torque (now 82 lb ıt at 3000 rpm) but not so with the Midget. Installation problems with the Triumph engine meant that a single outlet exhaust manifold rather than a twin unit had to be fitted. The result is a power figure no greater than that previously claimed (65 bhp (DIN) at 5500 rpm), though BL say that the current figure is more genuine than the old one. Torque is up by just over 4 lb ft (at 76.5 lb ft produced at 3000 rpm) and a noticeable improvement it is, too.

In fact both models are quicker than they were in their previous forms though neither is a true 100 mph car. Both will reach this speed if the wind and road conditions are right but such performance is rather mediocre for a 1500 sports car.

The Midget's top speed has gone up by 1.5 mph to 96.5 mph with a best quarter speed of 100 mph, while the Spitfire, which has benefited from raised overall gearing, is up by 7.2 mph to 98.5 mph. Its best quarter time was 103.4 mph.

The MG retains its 16.7 mph/ per 1000 rpm final drive ratio

The engines basically are the same but accessibility isn't. The Spitfire's bonnet and wings cant forward to provide unrivalled access to all the regular service items and more. The Midget's bay is a knuckle-scraper

while the Spitfire has been raised to 18 mph in direct top (22 mph in overdrive) so despite its lower power you'd expect the Midget to accelerate as quickly as the Spitfire. It does. Only one-tenth of a second separates the two from rest to 60 mph.

The MG's lower gearing really scores when it comes to acceleration in top, its time of 8.3 s for the all-important 30-50 mph increment being very respectable. And such is the engine's flexibility that in the MG it will pull from 600 rpm in the same gear without complaint.

The same can't be said of the Triumph as driveline vibrations and body booms inhibit the use of top below 1500 rpm. The car's 30-50 mph acceleration time is almost as good as the MG's though, at a creditable 9.3 s in direct top. In overdrive it's a rather laggardly 14.5 s.

The engine in both cars becomes very busy above 5000 rpm and both are noticeably short of breath at their 6000 rpm limits. Fan roar at high rpm is very noticeable in the Triumph. Wind noise prevented any similar assessment of the MG. What's needed is a viscous coupled fan to save noise and release some extra engine power.

ECONOMY

Big engines in small cars usually spell economy. The recipe works well for the Spitfire but less so for the lower-geared Midget. We achieved overall figures of 29.8 mpg and 27.3 mpg respectively using four-star fuel. The Spitfire's overdrive counts for a lot, as its computed touring fuel consumption is 35.4 mpg whereas for the Midget it's only 29.0 mpg.

To illustrate the benefit of the overdrive it's worth quoting a few steady speed figures. At 50 mph in overdrive top the Spitfire is returning 48.5 mpg—exactly the same as 40 mph in direct drive. Moreover, at 70 mph in overdrive the Spitfire's engine is spinning at little more than 3000 rpm and returning an impressive 36.2 mpg. At a similar speed the MG is practically 10 mpg worse.

TRANSMISSION

Think of a Marina gearshift. Conjure something not quite as slick and you'll probably be pretty close to imagining what the MG's gearchange is like. It's a bit notchy, first baulks frequently and reverse is very difficult to select and on the whole is not as slick as that fitted to the old A-series car. The Spitfire's shift is much better, even though it has the same Marina single-rail unit with synchromesh on all forward gears.

So why the difference? Possibly one gearbox was built better than the next. Maybe the Midget's shorter gear lever has increased the effort required. Maybe it just needed more miles to free up (the test car had covered 3000 miles). We don't know. But for the cars we tried the Spitfire gearbox was definitely more pleasant to use. Reverse is still a bit awkward to

obtain but the shift quality is generally superior.

An extra £122.85 on the Spitfire's price brings an excellent overdrive on third and top, giving you six ratios to play with rather than the MG's four. The gear-knob-operated overdrive slurs in and out very smoothly though doesn't cancel when you shift below third—a bad point as there's a very big gap if you shift from second to overdrive third. In the direct ratios the Spitfire is good for 6000 rpm maxima of 31, 50 and 77 mph; overdrive third gives a useful 97 mph. The MG's corresponding figures are a less effective 29, 47 and 70 mph.

BL say that they've considered an overdrive for the car but maintain that space is a problem.

HANDLING

If you regard fun as an opposite lock slide that can be controlled at will, the MG provides it. It's a car that really comes into its element along winding country lanes. By absolute standards it oversteers too readily (especially in the wet on Cinturato tyres and even in the dry it is outclassed by several sporty saloons) but the rack and pinion steering is so light, quick and responsive, that correction is easy. In fact there are few cars in the Midget's price range that can provide such a level of entertainment so readily, yet so safely. We liked this element of the car's behaviour very much.

The Spitfire isn't as much fun to drive under similar circumstances though it's just as safe.

The Spitfire's hood is excellent. Not only is it draught-free but its plastic rear panel can be unzipped for extra ventilation or better rearward visibility

The Midget's instruments are both informative and well placed but the black, crackle-finish facia looks dated and the switchgear isn't as good as the Spitfire's

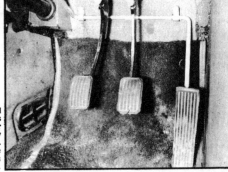

The Midget's pedal arrangement is good though our car had a slightly sticky throttle. Finish of the footwell area was bad.

TRIUMPH SPITFIRE 1500

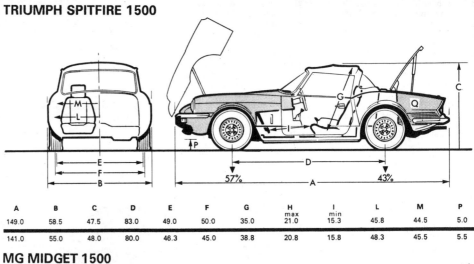

57%   43%

A	B	C	D	E	F	G	H max	I min	L	M	P
149.0	58.5	47.5	83.0	49.0	50.0	35.0	21.0	15.3	45.8	44.5	5.0
141.0	55.0	48.0	80.0	46.3	45.0	38.8	20.8	15.8	48.3	45.5	5.5

MG MIDGET 1500

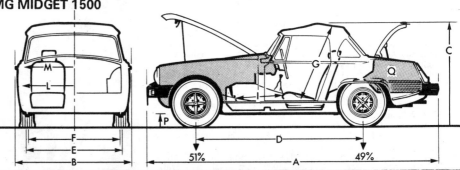

51%   49%

The Triumph's basic trait is mild understeer which either lifting off or applying more lock will negate. Lifting off doesn't invoke the sudden and quite vicious oversteer that was typical of earlier models. The car's swing axle rear suspension has been tamed by an ingenious modification to its transverse leaf spring layout. Now, all you notice if you do lift off in mid-corner is a slight twitch and wriggle from the rear.

Although the Spitfire's steering wheel is much smaller than the MG's unfashionably large one, the system is nowhere near as light or as responsive. In fact it posses a certain rubberiness which robs it of some feel. But what a fabulous steering lock! We wish all cars has the Triumph's small turning circle.

BRAKES

Both cars have disc/drum brakes without servo-assistance; it's just not required. Pedal pressures are firm and retardation is progressive.

In twin test convoy the cars did some quick braking from highish speeds and neither brake system faded. They're both good.

We were less than happy with the MG's handbrake though. It worked all right, getting to it was the problem! It's buried beside the transmission tunnel and passenger's seat and most awkward to reach.

The Spitfire's handbrake was much easier to get at, being a trifle heavy in use but none the less effective.

ACCOMMODATION

There's not much room inside either car. Both cars are strictly two-seater and you can throw a fair measure of bric-a-brac in the carpeted rear of either. A third person could be accommodated sideways in this area of both cars, but not for many miles.

Of the two the Spitfire has the more room. There's more rearward adjustment to the seats and a bigger area in the rear. The same can be said of the respective boot volumes. The Midget's boot lid opening is narrow whereas the Spitfire's is broad and the Triumph's boot interior accommodates about twice the amount of luggage. In fact the Midget is downright cramped in all departments.

RIDE COMFORT

As you'd expect of sports cars designed of long ago neither car has particularly comfortable suspension. The Midget has an independent front end and live-axled rear, located by semi-elliptic springs and controlled by lever-type dampers, while the Spitfire is independently sprung all round.

Both cars have a firm ride, the Midget being the harder of the two. In fact even on a smooth surface you're aware of a certain jitteriness in the ride. The Spitfire is better, though it only needs a slightly poor road surface to reveal what feels like lack of rigidity in the chassis/body unit.

Despite the extra inch of ride

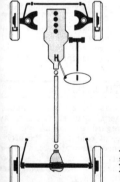

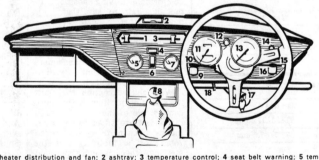

1 heater distribution and fan; 2 ashtray; 3 temperature control; 4 seat belt warning; 5 temperature gauge; 6 light switch; 7 fuel gauge; 8 overdrive; 9 choke; 10 dip and main beam control; 11 speedometer; 12 hazard lights; 13 rev-counter; 14 indicator warning light; 15 indicators; 16 wash/wipe; 17 ignition/steering lock; 18 trip zero

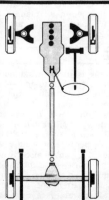

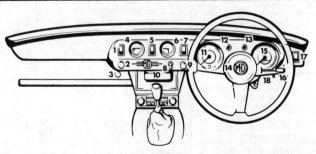

1 panel light switch; 2 temperature control; 3 bonnet release; 4 fuel gauge; 5 wiper switch; 6 temperature/oil pressure gauge; 7 light switch; 8 washer button; 9 choke; 10 interior light; 11 rev-counter; 12 left turn indicator; 13 right turn indicator; 14 horn; 15 speedometer; 16 indicators/headlamp dip and flash; 17 hazard flashers; 18 trip zero

STANDARD EQUIPMENT

SPITFIRE		MIDGET
	Adjustable steering	
●	Armrests	●
●	Ashtrays	●
●	Breakaway mirror	●
	Childproof locks	
	Cigar lighter	
	Clock	
	Coat hooks	
●	Collapsible steering	●
●	Dual circuit brakes	●
	Electric windows	
	Fresh air vents	
	Grab handles	
●	Hazard warning	●
●	Head restraints	●
	Heated backlight	
	Laminated screen	
●	Outside mirror	●
	Parking lights	
	Petrol filler lock	
	Radio	
●	Reversing lights	●
●	Rev counter	●
●	Seatbelts	●
●	Seat recline	●
	Seat height adjuster	
●	Removable hood	●
	Tinted glass	
●	Vanity mirror	
	Wash/wipe combination	
	Wiper delay	

TWIN TEST ● SPITFIRE/MIDGET

Make: Triumph
Model: Spitfire 1500
Makers: Rover Triumph, Coventry, CV4 9DB
Price: £1444 plus £120.33 car tax plus £125.15 VAT equals £1689.48.
Extras: overdrive, £122.85; luxury option pack, £42.18; laminated screen, £20.71; radio installation, £60.
Total as tested: £1935.22.

Make: MG
Model: Midget 1500
Makers: Austin Morris Group, Longbridge, Birmingham, B31 2TB.
Price: £1333 plus £111.08 car tax plus £115.53 VAT equals £1559.61.
Extras: head restraints, £18.27; radio installation, £60.
Total as tested: £1637.88.

SPITFIRE					MIDGET		
●	●	●	Performance	●	●		
●	●	●	●	Economy	●	●	
●	●	●	●	Transmission	●	●	
●	●	●	●	Handling	●	●	●
●	●	●	●	Brakes	●	●	●
		●	Accommodation (L)	●			
		●	●	Accommodation (P)	●	●	
		●	Ride comfort	●	●		
	●	●	●	At the wheel	●	●	●
	●	●	●	Visibility	●		
	●	●	●	Instruments	●	●	●	●
	●	●	●	Heating	●		
		●	Ventilation	●			
		●	●	Noise	●		
	●	●	●	Equipment	●	●	
●	●	●	●	Finish	●	●	●

PERFORMANCE

98.5	**Max speed mph**	96.5
77 (97 o/d) 6000 50 31	**Max in 3rd 2nd } rpm 1st**	70 } 6000 47 29
11.8	**0-60 mph sec**	11.9
9.3 (14.5 o/d)	**30-50 mph in top sec**	8.3
29.8	**Overall mpg**	27.3
35.4	**Touring mpg**	29.0
220	**Fuel for 10,000 miles £**	271
22 (L) 20.5 (R)	**Turning circle ft**	31.5 (L) 32 (R)
0.75	**Steering turns 50ft circle**	0.70
71	**True speed at ind 70 mph**	69

SPECIFICATION

In line 4	**Cylinders**	In line 4
1493/91 cu in.	**Capacity**	1493/91 cu in.
73.7/87.5 mm	**Bore/stroke**	73.7/87.5 mm
Ohv	**Valves**	Ohv
9.0 : 1	**Compression**	9.0 : 1
71 bhp (DIN) at 5500 rpm	**Max power**	65 bhp (DIN) at 5500 rpm
82 lb ft (DIN) at 3000 rpm	**Max torque**	76.5 lb ft (DIN) at 3000 rpm
4-speed manual with o/d	**Gearbox**	4-speed manual
18 in 4th or 22 in o/d	**mph/1000 rpm**	16.4
Separate steel box sections	**Chassis con**	Unitary
Independent by double wishbones, coil springs and telescopic dampers	**Front suspension**	Independent, coil spring upper arms cum damper levers and bottom wishbone
Swing axle, transverse leaf springs, dampers and radius rods	**Rear suspension**	Live rear axle, semi-elliptic leaf springs, lever dampers
Rack and pinion	**Steering**	Rack and pinion
Disc front, drum rear	**Brakes**	Disc front, drum rear
155 SR x 13	**Tyres**	145 x 13
19.17 cwt	**Weight**	20.1 cwt

height that the MG has been given because of its new set of Federal bumpers, the car still bottoms its exhaust loudly if you travel along a wavy road at speed. Under similar conditions the Spitfire tends to "float."

The MG rolls more than the Spitfire does.

VISIBILITY

The Spitfire scores, yet again, on visibility. Glass area is considerably greater and it has a set of wipers which scribe an arc across a wide section of the screen. The Midget's are poor. They're small and leave a big area of uncleaned screen to the driver's top right and an even greater unwiped area confronts the passenger who, in bad weather, practically can't see a thing. The MG's quarter lights also get dirty very quickly, effectively robbing you of any rearward vision through the door-mounted mirror.

The Spitfire's single pane of glass for either side window is much better in this respect and the car's hood has a plastic rear screen which will unzip to afford a clear view astern in addition to its primary benefit of extra ventilation.

In fine weather, with the hood down, visibility from within the MG improves considerably, but the folded hood obscures a great deal of your over-shoulder view so when reversing it's best to look out of the side window.

The lights on either car are just about adequate on main beam. On dipped lights the beams are rather scattered.

AT THE WHEEL

Neither car gives an especially comfortable driving position. In fact it's fair to say that both have had better seats in their time. Those in both cars are now rather formless, lacking sufficient lateral support. A couple of drivers complained of inadequate lumbar support from the Triumph's seats as well.

With that exception the Spitfire's driving position is the more comfortable of the two. Although the pedals are offset to the right there's much more legroom (even room for a footrest) and the steering wheel is more pleasant to handle, even though it is slightly heavy.

In the MG, once you've completed the struggle to get in, you're aware of several things: the close proximity of the screen; the poor rearward adjustment of the seats (the recline facility is worth very little unless you've very short legs) and the over-large steering wheel. Drivers sometimes found themselves banging their knuckles against the door as they shuffled the wheel from lock to lock.

As both cockpits are small there's practically nothing that isn't within arm's reach. Exceptions are the Midget's air distribution flaps situated in the bowels of each footwell. Unless you're a contortionist you have to stop the car and release your seat belt before you can reach the things.

INSTRUMENTS

The Triumph's matt finis wooden facia looks modern an attractive (unlike the Midget' black crackle finish dash) but th instruments aren't nearly as ir formative or as well placed a those in the MG.

For a start you don't get a oil pressure gauge, and wit your hands at "ten to two" o the steering wheel, the fuel gaug is obscured.

There are no such problem with the Midget. Moreover it rev counter and speedometer ar better calibrated (in increment of 100 rpm and 2 mph rathe than 500 rpm and 10 mph) with nicer needle.

HEATING

The MG's heating arrangement crude. Distribution control is vi very awkwardly placed flaps i either footwell and the heat regu lated over a narrow band by push-pull knob—by some desig quirk—can only be fan booste on maximum heat; result: toaste legs. It's a pity that the system isn't easier to control.

The Spitfire's heating arrange ment is simplicity itself and out put is excellent. There are tw facia-mounted slides—one fo temperature and another for dis tribution control including a effective fan boost.

Screen demisting was so muc easier with the Triumph. In th MG you had to play with th footwell flaps to direct air to th screen and of course, if the pas senger's flap is open, that entail having to clamber across th transmission tunnel to close i before the maximum amount o air can be channelled towards the screen. Very annoying, that.

Both rear screens tended to mist up readily. Provided i wasn't raining at the time, with the Spitfire you could at least unzip the panel for a clearer view of the rear.

VENTILATION

Both cars have folding hoods And that's about all you can say with regard to ventilation. The Spitfire, of course, has the afore mentioned removable rear screen and very often it was used, too, since the car's interior sometimes got rather fumey.

The Midget had ventilation al' its own, courtesy an ill-fitting hood which let in all manner o draughts, particularly around your neck.

NOISE

Neither car is quiet—wind nois from the hoods see to that—but the Spitfire is markedly better o the two. Cruising at the legal motorway limit was quite com fortable in the Spitfire but not in the MG which was practically unbearable because of wind roar.

In the MG you're also aware of engine noise—a combination of induction roar and genera mechanical clatter not to men tion a rather whiney gearbox and noisy exhaust. The Spitfire is better insulated from such sounds though engine fan roar is much in evidence at high rpm. The overdrive makes the Spitfire a generally more relaxing car to drive, particularly on motorways, but at over 90 mph (less if the wind conditions are right) the side windows would break their seal with the hood to create a significant increase in noise.

Tyre roar went unnoticed in either car (for obvious reasons) but crashing sounds could be heard from the suspension of both cars over rough ground.

EQUIPMENT

Even the flip-top ashtray which straddles the MG's transmission tunnel looks something of an afterthought, as does the under facia interior light which became standard on the Mk 3 version of the car in 1970. In fact when it comes to equipment there's not an awful lot one can say about the car. Screen washers are the manual, push/squirt sort and the wipers have only a single speed —slow. Our car came with optional head restraints (£18.25); the two door-mounted rear view mirrors are standard. The interior rear view mirror is the dipping sort but one great omission is a set of sun visors. The car badly needs them.

The Spitfire is better equipped. The screen washers are still the manual variety but at least they're incorporated with the two-speed wiper switch. For just over £42 you can also acquire a luxury option pack as fitted to the test car. This includes a central armrest, inertia reel seat belts, dipping rear view mirror, driver's door mirror, head restraints and a universally jointed map-reading light. And the car also has sun visors as standard!

FINISH

Here's where the Spitfire scores yet again. Its interior is tastefully designed and well executed with several nice touches—like foam-filled cushions round the edges of the transmission tunnel to prevent you from bruising your legs.

By contrast the MG's interior is spartan and plasticky and the carpeting is a poor fit and a bad contrast to the rest of the trim.

We had no quibbles regarding the paint finish of either car. The

These lidless views of both cars (top) illustrate just how better equipped and finished the Triumph is, especially if you opt for the £42 comfort pack which gives you things like the central arm rest, headrestraints, map reading light and several other niceties. By contrast the Midget's interior is rather stark and not so roomy. The lack of sun visors is a serious omission

Midget's screen did leak rather badly, though, and its hood was practically impossible to fasten in place without the aid of a second person.

The Spitfire's hood could be folded back or erected without even leaving the car.

CONCLUSION

Given the choice of either car some four or five years ago most of us would have opted for the MG. It's tremendous fun to drive, particularly around twisty country lanes. But nowadays the Spitfire gets you round corners just as quickly, albeit in a much more sober style. The Triumph is also quicker, appreciably more economical and substantially quieter. To our eyes it is also the more attractive of the two.

If one car is to suffer from the model rationalisation decreed by Sir Don Ryder then it must surely be the Midget, though we can't see it being axed while it's selling so well in the States. We'll be sorry to see it go.

MG MIDGET MARK IV

It's showing its age but the basic elements of
driving pleasure are still there

PHOTOS BY JOE RUSZ

ANYTIME THERE IS a discussion of sports cars, the name MG must come to the forefront. In the late Forties when the sports car movement first came to America, it was the MG TC that led the way and set the parameters of what a sports car should be. Almost 30 years later, MG may be sharing the market with a lot of other marques, but the basic sports car in this country has to be the MG Midget.

This diminutive roadster is the smallest and least expensive sports car available in the U.S. at this moment. The Midget has a long history going back to 1958 and the birth of the Austin-Healey Sprite, that odd-looking but lovable Bugeye that

represented a return to the basics. Over the past 18 years, the car has been updated several times, starting with the Sprite II in 1961 and the emergence of the MG Midget nameplate that same year, until today what we have is a car with roll-up windows, carpeting and relatively luxurious interior features compared to the original concept. (The Sprite name disappeared in 1970.) The engine has grown from the original 948 cc to 1493, the power from 45 net bhp to a high of 65 (with the 1275-cc engine) and now to 55.5 bhp (50 in California). And the price? It's gone from $1795 to almost $4000.

Despite the evolutionary changes that have taken place, the

132

Midget is, by any standards, an old-fashioned car. However, this quality leads to a simplicity that is rare today and helps keep the price at the bottom of the sports car scale, albeit that scale has taken a quantitative leap upward in recent years. However much automotive journalists and critics may call for a new design from British Leyland to replace the present Midget, it's unlikely that will happen unless or until there is a direct competitor for the car and it can no longer meet U.S. safety and emission standards through alteration rather than remaking.

Under the BL scheme of consolidation, the Midget now shares the same engine as the Triumph Spitfire: an overhead valve, inline 4-cylinder. With the displacement increase from 1275 to 1493 cc, the Midget has taken on a more relaxed attitude. It's really no quicker up to speed thanks to emission controls, but it doesn't work quite so hard and there is a little less of the busy, noisy effort of earlier Midgets. The larger engine's better low- and middle-rpm torque range accounts for the difference. Once the engine is taken over about 4000 rpm, however, it becomes a typically buzzy 4-banger. The 4-speed, fully synchronized transmission mates well to the engine and is a pleasure to use. Shifts can be accomplished crisply and with a relatively short throw, but we lament that there is no optional overdrive with the Midget as there is with the MGB

and Spitfire.

The Midget sits on an 80.0-in. wheelbase (11 in. shorter than the MGB) and has an overall length of 141.0 in. (18 in. shorter than the B and about the same length as the sub-compact Renault 5). Suspension is by lower A-arms, lever shocks as upper lateral arms, coil springs and anti-roll bar in front, with a very simple arrangement of live axle on leaf springs and lever shocks at the rear. The result is a ride that is firm and jouncy in the best tradition of British sports cars and with handling that is best characterized as a bit twitchy. The rack-and-pinion steering requires only 2.3 turns, lock-to-lock, and this gives the Midget a maneuverability factor that's hard to match. But the inherent understeer can change suddenly to final oversteer if the car is pushed hard enough. The first time out driving on the highway can be rather exhilarating if you're not prepared for all of this as the Midget will change direction quicker than you can say "God save the Queen!"

The brakes could stand improvement. After four ½g stops from 60 mph, the brakes had faded completely away. We repeated this test twice with ample time in between for cooling and recovery with no improvement. The brakes weren't very effective in our stopping distance tests either; the front wheels locked easily, causing the Midget to dart about. So the only thing to do was to use the pedal gently and pay the penalty

PRICE

List price, all POE $3949
Price as tested $4219

GENERAL

Curb weight, lb 1775
Weight distribution (with driver),
  front/rear, % 52/48
Wheelbase, in. 80.0
Track, front/rear 46.3/44.8
Length 141.0
Width 54.0
Height 48.3
Fuel capacity, U.S. gal. 7.5

CHASSIS & BODY

Body/frame .... unit steel
Brake system .... 8.3-in. discs front,
  7.0 x 1.1-in. drums rear
Wheels ....styled steel, 13 x 4½
Tires .... Pirelli Cinturato CF67,
  145 SR-13
Steering type .... rack & pinion
  Turns, lock-to-lock 2.3
Suspension, front/rear: lower A-
  arms, lever shocks as upper lateral
  arms, coil springs, anti-roll bar/
  live axle on leaf springs, lever
  shocks

ENGINE & DRIVETRAIN

Type .... ohv inline 4
Bore x stroke, mm ....73.7 x 87.4
Displacement, cc/cu in...1493/91.0
Compression ratio 9.0:1
Bhp @ rpm, net...... 55.5 @ 5000
Torque @ rpm, lb-ft....73 @ 2500
Fuel requirement.. premium, 96-oct
Transmission .... 4-sp manual
Gear ratios: 4th (1.00) 3.90:1
  3rd (1.43) 5.58:1
  2nd (2.11)................. 8.23:1
  1st (3.41) 13.30:1
Final drive ratio.................... 3.90:1

CALCULATED DATA

Lb/bhp (test weight) 39.1
Mph/1000 rpm (4th gear) 16.2
Engine revs/mi (60 mph)...... 3700
R&T steering index 0.70
Brake swept area, sq in./ton .. 214

ROAD TEST RESULTS

ACCELERATION

Time to distance, sec:
  0–100 ft 3.8
  0–500 ft 10.8
  0–1320 ft (¼ mi)............20.1
Speed at end of ¼ mi, mph ..67.0
Time to speed, sec:
  0–30 mph 4.8
  0–50 mph 10.7
  0–60 mph 15.5
  0–80 mph 36.5

SPEEDS IN GEARS

4th gear (5100 rpm) 83
3rd (6000) 70
2nd (6000) 48
1st (6000) 29

FUEL ECONOMY

Normal driving, mpg..............27.5

BRAKES

Minimum stopping distances, ft:
  From 60 mph 217
  From 80 mph 326
Control in panic stop ....fair
Pedal effort for 0.5 g stop, lb .. 50
Fade: percent increase in pedal effort
  to maintain 0.5g deceleration in
  6 stops from 60 mph .. see text
Overall brake rating .... poor

HANDLING

Speed on 100-ft radius, mph ..33.2
Lateral acceleration, g 0.737
Speed thru 700-ft slalom, mph..50.1

INTERIOR NOISE

All noise readings in dBA:
Constant 30 mph 72
  50 mph 81
  70 mph 86

SPEEDOMETER ERROR

30 mph indicated is actually ..31.0
60 mph 61.0
70 mph 71.0

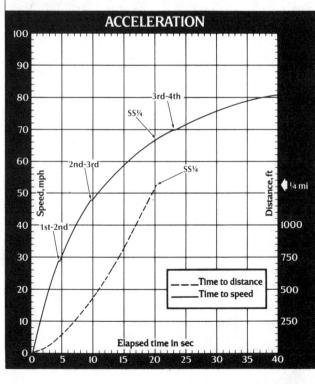

of very long stopping distances.

Keeping in mind the petite dimensions of the car, it's no surprise that it is not comfortable for anyone over about 6 ft. The quality of the interior finish is high and the soft top fits better than the last time we tested a Midget. There is still plenty of noise, mechanical and wind, and that means the car seems to be going fast at almost any speed. With the top down, and this is still not a simple task although it has been improved, the speed sensation goes up dramatically. And perhaps this is what the car is all about. All the elements are there for the young enthusiast: wind in the face, lots of gear changing, and a plethora of sports car noises. Power becomes rather secondary in this type of driving and responsiveness is of primary importance. The Midget also meets many of the other rudimentary requirements of a sports car: it has a proud name earned in road racing competition, there is an awareness of things mechanical going on all about you from the note of the exhaust to the whine of the gearbox, and there are gauges for monitoring vital functions rather than warning lights. All of these qualities come together in making a sports car something that demands to be driven with verve and expertise.

All in all, despite its outdated design and time-worn engineering, the Midget still provides that most important quality: it's fun to drive in the sports car tradition.

MG Midget 1500

1,493 c.c.

Smallest British Leyland sports car given much more punch by bigger engine. Quick, accurate steering but handling throttle-sensitive and inclined to oversteer. Harsh ride, excessive wind noise with hood up. Undergeared. Limited range

The Midget rolls considerably when cornered hard and the outside front wheel becomes heavily loaded as seen here. If at this point the steering wheel is held steady the car increasingly oversteers as the corner continues; lifting off the accelerator causes the tail to twitch sharply outwards

THERE was an outburst of lamentation from MG enthusiasts when the Midget 1500 was announced, apparently because the A-series engine had been replaced by a Triumph-designed unit. From an engineering point of view the change was almost inevitable. The Midget needed a bigger engine to counteract the effect of safety and antipollution equipment in America, where it sells in its greatest numbers; and at 1,275 c.c., the A-series unit was at the end of its "stretch potential". The answer was to instal the Triumph engine which, while of similar design and vintage, had long ago been given a longer stroke to bring its capacity to 1,493 c.c., its first application being the now-defunct front-drive Triumph 1500.

The purists may decry the move, but Triumph is a name long respected in the sports car business and there is no reason to suppose the Spitfire engine should be unsuitable for the Midget. It might be more in order to complain that a considerable increase in swept volume has resulted in a negligible increase in quoted power, from 64 bhp (net) to 66 bhp (DIN). On the other hand torque, a more important part of a sports car's character than most people realize, is increased by a greater margin. Against all this has to be balanced the greater weight of the new car, with a kerb weight (our measurement) of 15·3cwt compared with the 13·8cwt of the last 1,275 c.c. Midget we tested.

Performance and economy

The proof of the Midget 1500 is in the stopwatch, and there is no doubt it is substantially quicker than the late-series 1,275 c.c. car. Comparisons are valid because the final drive ratio remains unchanged at 3·9 to 1; the adoption of the single-rail "corporate" gearbox has meant some change in internal ratios, which are wider than before. Tyre size likewise remains the same.

The Midget 1500 is a genuine 100 mph car, and this represents a great advance on the 1275 which managed only 94 mph mean when tested in 1971. Unfortunately maximum speed takes the car over the red line on its rev counter, which over-read by a modest 100 rpm at maximum speed; clearly, therefore the Midget is substantially undergeared to make best use of its peak power, which falls at 5,500 rpm. Higher gearing would not only improve economy, but also permit higher speeds in the intermediate gears.

Although we ran the Midget beyond the 6,000 rpm red line to attain its ultimate maximum speed, we stuck to the limit in the lower gears with the result that first gear would not quite take the car to 30 mph, and third stopped just short of 70 mph. Our figures point up the considerable gap between second (47 mph maximum) and third, which is felt on the road to some extent but is disguised by the spread of useful torque.

Open sports cars always suffer in performance at the top end when they are run with the hood down, and the Midget was no exception. Lowering the hood took the maximum speed down to 94 mph – apart from making life very uncomfortable at that speed. We took no acceleration figures with the hood down, but there is no doubt they would be inferior to those obtained with the hood in place.

MG Midget 1500

All the Midget 1500 acceleration figures are far superior to those of the 1275, whether from a standing start or in any particular gear. Standing starts are best accomplished without a surfeit of revs and sudden engagement of the clutch, which tends to produce strong and uncomfortable axle tramp. A more gentle procedure, feeding in the clutch fairly fast from a 2,000 rpm starting point, trims half a second off the 1275 time to 30 mph, giving a respectable 3·7sec to this speed. The 1500 proceeds to 60 mph in 12·3sec (a 1·8sec improvement), and to 90 mph in 35·3sec, a better time by no less than 16sec. In like fashion, the standing quarter-mile now takes 18·5sec compared with 19·6 before.

In the gears, every single feature claimed by the 1275 is bettered by a substantial margin. Not only is the torque curve flatter; the 1500 does not run out of breath so quickly at the top end, while flexibility is improved to the extent of being able to pull away from 10 mph in top, which the 1275 would not tolerate.

Comparisons

MAXIMUM SPEED MPH
MG Midget 1500	(£1,560)	**101**
Ford Escort 1600 Sport	(£1,860)	100
Triumph Spitfire 1500	(£1,689)	100
Fiat 128SL 1300	(£1,791)	99
Renault 15TL	(£1,969)	94

0–60 MPH, SEC
Ford Escort 1600 Sport	10·3
MG Midget 1500	**12·3**
Fiat 128SL 1300	13·1
Triumph Spitfire 1500	13·2
Renault 15TL	13·6

STANDING ¼-MILE, SEC
Ford Escort 1600 Sport	17·9
MG Midget 1500	**18·5**
Fiat 128SL 1300	18·8
Triumph Spitfire 1500	19·1
Renault 15TL	19·3

OVERALL MPG
Renault 15TL	31·8
Triumph Spitfire 1500	29·1
Fiat 128SL 1300	28·5
MG Midget 1500	**27·9**
Ford Escort 1600 Sport	27·5

Performance

ACCELERATION SECONDS

True speed mph	Time in Secs	Car Speedo mph
30	3·7	30
40	5·8	40
50	8·5	50
60	12·3	61
70	17·0	71
80	24·0	82
90	35·3	92
100	—	102

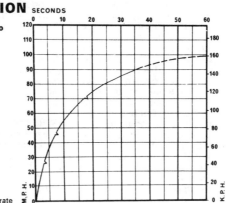

Standing ¼-mile
18·5sec 72 mph

Standing kilometre
34·9sec 90 mph

Mileage recorder: accurate

GEAR RATIOS AND TIME IN SEC
mph	Top (3·90)	3rd (5·58)	2nd (8·23)
10–30	9·8	6·2	3·9
20–40	9·2	5·8	4·0
30–50	8·7	5·8	—
40–60	9·6	6·7	—
50–70	10·2	7·9	—
60–80	12·5	—	—
70–90	19·3	—	—

GEARING
(with 145–13in. tyres)
Top	16·44 mph per 1,000 rpm
3rd	11·50 mph per 1,000 rpm
2nd	7·79 mph per 1,000 rpm
1st	4·82 mph per 1,000 rpm

MAXIMUM SPEEDS
Gear	mph	khp	rpm
Top (mean)	101	163	6,140*
(best)	102	164	6,200*
3rd	69	111	6,000
2nd	47	76	6,000
1st	29	47	6,000

*See text

BRAKES
FADE (from 70 mph in neutral)
Pedal load for 0·5g stops in lb
1	35		6	45–65
2	40–45		7	50–65
3	40–60		8	50–65
4	45–65		9	50–65
5	45–55		10	50–60

RESPONSE (from 30 mph in neutral)
Load	g	Distance
20lb	0·22	137ft
40lb	0·46	65ft
60lb	0·70	43ft
80lb	0·96	31ft
Handbrake	0·33	91ft
Max Gradient	1 in 3	

CLUTCH
Pedal 42lb and 4¾in.

Consumption

FUEL
(At constant speed – mpg)
30 mph	48·8
40 mph	44·5
50 mph	39·2
60 mph	34·2
70 mph	29·8
80 mph	26·2
90 mph	22·1
100 mph	17·6

Typical mpg 30 (9·4 litres/100km)
Calculated (DIN) mpg 32·5
(8·7 litres/100km)
Overall mpg 27·9 (10·1 litres/100km)
Grade of fuel Premium, 4-star (min 97RM)

OIL
Consumption (SAE 20W/50) 1,000 mpp

TEST CONDITIONS:
Weather: Fine
Wind: 0·3 mph
Temperature: 15deg C (58deg F)
Barometer: 29·95in. Hg
Humidity: 65 per cent
Surface: Dry concrete and asphalt
Test distance 883 miles

Figures taken by our own staff at the Motor Industry Research Association proving ground at Nuneaton.

All Autocar test results are subject to world copyright and may not be reproduced in whole or in part without the Editor's written permission.

Dimensions

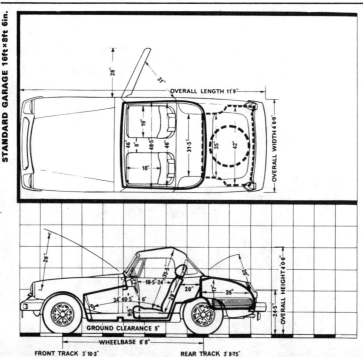

TURNING CIRCLES:
Between kerbs
L, 30ft 10in.; R, 31ft 11in.
Between walls
L, 32ft 2in.; R, 33ft 3in.
Steering wheel turns, lock to lock 2¾.

WEIGHT:
Kerb Weight 15·4cwt
(1,720lb–780kg)
(with oil, water and half full fuel tank)
Distribution, per cent
F, 53·7; R, 46·3
Laden as tested:
18·0cwt (2,020lb–917kg)

Where economy is concerned, one might expect the 1500 to be less economical because of its larger engine. On the other hand its economy should at least be comparable, because the car remains the same size and there is no reason why any more power should be needed to push it along. Two factors upset this tidy calculation. One is that the Midget in its new form is a good deal heavier; the other is its extra performance, which is used some if not all of the time. As a result, our overall fuel consumption emerged as 27·9 mpg compared with 29·6 mpg for the smaller-engined car. This is not a particularly good figure – worse than the Spitfire 1500 for instance, but then the Spitfire has higher gearing and, for our test, overdrive as well. It was noticeable, though, that the Midget's consumption stayed almost constant whoever the driver and whatever the journey, and at no time did it record a brim-to-brim figure of better than 30 mpg.

This is not to say that 30 mpg is unattainable. Our steady-speed figures show that cruising at a constant 60 mph (with the hood up!) enables the driver to better that figure with ease. If this limit were observed and fierce acceleration avoided, the Midget would prove quite economical; but it is not inherently so, still less the way it is likely to be driven.

Handling and brakes
The Midget sticks to its simple suspension arrangement with double wishbones at the front

Specification   MG Midget 1500

FRONT ENGINE, REAR-WHEEL DRIVE

Final drive	Hypoid bevel, ratio 3·90 to 1
Mph at 1,000 rpm in top gear	16·44

CHASSIS AND BODY
Construction	Integral, with steel body

SUSPENSION
Front	Independent: double wishbones, lever arm dampers, anti-roll bar
Rear	Live axle, semi-elliptic leaf springs, lever-arm dampers

STEERING
Type	Rack and pinion
Wheel dia	15½in.

BRAKES
Type	Disc front, drum rear
Dimensions	F 8·25in. dia R, 7·0in. dia, 1·25in. wide shoes
Swept area	F, 135 sq. in., R, 55 sq. in. Total 190 sq. in. (211 sq. in./ton laden)

WHEELS
Type	Pressed steel Rostyle, 4-stud fixing, 4in. wide rim
Tyres – make	Pirelli Cinturato (on test car)
– type	Radial ply tubeless
– size	145–13in.

EQUIPMENT
Battery	12 volt 40 Ah.
Alternator	28 amp a.c.
Headlamps	Sealed beam, 120/90 watt (total)
Reversing lamp	Standard

ENGINE
Cylinders	4, in line
Main bearings	3
Cooling system	Water; pump, fan and thermostat
Bore	73·7mm (2·90in.)
Stroke	87·5mm (3·44in.)
Displacement	1,493 c.c. (91·1 cu. in.)
Valve gear	Overhead: pushrods and rockers
Compression ratio	9·0 to 1. Min octane rating: 97RM
Carburettors	2 SU HS4
Fuel pump	SU mechanical
Oil filter	Full-flow, replaceable cartridge
Max power	66 bhp (DIN) at 5,500 rpm
Max torque	77 lb. ft. (DIN) at 3,000 rpm

TRANSMISSION
Clutch	Diaphragm-spring, 7·25in. diameter
Gearbox	4-speed, all-synchromesh
Gear ratios	Top 1·0
	Third 1·43
	Second 2·11
	First 3·41
	Reverse 3·75

Electric fuses	4
Screen wipers	Single-speed
Screen washer	Standard, manual plunger
Interior heater	Standard, water valve type
Heated backlight	Not available
Safety belts	Static type
Interior trim	Pvc seats
Floor covering	Carpet
Jack	Screw pillar type
Jacking points	One each side
Windscreen	Toughened
Underbody protection	Phosphate treatment under paint

MAINTENANCE
Fuel tank	7 Imp gallons (32 litres)
Cooling system	7½ pints (inc heater)
Engine sump	8 pints (4·5 litres) SAE 20W–50. Change oil every 6,000 miles. Change filter every 6,000 miles
Gearbox	1·5 pints. SAE 90EP. Check every 6,000 miles
Final drive	1·75 pints. SAE 90EP. Check every 6,000 miles
Grease	8 points every 6,000 miles
Valve clearance	Inlet 0·010in. (cold) Exhaust 0·010in. (cold)
Contact breaker	0·015in. gap.
Ignition timing	10deg BTDC (stroboscopic at 650 rpm)
Spark plug	Type: Champion N9Y. Gap 0·025in.
Tyre pressures	F 22; R 24 psi (normal driving) F 26; R 28 psi (high speed) F 22; R 26 psi (full load)
Max payload	420lb (190kg)

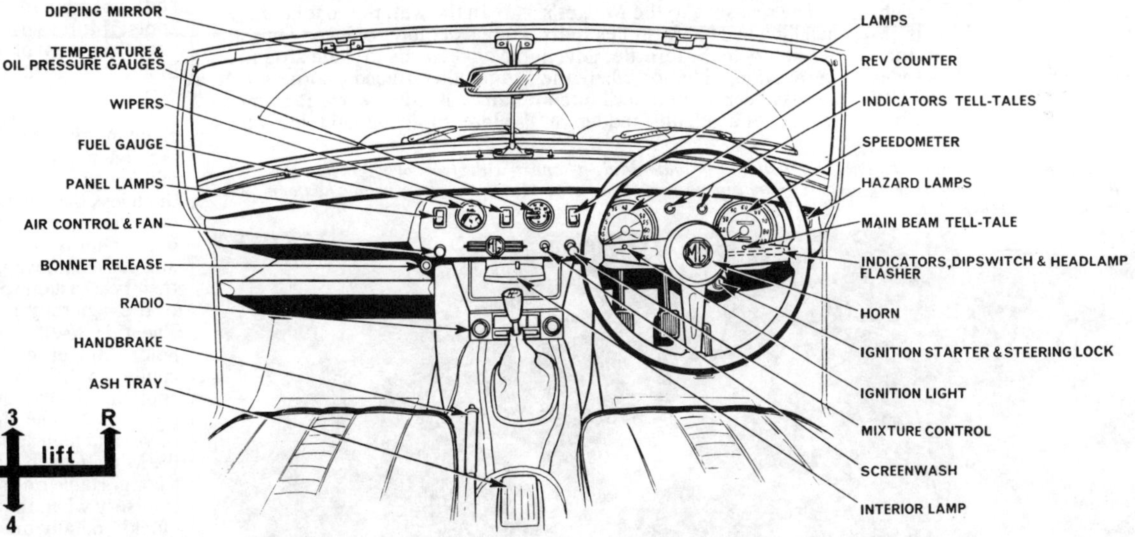

Interior/dashboard diagram labels:
DIPPING MIRROR, TEMPERATURE & OIL PRESSURE GAUGES, WIPERS, FUEL GAUGE, PANEL LAMPS, AIR CONTROL & FAN, BONNET RELEASE, RADIO, HANDBRAKE, ASH TRAY, LAMPS, REV COUNTER, INDICATORS TELL-TALES, SPEEDOMETER, HAZARD LAMPS, MAIN BEAM TELL-TALE, INDICATORS, DIPSWITCH & HEADLAMP FLASHER, HORN, IGNITION STARTER & STEERING LOCK, IGNITION LIGHT, MIXTURE CONTROL, SCREENWASH, INTERIOR LAMP

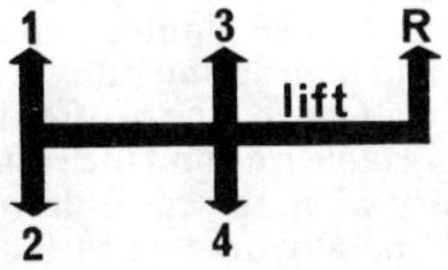

Gear shift diagram: 1 3 R / lift / 2 4

Servicing   6,000 miles

Time Allowed (hours)	3·5
Cost at £4.30 per hour	£15.05
Engine oil	£2.50
Oil Filter	£2.15
Air Filter	£1.08
Contact Breaker Points	£0.52
Sparking Plugs *	£1.48
Total Cost:	**£22.78**

*when required

Routine Replacements:	Time hours	Labour	Spares	TOTAL
Brake Pads – Front (2 wheels)	1·00	£4.30	£3.80	£8.10
Brake Shoes – Rear (2 wheels)	1·35	£5.80	£3.80	£9.60
Exhaust System	0·85	£3.65	£19.50	£23.15
Clutch (centre+driven plate)	8·00	£34.40	£12.83	£47.23
Dampers – Front (pair)	1·55	£6.65	£28.88	£35.53
Dampers – Rear (pair)	1·00	£4.30	£25.52	£29.82
Replace Half Shaft	0·55	£2.35	£13.80	£16.15
Replace Alternator	0·70	£3.00	£27.00	£30.00
Replace Starter	1·60	£6.90	£15.86	£22.76

MG Midget 1500

and a live rear axle located by semi-elliptic leaf springs with no other form of assistance. It worked well enough in the past, given the Midget's very limited wheel travel, but there are signs that the latest car needs something more sophisticated to cope with its greater torque and performance.

Part of the trouble lies in the fact that the Midget, like the MGB, has been given increased ride height at the back to compensate for the greater weight of its "5 mph" bumpers and associated structure. As a result, roll stiffness at the back end has been reduced and there is much more tendency to oversteer. This is despite the heavier engine which means the front wheels bear a greater part of the total weight.

The best feature of the Midget, as always, is its very quick and accurate steering. With less than three turns of the wheel between extremes of an average 32ft turning circle, the driver never has to tie his arms in knots to turn a corner or rescue a situation. Inevitably, there is some kick-back on rough surfaces, but this is by no means the most tiring feature of the car.

Straight-line stability is no better than average, except on ultra-smooth surfaces. Normally, the Midget feels willing enough to keep to a straight course but if the wheel is released for a moment it soon reveals its willingness to wander off-line. The feeling of stability is actually due to the driver

Massive front bumper makes the whole car look bigger than before; inset lights are well protected by lipped extensions. Door mirrors are part of standard equipment. Headlamps are sealed-beam units, not halogen

Standard number plate is mounted beneath the new "5 mph" bumper, rather than below the boot lid as in previous Midgets. Reversing lights are standard and boot lid can be left unlocked if the driver wishes

being barely conscious of the tiny but constant corrections he is applying.

The handling, as we have already said, holds the promise of oversteer. It is not evident at first, for in gentle driving the Midget stays very close to neutral. When driven harder into a corner, if the driver holds the wheel and accelerator steady, the tail will come out steadily until some of the lock has to be paid off before the car gets too sideways. In itself this is no bad thing, for it enables the Midget to be driven in distinctly sporting fashion by someone who knows what he is doing. At the same time it holds the seeds of danger for anyone less clever.

The real snag to the Midget's handling in 1500 form lies in its sensitivity to the throttle. Given the previous situation where the car has been wound hard into a long, tight bend, any sudden release of the accelerator will bring the tail out very smartly, calling for opposite lock to pin it down. Again, this is a situation beloved of some drivers but it means the Midget is much less predictable, and certainly calls for more skill, than many small saloons of equal performance *and* cornering ability. The drawback is compounded by limited roadholding, which can leave the car well-balanced fore and aft, but skittering sideways onto a wider line than desired. Despite the increased weight and torque, the tyre section remains the same as 145–13in., and it is difficult to avoid the conclusion that the 1500 is somewhat under-tyred.

In the wet, the roadholding is considerably reduced and the Midget tends to skate around on smooth-surfaced corners. In this case, however, it is much more forgiving and the quick

steering really comes into its own.

The brakes need moderate effort and generally work well, giving a well-controlled ultimate stop of 0·95g for a pedal effort of 80lb – well within reasonable limits. The brakes have good "feel", with no sign of sponginess, and no tendency to snatch when cold. Their fade performance is less reassuring with a near-doubling of effort for a 0·5g stop during our ten-stop test, and some smell of linings towards the end; but even then there is no increase in pedal travel.

The handbrake works well, our test car recording a 0·33g stop when the handbrake was used alone on the level. It also held the car well facing either way on the 1-in-3 test hill, on which a restart was easily achieved thanks to the low first gear – but not without a smell of clutch lining.

Comfort and convenience

The Midget could hardly be described as anything but cramped, with difficult entry and exit. It has always been so, and buyers have accepted it. But the statistics tell us that Britons are getting bigger – not to say Americans – and we are surely approaching the point where it may be too small for its own good. In fact our largest staff members (the largest of all scaling 16½ stone and 6ft 2in.) found the interior space just sufficient with the driver's seat moved to its back stop, but complained of their inability to shift position to relieve numb spots. More serious were the contortions involved in getting in and out, even with the hood down.

The seats do not look especially inviting, reminding one of the shapeless BMC equipment of a few years ago. This is doing them less than justice. Together with the generally tight confines of the interior they locate driver and passenger well, and they do their best to damp out the effects of the generally mediocre ride. The ride itself will not disappoint Midget enthusiasts and could only be described, euphemistically, as "good for the liver". The limited wheel travel and high spring rates give the Midget no chance of offering a comfortable ride and the result is misery when the car is driven quickly on any uneven surface, let alone a really rough one. On the credit side it is very rare for the suspension actually to bottom, and the 1500 is notably free of the crashes and bangs which afflicted some earlier Midgets, especially when their dampers were past the first flush of youth. Nor is the handling very much affected by suspension movement, so a driver fit enough to withstand the battering can make rapid progress along almost any British road.

Bigger Triumph 1500TC engine does not look unduly large under Midget bonnet, with plenty of length to spare and room for the massive heater trunking. Access to some items is good, but others (such as battery behind heater blower unit) are difficult to reach

Above: Black crackle-finished facia panel gives slightly vintage air to the interior. Rev counter and speedometer are widely separated but can still be seen inside rim of large steering wheel. Minor dials are less easily read

Left: Midget seats look rather stylized but not very well shaped; in fact they are quite comfortable, damping out the worst effects of the ride, while the small size of the interior ensures good location. Note the awkwardly-placed door handle by the occupant's shoulder

Boot lid is supported by a single self-locking strut. Capacity is strictly limited and there is a low sill over which luggage must be lifted. Spare wheel and fuel tank lie flat on the boot floor and beneath it respectively

The controls are not well laid out, but at least they are easy to understand and are clearly labelled. There are signs of penny-pinching in the single (too slow) speed wipers, the manual-plunger washer, the primitive heater control. Of the major controls, the steering wheel is larger than one might expect and close to the chest by modern standards; the pedals are understandably close together in their narrow tunnel. Clutch effort is high but pedal movement limited, though the clutch takes up sweetly enough. In the test car, however, the accelerator linkage was rather "sudden" and no help to gentle driving. The gearchange is precise but not as quick as some of its rivals.

A major drawback of the Midget is its high interior noise level. For the most part it is made up of wind noise, which drowns the other components to the extent where one is unsure how much contribution the engine is making until one switches off and coasts at high speed. The wind noise itself comes from the hood, and while this may seem inevitable there are other soft-top cars which do not suffer in the same way (or at least, not to the same extent). In the Midget's case it is noticeable that the car is much quieter with the hood down, and the radio easier to hear, at speeds as high as 70 mph. Indeed, with the hood up the radio is almost inaudible above this speed. The

engine actually makes a lot of noise at higher speeds – it simply can't compete with the wind roar. Induction and exhaust noise is high when the car is accelerating hard, at anything over 5,000 rpm; but when the car is driven more gently the 1500 unit is quiet and refined. Noisy or not, it is very smooth right up to the red line and beyond, in a way that may surprise MG diehards.

Even with the hood up, visibility is not bad. At first sight the windscreen is shallow but it seems to provide sufficient view for short and tall drivers; the hinged quarter-lights obstruct the front-quarter view a little, but the "over-the-shoulder" blind spot is cleared by two extra windows let into the hood. Two door mirrors are standard, but on the test car they continually flopped down to a useless position. The wipers clear only a small area of screen and are too slow to cope with heavy rain. Sealed-beam headlights give good illumination at night but the driver's low eyeline prevents him making the most of it. Reversing lights are standard.

The heater is a primitive affair with a single push-pull control for temperature; and a single-speed fan which can only be switched on when full heat is selected. There is no means of selecting airflow to screen or floor, the output being shared arbitrarily. However, the fan is quiet and the heater clears the screen quickly even in humid conditions. There is no direct-flow ventilation other than via the quarter-lights.

Living with the Midget 1500

By comparison with Midget hoods of a few years ago that of the 1500 is easy to contend with. It is not yet a simple one-handed operation either to stow or erect it, though, and in particular it is much easier to fit its leading edge to the windscreen rail if four hands are available. With the hood down one does not get too battered by the airflow, even at high speed, but one driver found that when driving open in light rain the inside of the windscreen soon became covered in droplets and the occupants of the car dampened.

A basic appeal of the Midget is its simplicity, and this is still so with the 1500 which is no more difficult to work on than its predecessors. The most awkward servicing point is the need

to reach the battery at the very rear of the engine compartment under the hinge line of the bonnet; the dipstick is not easy to find, especially in the dark. A link with tradition is the need to attend to eight grease points during the 6,000-mile service – but there are no intermediate service intervals, so an average car requires only twice-a-year attention.

A main drawback of the car is its small (7-gallon) tank, which gives a safe range of less than 200 miles. It is filled via a simple cap in the rear panel, and unlike many modern tanks can be filled quickly to the brim with no danger of blow-back.

There are few accessories to be added to the Midget from the MG option list. A hardtop is expensive but might prove an investment in terms of reduced wind noise and long-journey comfort; wire wheels are available for those who can face the chore of cleaning them; and head restraints may be specified. There is no overdrive option, far less an automatic. Static seat belts are standard – apparently there is no room for inertia-reel units.

In conclusion

There is no doubt that the performance of the Midget has been greatly improved by its change of engine, and there is now a spread of torque which allows the car to be driven sportingly or to be lugged along all the way in top gear by a lazy or tired driver. At the same time the handling has suffered in some respects and the car is no longer as predictable or forgiving as it was.

People are bound to differ on how badly cramped they find the interior (though few will argue with the infuriating difficulty of reaching the interior door handles), but few would quarrel with the conclusion that the ride is harsh and the noise level over-high.

Now that the Midget and the Spitfire share the same engine, the question of their joint survival must arise. For our money – and there is scant price difference between the two – the Spitfire is much more practical and civilized. There will always be those who will scorn it for precisely those reasons, but if further rationalization comes to pass it will be difficult to make out a case for the Midget *vis-à-vis* its stablemate. □

MANUFACTURER:
British Leyland UK Ltd., Austin-Morris Division, Longbridge, Birmingham

PRICES		Insurance	Group 5
Basic	£1,333.00		
Special Car Tax	£111.08		
VAT	£115.53	**EXTRAS (inc VAT)**	
Total (in GB)	**£1,559.61**	Wire wheels	£56.12
Seat Belts, static type	(standard)	Hard top	£112.09
Licence	£40.00	Head-restraints*	£18.27
Delivery charge (London)	£15.00	*Fitted to test car	
Number plates	£6.60		
Total on the Road (exc insurance)	**£1,621.21**	**TOTAL AS TESTED ON THE ROAD**	**£1,639.48**

COMPARISON:

The list of sports cars for less than $5000 is smaller now, but there are still four you can have without destroying your annual budget

The Affordable Sports Cars

In an era of $70,000 Rolls-Royces, $35,000 Maseratis, $30,000 Porsches and even $10,000 Volvos, one could be forgiven for coming to the conclusion that the price of other than simple transportation has finally been raised beyond the reach of mere mortals. Happily, thanks to the British and the Italians, that conclusion is not entirely accurate.

While England and Italy build the majority of the world's most expensive and exotic cars, they also seem able, in spite of spiraling worldwide inflation, to provide sports motoring for the less fortunate. In spite of all, they manage to keep coming up with the sort of car that one can take out on a lonely road and barrel the bejeezus out of, sampling small perils in controlled doses without spending the price of shelter for the privilege.

While it is true that the list of such cars has shrunk over the last couple of years, four are still available. While they reflect the inflation that has lofted the going price of even the most mundane of cars, they are still affordable if one considers the dividing line between reason and indulgence to be $5000. This is an admittedly arbitrary figure. We chose it simply because this is the top price you might logically set if you were looking for a normal, low-buck automobile with the more popular creature comforts and a bit of cosmetic verve. You could, perhaps, get away with less if you were willing to settle for absolute basic transportation for carrying you from Point A to Point B. However, we are speaking of having fun, not mere transportation with nil excitement quotient.

Where once there were a number of manufacturers of the kind of car we are talking about, there are now but two: Fiat and British Leyland. British Leyland has long specialized

in providing sports cars for the less pecunious and is still in there pitching. Three British Leyland sports cars are still under our arbitrary limit in spite of inflation and rising costs brought about by compliance with U.S. regulations: the MGB, Triumph Spitfire and MG Midget, in descending order of cost. Two others, the Triumph TR-6 and TR-7, are over the limit by about $500 and so are not treated here, but if you feel the pinch of indulgence outweighs the reason of affordability, they are well worth a look.

Fiat, that giant among European car manufacturers, is primarily engaged in bringing family transport to the world's masses, but it still finds time to indulge the adventurous. Inflation has done its work on Fiat, as it has on British Leyland, and the Fiat sports cars under our price ceiling add up to just one, the X 1/9. The popular 124 Spider is a healthy $800 over the 5-grand dividing line. Matter of fact, the X 1/9 just barely slides in under the line at $4947 plus $50 in dealer preparation charges.

It must be remembered that these cars are not family cars or even econo coupes in the accepted sense. They are sports cars, fairly pure and fairly simple, as sports cars are meant to be. Performing, as they do, on about the level of inexpensive sports cars of the early Fifties, they aren't even particularly fast in the straight line sense. What they do provide is light, sensitive steering, quick response to control inputs, better-than-average braking and a general feel of being in command of the automobile. In two instances there is also the *feeling* of speed, imparted by small size, a busy, buzzy engine, instant response, wind in the hair and the general exhilaration of top-down motoring. There is room

for two and a weekend's worth of light luggage. Period.

This is not to say these cars are utterly Spartan in terms of creature comfort. In comparison with sports car standards of recent memory, these cars are equipped like limousines, with a plethora of amenities. They all have heaters—that work—as standard equipment, optional radios that you can hear (if the top is right), interior courtesy lights and even cigarette lighters. They are also reasonably weatherproof, an attribute that was, not all that long ago, a seeming impossibility.

Your 32nd-degree sports car aficionado of the recent past, unless he was suffering from double pneumonia, erected a top only to ward off hailstones or snow, when parked under a tree or in the vicinity of seagulls, in which case a tonneau cover would do just as well. Perhaps the fact that sports car tops were fingernail-ripping abominations had something to do with it, or perhaps it was plain *machismo*. In any event, the tops on these cars are, while not effortless, a vast improvement.

The point is, the joy of a sports car lies not in the comfort it imparts but in the enthusiastic driving of it, a pleasure that transcends the lack of comfort so far as to make it nonessential.

MG MIDGET

In the beginning (almost) there was the Midget. MGs with the Midget designation have been built since 1929, when the first M-type rolled off the line. There was a six-year hiatus for World War II and another one from 1955 to 1961, the latter occasioned by the take-over of the parent Nuffield organization by Austin in 1955 and during which only the various MG-A models appeared.

The current MG Midget has had the longest life of all of the Midgets: 12 years. If you want to stretch the point, it actually began life in 1961, the product of a British practice called "badge engineering." When BMC did a redesign on the famous Austin-Healey Sprite, getting rid of the "bugeye" look just as it was catching on, management decided to revive the Midget name. With a slight change in trim and a small price increase, it hung the MG octagon on the new Sprite Mk. II and called it the Midget Mk. I. Whether it increased sales or not, history recordeth not, but the inevitable result was that both became interchangeably known as Spridgets. These Midgets were true roadsters with all that the name implies. They had hip, shoulder and leg room for 6-footers and were light and responsive, if not overly fast. As a matter of fact they were a shade too responsive, thanks to the trailing quarter elliptic rear springs inherited from the Sprite.

As a result of this over-response and dealer pressure for more of the amenities, a new Midget, the Mk. II, appeared in 1964, along with the Sprite Mk. III. With the new car came a new rear end with semi-elliptic springs similar to that of the MGB and an engine displacement increase from 948 to 1098 cc. To the dismay of the purists, BMC also added heavier seats and roll-up windows which meant heavier, thicker doors. The new car didn't dart unpredictably about on minor wheel and throttle inputs any more, it was reasonably dry in the rain if you remembered to roll up the windows before you shut the doors, and it didn't have room for 6-footers anymore. The Sprite nameplate has been off the market for nearly a decade now, but the Midget in this configuration with various add-ons and deletions is with us to this day.

The first of the changes was for the better. To make up for smog tuning, the engine was given more displacement to 1275 cc, about maximum for the BMC A-type engine. This gave it sufficient low-end torque to play games with larger cars without embarrassment and also gave it tuning potential to make it a successful contender in SCCA production class racing. However, as the emissions regulations tightened up, the upper-end power was slowly eroded by the required progressive detuning. It wasn't detectable at first without a stopwatch, but by 1973 you could tell the difference without help.

With the stringent 1975 emissions requirements in the immediate future, a change was dictated. The 1275cc engine was at its displacement limit,

The MG Midget is the least expensive of the four "affordables," but that doesn't change the fun—only the style. The cockpit has shrunk over the years, so that it is a tight fit for 6-footers. If you can do without the spare tire, the trunk will carry a fair amount of luggage, but otherwise it, like the cockpit, is tight. A good learner's car, the Midget is forgiving and can be tossed around with a fair amount of abandon, thanks in part to the use of the 1500 Spitfire engine.

Triumph's Spitfire is the exact equal of the Midget in straight-line performance, but it's a touch more sophisticated. The cockpit was designed around roll-up windows, so it is roomier than the Midget. The trunk is deep, even with the spare, and without will carry a lot of gear. It, too, is a learner's car, but due to its all-independent suspension requires more tidy driving than the Midget. Precision pays off in better performance. Engine is single-carbureted with 1496 cc.

The MGB has been raised on its chassis and has new, heavy safety bumpers. The result is that it has considerable lean and feels less stable than before. Its cockpit is the roomiest of all and is well-instrumented and comfortable. The trunk, on the other hand, is unfinished and crowded by the spare. Though the handling suffers by comparison to earlier versions, the MGB is still fun to drive and forgiving in its road manners. Use of single carb has cut power and revs.

The Fiat X 1/9, with its mid-engine configuration, is easily the most advanced of the quartet, with superb road manners and precise handling. In spite of its smaller engine, it also is the fastest of the four. The cockpit is roomy and exceptionally well-appointed. Luggage space is ample with a deep compartment under the nose, unencumbered by a spare. A second, smaller compartment is at the rear of the engine bay. The 1290cc SOHC engine is tucked in sideways.

and there were only two solutions: a bigger engine or an entirely new one with greater efficiency. Management opted for the former course, and the 1493cc Triumph Spitfire engine was adapted. This has brought back the low-end torque, but emissions requirements dictate that it be equipped with only one carburetor instead of the pair that had graced MGs and Midgets since time immemorial. The result is that it's out of steam between 4500 and 5000 rpm. There is one improvement that went with the new engine, and that is the Spitfire all-synchro transmission. The 1275cc Midget was perhaps the last car in the world with a 4-speed gearbox to come without a synchronized low gear, and the new gearbox has finally ended that abomination, giving the Midget a flexibility it never had before. A 20-plus percent gain in highway fuel mileage doesn't hurt a bit either.

The safety regulations have also had their influence on the Midget. In 1975, safety bumper regs finally caught up with it, and now a large, plastic-covered bumper-cum-snout has been appliqued over the front, and an equally massive black ledge is mounted on the rear. This added weight would be bad enough stuck out on the ends of the car, but to insult is added the injury of a height requirement, necessitating the raising of the chassis. The rise in height, fortunately, is minimal in the Midget's case, and handling does not suffer except for the feeling of high polarity imparted by the extra weight that tends to give a spooky dumbbell effect.

It's easier to find the differences between the current Midget and the one just past on the track than it is on the road. Up to 60 mph the new Midget is quicker than the previous one by just short of 2 seconds. It is also quicker to 30 mph by a full second. As a consequence, the car feels, and actually is, stronger at all traffic speeds than it was before. After 60 mph, however, the single carburetor makes its presence known by a flattening out of the acceleration curve, with the result that the standing quarter mile time and speed is almost what it was with the older engine, or just a touch less. What it all amounts to is that the added torque from the increased displacement makes itself known at the lower end, but the ability to rev has been effectively choked off by reduced ability to breathe.

In the handling department, the stopwatch and g-meter tell the real story. The current car is slower through the slalom than its predecessor by an average half-second, and transient g-forces are less, thanks to the weight shift brought about by raising the chassis. You need instruments to pinpoint it, but it's there.

There is now, and always has been, one endearing aspect about the Midget: It feels like it's going faster than it really is. Combined with road-holding and responsive handling that is surprising, considering the elementary suspension, it is possible to go out and have a ball on country roads without getting in over your head. The Midget has always been considered a sports car for people who want to learn how to drive sports cars. It still is.

SPITFIRE

When first introduced in 1963, Triumph's Spitfire was designed primarily to do one thing—to take a piece of the market owned by BMC's MG Midget and Sprite. Built to a price of $2000, give or take a buck or two, it was designed around Triumph Herald bits and pieces, at least insofar as the suspension and engine were concerned. It was not without its crudities as a result, but it had a number of things going for it as well. The cockpit was far more roomy than that of the Spridget, it had roll-up windows as an integral part of the design, it had a top you could put up without the help of a pit crew, and it had a better ride insofar as normal street driving was concerned. These attributes are still part of the package, remaining unchanged through

13 years and four model updates.

Perhaps the most significant of the improvements over the years was a rear axle change that took place with the second update which brought forth the Mk. III. The original Spitfire had swing axles taken directly from the Herald. Calling the rear axle behavior mere tuck-under when hardpressed was charitable. The car would stick up to a point and then let go with a sort of slingshot effect that could have you quickly pointing the way you had just come if you weren't quick enough to catch it. With the MK. III that became a thing of the past. The rear axle is still a swing type, but it has now been so

Specifications:

GENERAL	MG Midget	Triumph Spitfire	MGB	Fiat X 1/9
Importer	British Leyland Motors, Inc. 600 Willowtree Rd. Leonia, NJ 07605	British Leyland Motors, Inc. 600 Willowtree Rd. Leonia, NJ 07605	British Leyland Motors, Inc. 600 Willowtree Rd. Leonia, NJ 07605	Fiat Distributors, Inc. 155 Chestnut Ridge Rd. Montvale, NJ 07645
Number of U.S. dealers	467	383	467	647
Warranty	12 months/12,000 miles	12 months/12,000 miles	12 months/12,000 miles	12 months/12,000 miles
Base list price POE	$3949	$4295	$4795	$4947
Options on test car	Wire wheels (painted), $135; Tonneau cover, $50	AM/FM radio, $150; Tonneau cover, $50	AM/FM radio, $150; Tonneau cover, $50	AM/FM radio, NA
Price as tested	$4134	$4495	$4995	$5190
POWER UNIT				
Type	OHV 4-cyl	OHV 4-cyl	OHV 4-cyl	SOHC 4-cyl
Bore & stroke	2.90x3.44 in./ 73.7x87.5 mm	2.90x3.44 in./ 73.7x87.5 mm	3.16x3c5 in./ 80.2x88.9 mm	3.39x2.19 in./ 86x22.5 mm
Displacement	91.1 cid/1493 cc	91.1 cid/1493 cc	110 cid/1798 cc	78.7 cid/1290 cc
Maximum net HP	55.5 @ 5000 rpm	57.5 @ 5000 rpm	62.5 @ 5000 rpm	61 @ 5800 rpm
Maximum net torque	73.3 lb/ft @ 2500 rpm	74.5 lb/ft @ 2500 rpm	86 lb/ft @ 2500 rpm	67 lb/ft @ 4000 rpm
Compression ratio	9.1:1 (7.5:1 Calif.)	9.1:1	8.0:1	8.5:1
Carburetion	One S.U. sidedraft	One S.U. sidedraft	One S.U. sidedraft	Single 2-bbl
DRIVETRAIN				
Transmission type	4-spd manual	4-spd manual	4-spd manual	4-spd manual
Final drive ratio	3.9:1	3.89:1	3.9:1	4.41:1
CHASSIS				
Body/frame	Unit body	Body on backbone frame	Unit body	Unit body
Suspension, front	Ind, coil springs, lever shocks	Ind, coil springs, tube shocks	Ind, coils, lever shocks	MacPherson struts
rear	Live axle, leaf springs, lever shocks	Ind, transverse leaf springs	Live axle, leaf springs, lever shocks	Chapman struts
Brakes, front	Disc	Disc	Disc	Disc
rear	Drum	Drum	Drum	Disc
Steering system	Rack & pinion	Rack & pinion	Rack & pinion	Rack & pinion
Steering ratio	2.25 turns lock to lock	2.75 turns lock to lock	2.93 turns lock to lock	3.0 turns lock to lock
Tire make & size	Pirelli 145SR x 13	Dunlop 155SR x 13	Pirelli 165 SR x 14	Pirelli 145 HR x 13
DIMENSIONS				
Wheelbase	80.0 in./203.2 cm	83.0 in./210.8 cm	91.3 in./231.9 cm	86.7 in./220.4 cm
Track, front	46.31 in./117.6 cm	49.0 in./124.4 cm	49.0 in./124.4 cm	52.5 in./133.3 cm
rear	44.75 in./113.6 cm	50.0 in./127.0 cm	49.25 in./125.1 cm	52.9 in./134.3cm
Length	141 in./358.1 cm	156.3 in./397.0 cm	158.25 in./401.1 cm	158.5 in./402.6 cm
Width	60.25 in./153.0 cm	58.5 in./148.6 cm	59.9 in./152.1 cm	61.8 in./156.9 cm
Height	48.25 in./122.5 cm	45.6 in./115.8 cm	51.0 in./129.5 cm	46.1 in./117.1 cm
Weight	1825 lb/827.8 kg	1780 lb/897.4 kg	2275 lb/1032 kg	2050 lb/930.5 kg
Fuel capacity	7.5 gals.	8.7 gals.	12.25 gals.	12.7 gals
PERFORMANCE				
0-30 mph	4.8 sec	4.8 sec	5.5 sec	4.1 sec
0-60 mph	16.4 sec	16.4 sec	18.5 sec	14.0 sec
40-60 mph	8.4 sec	8.8 sec	10.1 sec	6.9 sec
Quarter mile	20.7 sec	20.3 sec	21.0 sec	20.8 sec
MPH	65.2	65.8	62.3	73.2
Braking, 30-0 mph	35.3 ft	34.2 ft	33.7 ft	31.5 ft
60-0 mph	145.4 ft	136.5 ft	150.2 ft	126.5 ft
Fuel economy, 73-mile loop	30.4 mpg	27.9 mpg	25.2 mpg	28.6 mpg

well located that, while the wheels still look ready to tuck under when the car is going around a corner, they aren't. A new Spitfire will produce a lateral acceleration figure of more than .7 g around a 200-ft circle and buzz through our lane-change slalom in less than 14 seconds.

The Spitfire has had only one major engine change during its relatively long lifetime. Originally equipped with a 1296cc OHV engine with two 1¼-in. SU carburetors, it had to be detuned by having the spark retarded to 6 degrees *after* top dead center and by the replacement of the dual carburetion with a single 1½-in. SU, which weakened it greatly. A little performance was regained by increasing the displacement to 1493 cc. That increased low-end torque, but a single inch-and-a-half carburetor simply can't sufficiently feed a 1500cc engine at high revs. (As an aside, there's nothing—except in California—that says you can't bolt the old dual-carb setup on your 1500. It fits perfectly.)

As they come out of the box, there is little to choose between the performance of the Spitfire and the Midget, which isn't surprising, since they share the same engine. Both will do a 0-60 mph run in 16-and-a-fraction seconds, and both will put 66 mph into a standing quarter mile in 20 seconds. Both exhibit enough torque to stay with traffic at normal speeds. In any kind of a drag race between the two cars, it would be the driver with more skill in getting off the line and picking the right shift points who would emerge the winner. Since they are geared basically the same, they both exhibit that choked-off feeling at the high end of the rev scale, and both cars will reach a top speed of only 80 (a little more with a tail wind). There is a slight weight difference in favor of the Midget, but the Spitfire's more slippery shape seems to cancel that out.

The major difference between the two cars, other than the fact that the Spitfire will accommodate 6-footers, lies in the handling. Thanks to the slightly more sophisticated suspension, the Spitfire sticks better both in steady-state turns and in the slalom. Where the Midget does well to get through the single, double, triple lane change problem in 15 seconds, the Spit will do it handily at 14 seconds flat. It would probably do it even quicker but for a difference in the original-equipment tires. The Midget's Pirelli CN36 radials have an edge over the Spitfire's Goodyear G800 radials. On the open road, a Midget will stay with a Spitfire, but the Spit-

fire driver will be merely motoring briskly, while the Midget driver will be working at it.

The Spitfire, like the Midget, is a car for those who want to learn how to drive a sports car properly, but with a difference. The Midget, with its live axle and elementary suspension, is a car you can toss around. The Spitfire is a little different, since it sticks a bit better and it's best driven through a turn rather than being tossed into it. You can learn skills with it that you probably won't learn with a Midget since, without a gob of torque or a live axle to slide with, it must be driven tidily to get the most out of it. The practice can only teach precision, an attribute in any car.

MGB

We have long been defenders of the MGB against those who have put it down for its dated suspension. Unfortunately, we now have to defer, not so much for its basic design, but for the modifications that have been forced upon it. It is a perfect example of the fact that if you mess about overmuch with a tradition, you no longer have a tradition but an anachronism.

The MGB has been with us since 1962, a long run for a single model with so few changes, at least until recently. For the first dozen years of its 14-year lifetime, the B remained almost untouched by emissions and safety regulations. If anything, the later MGBs rode better and handled better than their predecessors.

True, you could not corner a box-stock MGB on a controlled transient lane change test or a steady-state 200-ft circle with a Dino or a Lotus, but you could come as close as would be comfortable on the road. In point of fact, the "crudeness" of the MGB's behavior tends to make it more forgiving than some more sophisticated cars, allowing for a certain amount of unskilled *brio* that more advanced designs won't allow.

Unfortunately, emissions and safety regulations have caught up with the MGB all in one large, unpalatable lump. The 1975-76 emissions rulings finally outstripped the ability of the tuners to cope as they had since 1968. The most noticeable change is in the carburetion. A single 175 SU CDSE carburetor replaces the pair of 1½-inch SU carburetors the car has had since the beginning. The result is a reduction not only in horsepower but in the engine speed at which peak horsepower is developed, i.e., a loss of usable revs along with power.

In 1974 the rated power was 78 bhp at 5400 rpm; it is now 62.5 bhp at 5000 rpm. In actual practice it starts running out of air at not much more than 4500 rpm. The result is that both the Midget and the Spitfire will outdo it in the standing quarter mile by 4 mph and a significant fraction of a second. It will eventually reach 80-and-a-bit mph.

The power loss would be acceptable if that were the only problem with the current model. The old practice of rubber bumper over-riders will no longer meet safety requirements. As with the Midget, a large bumper-cum-snout was added to the front, and a massive, plastic-covered bumper was added at the rear. The high polarity or dumbbell effect these impart would have been noticeable in any event, but there is also a bumper and headlight height requirement. This necessitated either a major body change, for which B-L wasn't really ready, or the simpler expedient of raising the car higher on the suspension. The latter was chosen here as with the Midget. The result is the raising of the center of gravity by a significant amount and the consequent loss of the flat cornering that has always marked the B's behavior. The ride is still as good as it was, but the car now rolls severely, and there is a definite loss of adhesion. Both the 200-ft circle and slalom test confirmed this seat-of-the-pants feeling. The g-force generated on the circle is now down to an average of .68 g, and on the slalom the transients, always higher than steady-state figures, are barely .75 g. It still sticks better than your average sedan, and by that token it's still a sports car in behavior, but by comparison to previous Bs it is sadly softened.

This is not to say you can't still go out and have fun with it. You can. It's just that it isn't quite the same as before, and a truly shriven MGB owner is advised to hang onto his '74 or earlier or be prepared to make some modifications to the new one.

It is also unthinkable that the men of Abingdon will let this state of affairs go on overly long; after all, they and their works are a tradition, and a fix for the situation will undoubtedly be made. Speed the day.

FIAT X 1/9

Fiat's delectable little confection, the X 1/9, is as contemporary as the other cars in the category are traditional. Nothing, but nothing, handles as well as a properly designed mid-engine sports car. Normally the mid-engine configuration means a price in the five-figure bracket, but the X 1/9 brings the precise handling, if not the sizzle, of the mid-engine sports within reach the of "masses."

After driving the X 1/9, it's a little clearer why some enthusiasts will lay out the price of a small house for the Ferrari Dino. The X 1/9 certainly lacks the Dino's power, but there is the same solid feeling, the same neutral handling, the same precision of control and the air of being at one with the car. There is a tendency on the part of some reviewers, including some members of the MT staff, to downgrade the straight-line performance of the X 1/9. It's understandable, because the car, unlike others in the "affordable" category, doesn't seem to be going as fast as it is. This is, in part, due to its excellent and unflappable road manners and the transverse engine position.

The rocking couple of the engine is in line with the fore and aft line of the car, and there is no feeling of twist when the throttle is applied. The result is that you don't really feel the acceleration as you do in those cars with the more normal engine position. The effect is visual, and it is only when you see you are pulling away from other traffic that you realize the car is doing quite creditably. As a matter of fact the X 1/9 is both quicker and faster than any of the other cars in this group. What feels like moderately brisk motoring in the X 1/9 feels like breaking the sound barrier in the Midget or Spitfire. In a sense, such a comparison is a bit unfair, because those two cars are not peers of the X 1/9, either in price or performance. Its real peers are the earlier MGB, the current TR-6 and the California version of the TR-7, at least insofar as performance.

Because it is of the so-called Targa design—a coupe with a removable roof section, rather than a roadster—the X 1/9 has more of the creature comforts than the others. It also has a bit more storage space. There is a fair-size storage bay in front that isn't crowded by a spare tire, which is nestled behind the drivers seat, and a smaller, narrower compartment all the way at the rear capable of carrying a couple of small overnight bags and the oddment of soft luggage.

There is only one small problem with the X 1/9. In certain areas, primarily the East and West Coasts, the car is so much in demand that some dealers find it irresistible to load it with extras, kicking the price up more than a little. However, if you look around you can find one without the full load. The X 1/9, as it comes from the store, is very desirable property and the most sophisticated of the affordable's

CONCLUSIONS

Even though the list is short, there is an interesting variety in this mix of cars. The Midget is the least expensive of the lot and is, in some ways, less car. There is less cockpit space than in any of the others, so that anyone who measures more than about 5 ft, 10 in. had best look elsewhere. There are pluses and minuses in the handling. It doesn't stick as well as the others and is the least sophisticated in its suspension, but on the other side of the coin is the fact that it is so forgiving and predictable it can be tossed around with a certain amount of disregard for the finer points of fast driving.

The Spitfire's more complex suspension requires a more precise driving style. It is roomier and more comfortable than the Midget. There is little or no difference from the Midget in straight-line performance, but on a twisty piece of road it takes less effort when in a hurry. For those who wish for a bit more room, a bit more sophistication and a good training car before stepping up to a fast, modern sports car (Porsche 911, for example), it is a fair choice—especially if you happen to be 6 ft tall.

The MGB has just about reached the end of its road, emissions and safety regulations having ganged up on it in one indigestible lump. In some ways—comfort and ride, primarily—it's more car than the other two British Leyland offerings, but both of them will outdo it on a back road. If you are out for pleasurable individual motoring, the B will fit your bill, but if it is informal competition with your peers that you want, best look for a used one *circa* 1973.

The Fiat X 1/9 is, on the other hand, a thoroughly modern motorcar, sophisticated and superb in its road manners. While it won't exactly give you nosebleeds from acceleration, it is the fastest of the four. There is really nothing quite like it within $5000 of its price that will give you the solid, glued-to-the-road feeling.

If you want something basic to knock around in, you'll probably opt for one of the British Leyland offerings, but if you want to sample the precision of a modern racing car in small doses, you'll take the Fiat without question. In many ways, it's the bargain of the decade. ∎

THE HERITAGE MOTOR CENTRE

Situated at Gaydon in Warwickshire, just 3 minutes from junction 12 of the M40 motorway, the Heritage Motor Centre is the home of the British Motor Industry Heritage Trust (BMIHT) and is the largest purpose-designed road transport museum in the UK.

The stunning, art deco-style building houses the largest collection of historic British cars anywhere in the world, bringing together the world famous marques of MG, Rover, Austin, Wolseley, Land Rover, Triumph, Morris, Riley, Standard and Austin Healey.

From the moment you arrive and board one of the specially-designed Land Rover shuttles you begin to discover that this is no dusty, static, "traditional" motor museum. Here you will find a whole world on wheels brought vividly to life in a range of displays that are both entertaining and informative.

The Centre has been designed with both enthusiasts and family visitors in mind with a wide range of indoor and outdoor activities.

Other facilities and attractions include the Lucas and Corgi museum collections, computer-controlled audio/visual display, a range of themed exhibitions, public reading room (with access to some of the Trust's vast archive of rare drawings, photographs and records), well-stocked gift shop, cafeteria, picnic area, nature reserve, children's adventure playground and a spectacular 4-wheel-drive demonstration circuit.

The Centre also has a range of meeting and conference rooms as well as providing a full educational service with full time teaching staff and purpose-built classrooms.

Special events, including numerous car club rallies, are held throughout the year.

For further information
telephone : 0926 641188 (24 hours)
or write to:
**The Heritage Motor Centre,
Banbury Road,
Gaydon,
Warwickshire CV35 0BJ**

by John Bolster

Midget takes a lot of beating

The small, open, sports two-seater was invented by the French in the nineteen-twenties. In earlier times, sports cars were apt to be huge, chain-driven, and German, but the French, having organised many races for *Voiturettes* produced a marvellous range of racy little sports *bolides*, Bugattis, Salmsons, Amilcars, Senechals, Rallys, BNCs, Lombards, Ratiers—but I could go on for the rest of the page.

It is history that Britain took over the sports car market and in the nineteen-thirties an open sports car usually carried a GB plate, while large numbers of them also exhibited an octagon badge, containing the magic letters, MG. After the war, the Americans belatedly discovered the sports car and the MG became a mighty dollar earner. Since then, the USA has adopted a plethora of 'safety' regulations, most of which make a car more dangerous by spoiling its handling and reducing its acceleration.

To build a sports car that will fulfil all these crazy requirements is difficult indeed and MG are to be congratulated on getting through the labyrinth, while other sports car manufacturers have given up in despair. Unfortunately, the cars for the USA and UK markets come off the same production lines, and so we must buy our Midgets weighed down with huge American bumpers, or go without.

This is a pity, but nothing can compare with a real open car on a summer's day, and the Midget is still an attractive little machine. Though its weight has gone up, it now has a 1493cc Triumph engine instead of the 1275cc A-series unit, which enables it to out-perform such modern competitors as the Fiat X1/9. In the vintage era, the MG would have been called a drophead coupé, because it has winding windows and a folding hood. Though it is appreciably faster with the top up, it is as an *open* sports car that it really appeals.

In open form, the Midget is surprisingly quiet and not at all draughty. There's some luggage space in the boot and a lot more behind the seats, so this is an ideal holiday car for two. When parking, one can quickly button on the cockpit cover, in case of rain. In passing, may I ask manufacturers if they will please, please not refer to this useful accessory as a tonneau cover? The tonneau is the rear half of an open four-seater, so you can't have a tonneau cover on a two-seater car!

In closed form, the MG is completely weather-proof and very cosy, a useful small town car,

in fact. It is also extremely noisy at high speeds, most of the general hubbub being generated by the wind passing over the fabric. It is possible to make a quiet hood, but it needs careful profiling and support in exactly the right places. The hood of the MG has evidently not been developed in the wind tunnel, and it shows. This is a splendid hood for moderate speeds around town, but it simply isn't acceptable for a long, fast trip.

I found the MG very easy to enter, though it is perhaps a little difficult for portly persons to place their posteriors; I judged the driving position comfortable and a shorter driver was equally at home. The gearchange is rapid and simple, all the controls being well-placed, and though the younger generation might like a smaller wheel, set rather further away, I would not quarrel with the present arrangement. The engine starts instantly, hot or cold, and only becomes noisy when pressed towards its limit. However, there's plenty of torque if one changes up a little earlier than that.

The steering is quite high-geared and pleasantly light to handle, but the car needs more holding to a straight course than is usual nowadays. On corners it tends to oversteer, especially on lift-off, which calls for rapid correction. Some drivers enjoy handling a car that is set up in this way, and it's fun to apply bags of opposite lock. On the other hand, oversteer is a condition of instability, and some modern drivers, who have never met it before, might be caught out. I believe that this characteristic stems from a raised suspension height, which is part of the American package, but certainly the fabulous controllability of earlier Midgets seems to have been lost to some extent. The brakes are well up to their work and smooth in action.

The latest Midget has a good performance—it's a genuine 100mph car—and as an open car for enjoying the fresh air it takes a lot of beating; detachable "Targa" tops or sliding sunshine roofs are poor substitutes. Many sports car drivers prefer a hard ride, and they will appreciate this machine, but I would ask for more suspension travel, and there are parts of France and Spain where the MG would be almost unbearable if driven at all fast. However, for the better roads of England it does quite well and I enjoyed driving it enormously in the beautiful summer sunshine; it looked the part in its brilliant yellow paint job, too.

Above: our Technical Editor aboard the MG Midget—it still takes a lot of beating if you appreciate fresh air An enormously enjoyable little car.

Specification and performance data

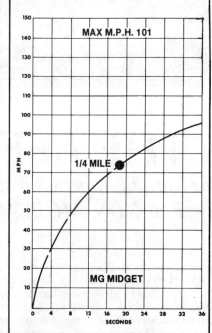

MAX M.P.H. 101

1/4 MILE

MG MIDGET

Car tested: MG Midget sports 2-seater, price £2,647.
Engine: Four cylinders 73.7 × 87.5mm (1493cc). Compression ratio 9 to 1. 66bhp DIN at 5500rpm. Pushrod-operated overhead valves. Twin SU carburetters.
Transmission: Single dry plate clutch. 4-speed synchromesh gearbox, ratios: 1.0, 1.43, 2.11, and 3.41 to 1. Hypoid rear axle, ratio 3.9 to 1.
Chassis: Integral steel construction. Independent front suspension by wishbones and coil springs with anti-roll bar. Rack and pinion steering. Live rear axle on semi-elliptic springs. Disc/drum brakes. Bolt-on steel wheels, fitted 145-13 tyres.
Equipment: 12-volt lighting and starting. Speedometer. Revcounter. Water temperature, oil-pressure, and fuel gauges. Heating and demisting. Windscreen wipers and washers. Reversing lights.
Dimensions: Wheelbase 6ft 8in, track 3ft 10.3in/3ft 8.75in. Overall length 11ft 9in. Width 5ft 0.25in. Weight 15.4cwt.
Performance: Maximum speed 101mph. Speeds in gears: third 70mph, second 47mph, first 28mph. Standing quarter-mile 18.4s. Acceleration: 0-30mph 3.9s, 0-50mph 8.6s, 0-60mph 12.2s, 0-80mph 23.8s.
Fuel consumption: 28 to 34mpg.

THE AFFORDABLES
A head-to-tail confrontation between six moderately priced sports cars: Fiat 124 Spider, Fiat X1/9, MGB, MG Midget, Triumph Spitfire and Triumph TR7

PHOTOS BY JOE RUSZ & JOHN LAMM

NOT TOO MANY years ago you could have bought a lot of sports car for $3500. The Datsun 240Z, Fiat 124 Spider, Porsche 914, MGB and Triumph TR6 all hovered around that price. And if you only had $2500 or so, you could buy more basic sports cars like the Triumph Spitfire and the MG Midget. If you've checked new car prices recently, however, you have to be astonished and dismayed at the havoc world inflation has wrought. The least expensive sports car sold in America in 1976, the MG Midget, lists for $3949, and over the past four years the 280Z and 914 have almost doubled in price!

The popularity of our Used Car Classic series and the record or near-record sales posted by British Leyland and Fiat in 1975 attest to the fact that a lot of car enthusiasts are also sports car enthusiasts. But more so today than ever before they are carefully looking for value for the dollar. Which is where R&T comes in. With what has happened to prices the last four years, coupled with the introduction of completely new sports cars like Fiat's

X1/9 and Triumph's TR7 we decided it was time to take a fresh look at the various options available to a potential sports car buyer. Obviously this runs the gamut from the Porsche Turbo, the Maserati Merak and similar cars only the very rich can afford, all the way down to the diminutive Midget. What we were most interested in, however, were those cars within the reach of the average R&T reader.

After much discussion we decided to limit the test to those sports cars costing less than $6000. If that seems high (it did to us at first) consider this: only seven sports cars fall below that figure and they are Fiat 124 Spider, Fiat X1/9, MGB, MG Midget, Triumph Spitfire, Triumph TR6 and Triumph TR7. We included six of those seven cars in our comparison test, leaving out the TR6 because it is not sold in California and we ran into insurmountable logistical problems in trying to borrow one.

The price spread of the six cars—from $3949 for the Midget to $5845 for the Fiat 124 Spider—is larger than usual for our

X1/9 is unique in having a midship engine, naturally with independent suspension. To transmit power the 124 has a 5-speed gearbox while all the others have 4-speeds. Overdrive is an option with the MGB and the Spitfire, however, and later in the year the TR7 will be available with automatic. When that happens the TR7 will replace the 280Z as the lowest priced sports car offered with that option. Both Fiats have 4-wheel-disc brakes; all the English cars have front discs and rear drums. Probably the greatest similarity between the six cars is their common purpose of providing driving pleasure.

None of the six cars is a new model, all having been tested by us at least once before in separate road tests. Although their basic character has not changed there have been detail changes in all of them since we last tested them. Still, there's nothing like taking a trip and comparing them head to head for making an accurate assessment of the practical, functional and aesthetic qualities of each and to arrive at an overall rating of preference.

So a test crew of eight (including Editor-at-Large Henry Manney whose sometimes caustic wit and overall irreverence tempered the more routine approach of the others) took turns behind the steering wheels and in the passenger seats during a 2-day jaunt that put the cars through the sort of use their owners might. We filled the fuel tanks at San Juan Capistrano and headed out the Ortega Highway to Lake Elsinore. This highway is a nicely surfaced, 2-lane route with a delightful variety of turns and hills as it winds through some of southern California's finest country. From Lake Elsinore we headed southeast through Temecula and Warner Springs into the Anza-Borrego Desert where we spent the night. Next day we headed back toward San Juan Capistrano over the desert and along some wonderfully twisty roads at speeds dictated by road conditions and car capability rather than artificial limits, passing through Banner, Rincon Springs and Pala along the way. At Oceanside we hooked up with the San Diego Freeway for a leisurely 55-mph drive back to San Juan where we again topped up the fuel tanks. A large portion of this trip did involve sports car country and we drove these cars hard for miles on end so the trip fuel economy figures are a bit on the low side. Prospective buyers of any of the six can expect to get more miles per gallon in daily use.

Back at the office we set about scoring the cars. Each driver had a score sheet with 20 different categories in which to rate the cars, and after the trip each sat down immediately with clipboard in hand, the six cars nearby and the pages of notes each had made at our various meal, rest and driver-change stops on the trip. All the categories could be scored on a 1 to 10 basis, 10 being the score of a topnotch performance and 1 being the lowest score possible. These scores were then totaled for each driver and for the entire group to get an overall rating score for each car.

In addition, each driver was asked to rank the cars in the order of his or her personal preference—disregarding, if necessary, the separate ratings of the car's various aspects. Here's how the ratings turned out. Of a possible 1600 points, the scoring was as follows: Fiat X1/9 1371; TR7 1247; Fiat 124 1214; MGB 940; Spitfire 920; Midget 761. In individual driver scoring the X1/9 garnered the highest number of points from all eight drivers and everyone rated it his personal favorite. Next came the TR7 with six drivers rating it second in points and two drivers placing it third. For personal perference the TR7 scored six second places, one third and one fourth. The 124 was a solid third-place finisher. Six drivers had it third in points, two drivers had it second. These same two drivers also gave it second place in personal preference while one of the other six had it fifth on his most favorite list.

A clear step below the two Fiats and the TR7 came the MGB and the Spitfire. In the points standings both had four fourth-place finishes and three fifth places. One driver had the MGB in a third-place tie with the 124 and another had the Spitfire last. On the personal favorites list four drivers had the MGB fourth and four had it fifth. The Spitfire was well enough liked to be scored third favorite by two drivers; the other six voters were evenly split between fourth and fifth places.

Finally we come to the Midget, clearly trailing the pack by a wide margin. Seven of the drivers had it last in points; its lone

comparison tests. But the cars are quite dissimilar with features and characteristics that might strongly appeal to some drivers but not to others. And even among the staff there wasn't universal agreement as to whether or not a higher price tag would necessarily mean a better car.

Three of the cars—MGB and Midget and Spitfire are what we would consider classic roadsters in the Best British Tradition. The 124 would probably be considered by most to be a more civilized sports car done up with the usual Italian flair.

The TR7 represents a complete break from the past. Though based on an existing sedan series—as sports cars usually are—it is a new car for all practical purposes that draws on contemporary engineering practice to combine its performance and handling with a high degree of comfort. It's the only car in the group without a removable top. But British Leyland will remedy that situation later in the year by offering a large sunroof similar to the Renault 17 Gordini coupe/convertible design.

The Fiat X1/9, the only mid-engine car in this group, is also a trendsetter in some respects. It's the first good-looking open mid-engine roadster available to buyers of moderate means.

The six cars differ greatly in specifications as well as vintage. Both MGs and the Spitfire have undersquare overhead-valve 4-cyl engines; the TR7 and the X1/9 have decidedly oversquare 4-cyl engines with a single overhead camshaft; the 124's 4-cyl is an efficient dohc design. In chassis design the 124, both MGs and the TR7 have unit bodies with live rear axles, the Spitfire has a separate body and frame with independent suspension and the fifth place was by one point over the Spitfire. And all eight drivers had it last in their personal ratings.

Fiat X1/9

Now let's take a closer look at all six cars. The Fiat X1/9 was rated best in 13 of the 20 categories: handling, ride, quietness, braking, steering, gearbox, driving position, exterior and interior styling, exterior and interior finish, luggage space and loading and solidarity of its body structure. Its lowest placing in any category was a third in instrumentation and even there it scored a total of only three points less than the top-rated TR7. Overall balance is definitely the X1/9's forte and it's obvious that Fiat engineers really did their homework in coming up with what we consider the most significant sports car since the Datsun 240Z.

The X1/9 has the smallest engine but it makes every cubic centimeter count as only the 124 and TR7 out performed it to any degree. And what the X1/9 lacks in all-out straight-line acceleration it more than makes up for with its impressively smooth, quiet

and easy revving engine.

The ride, steering, braking, handling and roadholding are all first rate with the usual Fiat expertise applied to the always potentially outstanding mid-engine layout. There's an almost perfect blending of springing, damping and wheel travel, so the ride, though firm, is not harsh like the 914's. The body is solid and rattle free and the steady-state cornering is on a par with much more expensive sports cars. But what makes the X1/9 such an excellent road car are its transient characteristics. There's minimal roll and even if you lift off the throttle in a tight turn there's no abrupt change in attitude as sometimes happens with rear-heavy cars. The front tucks in a bit but there's no abrupt change to oversteer.

Designed by Bertone, the X1/9 has clean, taut lines and an aggressively agile appearance marred only by ugly safety bump-

ers. The handsome interior is comfortable for driver and passenger but we are a bit dismayed that Fiat has fitted only lap belts and not a safer lap-shoulder belt system. One other complaint: Engine accessibility seems rather appalling and in these days of $22 an hour labor rates in sections of the country this can be important.

The X1/9 is a thoroughly professional effort: small, light, frugal, immensely entertaining to drive and yet comfortable and practical. It's no wonder that driving the X1/9 elicited such comments as, "Bloody nice little car," and, "It sounds like it's having fun too."

Triumph TR7

The TR7 is proof that in between labor strikes British Leyland can design modern sports cars when it wants to. It placed highest in five categories: engine, controls, instrumentation, ventilation and ease of top removal and installation. The latter was not voted facetiously despite what you might think. The car we tested didn't have a sunroof but we studied a photo of the sunroof car and a description of its operation found in the owner's manual before voting the TR7 best in this category. In every other category except outward vision the Triumph was a consistent second or third place finisher. In outward vision the Triumph fell to last place because the forward extremities are largely invisible and the wide sail panels interfere with rear-quarter vision. We were somewhat surprised after totaling the sums to discover the TR7 rated third in exterior styling, but it scored fewer points in this category than in any other area under consideration except outward vision and it was a distant third behind the two Fiats. The Triumph's strange and stubby appearance sort of grows on you after a while but one of the staff wags summed it up best when he said the TR7 looks like an X1/9 with a bad case of the mumps.

TR7 answers the cry for an open car with this sliding sunroof.

Triumph Spitfire Mk IV 1500.

MG Midget Mark III.

If the exterior styling is a bit offputting, Triumph certainly did the right things inside. The interior is spacious and luxurious, the gauges and controls are all in the right places and the fabric-covered seats are comfortable with easily adjustable backrests. Our 1975 road test car had foot pedals located so enthusiastic drivers could heel and toe easily. In this latest example, however, the space between the brake and throttle pedals has been widened, making double-clutching while downshifting a difficult proposition. Strange.

The TR7's engine, at least in the 2-carburetor 49-state version we tested, is by far the strongest runner in this group. The Triumph isn't particularly quick off the mark because 1st gear is surprisingly tall and this requires a bit of clutch slip to get the car moving from rest. But once underway the TR7 quickly puts a wide expanse of pavement between itself and the next most lively car, the 124 Spider. The gear change suffers from a recalcitrant reverse gate and a slight graunch whenever you downshift into 1st gear but is otherwise quite satisfactory. The brakes are very good both for pedal modulation and stopping distances and the handling is very driver friendly: understeer is the prevailing trait but just enough to keep the novice driver safe and not enough to bother the expert. The steering is neither terribly quick nor light but it is precise and it does lighten up at speed. The ride is well controlled and comfortably supple but at high speeds on undulating pavement the front end gets a little floaty.

Even though it blazes no new trails in the evolution of the sports car, we think Triumph has done a generally nice job with the TR7. The handling-ride-braking combination is most pleasing, it's reasonably light and economical of fuel, it's an exceptionally comfortable car with a wide, deep and regularly shaped trunk, and it's entertaining to drive. You couldn't ask for much more than that.

Fiat 124 Spider

ALTHOUGH IT dates back to 1968 the Fiat 124 Spider is still a very civilized sports car and of the four "vintage" cars in this test it has aged the most gracefully. That was made very clear in the scoring because the 124 was a close third behind the considerably newer TR7. The 124 was voted best in two categories—heating and outward vision—and scored no lower than third

Fiat 124 Sport Spider.

in any area except for fourth place finishes in ventilation and braking (more about that later) and a fifth in driving position.

Keeping up with emission requirements has severely weakened Fiat's once strong dohc 4-cyl, but nevertheless it is still a satisfying piece of machinery: quiet, very smooth for a 4-cyl and willing to rev to its 6500-rpm redline. And in this group of cars it was still second fastest. The 124 has the only 5-speed gearbox; although it requires longer throws than the British 4-speeds, the shifter is quite precise in its action.

Probably the most controversial aspect of the 124 is the driving position. Either you love driving with your arms extended 'way out and the pedals close or you hate it. In this case it was a split decision, four voting yea and four nay. Otherwise there's little to complain about inside. The instruments are easy to read, the controls well laid out and stowing and raising the soft top is utter simplicity. And the top provides far better weather protection than any of the British roadsters.

The Fiat's basic understeer and low-speed steering heaviness are not appreciated at first; after miles of fast driving the Fiat's excellent transient cornering and good absolute adhesion make it a most enjoyable car. It's a supple riding car in the best Italian tradition with exceptional axle control over rough pavement.

The brakes are an enigma. They achieved creditable stopping distances in our simulated panic stops, although the front discs locked easily and unequally causing the car to pull to the left. They faded more than we expected for an all-disc design but not to an alarming degree. But while driving through Anza-Borrego our first day out, the brakes faded completely away during one hard downhill stop from 70 mph and were never completely right thereafter. This is obviously not characteristic behavior because we have found Fiats to have better than average brakes.

There's no disputing the fact that the 8-year-old 124 is outdated in some ways. However, the Italians design sports cars with so much feeling for the car and the driver that many of their cars are endowed with a timeless quality that makes them enjoyable to drive despite their age.

Triumph Spitfire

IN THE individual points scoring the Spitfire's best showing was four fourth-place finishes. On the personal preference lists, however, the Spitfire found itself with two third place votes, one driver placing it ahead of the TR7 and one ahead of the Fiat 124. And in the overall scoring it had only 20 fewer points than the MGB. The Spitfire's highest placing in any of the individual categories was a second place in braking. It also scored four worsts: instrumentation, ventilation, ease of top removal and installation and body structure, but only in the latter was it far

GENERAL DATA

	Fiat 124 Spider	Fiat X1/9	MG B	MG Midget	Triumph Spitfire	Triumph TR7
Basic price	$5845[1]	$4947	$4795	$3949	$4295	$5649
Price as tested[2]	$6045	$5147	$4995	$4299	$4495	$5847
Layout	front engine/ rear drive	mid engine/ rear drive	front engine/ rear drive	front engine/ rear drive	front engine/ rear drive	front engine/ rear drive
Curb weight, lb	2255	2045	2275	1775	1750	2220
Test weight, lb	2635	2420	2645	2170	2120	2580
Weight distribution (with driver), f/r, %	51/49	41/59	50/50	52/48	53/47	55/45
Wheelbase, in.	89.7	86.7	91.1	80.0	83.0	85.0
Track, f/r	53.2/52.0	52.5/52.9	49.0/49.3	46.3/44.8	49.0/50.0	55.5/55.3
Length	163.1	158.5	158.3	141.0	156.3	164.5
Width	63.5	61.8	59.9	54.0	58.5	66.2
Height	49.2	46.1	50.9	48.3	45.6	49.9
Wheel size	13x5	13x4½	14x4½	13x4½	13x4½	13x5½
Tires	Goodyear G800 Grand Prix, 165HR-13	Michelin XAS, 145HR-13	Dunlop SP68, 165SR-14	Pirelli Cinturato CF67, 145SR-13	Goodyear Custom G800 Rib, 155SR-13	Michelin X, 175/70HR-13
Fuel capacity, U.S. gal.	11.4	12.7	14.0	7.5	8.8	14.5

[1] Price varies according to port of entry.
[2] As-tested price includes: for the Fiat 124 Spider, AM/FM radio ($200); for the Fiat X1/9, AM/FM radio ($200); for the MGB, AM/FM radio ($150), tonneau cover ($50); for the MG Midget, AM/FM radio ($150), wire wheels ($135), tonneau cover ($50), anti-roll bar ($15); for the Triumph Spitfire, AM/FM radio ($150), tonneau cover ($50); for the Triumph TR7, AM/FM/tape ($198).

Raising or lowering the top on the English roadsters was an exercise in frustration.

behind the fifth place car.

The Spitfire surprised a lot of people. Drivers commented, "The handling is damned impressive," "The suspension, steering, ride and roadholding are much better than I suspected," and "It's a surprisingly good car." On external styling one driver said it best: "The Spitfire has aged very well and has grown into the safety age (it was introduced in the U.S. in 1963) better than any of the others that were around before The Great Silliness. And when you consider what the first Spitfires looked like this is a great improvement."

The Spitfire is the only car with a separate body and frame and is not as solid feeling as the unit-body cars. The hood shakes, the chassis seems to flex a bit and there is excessive steering feedback on rough roads through the otherwise excellent rack-and-pinion steering. The Spitfire's independent rear suspension is a relatively unsophisticated swing-axle design but some clever re-engineering in 1971 improved the handling enormously. Only the main spring leaf of the Spitfire's transverse leaf spring is clamped to the differential so that it can contribute roll stiffness; the other leaves contribute practically nothing to roll stiffness. Furthermore, the whole spring assembly has a higher 2-wheel jounce rate—roughly double what it was—so that camber change under acceleration and braking is reduced. This design decreases the oversteer and jacking of the rear wheels that was characteristic of earlier Spitfires.

The Spitfire's engine is rough as old boots when revved above 5000 rpm (redline is at 6000) and it's noisy as well in the upper speed ranges, but it provides peppy performance otherwise, especially in the lower three gears.

The Spitfire's seats drew mixed reviews as the seat cushions are short and don't provide enough thigh support. It also has less instrumentation than the other cars but otherwise the interior is

PERFORMANCE

	Fiat 124 Spider	Fiat X1/9	MG B	MG Midget	Triumph Spitfire	Triumph TR7
Lb/bhp (test weight)	30.6	36.9	42.3	39.1	36.9	28.7
Acceleration: time to speed, sec						
0–30 mph	4.9	5.3	5.5	4.8	4.8	4.3
0–60 mph	14.8	16.3	18.3	15.5	15.3	11.5
0–70 mph	20.5	23.7	26.5	22.8	22.3	15.7
0–80 mph	30.4	34.7	39.0	36.5	32.3	20.9
Standing ¼ mile, sec	20.0	20.4	21.5	20.1	20.2	18.5
Speed @ ¼ mile, mph	69.5	66.5	64.5	67.0	67.5	76.0
Top speed, mph	100	90	90	83	94	105
Trip fuel economy, mpg	22.0	26.0	19.5	29.0	25.0	22.5
Braking: stopping distance, ft, from						
60 mph	170	151	177	189	167	169
80 mph	285	280	320	321	304	289
Control in panic stop	fair	excellent	fair	very good	very good	excellent
Pedal effort for 0.5g stop, lb	25	38	25	38	50	32
Fade, % increase in pedal effort in six 0.5g stops from 60 mph	40	58	60	97	10	9
Overall brake rating	good	very good	fair	fair	good	very good
Cornering capability, g	0.737	0.791	0.698	0.737	0.731	0.760
Speed thru 700-ft slalom, mph	55.8	57.4	53.0	50.1	58.1	58.6

INTERIOR NOISE

	Fiat 124 Spider	Fiat X1/9	MG B	MG Midget	Triumph Spitfire	Triumph TR7
All noise readings with top up, dBA:						
Idle in neutral	59	59	61	61	61	60
Maximum, 1st gear	87	82	87	87	87	88
Constant 30 mph	72	67	70	72	74	67
50 mph	75	72	75	81	79	71
70 mph	83	79	82	86	87	77

ENGINE & DRIVETRAIN

	Fiat 124 Spider	Fiat X1/9	MG B	MG Midget	Triumph Spitfire	Triumph TR7
Engine type	dohc inline 4	sohc inline 4	ohv inline 4	ohv inline 4	ohv inline 4	sohc inline 4
Bore x stroke, mm	84.0 x 79.2	88.0 x 55.5	80.3 x 89.0	73.7 x 87.4	73.7 x 87.4	90.3 x 78.0
Displacement, cc	1756	1290	1798	1493	1493	1998
Compression ratio	8.0:1	8.5:1	8.0:1	9.0:1	9.0:1	8.0:1
Bhp @ rpm, SAE net	86 @ 6200	65.5 @ 6000	62.5 @ 5000	55.5 @ 5000	57.5 @ 5000	90 @ 5000
Torque @ rpm, lb-ft	90 @ 2800	67 @ 4000	72 @ 2500	73 @ 2500	75 @ 2500	106 @ 3000
Carburetion	one Weber (2V)	one Weber (2V)	one Zenith-Stromberg (1V)	one Zenith-Stromberg (1V)	one Zenith-Stromberg (1V)	two Zenith-Stromberg (1V)
Fuel requirement	unleaded, 91-oct	unleaded, 91-oct	unleaded, 91-oct	premium, 96-oct	premium, 96-oct	regular, 91-oct
Transmission	5-sp manual	4-sp manual	4-sp manual	4-sp manual	4-sp manual	4-sp manual
Final drive ratio	4.30:1	4.08:1	3.90:1	3.90:1	3.89:1	3.63:1
Engine speed @ 60 mph, rpm	3330	4100	3320	3700	3500	3300

much more roomy and livable than the Spitfire's direct competitor, the Midget. Overall we'd have to say that although it has its failings, these days the Spitfire is the cheapest way to get into an acceptable new sports car.

MGB

WE'VE HEARD that British Leyland is simply letting the MGB run its historic course; when it can't be sold anymore they'll drop it and that's that. The car seems to bear it out. Meeting the U.S. crash-safety regulations was done by laying an ugly, add-on instrument panel over the existing one and the little bit of styling facelift has been done in a haphazard way.

It's truly a car of the past. Everywhere there's evidence of a sports car designed and built in the traditional manner—in a rather homemade way, to be blunt...

Think you've heard that said somewhere before? You're right. The previous two paragraphs are a direct quote from a 1971 test comparing the Datsun 240Z, Fiat 124 Sport, Opel GT, MGB GT and Triumph GT6. And it's truer today than it was five years ago. To meet bumper crash regulations British Leyland grafted on ugly rubber appendages to both ends of the car. These look bad enough but because the MGB still couldn't meet bumper height requirements the body was raised on its springs about 3 in. adding injury to insult. Not only does the MGB look like a candidate for the Baja 1000 but the car rolls excessively and the handling has deteriorated severely.

If the MG's pushrod engine never produced a lot of power it did have lots of torque. Now even that is gone. The redline is at 6000 rpm but nothing is gained by pushing it above 4000. The engine always sounds like it's straining and wheezing, leading one driver to comment, "The engine performance makes the car feel like it weighs nine tons." It was no surprise in tallying the scores to discover the MGB mired in last in the engine category.

Even though it doesn't go and it doesn't handle, the MGB is still a reasonably comfortable car. The seats are comfy, the pedals are well positioned and the instruments are readable and the steering wheel and gear shift lever fall easily to hand.

But these virtues can hardly compensate for the antique qualities of the rest of the car. Perhaps British Leyland will have the last laugh. The MGB could be the first replicar that never went out of production!

MG Midget

THEN WE come to the Midget. Fun to drive? Maybe. But a modern car, hardly. The Midget scored as many worsts as the X1/9 did bests, 13, and in no category did it score higher than fifth. That about sums it up: a seriously outdated automobile in striking contrast to the throughly modern X1/9.

The Midget's handling is, well . . . interesting and entertaining. There's an excessive amount of rear-wheel steering so the car darts around a lot. The steering is very quick but a little numb and the driver is constantly making little corrections and overcorrections to keep the car headed approximately in the right direction. The short wheelbase and the British cart springs cause the car to hop about even over small road irregularities. Blame the bumpers for part of the Midget's idiosyncrasies; British Leyland chose the same "solution" for the Midget as it did for the MGB.

The brakes, however, were better than on the Midget tested last month. They still fade excessively and the panic stopping distances are long but at least the control was very good.

This latest Midget uses the Spitfire engine, but to fit the narrow confines of the Midget's engine compartment the exhaust manifolding had to be made more restrictive so in Midget trim it produces two less horsepower. Like the Spitfire, the Midget was a 49-state car requiring premium fuel for its 9.0:1 compression ratio ohv engine. As might be expected from two cars differing in curb weight by only 50 lb the straightline performance is virtually identical up to around 70 mph when the Spitfire's better breathing and better aerodynamics afford it an advantage.

The Midget is aptly named for inside it's a hopelessly cramped car. This didn't seem to bother one driver who commented, "Once inside it isn't too bad. It gives me the impression of wearing the car, which lends a nice touch and feel to it all." Others were less kind, complaining about lack of seat travel, limited shoulder room and awkwardly positioned door handles. We all agreed on one point, however. Anyone who would buy a Midget when the X1/9 was available for only $1000 more would have to be a complete masochist.

Conclusion

IF THERE'S one thing this test proves conclusively it's that time and automotive engineering stand still for no car. A car that might have been perfectly adequate and more than acceptable 10 to 15 years ago when stacked up against its peers, can't hope to compete against a design that has benefited from the latest in automotive innovations and technology.

Thus we find the thoroughly up-to-date X1/9 and TR7 leading this comparison test. The Fiat 124 is one car that seems to disprove the above rule, but then the Italians always seem to design sports cars with more finesse than other manufacturers and there's no denying that with the passing of time it too is becoming dated. There's little hope for the three other British cars despite how much we enjoyed the Spitfire. The only thing left is for British Leyland to start all over with a clean sheet of paper.

MG Midget

Sports cars, living-legend department. Get one while they're last.

• There are lots of things you can say about an MG Midget. Like it sure is small. And it's really slow. And it's simple to the point of bare necessity. And it wanders a bit under hard braking. And it wanders a bit in crosswinds. And it is pure, unadulterated automobile fun. Most of all it's fun.

MG Midgets have been with us since late in 1928, when the M-type went into production at the old Abingdon facility. Of course there was a bit of an interruption when the Hitler war turned Britain's automobile producers to more pressing business, but within five weeks of the official end of hostilities, MG an-

nounced the first TC Midget and the string began again.

And it *was* called the TC *Midget,* and that's something to add to your collection of little-known facts that win bets in bars. But there's more. The equally famous TD and TF were also Midgets. The MGA and the MGB of more recent

vintage were of another breed altogether. And one final bit of esoterica: 10,000 MG TC Midgets were produced, and exactly 2001 exported by MG to the U.S. So the car that "started it all" in this country did so with a rather small expeditionary force.

Although that little orange Midget sitting in the *Car and Driver* parking lot right now may not seem like what a living legend should come to, it nonetheless is one. And it is also the last of its kind. In all its marketing wisdom, MG's parent company—called Jaguar Rover Triumph this week—has decided to stop Midget production this summer.

The Triumph Spitfire will be the company's only low-ball sports car.

So there you are. The end of another automotive era. Get your living legends while they're last.

Testing the Midget has turned out to be quite an adventure in automotive history. Not only is there great historical significance attached to this representative of a dying breed, the car itself is more historic than contemporary. It is the past. And if you're more of the past than of the present, any changes in the good name of technological advancement, any moves toward the contemporary will be at best only grudgingly made. Of course the Midget has a DOT-proper set of bumpers front and rear; there's a three-point harness; non-protruding rocker switches have replaced the traditional toggles; there are three wipers to ensure legal coverage of the glass; and you can bet that hidden in the doors are side-guard beams. And of course the poor thing has been forced to lug around a catalytic converter to clean its breath. But there's precious little else to indicate the Midget has been squirting off the MG production line right up to the bitter end, rather than being shoved out the door of a barn somewhere in England where the last ones were stored fifteen years ago.

To love the little dear you have to be a lover of simple machinery, because the Midget is really little more than a simple machine that happens to roll down the road on four wheels when it's doing its simple-machinery task. It is to a Chevrolet Citation what a wheelbarrow is to a Bucyrus-Erie earthmover.

To love a Midget, you have to love simple machinery. That's what it is. A simple machine that happens to be a car.

Also, to love a Midget you have to be rather supple, because slipping in through the doorway while angling your legs under the steering wheel is not a game for the creaky of joint. And the bracing, twisting, and writhing to get out are as close as you can come to automotive isometrics. It's called a Midget for a reason, you see.

Although the top goes up and down quite easily—3.5 minutes from boot-on to top-up was the time actually recorded by an agile driver caught in a sudden shower—when it's up there are spaces around the door large enough to pass a Big Mac through. And the snaps for the rear edge of the top are the same nail-breakers that broke the nails of countless TR3 owners fifteen years ago. MG's concession to modern top technology was to add a little Velcro at a couple of points where the top joins the body. Take that, revisionists.

However, top-up is the Midget at its

worst. It may be mostly psychological, but when the roof is raised, life in the Midget gets very frustrating. All the controls are too close and too close together. And it's claustrophobic in there. The windshield has about the same dimensions as a machine-gun port in a small bunker.

But put the top down and you and your Midget are transformed. Suddenly the cockpit is not only livable, it's a nice place to be. And when you move off down the road, you're not just driving, you're motoring. The little devil will cruise the world's freeways at an almost effortless 70 mph if you must. But better you should enjoy flinging it around corners in town, frightening your dog and squeezing suitable squeals out of your lady; or cruising through warm summer nights. Or maybe find a piece of countryside to charge through. And please don't worry about its taking a

With the top down, the car is transformed.

sedate sixteen seconds to get up to 60 mph, or that its quarter-mile acceleration capabilities have it in the Christmas, Slow As, category. It sounds as if it's going fast, and the tactile messages coming through the steering column are telling you you're going fast, and if your hair is whipping itself into knots and you're smiling from ear to ear, then dammit, you are going fast. Or at least fast enough. Right?

Continued

"Safety Fast" was the MG motto, but "Fun Slow" might have been more appropriate.

• The first brand-new car I ever purchased was a 1953 MG TD, metallic tan with red leather in the cockpit. I got a pair of Brooklands windscreens from Vic Derrington in England, along with a very *pur sang* Brooklands steering wheel. I sent away to Dale Runyan for a louvered hood, which I installed without the side panels and held down with a red leather strap. There was a badge bar on the front, which carried a Lucas "Flamethrower" pencil-beam road lamp and cloisonné badges for the MG Car Club, the Sports Car Club of America, the Detroit Region of the Sports Car Club of America, and the 1953 Press On Regardless Rally. A local top shop made me a zipper tonneau cover and then I painted the car white, with red underfenders, white wheels, and

a red-and-white checked grille. The *pièce de résistance* was a Boyce Motometer that actually worked, screwed into the removable radiator cap.

The engine was bored .030 oversize, the head was milled, and the ports polished. I scrounged a set of inch-and-a-half SU carburetors to replace the stock inch-and-a-quarters, and dressed them up with chromed Hellings air cleaners. The engine also wore a polished aluminum valve cover and side plate. The exhaust system was removed from the manifold back, and in its place was an inch-and-three-quarter copper straight pipe. Most of the time the pipe's song was muted by a chrome "racket buster," a short muffler that clamped onto the business end, but could be slipped off easily when my youthful blood was up.

Several of my friends owned MG TCs, and most of these were outfitted much like my TD, except that the TC had nineteen-inch wire wheels and fashion dictated that the rears be cut down to sixteen inches and, if possible, laced on a wider rim. The best TD in the world—and mine was a good one—was an innocuous little car that didn't go very fast and didn't do a very good job of keeping the rain and snow off the occupants. The TC was essentially the same, except that it didn't ride at all as a car was supposed to, and the steering required the strength of Sylvester Stallone. The TD was a better car

in almost every respect, but the TC had the advantage of the most rakish appearance seen on this side of the Atlantic since the Army Air Corps stopped flying biplanes.

We raced these cars, rallied them, ran gymkhanas and British-style trials in muddy, rocky farmland, and drove them to work every day. The fact that they were not as reliable as the American cars of the period was offset by their ease of maintenance. We did our own brake jobs, valve jobs, rebuilt the SU carburetors once a month, and got out to whack the SU fuel pump back to life every time it quit ticking, which was regularly. Our small talk dealt mainly with the vagaries of Lucas electrical systems. The fact that a T-series MG Midget was slow, heavy, and about as agile as a McCormick reaper never occurred to us. They were sports cars and we were sports. Only the arrival of significant numbers of 1500cc Porsches among U.S. enthusiast ranks caused us to doubt the ability of our little MGs to do anything we asked of them. Porsches did things that had never occurred to us. Nonetheless, the postwar Midgets rent the veil of the Detroit temple, we saw fundamental automotive truth revealed, and we never turned back. —*David E. Davis, Jr.*

But alas, what it comes down to is just how much you are willing to pay for a fair-weather friend, a toy. The Midget simply isn't a serious car anymore. Sure, the heater will keep you warm, you can actually hear the radio at 70 mph, and all the bits and pieces seem to be screwed together with some thought to durability. But the Midget asks a little too much of us. The handling is really rather dodgy for today, under hard braking each wheel takes a turn at trying to get things slowed down, there's just enough room in the trunk for a cheese

sandwich, and our best guess is that after a few months of intimacy—including one old-fashioned wet, slick, and cold winter—all that nostalgia-fueled fun motoring will hardly be worth the effort. Or $5395. Pity.

There may always be an England, but this is it for Midgets. Maybe you'd better get one while they're last. And worry about winter when it gets here.

—*Mike Knepper*

COUNTERPOINT

• This thing is trash, and I for one won't be sad to see it go. The state of the automotive art will lurch smartly upward just from the riddance of the MG Midget. Perhaps the British will find a way to produce a few extra Spitfires or TR7s in its place, both of which I consider infinitely more desirable, price notwithstanding.

You see, the Midget never really enjoyed any development, a predicament I consider inexcusable. This car will fade from production with the same wretched, hanky-in-the-wind top it was born with. Along the way, Jaguar Rover Triumph (hey! what happened to MG?) did jack up the ride height, slap on ugly bumper masks, and drain all the horsepower out of the Midget's engine. Please excuse me if I don't consider these either improvements or developments. However, credit should be given for the compassionate excision of this car's bug-eye birth defect, and the addition of synchronizers in the transmission a few years back. In farewell, I can offer nothing more than a kick in the behind, and this goodbye to such a crude little coal cart of a car: "Get outa here, you knucklehead!" —*Don Sherman*

Everything under the sun is wrong with the Midget until you put the top down; then it's perfect. With the top up, I could barely get in, much less drive, and I found that no matter how deftly I attempted to operate the various controls and switches, one or another of my knuckles and thumbs was constantly making painful contact with some other part of the little bolide. Owning a Midget is a character-building experience. One very quickly finds out whether or not one is suited for the sporting life. It is small and uncomfortable. It doesn't go very fast, nor does it handle very well. It represents about

the same level of automotive sophistication as a Japanese pickup truck. But if you're the right sort of person, none of that will make much difference when the sun is out and the top is down. And then, if you can still bear it at the end of a long, cold winter, you are destined for automotive greatness. This is where beginning car nuts get their feet wet in the sport. This is the car that introduces one to the automotive alternatives. By no stretch of the imagination is it a Porsche or a Jaguar, but it's a very nice first step in that direction, if you're tough.

—*David E. Davis, Jr.*

Decades ago, when God instructed the British about sports cars, He laid down an absolute formula, to be followed, no matter what, with a stiff upper lip. The design staff at MG has, by God, the stiffest upper lip this side of Alice McDaniels. But that's another story. MG's lack of progress is of no importance here, because there is no modern rationale for a little dart game like the Midget. It's not supposed to make sense and never has. This shrunken buzz bomb has got some real *whoopeee!* ballistics. It converts every tight corner, small crosswind, and big truck into a madcap change of direction, like an atomic mouse in an elephant compound. It has Woody Allen's vaguely wild-eyed approach to life, but for following Diane Keaton to the ends of the earth, you'll want something else, because this teensy car gets familiar with every corner of your body, and the seats are squishy. Forget all that. The Midget is absolutely alive and utterly tingling with the road. Every decisive move in the cockpit makes something dramatic happen. If you haven't driven an X1/9, maybe you can love a Midget. If you can fit. Maybe. —*Larry Griffin*

ACCELERATION standing ¼ mile, seconds

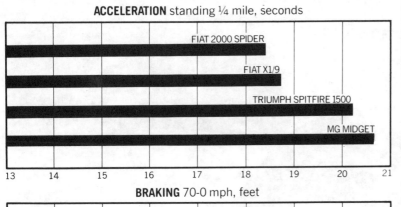

FIAT 2000 SPIDER
FIAT X1/9
TRIUMPH SPITFIRE 1500
MG MIDGET

13 14 15 16 17 18 19 20 21

BRAKING 70-0 mph, feet

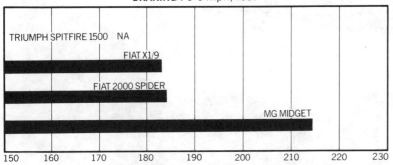

TRIUMPH SPITFIRE 1500   NA
FIAT X1/9
FIAT 2000 SPIDER
MG MIDGET

150 160 170 180 190 200 210 220 230

FUEL ECONOMY EPA estimated city mpg

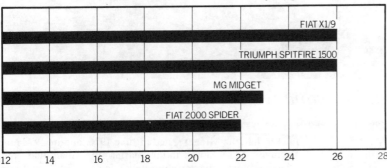

FIAT X1/9
TRIUMPH SPITFIRE 1500
MG MIDGET
FIAT 2000 SPIDER

12 14 16 18 20 22 24 26 28

CURRENT BASE PRICE dollars x 1000

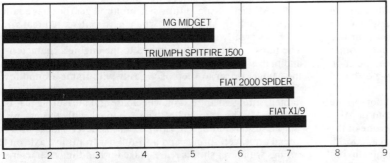

MG MIDGET
TRIUMPH SPITFIRE 1500
FIAT 2000 SPIDER
FIAT X1/9

1 2 3 4 5 6 7 8 9

INTERIOR SOUND LEVEL dBA

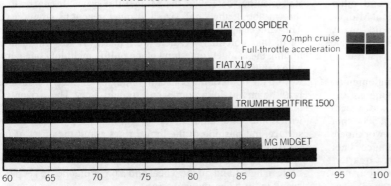

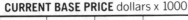
70-mph cruise
Full-throttle acceleration

FIAT 2000 SPIDER
FIAT X1/9
TRIUMPH SPITFIRE 1500
MG MIDGET

60 65 70 75 80 85 90 95 100

MG MIDGET

Importer: Jaguar Rover Triumph, Inc.
600 Willow Tree Road
Leonia, New Jersey 07605

Vehicle type: front-engine, rear-wheel-drive, 2-passenger, 2-door convertible

Price as tested: $5597.50.

Options on test car: base MG Midget, $5395; tonneau cover, $70; AM/FM radio, $132.50.

ENGINE
Type: 4-in-line, water-cooled, cast-iron block and head, 5 main bearings
Bore x stroke ....2.90 x 3.44 in, 73.7 x 87.5mm
Displacement ....91.0 cu in, 1493cc
Compression ratio 7.5:1
Carburetion ....1x1-bbl Zenith Stromberg
Valve gear ....pushrods, overhead valves, solid lifters
Power (SAE net) ....50 bhp @ 5000 rpm
Torque (SAE net) ....67 lbs-ft @ 2500 rpm
Redline ....6000 rpm

DRIVETRAIN
Transmission 4-speed
Final-drive ratio 3.72:1

Gear	Ratio	Mph/1000 rpm	Max. text speed
I	3.41	5.1	28 mph (5500 rpm)
II	2.11	8.2	45 mph (5500 rpm)
III	1.43	12.1	67 mph (5500 rpm)
IV	1.00	17.3	86 mph (4950 rpm)

DIMENSIONS AND CAPACITIES
Wheelbase ....80.0 in
Track, F/R ....46.5/45.0 in
Length ....141.0 in
Width ....55.5 in
Height ....48.2 in
Ground clearance ....3.2 in
Curb weight.......................................1820 lbs
Weight distribution, F/R..................51.6/48.4 %
Fuel capacity ....7.5 gal
Oil capacity ....4.8 qt
Water capacity ....5.7 qt

SUSPENSION
F: .ind, unequal-length control arms, coil springs, anti-sway bar
R: ....rigid axle, semi-elliptic leaf springs

STEERING
Type ....rack-and-pinion
Turns lock-to-lock....................................2.9
Turning circle curb-to-curb ....31.7 ft

BRAKES
F: ....8.2-in dia disc
R: ....7.0 x 1.2-in cast-iron drum
Power assist ....none
Brake effort for 0.5-g deceleration ....43 lbs

WHEELS AND TIRES
Wheel size ....4.5 x 13 in
Wheel type ....stamped steel
Tire make and size ....Dunlop SP4 Radial, 145SR-13
Test inflation pressures, F/R ....26/30 psi

INTERIOR SOUND LEVEL
Idle..59 dBA
Full-throttle acceleration ....90 dBA
70-mph cruising ....87 dBA
70-mph coasting ....85 dBA

PERFORMANCE

Zero to	Seconds
30 mph	4.6
40 mph	7.1
50 mph	11.5
60 mph	16.3
70 mph	24.1
80 mph	35.4

Standing ¼-mile ....20.7 sec @ 67 mph
Top speed ....86 mph
Braking, 70–0 mph ....214 ft
EPA estimated fuel economy ....23 mpg, city driving

MG MIDGET

Why would anyone want one?

PHOTOS BY RON WAKEFIELD & JOE RUSZ

BACK TO BASICS is the phrase that most readily comes to mind in describing the MG Midget: It retains its unenviable position as the most basic sports car offered in the U.S. market. MG broke the barrier some 30 years ago and earned the affection of American sports-car enthusiasts, popularizing an entirely new genre of driving pleasure—small, lightweight, open 2-seater automobiles with an allure virtually unknown on this side of the Atlantic before then. There would be many other marques to follow and eventually MG's preeminent position would decline, but no other manufacturer would ever be able to take away the British carmaker's firstborn status.

The Midget was introduced in 1961 as an offshoot of the Austin-Healey Sprite Mk II, which had made its debut in Mk I ("Bugeye") form in 1958; thus the diminutive MG has one of the longest continuous production runs in the sports-car world. There have been many changes in the Midget since its birth, but it's still the same type of car it's always been: basic roadster. True, now there are windup windows, plush carpeting and other amenities scarcely dreamed of in the days of the original Midget, and U.S. safety and emission regulations have mandated many revisions and alterations, but a drive in the Midget is a nostalgic experience. Or, as the less charitable put it, the car is seriously outdated and old-fashioned.

Within the framework of the British Leyland conglomerate, the Midget shares the same inline 4-cylinder engine as the Triumph Spitfire. It's an overhead-valve design with a displacement of 1493 cc that in current form develops 50 bhp at 5000 rpm and 67 lb-ft torque at 2500 rpm. The powerplant is a workhorse "tractor-type" engine in a mild state of tune. Performance is not startling, with a 0–60 mph time of 14.3 seconds and a quarter-mile clocking of 20.3 sec at 69.5 mph (measured with our new lightweight test equipment). That 0–60 mph time is 1.2 sec

quicker than the Midget tested in June 1976, but the 1978 model is actually 0.2 sec slower in the quarter mile. Chalk that up to a reduction in compression ratio (9.0:1 down to 7.5:1) and horsepower (55.5 down to 50.0) since our 1976 test.

The Midget's 4-speed fully synchronized gearbox has a notchy feel and a high shift effort when new, but as it breaks in it improves greatly and is crisp and positive wihout being too stiff. The transmission is well matched to the engine's characteristics and makes good use of the low- and mid-range torque, enabling the Midget driver to keep pace easily with traffic around town.

A perusal of the Midget's dimensions reveals that it's aptly named, sitting on an 80.0-in. wheelbase and measuring just 143.0 in. overall. The short wheelbase, coupled with the essentially simple suspension design (lower A-arms, lever shocks as upper lateral arms, coil springs and anti-roll bar front; live axle on leaf springs with lever shocks rear), make for handling characteristics that are entertaining to some and nerve-jangling to others. One staff member described the Midget this way: "It can really be thrown about; the small size and quick reactions grow on you. The Midget's potential may be fairly low, but it's very easy to use all of that potential." Others were markedly less enthusiastic, finding the Midget something of a handful, including one person who described it in nautical terms as "very much like tacking my way up the boulevard," constantly nudging the steering back and forth to maintain a somewhat straight line. The driver who masters the Midget's handling idiosyncracies will be rewarded with some entertainment on a winding road with a smooth surface, but pushing to the limit brings about the onset of final oversteer, requiring quick driver reactions and a deft touch. The fast (2.3 turns lock-to-lock) rack-and-pinion steering also necessitates a light hand on the wheel and a bit of practice to keep from overdoing it when maneuvering.

The ride manners of the Midget are rather unpleasant. As a runabout, it's quite acceptable and the firm and jouncy nature of the car seems appropriate. For anything more than a short drive, however, the stiff-legged feel becomes tiresome.

Inside, the Midget can be described at best as cozy, at worst as claustrophobic. Perhaps it's a natural law of selection that this car is most suited to young and lithe people who don't mind contorting themselves a bit to get behind the wheel. Once there, though, they will find that leg, hip and shoulder room are restricted for anyone taller or more portly than average. The controls and instruments are well laid out and most everything (including the opposite door handle and window crank) is within easy reach—many of our staff members expressed the feeling that it's more like wearing a car than driving one. There is insufficient space to move the seat far enough rearward for most drivers more than about 5 ft 8 in. tall; one short driver found that when the seat was close enough to depress the clutch pedal fully, she had great difficulty reaching back to use the door handle to get out! One quite serious problem concerns the safety belts—the inertia reels stick badly as you try to put on the belts, and when the convertible top is down it interferes with them so much that it becomes a major task to adjust and fit them. The reel covers won't stay on the reels, further interfering with one's good intentions to belt up. Also, the receptacles for the belt latches on the inboard side of the seats present a dangerous and hard surface to many people's hip bones. The convertible top provides

Current Midgets share their engine with the Triumph Spitfire.

MG Midget's cockpit is one of the tightest known to man.

a reasonably snug, closed environment but there is considerable wind leakage around the edges and the Midget is a car best reserved for a sunny day when the top can be left down and the driver is free to enjoy open-air motoring in the old style.

Putting the top up and down is easier than it used to be, but there are still far too many steps required, snaps to be fastened, etc. Other carmakers have found much simpler solutions to the convertible top (the Fiat 124 comes to mind) and there's no reason why British Leyland couldn't follow suit.

All in all, we find far more minuses than pluses with the MG Midget. Small, lightweight sports cars can and should be great fun to drive. Perhaps many people can and will experience that sort of fun with the Midget. But there is ever so much room for improvement, badly needed to return to MG the rightful crown as builder of exciting sports cars. As it stands, the marque has fallen into a state of disrepair. 🔘

PRICE

List price, all POE...............$4850
Price as tested $5260

GENERAL

Curb weight, lb 1835
Weight distribution (with
  driver), front/rear, % 52/48
Wheelbase, in. 80.0
Track, front/rear 46.3/44.8
Length 143.0
Width 54.0
Height 48.3
Fuel capacity, U.S. gal. 7.5

CHASSIS & BODY

Body/frame ....unit steel
Brake system ....8.3-in. discs
  front, 7.0 x 1.1-in. drums rear
Wheels .... styled steel, 13 x 4½
Tires....................Pirelli Cinturato
  CF67, 145SR-13
Steering type .... rack & pinion
  Turns, lock-to-lock 2.3
Suspension, front/rear: lower A-
  arms, lever shocks as upper lat-
  eral arms, coil springs, anti-roll
  bar/live axle on quarter-elliptic
  leaf springs, lever shocks

ENGINE & DRIVETRAIN

Type ....ohv inline 4
Bore x stroke, mm........ 73.7 x 87.4
Displacement, cc/cu in. .. 1493/91.0
Compression ratio 7.5:1
Bhp @ rpm, net .... 50 @ 5000
Torque @ rpm, lb-ft ... 67 @ 2500
Fuel requirement ..unleaded, 91-oct
Transmission .... 4-sp manual
Gear ratios: 4th (1.00) 3.72:1
  3rd (1.43) 5.32:1
  2nd (2.11) 7.85:1
  1st (3.41) 12.69:1
Final drive ratio.................. 3.72:1

CALCULATED DATA

Lb/bhp (test weight) 40.1
Mph/1000 rpm (4th gear) 17.9
Engine revs/mi (60 mph) 3360
R&T steering index 0.70
Brake swept area, sq in./ton .. 232

ROAD TEST RESULTS

ACCELERATION

Time to distance, sec:
0-100 ft. 3.9
0-500 ft 10.6
0-1320 ft (¼ mi) 20.3
Speed at end of ¼ mi, mph ...69.5
Time to speed, sec:
0-30 mph 4.4
0-50 mph 10.2
0-60 mph 14.3
0-70 mph 20.7
0-80 mph 33.4

SPEEDS IN GEARS

4th gear (4500 rpm) 85
3rd (5500) 68
2nd (5500) 47
1st (5500) 29

FUEL ECONOMY

Normal driving, mpg 28.5

BRAKES

Minimum stopping distances, ft:
  From 60 mph 189
  From 80 mph 321
Control in panic stop........very good
Pedal effort for 0.5g stop, lb 38
Fade: percent increase in pedal ef-
  fort to maintain 0.5g deceleration
  in 6 stops from 60 mph 97
Overall brake rating..................fair

HANDLING

Speed on 100-ft radius, mph ..33.2
Lateral acceleration, g............ 0.737
Speed thru 700-ft slalom, mph....50.1

INTERIOR NOISE

All noise readings in dBA:
Constant 30 mph 72
  50 mph 81
  70 mph 86

SPEEDOMETER ERROR

30 mph indicated is actually....31.5
60 mph 60.5
70 mph 69.0

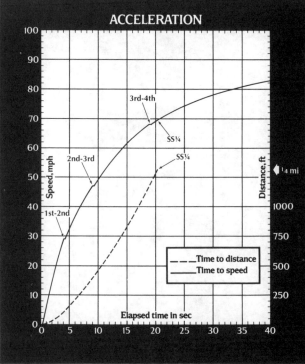

ACCELERATION

SPRITE/MIDGET
CLASSIC CHOICE

Austin-Healey or MG? Frogeye or later Midget/Sprite body? Chrome or black bumpers?
Whichever you choose, you can't go wrong – the long-running 'Spridget' is one of the
most popular Classics of all

MG enthusiasts won't like this, but they have to thank Donald Healey for the birth of the modern Midget. Without Donald Healey there wouldn't have been a Sprite, and without the Sprite there wouldn't have been a Midget.

The Sprite was an appealing little car, which arrived at exactly the right time. Along with the Midget which evolved from it, these two cars brought back motoring fun to those who couldn't afford larger sports cars. For all such people, the Sixties and Seventies were very happy times.

There's no doubt that BMC *needed* a tiny car like the Sprite, for in the Fifties its sports cars had been growing too fast. The T-series MG Midget had been small, but the MGA which replaced it was a lot bigger. The Austin-Healey 100s were even larger and more expensive.

For more than 20 years, BMC (and British Leyland) got it right. They offered a small sports car with simple engineering, agile handling, and bags of character. Not even the onset of USA legislation could spoil that.

Die-hards blame British Leyland for neglecting the Midget. Others will never forgive them for imposing Triumph engines in the Seventies. Never mind – everyone agrees that the Spridget's character stayed alive to the end. The sales figures prove it – after all, 355,000 buyers can't be wrong. . . .

Donald Healey's A90-engined 100 was such a success that BMC's Len Lord invited him to repeat the trick. Lord saw the potential for sales of a tiny sports car in the USA – a chance to repeat the success of the old T-series MG. Healey designed a new small sports car at Warwick in 1956, MG developed it in 1957 and 1958, and Abingdon put it into production in 1958.

The original version was the 'Frogeye' Austin-Healey Sprite, but from 1961, when the first restyle took place, it was joined by an MG-badged Midget. For the next 10 years both types were sold by different dealer chains. The greatest sales success, as expected, was in North America.

By 1963 there was major competition from Triumph, with the Spitfire, and after 1968 the two cars became part of the same British Leyland conglomerate. The Austin-Healey franchise was abandoned in 1971.

Later in the Seventies the two rival cars were rationalised, but they always competed against each other. All in all, BMC's 'sports car factory' spent more than 20 years refining and improving the Spridgets, which were only killed off when top management decided that sports cars were no longer profitable, and that Abingdon would have to be closed.

Model history

In the beginning, only the Frogeye design, badged Austin-Healey Sprite, went on sale in 1958. The basic design featured a BMC A-series engine, gearbox and rear axle, with modified A35 front suspension, and cantilever leaf spring rear suspension. Pressed Steel produced the chunky little monocoque, which had no external boot access, and where the entire front end – bonnet, nose and front wings – lifted up for engine access.

From 1961 the structure was restyled, with a conventional front end, with a bootlid – and with a choice of Austin-Healey or MG badges. For the next decade two near-identical cars were built at Abingdon.

Regular updates followed. A 1.1-litre engine was adopted for 1963, half-elliptic spring rear suspension and wind-up windows were standardised in mid-1964, and a beefier 1.3-litre engine followed for 1967.

Corporate upheavals followed in the Seventies. The Austin-Healey franchise was dropped at the end of 1970, there was a short-lived run of 'Austin' Sprites, but after that MG reigned supreme.

USA's new legislation then hit hard at the Midget, the result being that for 1975 a Triumph 1.5-litre engine was fitted and large energy-absorbing black

Above, 1980 and the last of the breed after 21 years – the 1,500cc rubber-bumper Midget. Right, the Frogeye popped up in 1958. This is a restored 1959 example

bumpers were specified. Traditionalists hated it, USA customers tolerated it, and the Midget was granted five further years of production. The end came at the end of 1979.

Nothing, they say, could replace the Midget – and nothing has.

What to look for

Although Sprites and Midgets are agile little sports cars, their monocoques tend to rot away rapidly in old age, and a considerable amount of work usually needs to be done when tackling a restoration today.

To help us compile this section, we not only drew on our own records and experiences, but also talked to Rod Dunnett of Harrogate, who tackled the restoration of a 1963 MG Midget a few years ago as his first Classic car rebuild. Rod has preserved all the 'before-and-after' pictures of this job, and has a great deal of practical experience of this task.

Rod's particular car is a 1,098cc example, with wire wheels and a soft-top. The restoration took 19 months of spare time work; everything except the actual respray (from Harvest Gold to Clipper Blue) was carried out in his own small garage at home. Rod told us that he found much more trouble than he bargained for.

It was fascinating to compare our own views on the car's problems with those which Rod experienced.

Structure

The Frogeye, with its hinge-up front-end structure, is the odd-man-out here. The bonnet is heavy, and prone to flexing and rust damage at panel joints. Rust is often found where the front end curls round under the nose, and in the area of the headlamp pods and cut-outs. Because the hinges have an arduous job to do there is often rust at the bulkhead and on the bonnet assembly close to the fixings. If the bonnet assembly is damaged you are in trouble, because replacement assemblies are not available.

All other models share the same general problems, and in almost every case new sections, repair patches or panels can be found to help a rebuild.

The main strength of the monocoque is in the sills, and this is where almost all cars need work at restoration time. Because this is an open-top shell it must be properly supported when any cutting or welding is done, or serious sagging and distortion may take place.

Look for trouble in outer and inner sills, and be prepared to replace both items. Close by, inspect the floorpans, especially the box section members which lie underneath the seats.

There may be awful corrosion trouble at the rear, especially at the rear bulkhead on earlier cars where the quarter elliptic leaf springs are fixed; you'll notice this by rolling back the floor covering inside the car and inspecting the fixing.

The rear wings tend to rust around

their edges, and the inner wheelarches may be just as bad. It's also likely that the boot floor panel near the rear cross-panel will also have rusted through due to long-standing water in the tail.

The passenger foot tunnels are often in a terrible state, particularly at the sides where they meet the sills, and on the floor panel itself. The door pillar (or 'A' post) rots away from its welded joint with the sills, this often showing up as a less than rigid support for the doors themselves. Doors tend to go frilly around their lower edges, and the inner panels also tend to go rusty at the bottom.

The main 'chassis legs' should still be sound, as should the main front bulkhead and the front inner wheelarches, but the bonnet itself may rust at its front end, while the front wings usually corrode around their wheelarch edges, close to the joint with the sills, and around the headlamp apertures.

The front cross-panels (above *and* below the grille opening) also rust at their edges, close to welded joints.

Engines

The A-series engine (used in all models except the Midget 1500) is a well-known unit, which seems to last well if it has been regularly serviced. When Rod was rebuilding his own 1.1-litre unit (which had been 'stored' outside, in a stinging nettle patch, for some years!) he used the original head and block castings, had the block rebored, kept some other components, but invested in new pistons, valve springs, rocker shaft, oil pump, water pump, primary chain, and a new gasket set. Apart from painting it all the wrong colour at first, the rest, he says, was easy!

Rod now admits that he should also have changed the spigot bush in the crankshaft – which lines up the gearbox first motion shaft – he had to do this later.

Old age and wear show up as clattery valve gear and excessive oil consumption, but the unit is so simple that a rebuild is straightforward. After reassembly, take great care to set up the balance of the twin SU carburettors, not only for optimum performance, but for optimum fuel efficiency.

The die-hards complain that Triumph Spitfire-type engines, as used in the Midget 1500s, don't last anything like as

Above and right, in its element in the lanes, a 1965 MkII Midget

Left, the Frogeye was replaced in May 1961 by the MkII, which had squared off lines and a proper bootlid

long as A-series units, but Triumph rebuilders disagree. The evidence is that properly kept 1500 engines are not only as reliable as A-series units, but they are more powerful as well. As with the A-series, the Triumph engine is simple to rebuild, and almost all replacement parts are available.

If you have difficulty in sourcing expertise and parts from a rebuilder who doesn't like Triumph engines, why not swallow your pride and consult one of the Triumph experts instead?

Transmissions

There are two types of gearbox to be considered – the A-series 'box for A-series engines, and the Marina/Spitfire type of 'box for Midget 1500s.

A-series 'boxes were working near their limit on the more powerful 1,275cc Midgets, and may need a lot of restoration work at rebuild time.

The layshaft may be worn, as may the mainshaft main bearings and the needle rollers. If the first motion shaft (also known as the 'input shaft') is worn, the bad news is that replacements are not available, so metal spraying and regrinding may be necessary to regenerate bearing surfaces.

Other components which may need

Above, chrome-bumper Midgets lasted through to 1974 by which time many styling changes had been made

replacement are the synchromesh cones, the rear brass bush and the oil seal close to it. Except that first gear usually goes noisy, the gears themselves seem to last well. Oil leaks from the bell-housing usually signal a worn or misaligned scroll at the front end of the gearbox itself. The gearchange should normally feel crisp and positive. If not, it means that selectors or joints have worn, and should be renewed.

The change on Triumph-type gearboxes is more notchy than the A-series, but it is inherently stronger. Synchromeshes tend to wear away by 50,000-70,000 miles, and the same bearing replacement programme may be needed as for the A-series types.

The rear axles rarely seem to give trouble. Just so long as they are not persistently 'leaky', they should not need expensive work.

Running gear

The front end is based on that of the Austin A35. Naturally all bushes and bearings wear, so at restoration time these should all be renewed as a matter of course. Check, in particular, for wear in steering ball-joint ends, though the steering rack itself should be OK.

Rod considered buying a king pin replacement set, but eventually invested in a complete pair of stub axles, reckoning that these were good value, and even simpler to exchange on the car. He also bought two new front coil springs at the same time.

Check for front (lever-arm) damper leaks. Replacements are freely available; unless you're an originality fanatic it isn't really worth rebuilding the worn components.

If regular greasing has been neglected, the bottom fulcrum pins may be worn; the old ones may be difficult to remove, but do persevere, as replacement adds to steering accuracy and to tyre life.

At the back end, the lever-arm dampers may need replacement, while the bushes at each end of the radius arms on '¼-elliptic spring' cars are almost always badly worn; according to Rod, they are very difficult to remove. Springs give little trouble, though you should check the condition of their fixing bushes.

Brake installations are very simple. The front calipers (first fitted to 1963 models) may suffer sticking cylinders, while discs are often badly scored. Don't try to have the discs skimmed, but have them replaced.

Drums, in general, sometimes suffer from sticking cylinders, and (at the rear) from wear at the handbrake pivots. In addition, the pins in the handbrake mechanism rod ends may also have worn, which sets up rattles and may eventually lead to the linkage parting.

Interiors

Interiors are 'cheap and cheerful', which means that many old cars will have torn or warped trim panels, scruffy carpets and a generally doggy appearance.

Sliding-panel side-screens seem to last quite well, and replacements are available. Remanufactured soft-tops (hoods) are now available in all original colours.

The carpets may be damp (or often wet and rotting) – this being due to water getting in around the hoods, sidescreens or through rusty holes somewhere in the footwells or the side panels.

Water in the boot sometimes causes trouble to trim panels and floor coverings, which in any case get scuffed by the contents over the years.

Supplies of correct colour/specification trim panels and carpets are available from specialists for most models.

Most electrical items are still being produced by Lucas. A visit to the local Lucas supplier, with the correct details of what you require, is usually rewarding.

Re-chroming of bumpers is straightforward enough, but bringing the 'black bumpers' back to health takes more time. In a reader's restoration feature we published in 1986, Trevor Smith recommended black shoe polish followed by Simoniz Black Diamond. . .

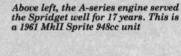

Above left, the A-series engine served the Spridget well for 17 years. This is a 1961 MkII Sprite 948cc unit

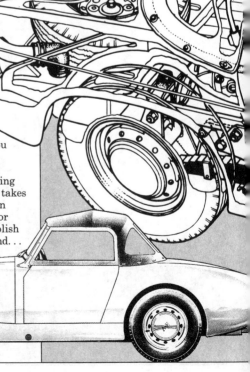

*Brothers under the skin; the MkII
Austin-Healey Sprite and the MkI
Midget were little different*

*Left, small but perfectly
formed; the MkI Sprite was
produced for three years*

167

Specification

Except for quoted details, all Sprites and Midgets had the following basic specifications for UK sale:

Layout: Unit-construction steel body-chassis, with front engine/rear drive, in two-door/two-seater open sports style. Optional removable hard top.

Engine: Four-cylinder, ohv, two SU carburettors.

Transmission: Four-speed gearbox (first gear synchromesh only on 1.5-litre model of 1974-1979).

Suspension, steering and brakes: Independent front suspension by coil springs and wishbones; beam (live) axle rear suspension, quarter-elliptic leaf springs/radius arms at first, half-elliptic leaf springs from 1964-1979. Rack-and-pinion steering. Front drum brakes at first, front discs from late 1962, rear drum brakes.

Major dimensions: Width 4ft 5in; height 4ft 2in; wheelbase 6ft 8in.

Detail differences were:

Sprite MkI ('Frogeye'): 948cc, 43bhp (net) at 5,200rpm. Length 11ft 5.25in.

Sprite MkII/Midget I: 948cc (1961 and 1962), 46bhp at 5,500rpm. Length 11ft 6in. From late 1962: 1,098cc, 56bhp at 5,500rpm.

Sprite MkIII/Midget II: 1,098cc, 59bhp at 5,750rpm. Length 11ft 6in.

Sprite MkIV/Austin Sprite/Midget III: 1,275cc, 65bhp at 6,000rpm. Length 11ft 6in.

Midget 1500: 1,493cc (Triumph), 66bhp at 5,500rpm. Length 11ft 9in.

Parts supply

Because the Sprite/Midget range used many components which were also to be found on BMC/British Leyland family cars, many of the mechanical parts are still available.

On the other hand, because the last Midget was built 12 years ago, the stock of body panels and trim items, particularly those for earlier models, is running down.

However, because so many of these cars are still in use and actively being restored, almost every one of the 'missing' parts is now being remanufactured by specialists. No-one, as far as we know, has had to abandon a rebuild because he or she cannot find parts.

The clubs and the specialists can all provide detail information on parts supply. In the search for factory-made parts, you should arm yourself with the exact part number, along with the chassis number of the car in question, then visit a Rover dealer to see if Unipart can help. Unipart's HQ is at: UGC Ltd, Unipart House, Garsington Road, Cowley, Oxford OX4 2PG. Tel. 0865 778966.

Production

Frogeye Sprites were built from 1958 to 1961, and restyled Sprite/Midgets were produced from 1961 to 1979. 'Austin' Sprites were only built in 1971.

Production of each model type was as follows:

Austin-Healey Frogeye Sprite MkI	48,999
Austin-Healey Sprite MkII (948cc)	20,450
Austin-Healey Sprite MkII (1,098cc)	11,215
MG Midget MkI (948cc)	16,080
MG Midget MkI (1,098cc)	9,601
Austin-Healey Sprite MkIII	25,905
MG Midget MkII	26,601
Austin-Healey Sprite MkIV	21,768
MG Midget MkIII	100,345
Austin Sprite (1971 only)	1,022
MG Midget (Triumph engine)	73,899
TOTAL	355,885

Chassis identification

The basic Sprite/Midget family of sports cars was in production for 21 years. At the end of the run the same basic car had different styling, a different engine, transmission and rear suspension. Here's how to identify the different cars:

	Series	Chassis No.
May 1958: 'Frogeye' Sprite introduced, with unmistakable nose style, and no external boot access:	H-AN5	...501
May 1961: 'Frogeye' Sprite dropped:	H-AN5	.50116
Restyled car, with squared-up nose and tail style plus external bootlid, in two types:		
Austin-Healey Sprite MkII	H-AN6	...101
MG Midget MkI	G-AN1	...101
October 1962: Both cars given 1,098cc engine, front-wheel disc brakes, at:		
Austin-Healey Sprite MkII	H-AN7	.24732
MG Midget MkI	G-AN2	.16184
March 1964: Substantial redesign, with half-elliptic spring rear suspension, wind-up windows, more power, at:		
Austin-Healey Sprite MkIII	H-AN8	.38829
MG Midget MkII	G-AN3	.25788
October 1966: Further redesign, with 1,275cc engine, at:		
Austin-Healey Sprite MkIV	H-AN9	.64735
MG Midget MkIII	G-AN4	.52390
October 1969: Minor cosmetic changes for 1970, at:		
Austin-Healey Sprite	H-AN10	.85287
MG Midget	G-AN5	.74886
January 1971: Last 'Austin-Healey' badged car, at:	H-AN10	.86803
First 'Austin' badged car at:	A-AN10	.86804
1971: Last 'Austin' badged car was:	A-AN10	.87824
October 1974: Last 'chrome bumper' MG Midget was:	G-AN5	153920
For 1975, Midget substantially redesigned, with black bumpers, 1.5-litre engine, all-synchromesh gearbox, at:	G-AN6	154101
November 1979: Last MG Midget built was:	G-AN6	229526

Introduced in late 1966, the MkIV Sprite

Clubs

Sprite and Midget owners have a lot of choice when they are looking to join a one-make club. In every case Midget owners may join Austin-Healey clubs, or Sprite owners may join MG clubs.

There are three major organisations. The biggest club, and the one which concentrates on parts supply, technical advice, and restoration matters, is the MG Owners Club. This has more than 50,000 members and an organisation to match. The annual subscription is £18 per year, with a joining fee of £4. More details from: Membership Secretary, MG Owners' Club, 2/4 Station Road, Swavesey, Cambs CB4 5QZ. Tel. 0954 31125, fax 0954 32106.

The MG Car Club is the oldest of the specialist clubs (it was founded in the Thirties), and has now relocated to part of the original factory buildings at Abingdon. Nostalgia means a lot to this club – the PO Box number is the same as the factory's original phone number. There are 10,500 UK members and more than 40,000 affiliated from overseas clubs. The annual membership fee is £23 per year. There is a Midget Register. More details from: Lyn Jeffrey, MG Car Club Ltd, Kimber House, PO Box 251, Abingdon, Oxon OX14 3FA. Tel. 0235 555552.

The Austin-Healey Club has also been in existence since the Fifties, and because of the affinity of the Midget to the Sprite, MG Midget owners are welcomed.

There are around 2,500 members. The UK membership fee is £20 per year (or £21 for a two-member family), and there is no joining fee for new members. For all membership details, contact: Mrs Colleen Holmes, 4 Saxby Street, Leicester LE2 0ND.

Road tests

Every tester, everywhere in the world, got to drive these cars. Almost without exception they loved the cars' character, zest and handling. On the other hand, they all thought the cars had an interior which was too small. Later in life, every restoration pundit has pointed out the Bad News and the Good News – corrosion-prone structures, but easily available parts.

In June 1958 *The Autocar* summed up well: '. . .while acceleration and speed at first glance seem modest, the character, behaviour, economy of operation and, not least, the low initial cost combine to make a very rewarding total.'

'The Sprite is at its most satisfying on winding roads . . . rack-and-pinion steering is very precise; at first it feels almost over-sensitive . . . the way in which the Sprite goes round a corner is a delight . . . the ride is firm to the point of being a little harsh.'

Overall, testers were impressed: 'The little Austin-Healey Sprite has the sort of charm that grows with acquaintance. It exhibits so many pleasant characteristics on the road, does much more – and does it better – than the specification suggests. . .'

The accent, in future years, was to judge the improvements. In 1961, when the car had been restyled, *The Autocar* wrote that: 'Cornering on rough surfaces causes the rear wheels to bounce outwards and the rear axle struck its bump stops rather too easily . . . the new gear ratios have improved the versatility of the car. . . That the car now has a completely lockable (boot) compartment greatly increases its potential. . . It does everything its predecessor did with a little more refinement – it is, therefore, a very worthy successor.'

The big advances came in 1964, with the arrival of wind-up windows and half-elliptic spring rear suspension: 'It doesn't take one many miles . . . to appreciate that this car's recent revisions must have been devised by designers who really drive. . . The new Sprite is faster, holds the road better, rides more comfortably and is more habitable.'

In more detail: 'Front disc and rear drum brakes by Lockheed are right up to the standard set by the rest of the car . . . the half-elliptic (rear springs) allow more travel at a softer rate, which means improved comfort and a reduction of axle hop over bad surfaces; more important, they cut out "rear-wheel steering" and the over-sensitivity of control that were criticised in previous Sprites. . . Winding side windows and hinged quarter vents . . . have done much for the Sprite's appearance as well as for its travelling comfort.

The late-model 1,275cc-engined Midget was still well liked, but the lack of first-gear synchromesh was now emphasised, and the interior was described as 'cramped'. Specifically: 'All the indirect gears, particularly bottom (with straight-cut gears) are noisy, and somewhat harsh. . . The latest driving

The redesigned facia of the MkII Midget of 1964. At this time Spridgets gained wind-up windows and improved suspension

position is disappointing and somewhat cramped. Late model MkII Midgets were given revised seats. . . Their backrests are thicker than before, with less bucket shaping . . . drivers taller than 5ft 8in find it difficult to get comfortable.'

By the mid-Seventies the car had been given a Triumph-built engine, and all-synchromesh gearbox, plus raised suspension. By this time, though, *Autocar* testers thought the car outdated, with a summary which included: '. . .inclined to oversteer. Harsh ride, excessive wind noise with hood up. Undergeared. . .'

However: 'there is no doubt it (Midget 1500) is substantially quicker than the late-series 1,275cc car . . . a genuine 100mph car, and this represents a great advance on the 1,275. . .'

Greatest criticism was reserved for the suspension which: '. . .worked well in the past, but there are signs that the latest car needs something more sophisticated to cope with its great torque and performance. Part of the trouble lies in the fact that the Midget has been given increased ride height at the back.'

Unhappily for MG enthusiasts, testers reached this conclusion about the Midget 1500: 'For our money the Spitfire is much more practical and civilised. There will always be those who scorn it for precisely those reasons. . .'

Do you agree with them today?

Prices – then and now

When the Frogeye Sprite went on sale in 1958 it cost £679, but in mid-1961 when the Midget was introduced prices were £669 (Sprite) and £660 (Midget). Price increases in the Sixties were countered by purchase tax reductions, such that when the 1,275cc engine was introduced for 1967 they had only crept up to £672/£684.

The rush came in the Seventies, with the Midget 1500 being introduced at £1,560. By the end of 1979, however, this price had leapt to £3,821.

Classic values were higher in 1989 than they are today. In general terms we feel that Sprites and their equivalent Midgets now have the same values – in other words 'the badge' means nothing. The spring 1991 edition of *Collectors Cars*, makes these estimates about present values:

	Cond. B	Cond. A
Sprite Frogeye (1958-1961)	£4,500	£8,000
Spridget 948cc/1,098cc	£2,500	£4,000
Spridget 1,275cc (1966-1972)	£3,250	£5,000
Midget 1,275cc (round wheelarch, 1972-1974)	£3,000	£4,500
Midget 1500	£2,850	£4,250

Performance

	Sprite MKI	Sprite MkII	Midget MkII	Sprite MkIII	Midget MkIII	Midget 1500
Engine power (ltr/bhp)	0.95/43	0.95/46	1.1/56	1.1/59	1.3/65	1.5/66
Top speed (mph)	80	85	90	92	94	101
0-60mph (sec)	20.9	19.8	17.2	14.5	14.6	12.3
0-80mph (sec)	—	51.8	36.9	31.5	33.2	24.0
Standing ¼-mile (sec)	21.7	21.8	21.1	19.4	19.7	18.5
Typical mpg (overall)	38	38	32	30	30	30
Weight (lb)	1,463	1,540	1,596	1,561	1,589	1,720
Tested in:	*Autocar*	*Autocar*	*Autocar*	*Autocar*	*Autocar*	*Autocar*

This table shows an honest progression over the years. Each time the engine was enlarged, or made more powerful, the performance increased. Top speeds increased from 80 to 101mph in 21 years, while fuel efficiency slumped from about 38mpg to 30mpg. Along the way weights went up from 1,463 to 1,720lb. Faster, heavier cars use more fuel – that's normally a fact of motoring life.

First timer

Danny Fenton had never carried out welding or spraying until he
restored a wrecked MG Midget into a unique prototype replica.
Nick Larkin hears his story   Photos by **Dave Wigmore**

ABLACK and white photo of a unique Austin-Healey scrapped 30 years ago seized Danny Fenton's imagination so much that £4000 and 4000 hours later he'd recreated the car.

Danny was leafing through Eric Dymock's work *The Sprites and Midgets* when his eye caught the picture of a prototype, scrapped 30 years ago, which could have been a replacement for the immortal 'Frogeye'.

'I knew immediately that this was a car BMC *should* have built. It looked exactly right. I immediately thought of making a replica,' said Danny, a 32-year-old computer engineer from Bristol.

The car is described unofficially as an Austin Healey Mk 1½; basically it retains the Frogeye's back end but the front is virtually identical to the Mk I MG Midget and Mk II Sprite which arrived in 1961.

'Had it gone into production, the prototype would have been a pure Healey design. In the pre-production cars, the rear was done by MG and the front by Healey,' explained Danny.

Several factors fell into place to make Danny's dream a reality.

Firstly, he already had a 1973 MG Midget which was well past economic restoration but could form a basis for the replica. 'Obviously I didn't want to hack

'I knew immediately that this was a car BMC *should* have built. It looked exactly right'

Frogeye-style rounded rear was made by a boatbuilder in glassfibre and faired into the MG Midget front end

Interior is pure Sprite: functional but comfortable, and very sixties. Note Austin-Healey crest on steering wheel hub

a good Frogeye around, but thought it would be okay to do something with one which would otherwise have gone to the scrapyard,' Danny said.

Secondly, discussing the matter with staff at the Bristol Sprite and Midget Centre revealed a source which could produce a glassfibre replica 'Frogeye' rear at reasonable cost – a boatbuilder on the Isle of Wight.

No longer was the project merely a dream. Danny's down-at-heel Midget was about to undergo a transformation!

Looking at the car would have made the most dedicated restorer think again. It had 'cartwheeled' in an accident and the then-owner had crudely attempted to hammer out the damage before using bodyfiller to make it look presentable.

Most of what wasn't filler on the car had sprouted rust, and large areas of the floor were absent altogether. In other words, it wasn't a straight, original car!

But Danny got down to work. He began by removing everything removable, enabling the car to be tipped on its side when required. Stripping down was a relatively easy task, with Danny adopting his own method to speed things up.

'I have a philosophy about nuts and bolts. Unless they're special items you can't get again very easily you may as well just grind them off if they don't undo easily. It saves a lot of time and you'd probably have replaced them with new anyway,' he explains.

Danny had never attempted welding before, but that wasn't going to stop him. He bought an SIP Migmate welder, practised on a few pieces of scrap metal and got down to work. 'I was surprised how easy it was under the circumstances,' he said.

There was a major task ahead. 'For a start, the boot floor was only attached to the car on one edge. I tried to repair it initially, but after a week I gave up.' A replacement came from Wheeler and Davies, and had to be modified to accept the Midget's semi-elliptic rear springs.

New sills and assorted floor sections were bought, and Danny was lucky enough to find a set of factory front wings, though these were for a later car so the sidelight mouldings had to be altered.

A new front valance was bought after an unsuccessful attempt to make one out of three scrap examples.

The car's inner wheelarches, and the rear arches at the leading rear spring hangers had all suffered particularly badly, and as Danny couldn't get some of the original panels he had to hand beat them, folding them as necessary in a vice.

A bonnet from a rolled 1500cc Midget was found in a scrapyard: 'It was in excellent condition, but there was a great ridge in the middle of the bonnet where the engine had tried to escape,' Danny recalled. Careful panel beating was needed to rectify this.

Surprisingly even for a car in this condition, rust had taken a hold in the transmission tunnel, which meant Danny had to cut a large hole in the underneath so he could get at it. Once the corrosion had been removed he welded the hole shut again.

A further large-scale job was strengthening the front bulkhead with thick gauge steel to take the heavier Frogeye-style windscreen. Danny also had to make up special brackets for the screen.

Ready-made repair sections were used to revive the A-posts, but the B-posts were to present problems. Danny eventually made pieces to fit them by shaping metal over a piece of wood in his vice.

Danny paid £40 for a pair of rusty Frogeye doors from a scrapyard, which were repaired with Midget lower skins.

There was now a sound car, but by far the worst was still to come. How was Danny going to

Engine is in fact 1275cc rather than correct 948cc unit, but Danny has modified it externally to look original

fit the new glassfibre rear to the car? The panels were not particularly well made, and Danny spent more than a week sanding and filling them before he was satisfied. He also had to remove all the flanges from the new section if there was to be any chance of it fitting.

He devised a novel solution. First he welded a strip of 18 gauge steel from the back of the B-posts, around the wheelarches and the boot floor. The glassfibre item was then attached to this using self-tapping screws at two-inch intervals.

Danny understandably winces at the memory of what followed, a truly horrific task. Frogeyes don't have an opening boot, so Danny had to crawl headfirst from the interior of the car into the new boot section, armed with a large bucket of glassfibre resin and matting to stick the new section to the framework he'd made up. 'Simon Hawkes, a friend who helped me do this, wondered if he should go home and get his aqualung. It was dark, cramped and stuffy inside there,' Danny laughs. Danny would like to thank Simon, who has also restored an MGB to top show condition, for his help.

Once this onerous job was complete, the self-tapping screws were removed and the holes filled in.

'Well it worked. The rear section is still attached!,' Danny points out.

So, a sound car at last. A month, including a week's holiday, was spent preparing the bodywork; filling and sanding. Aged underseal was removed with the help of a blowlamp from what remained of the car's original underneath.

Danny initially used 80-grit glasspaper, then 180-grade wet and dry. A coat of yellow paint was sprayed on to locate any high spots in the finish, which were then dealt with.

Finally, the shell was ready for painting. Danny had never sprayed before but, again,, practising on old metal soon gave him confidence.

Two coats of primer filler and a coat of grey primer followed, getting the car ready for its first top coat.

Danny chose primrose yellow. 'I'd always wanted a red sportscar, but the photo in the book showed it was a light colour. The yellow was simply available at the time,' he said.

On went a first topcoat, mixed 50/50 with thinners. Sadly, this reacted with the primer, perhaps because of the atmoshere of the industrial area in which Danny lives. Sanding back the paint and trying again led to a similar result, so finally an ICI isolator, plus three coats of primer, followed.

Danny applied 12 coats of cellulose in all, initially 50/50 with thinners, then 30/70 and 10/90. Rubbing down was accomplished with 1200 wet and dry.

The dashboard needed considerable attention to convert it to Mk I Sprite style. Holes left by various accessories had to be filled in, and an array of suitable switches and dials, found at autojumbles over the years,

Left, Danny had to crawl into the boot to fix the new rear section to the front

Below, an angle grinder was used extensively for dressing welds and removing rusty bolts

Danny's unique Austin-Healey replica may be based on a Midget but looks totally right in its yellow livery with wires

fitted in their place. A vinyl covering was fitted using Evostick and a hairdryer!

A new wiring loom for the car was made from two old Mini ones – Danny's neighbour races these cars, and was also able to provide a set of headlamps for the Sprite.

Danny next turned his attention to the gearbox. Accidentally dislodging the selector mechanisms inside meant two evenings spent delving into the 'box innards with spring pullers to get everything back together again.

A further task was

Middle picture, Danny Fenton reckons there's nothing to beat a good Sprite or Midget

Above, he had to buy each wire wheel individually to afford a complete set!

Right, distinctive front grille with its crinkly slats is a modified Austin 1100 part

'It certainly defeats all the know-alls at shows, who think I've converted a Frogeye!'

reshimming the steering rack, taking out the excessive play which had been a notable feature of the car before restoration.

The engine fitted to the Midget was in excellent condition, though it had been bored out to plus-40 thou at some stage.

New big-end shells, rocker shaft and valve guides were fitted, and the cylinder head was skimmed. Two new valves were needed.

Danny decided to retain the Midget's 1275 engine instead of getting a Frogeye-spec 948cc unit. 'To be honest, it was for performance reasons as much as anything,' Danny said.

However, he went to great lengths to make the unit appear as much as possible like the earlier unit. He painted it in BMC green engine paint and converted it to dynamo operation, mounting the coil on the dynamo as was the case with early Sprites. An early sixties radiator completed the effect.

A front grille from an Austin 1100 was adapted to fit the car, and the Midget's bumpers were rechromed. Danny bought one wire wheel a month from Moss, until he had a complete set!

The seats presented further

problems. Eventually a set of extremely unhappy Frogeye ones were found. The metal frames had to be welded up, and replacement base frames made from three different thicknesses of marine ply. The original foam backing was beefed up with carpet underlay, cotton wadding and horsehair. To save a lot of trouble, new seat coverings were bought from Moss.

The hood was also new, but required much modification and jiggling to fit.

Meanwhile, the rear axle and diff were stripped for inspection, but had to be put back together by a specialist who had the necessary tools.

Danny made up door trims using hardboard and a vinyl covering. 'Just like they did originally.' A new carpet set completed the picture.

Finally, the Sprite was complete: 'Driving it was an amazing feeling. The first 300 miles I covered were just around Bristol, making sure everything was settling in properly. As I began to stretch my journeys I gradually realised nothing was going to fall off the car and it was going to be reliable,' said Danny, who has already picked up several major awards with the car.

'It certainly defeats all the know-alls at shows. First it doesn't register with them, then they think I've converted a Frogeye!' he laughs.

There have been Midgets and Sprites in Danny's family for years: 'There is nothing else like them. You just can't get into one without a smile on your face.'

What better way of summing up Danny's car, the result of a magnificent restoration! ∎

Same wine, new bottle

The Heritage bodyshell for the Sprite and Midget is here – and could save you money and a lot of grief if your old Spridget needs restoration. Top expert Graham Paddy of Moss Europe shows you how to tackle the re-shell operation. Story: Jon Pressnell

The arrival of the Heritage bodyshell for the Sprite and Midget is a major event in the classic car world. It's probably more important than the launch in 1989 of the MGB shell, because it's targeted much more at the relatively impecunious first-timer. But how easy is a re-shell.

To find out, CLASSIC AND SPORTSCAR got together with the man who knows more about Spridgets than just about anyone else – Graham Paddy, founder and managing director of the long-established Sprite & Midget, B,C, V8 Centre, now part of Moss Europe.

Graham agreed to carry out a re-shell for us

– on a budget. The car: a 1969 Midget owned by Moss's graphic artist, Peter Taylor, himself the veteran of six or so Spridget rebuilds. Joining Graham and Peter for the exercise was Mike Inmon, who's put together a couple of Spridgets back in his native America.

The donor car had been off the road for two years, but before that had been an MoT'd runner. Superficially not too bad, it was in fact structurally very weak, with the all-important front 'H' frame needing replacement and with holed inner sills and a boot floor you could put your fist through.

"It would have been recoverable but it

plete assemblies, for example.

"With the shell home, check it thoroughly: make sure all the holes you'll need are there, and make a note of any surplus ones that will need to be filled. Trial-fit the rear lamps, too, in case their plinth on the shell needs building up with lead for a good fit.

"Think carefully before deciding to spray the shell yourself. If you do it badly you'll lower the value of the vehicle. And if you make a mess you'll still have spent around £150 on materials — that's a lot of money to have thrown down the drain. I'd recommend you leave the job to a professional, and budget for £600 or so. If it's less than £500 you're wasting your time.

"To avoid damage to the freshly-painted shell, make sure all the panels are tied down with bungee straps before transporting it, and fit short lengths of rubber door seal to the panels to prevent chafing."

Front end mechanicals

It was with everything outlined in the previous section carried out, and the MG back from the Midhurst Engineering paintshop, that CLASSIC AND SPORTSCAR started to follow through the re-shell — at the point where Mike was going round the body with a set of taps, cleaning up all the various threads that had become clogged with paint. This is an important prelude to starting work.

Spridget front suspension is not particularly long-lived, and you should expect to replace everything — as was indeed necessary on Peter's car. It wasn't an easy job, not helped by everything being seized and by a duff batch of wishbone outer fulcrum pins. You'll be lucky indeed if you can get away with just fitting new wishbone rubber bushes.

Graham managed to hammer out the inner wishbone fulcrum bolts, but it was touch-and-go: he came close to giving up and sawing them through — which isn't an easy job at all. A handy tip is to remove the bumper irons, so you can gain access through the front apron.

"There was side-to-side play in the kingpin. If there's play there's no sense in just putting a new pin in — replace the pin and the wishbone pan. It's not worth taking a short cut with suspension — it could be a recipe for disaster," says Graham.

"You can bet that the top fulcrum pin will

be seized, too, so leave it on the damper and take the whole assembly to the bench — you'll never get it out otherwise.

"Trial-fit everything, and when you're putting it back together, make sure the inner wishbone fulcrum bolts are inserted from the *inside* out. If you do it the opposite way the tabs on the washers won't engage in their slots and the suspension will move around. To help the wishbones slide in, I open out the chassis brackets a little with a hammer, and when the pans are in place I tap them back. And make sure the top trunnion is the correct way round, with the boss facing outwards.

"Before tightening the fulcrum bolts, jack the suspension up to its normal operating height, to avoid twisting the rubber bushes."

With the front suspension sorted, Graham and Peter moved onto the brakes.

"Unless you know the car, always replace brake components," Graham stresses. "It's not sensible to save money on safety-related items — and re-rubbering is a pain in the neck. It's better to go for a new master-cylinder than a new bumper, if cash is short. And always replace brake pipes and hoses regardless — nine times out of ten the brake lines will be internally corroded."

On Peter's car the front calipers were retained, as the pistons were operating correctly and there were no leaks, but the badly corroded discs went in the bin.

The steering was fine, but Graham replaced all Nyloc nuts as a matter of course. He also kept the rack securing bolts loose, to enable the column splines to align correctly with those on the pinion shaft when later fitting the column. Bolt the rack up tight and you may end up damaging the splines as you try to fit the column.

Rear end mechanicals

Having drained the gearbox, Graham and Peter removed the rear axle as a unit, complete with the springs on their mounting plates and with the propshaft still attached.

"It's a lot easier, and it enables you to strip everything more comfortably, off the car," says Graham. "Keep the wheels on, and you can wheel it around as well. I cut the brake pipes and the check straps — which were frayed anyway — because it's not worth messing around with such low-cost items.

"It's advisable to replace all spring shackle

would have needed jigging-up before welding, and you'd have reached the point where you'd have been spending £1500 on panels alone," says Peter.

"You'd have to be a fool to want to rebuild a shell like this — at £2200 the new body really is a bargain."

Preparation and spraying

"Before you start, you must work out a plan of action," says Graham. "It's best to transfer bits from the donor car to the new shell as you go along — that way you know where everything goes. If you completely dismantle the old car and put everything in little boxes you're giving yourself a lot of grief. But if there's no alternative, take as many detailed photos as you can, along with lots of drawings of how things are arranged. And don't strip everything down — keep the doors as com-

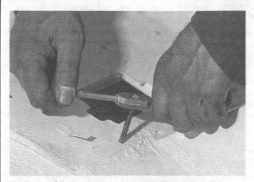

An important preparatory step is to tap out paint-coated threads on shell (above). Suspension is likely to need full rebuild — inner fulcrum pin must be correctly inserted, and top trunnion right way round; note anti-roll bar

bushes, 'U' bolt rubbers and damper bushes as a matter of course, lubricating them first with the correct rubber grease. And always put new nuts on the 'U' bolts. If the springs had a decent curve to them when taking the full weight of the car, there's no sense in replacing them".

Peter had fitted telescopic dampers at the rear, and, in common with the front lever-arms, they were in good order.

"Rear telescopics are a good idea if you need new rear dampers, and at the front I'd recommend brand-new dampers rather than reconditioned ones," says Graham. "A ⅝in front anti-roll bar makes a lot of difference, too – but make sure beforehand that you've bought genuine Spridget wishbones with all the holes and reinforcements for the bar"

Despite its lack of complication, the rear end wasn't all plain sailing: the brake adjusters were seized and had to be freed off with oxy-acetylene and the splined hubs had to be replaced – complete, Peter reminded us, with the lock tab straps for the drums.

One final tip: if you're removing the half-shafts, do remember to put them back in the same side. If you don't, you'll reverse the direction of rotation, and thus of stress, and soon have a breakage on your hands...

Wiring loom & petrol tank

Tank and loom – the two go together. The reason's simple: before fitting the tank you need to install not only the fuel gauge sender unit but also its wiring. Forget this, and you'll have to drop the tank later.

"It's a false economy not to put a new loom in", says Graham. "The original is bound to have been bodged over the years. But don't wrench the old loom out in a burst of enthusiasm. Keep it in place as a guide, cutting the cables just short of their terminals, so you can tell what goes where by the stub of cable left behind".

As is common on Spridgets, Peter's tank had rusted through on the top, so a new one was fitted complete with new seating strips, often forgotten when a tank is installed.

As the loom comes in two parts, Peter could have got away with just fitting the rear loom at this stage, but chose to complete the job in one by fitting the whole loom. With the loom fitted he also took the opportunity to install the tail and reversing lights.

Petrol & hydraulic lines

With the tank in, on went the rear-mounted electric pump – which had been checked beforehand for correct operation. There are two things to remember here: first, that the part of the pump marked 'top' is indeed mounted uppermost and second, that the pump's two vent pipes are fitted. The fuel line followed, Peter taking care to secure the pipe with suitable clips, and to sleeve it where necessary with lengths of rubber hose.

And so to the brake lines – which are best fitted early on: leave them until the engine and gearbox are in place and you'll have the devil of a job, as the main run is *inside* the transmission tunnel. Also, if you fit them at this stage you can move on to fit the master cylinder and then finish off the braking installation by adding fluid and bleeding the whole system.

Engine bay fitting-up

It's a big morale-booster getting a few shiny components bolted in place under the bonnet – but Graham advises a little caution:

"A lot of people replace components just because they look tatty. By taking the time to clean them up and repaint them you could probably save quite a bit of money".

Whether you renovate or replace, there are certain jobs that *have* to be done at this stage. Strictly speaking they're not under-bonnet items, but are part of under-bonnet assemblies. These are the wiper mechanism and the heater ducts. Fitting these under the scuttle after you've fitted the windscreen is a near impossibility, so do it now. By the same token also fit the tonneau studs – *before* going on to bolt in the cockpit crash rail and the washer jets and tubing.

Doors, windscreen & dash

Again, there's a sequence to be observed here: doors before screen before dashboard. This is because the doors form the datum point for correct alignment of the screen – a reason also why you should begin by fitting the door rubbers, as these will slightly alter the attitude of the doors.

Fitting up the doors proved a time-consuming and infuriating job, despite Graham's expertise. The main problem was the catch mechanism, which – along with the locks – needed replacing. Although the catches are still made on the original tooling, tolerances have slipped somewhat, and it took a while for Graham to find a new unit that worked correctly. Even then, he had to bend the arm on the lock barrel before it could engage properly with the catch mechanism.

"If a lock isn't working, sit down and try to understand how it operates," says Graham. "Once you've worked this out, you'll be able to do something about the problem. So if the lock on the other side is OK, take it off and see how it works.

"Don't expect everything you transfer to fit perfectly and work perfectly straightaway, either. Because you've taken it off an old car and disturbed it, Murphy's Law says it won't work when you put it back. With the locks, in particular, make sure everything works *before* you start putting in the window mechanism."

Moving on to this stage, the first step is to secure the window guide at the rear edge of the door by its top bolt. Only then bolt in place the vinyl-covered top rail and install the inner weather excluder. You can then slide in, at an angle, the quarter-light assembly. With this wedged in the door, fit the quarter-light locating 'L' bracket; if you try to do this with the assembly fully in position you'll find it impossible.

With the quarter-light in place, but not bolted in tight, the window glass and the regulator can be slid in – sliding the regulator along its guide channel on the window from front to back. Only with everything in place should you bolt the quarter-light assembly up tight, when you've satisfied yourself everything works smoothly.

"Keep the window mechanism loose, though, and the trim off the doors, until the car is on its wheels, in case adjustments are needed when the car is supporting its full weight," advises Graham.

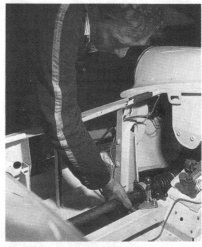

Replace rack if play excessive; keep clamps loose until column fitted on splines

Unless master cylinder is fairly new is best replaced – don't take risks with brakes

Badly corroded front discs were replaced (new disc on right); worn hubs discarded

Putting in the screen is a two-man job. First step is to ensure you fit the correct number of shims to the screen pillars. Leave these out, and as you tighten up the windscreen the glass will crack.

Begin by loosely fitting the scuttle-top bolts, and then with one person leaning on the screen put a screwdriver through the top bolt hole on one side and lever the screen down until you can install the lower nut and bolt; repeat on the other side and then fit the upper bolts. Tighten up to align with the quarter-light leading edges.

Now – at last! – the dashboard can be connected to its wiring and fitted in place. Peter's was reasonably respectable, so was installed without further work, but if yours is tatty there's no need to splash out on an exchange unit: an afternoon with a can of Sperex black-crackle paint will have your dashboard as new.

Although re-shell was carried out in Moss Europe's Cox and Buckles workshops, all procedures used are applicable to home restorer. Graham Paddy (back to camera, left) used to rebuild ten Spridgets per year on average...

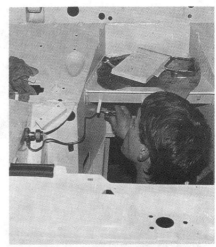

Rear end was removed as a single unit, with the propshaft; note non-standard telescopic dampers. Only problem with diff likely to be excessive noise

Brake pipes run down inside of tunnel, so should be fitted early on; replace piping

Good idea to check halfshaft splines for damage – but make sure shafts go back correct side

Keep old loom in place, and just cut off cables at dash, leaving stubs in place

Tonneau studs, heater ducting and wiper drive need to be fitted before screen and dash

New tank may be needed. Fit sender, wiring and seating strip before installation

Rear-end fitting-up under way; check if lamp plinths need lead-filling pre-paint

Fitting up the doors can be a fiddle – allow at least three hours a side, and don't rush

GRAHAM PADDY'S TOP TEN TIPS

1. You've got to enjoy doing it. If you're not going to enjoy it, don't start. You shouldn't treat it as a chore – look forward to doing it, and have some fun.

2. Don't work to a tight timetable. Regard it as a project for six months rather than as a two-week marathon.

3. Buy the parts you need from the people who supplied the shell, even if it costs a bit more – they will then be more willing to help you if you're in trouble.

4. At every stage refer to a parts catalogue such as our own and to a proper BL parts list, so you can see what's supposed to be there – when you take a car to bits you shouldn't assume it's still as the manufacturer intended. Clips may have rusted away or been lost, for instance, and it's always the tuppeny-halfpenny items that end up destroying the expensive bits...

5. Check the condition of as much as you can before taking the car to bits – a steam-clean before you start isn't a bad idea here. Maybe even have the car MoT'd, so you know what it'll fail on.

6. Think long-term: spend £20 now rather than £50 later.

7. Take units out in as big chunks as you can – it's a lot easier dismantling it all on the bench.

8. Whatever you're putting on the new shell, put it on and finish the job. Don't think you'll go back and finish it later. I guarantee you'll forget it...

9. Clear up as you go – keep car and workshop clear of rubbish.

10. Don't think it's going to be a straightforward job: things are going to go wrong. If they do, take a break – a fresh look usually helps.

Space for engine removal and reinstallation is tight. Unit needs to be angled sharply to slot in place

This exhaust mounting strap is often missing; omit it and your exhaust downpipe will fracture

Getting there! Tighten manifolds from inside out, or exhaust manifold will bow

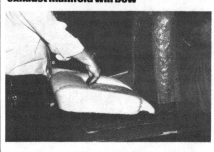

Polythene cap (dustbin bag will do) enables cover to be slid on. Use glue sparingly. All seat covers are available to original patterns; trial-fit before committing yourself

Engine/gearbox/prop

"If you're sticking with the units you have, split the engine and 'box and inspect the clutch. Unless it has been renewed recently, replace it – it's not worth messing around," says Graham.

"Fit a new press-in bearing to the clutch release arm if there's play, and don't forget to fit a new spigot bush in the middle of the flywheel. Also, if the clevis pin on the clutch pushrod is oval, the lost motion will reduce travel of the clutch pedal. If this is a problem, you can buy a new pushrod, but you'll have to have the eye on the clutch pedal welded up and re-drilled."

Fit new engine and gearbox mounts as a matter of course, and take the time to trial-fit them before installing the engine. Graham didn't do this, and found he had to close up the legs of one front mount before it would

align with its fixing holes. Don't forget, too, that there's a clip for the fuel line attached to the nearside front mount.

With the gearbox mounting crossmember attached to the gearbox, the engine and gearbox can be hoisted into place. The trick, as with removing the engine, is to have the right-hand engine mount bolted in place on the shell but to leave the left-hand mount totally off both engine and body; with engine removal, the right mount is merely unbolted at the engine, while the left mount is unbolted both at the engine and at the chassis.

The engine/gearbox goes in at a sharp angle, and once in position is supported on the hoist while the right mount is bolted to the engine and the fully-assembled left mount is slid into place and bolted down. The rear mounts can then be bolted in place, still with the weight off the engine; a beefy crosshead screwdriver is handy to lever the mounts into alignment with the bolt holes.

Graham's no great lover of upholstery and trim work, so we called in Chris Maddox and Paul Stringer of Callow & Maddox – trim supplier to the motor industry and manufacturer of all Moss Europe's original-pattern seat and trim kits.

Paul laid down various basic principles – the first of which is to work in well-ventilated conditions and always to disconnect and remove the battery.

Take this advice seriously: Paul was once working on a Big Healey when his scissors fell across the battery terminals. The spark ignited the vapour from the glue he was using, and within seconds the car was ablaze, with flames reaching the workshop roof.

"Be patient, take your time, and above all trial-fit everything," says Paul. "Assume that whatever you've got you'll have to use again. Some foams aren't available, for instance, so don't go crazy and just rip them out – put some hose on the end of a kettle and gently steam them free of the seat covers."

Paul also advises prudence with glue – it's better to use the Dunlop Thixofix type than the spray-on variety that is more convenient but apparently of limited life. Use a spreader, he suggests, and don't apply too much, otherwise it will set into lumps.

Other tips are to fit a polythene cap around the outer edge of the seat back to help the cover slide over, to be generous in the amount of surplus material you leave in place, and to use clips that aren't so tight they'll tear the material. Think, too, about whether any previous re-trims have seen the disappearance of vital items such as protective edging to sharp corners.

Trim and hood

As with the seats, Chris stresses the importance of trial-fitting: once carpet is glued in place you'll wreck it if you try to pull it off.

The trickiest part of the trimming is fitting the carpet over the rear wheelarches. Chris's approach is to fit the chassis-rail section and then the section over the arch, cutting away the overlap with a Stanley knife to give an imperceptible join.

As for the trim panels, always use cup washers behind the securing screws, and use a bradawl rather than a drill for making holes, as a drill bit will wrap itself around the padding inside and twist it around.

To show how the hood is fitted, we enrolled Peter Randle and Andy Monger of Tickford Ltd – maker of the original hoods and supplier of weather equipment to Moss Europe.

The first thing to do is measure across the rear of the body and find the centre of the hood mounting flange. Holes can then be drilled 4/10in down and the hood attached, mounting strip; don't drill the flange for the lift-the-dot studs at this stage.

With the hood frame loosely bolted in place, Andy and Peter attached the header rail to the frame and trail-fitted it to the screen. With it satisfactorily positioned they tightened the hood mounting bolts and roughly slotted in place the sealing rubber.

Glue was then applied in a broad line to the outer edge of the header, and the hood pulled tautly into place, using the screen stay as a datum point for the hood centre – which is

For good adhesion use a soft-faced hammer to bed down carpet on tricky sections

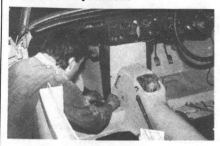

Various bits of vinyl are used to hide metal; check on old car to see where they should go

Header has to be fitted to frame and offered up before frame bolted in tightly

Pretty impressive, huh? Finished car shows off its taut hood. Use masking tape guide to position the chrome trim

already marked. Peel back the hood after this operation and a line of glue on the fabric will indicate where to apply adhesive to stick the hood to the header. When the glue has dried you can pull the fabric into place, checking that the sides of the hood are level with the bottom of the header rail.

All that remains now is to fold the hood back and glue it to the outer edge of the header, working the fabric down firmly. Attachment of the mounting strip for the sealing rubber follows, and you can then trim off surplus fabric and fit the rubber.

The final and crucial step is to screw the draught-excluder side-pieces to the header, inboard of their studded tabs. If you don't do this – using cup washers – you'll end up slowly pulling the stitching apart in use. Now you can fit those lift-the-dots to the sides...

Detailing

With the car so tantalisingly close to being finished, this is the stage where it's easy to get carried away, and make silly slip-ups.

A common mistake on pre-1970 Midgets, says Graham, is to position the chrome side strips wrongly, through not taking into account the way the strip curves down at the rear: if the strip seems too long, it's in the wrong place...

Over-enthusiasm can also lead to mis-judgements such as winding the tap in too far when cleaning the captive nuts for the bonnet hinges, and as a result putting a dimple in the bonnet.

Testing and adjustments

"If you have to tow it round the block to start it, forget it – something's wrong," says Graham – who also stresses the importance of first spinning the engine with the plugs out, to get the oil pressure up.

"And don't forget to fit the bonnet safety catch in your hurry to get the car on the road – I know of several people who've come back from their first test run with the bonnet having sprung up and damaged the car."

Problems encountered on our test run are a good guide to the snags you could come up against: a loose fuel filler neck, a carb out of adjustment, the fuel gauge not connected, the steering wheel slightly out of alignment, and noisy starter engagement. Not bad!

The Heritage shell

The Heritage shell is made by British Motor Heritage, using the original tooling and presses. It is currently available for all models from the 1966 Midget MkIII/ Sprite MkIV. The shells are phosphated, electrophoretically dipped, seam-sealed and primed. You can buy them either without front wings and front panels or with these items already fitted. Prices start at £1568 including VAT for shells less the front end; for a full shell for rubber-bumper cars the price is £2291 including VAT. All shells come with doors, boot lid and bonnet ready fitted.

What it cost

Heritage body shell	**£2185**	**Fuel tank/pump parts**	**£109**
Spray in two-pack	**£600**	...including tank	£53
Brakes and suspension	**£431**		
...including 2 splined hubs	£129	**Hood assembly**	**£112**
2 brake discs	£33	...including hood	£82
2 wishbone pans	£46		
		Seats	**£126**
Wire wheels (4, new)	**£249**	...including seat covers	£82
Engine/gearbox/clutch	**£221**		
...including carb parts	£75	**Interior trim**	**£225**
clutch parts	£80	...including trim kit	£117
		carpets	£70
Electrics	**£340**		
...including two-part loom	£129	**Miscellaneous**	**£166**
wiper parts	£101		
		TOTAL COST	**£4764**

All prices include VAT and are using parts supplied by Moss Europe. If an exchange engine and a reconditioned gearbox were to have been fitted, additional costs would have been around £525 and £250 respectively, VAT included.

The Sprite & Midget, B, C, V8 Centre is at 22-28 Manor Road, Richmond, Surrey TW9 1YB (tel: 081-948 6666). Our car was painted by Sussex specialist Midhurst Engineering; contact the firm on 0730 812162/3. New wire wheels were supplied by Motor Wheel Services, which is on 0753 49360.

BRITISH MOTOR HERITAGE

OFFICIAL TECHNICAL BOOKS

Brooklands Technical Books has been formed to supply owners, restorers and professional repairers with official factory lilterature.

Workshop Manuals

Model	Orig. Part No.
Midget TC (instruction manual)	n/a
Midget TD/TF (SC)	AKD580A
Midget TD/TF (HC)	AKD580A
MG M to TF 1500 (Blower)	XO17
MGA 1600/1600 Mk.2 (SC)	AKD600D
MGA 1600/1600 Mk.2 (HC)	AKD600D
MGA Twin Cam	AKD926B
Midget Mk.1,2 & 3 & Sprite	AKD4021
Midget 1500	AKM4071B
MGB (pub. '76)	AKD3259
MGB GT V8 WSM Supp.	AKD8468
MGC	AKD3259

Owners Handbooks

Model	Orig. Part No.
MG Midget TF & TF 1500	AKM658A
Midget TD	n/a
MGA 1500	AKD598G
MGA 1600	AKD1172
MGA 1600 Mk.2	AKD195A
MGA Twin Cam	AKD879
MGA Twin Cam (3rd edn.)	AKD879B
Midget Mk.3 (pub. '71)	AKD7937
Midget Mk.3 (pub. '73)	AKD7596
Midget Mk.3	AKM3229
Midget Mk.3 (US)	AKM3436
Midget Mk.3 (US)	AKM4386
MGB Tourer (pub. '65)	AKD3900C
MGB Tourer (pub. '69)	AKD3900J
MGB Tourer & GT (pub.'74)	AKD7598
MGB Tourer (pub. '76)	AKM3661
MG GT V8	AKD8423
MGB (US)(pub. '68)	AKD7059
MGB (US)(pub. '71)	AKD7881
MGB (US)(pub. '73)	AKD8155
MGB (US)(pub. '75)	AKD3286
MGB (US)(pub. '80)	AKM8098
MGB Tourer & GT Tuning	CAKD4034L
MGB Tuning (1800cc)	AKD4034
MGC	AKD4887

Parts Catalogues

Model	Orig. Part No.
MGA 1500 (HC)	AKD1055
MGA 1500 (SC)	AKD1055
MGA 1600 (HC)	AKD1215
MGA 1600 (SC)	AKD1215
Midget Mk.2 & 3	AKM0036
Midget (owners edn.) (pub.61)	AKD1909A
MGB Tourer GT & V8 (to Sept. '76)	AKM0039
MGB Tourer GT (Sept. '77)	AKM0037

Note: SC - Soft Cover   HC - Hard Cover

From specialist booksellers or, in case of difficulty, direct from the distributors:

Brooklands Books Ltd., PO Box 146, Cobham, Surrey KT11 1LG, England
Phone: 0932 865051 Fax: 0932 868803
Brooklands Books Ltd, 1/81 Darley St., PO Box 199, Mona Vale, NSW 2103, Australia
Phone: 2 997 8428 Fax: 2 997 8428
CarTech, 11481 Kost Dam Road, North Branch, MN 55056, USA
Phone 800 551 4754 & 612 583 3471 Fax: 612 583 2023